TEACHER'S RESOURCE BOOK CONTENTS

STUDENTS' BOOK CONTENTS

Comyns Carr

with Gabby Maguire

speakout

Starter
Teacher's Resource Book

LISTENING/DVD	SPEAKING	WRITING
listen to personal introductions	introduce yourself	learn to use capital letters
	ask questions about people and places	
listen to conversations at reception	learn to check spelling; exchange personal information	
Around The World: watch an extract from a documentary about people around the world	talk about yourself and your country	write a personal introduction
listen to someone talk about family photos	talk about photos of family and friends	learn to use contractions
	check information about people	
listen to people making suggestions	learn to respond to suggestions; make suggestions about where to go	
The Royal Wedding: William and Catherine: watch an extract from a documentary about a royal wedding	talk about five people in your life	write a description of people in your life
listen to conversations at a festival	ask personal information; talk about your family	
listen to conversations in offices	ask for the names of things in English	
	talk about clothes	link sentences with *and* and *but*
listen to conversations in a café	learn to say prices; do a role-play in a café	
Francesco's Mediterranean Voyage: watch an extract from a travel programme about a market	do a role-play in a market	write a description of a market
listen to people talk about life in the USA.	talk about things you have in common	link sentences with *and* and *because*; write a blog about your life
	find differences in pictures	
listen to conversations about times	tell the time; learn to check times; ask people to come to events	
Human Planet: Rivers: watch a documentary about rivers	talk about your favourite season	write a forum reply about your favourite season
listen to a conversation about a woman's favourites	talk about your favourite thing; guess the jobs	
listen to conversations about people's bad habits	talk about habits that drive people crazy	
	answer a questionnaire about your daily routines	link sentences with *first, then, after that, finally*
enquiries in a hotel	learn to show interest; do a role-play at a tourist information desk	
Doctor Who: watch a drama about a time-travelling doctor	talk about food to take to a desert island	write a forum entry about food to take to a desert island

COMMUNICATION BANK page 148   AUDIO SCRIPTS page 154

LISTENING/DVD	SPEAKING	WRITING
conversations at a station	ask about places; find differences between two pictures	learn to start and end an email
	ask and answer questions about transport; compare cities' transport	
listen to someone buy a bus ticket	learn to check numbers; do a role-play at a train or bus station	
BBC **Visions Of India: Rush Hour:** watch an extract from a documentary about India	talk about travel in your country	write a travel forum entry
listen to problems in different situations	role-play problems in different situations	
listen to conversations about New Year 2000	ask where people were in the past	improve your punctuation
	talk about what you/others did in the past	
listen to people giving opinions	give your opinion; learn to show feelings	
BBC **The Chilean Miners' Rescue:** watch an extract from a documentary about the Chilean miners' rescue.	do a history quiz	write a history quiz
	talk about first meetings	
listen to a radio programme about holidays	talk about a good holiday	link sentences with *so* and *because*
listen to people ask directions in a supermarket	do a role-play in a supermarket; learn to use examples	
BBC **Little Britain Abroad:** watch an extract from a comedy about tourists in Spain	tell a bad holiday story	write a story about a bad holiday
listen to people talk about the crime	find differences in two students' stories	
	talk about likes and dislikes; choose an activity gift for a student	
listen to a radio programme about shopping mistakes	talk about shopping	write captions for your photos
listen to someone shopping	learn to use hesitation phrases; choose a birthday present	
BBC **Days That Shook The World: Into The 21st Century:** watch an extract from a documentary about the arrival of the MP3 player	describe a possession	write about a favourite possession
listen to job interviews	talk about ability; do a quiz to find the best job for you	
listen to street interviews about people's goals	discuss your plans and goals	learn to check your work
listen to people start and end conversations	learn to respond naturally; do a role-play at a party	
BBC **Miranda:** watch an extract from a comedy about a woman who wants to change her life	talk about learning something new	write a magazine interview about learning something new
listen to students talk about learning English	discuss ways of improving your English; play the Speakout Game	

COMMUNICATION BANK page 148

AUDIO SCRIPTS page 154

Before we started writing *Speakout*, we did a lot of research to find out more about the issues that teachers and students face and how these can be addressed in a textbook for the 21st century. The issues that came up again and again were motivation, authentic content and the need for structured speaking and listening strategies.

As English teachers, we know how motivating it can be to bring the real world into the classroom by using authentic materials. We also know how time consuming and difficult it can be to find authentic content that is truly engaging, at the right level and appropriate for our students. With access to the entire archive of the BBC, we have selected some stunning video content to motivate and engage students. We have also created tasks that will encourage interaction with the materials while providing the right amount of scaffolding.

We realise that the real world is not just made up of actors, presenters and comedians, and 'real' English does not just consist of people reading from scripts. This is why *Speakout* brings real people into the classroom. The Video podcasts show people giving their opinions about the topics in the book and illustrate some of the strategies that will help our students become more effective communicators.

Speakout maximises opportunities for students to speak and systematically asks them to notice and employ strategies that will give them the confidence to communicate fluently and the competence to listen actively. While the main focus is on speaking and listening, we have also developed a systematic approach to reading and writing. For us, these skills are absolutely essential for language learners in the digital age.

To sum up, we have tried to write a course that teachers will really enjoy using; a course that is authentic but manageable, systematic but not repetitive – a course that not only brings the real world into the classroom, but also sends our students into the real world with the confidence to truly 'speak out'!

From left to right: Frances Eales, JJ Wilson, Antonia Clare and Steve Oakes

STUDENTS' BOOK

- Between 90 and 120 hours of teaching material
- Language Bank with reference material and extra practice
- Photo Bank to expand vocabulary
- Audioscripts of the class audio

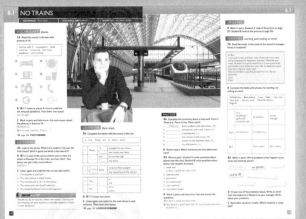

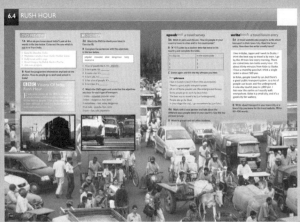

CLASS AUDIO CDs

- Audio material for use in class
- Test audio for the Mid-course and End of Course Tests

DVD & ACTIVE BOOK

- DVD content
- Digital Students' Book
- Audio, video and Video podcasts

WORKBOOK

- Grammar and vocabulary
- Functional language
- Speaking and listening strategies
- Reading, writing and listening
- Regular review and self-study tests

AUDIO CD

- Audio material including listening, pronunciation and functional practice

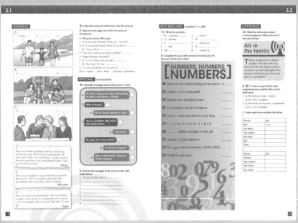

MYSPEAKOUTLAB

- Interactive Workbook with hints and tips
- Unit tests and Progress Tests
- Mid-course and End of Course Tests
- Video podcasts with interactive worksheets

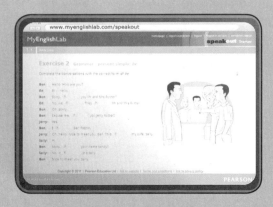

TEACHER'S RESOURCE BOOK

- Teaching notes
- Integrated key and audioscript
- Four photocopiable activities for every unit
- Mid-course and End of Course Test

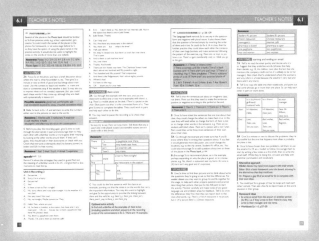
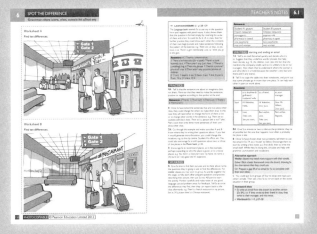

SPEAKOUT ACTIVE TEACH

- Integrated audio and video content
- Video podcasts
- Test master containing all course tests
- Answer reveal feature
- Grammar and vocabulary review games
- A host of useful tools
- Large extra resources section

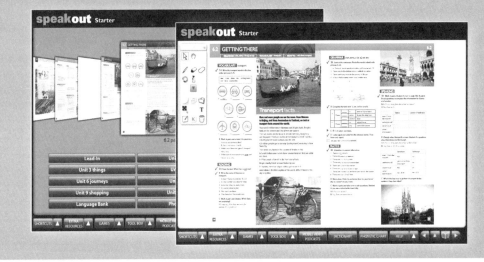

SPEAKOUT WEBSITE

- Information about the course
- Sample materials from the course
- Teaching tips
- Placement test
- A range of useful resources
- Video podcasts

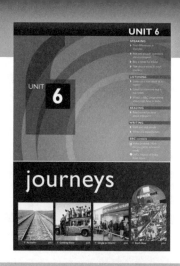

UNIT OVERVIEW

Every unit of Speakout starts with an Overview, which lists the topics covered. This is followed by two main input lessons which cover grammar, vocabulary and the four skills. Lesson three covers functional language and focuses on important speaking and listening strategies. Lesson four is built around a clip from a BBC programme and consolidates language and skills work. Each unit culminates with a Lookback page, which provides communicative practice of the key language.

INPUT LESSON 1

Lesson one introduces the topic of the unit and presents the key language needed to understand and talk about it. The lesson combines grammar and vocabulary with a focus on skills work.

The target language and the CEF objectives are listed to clearly show the objectives of the lesson.

Every pair of input lessons includes at least one writing section with focus on a variety of different genres.

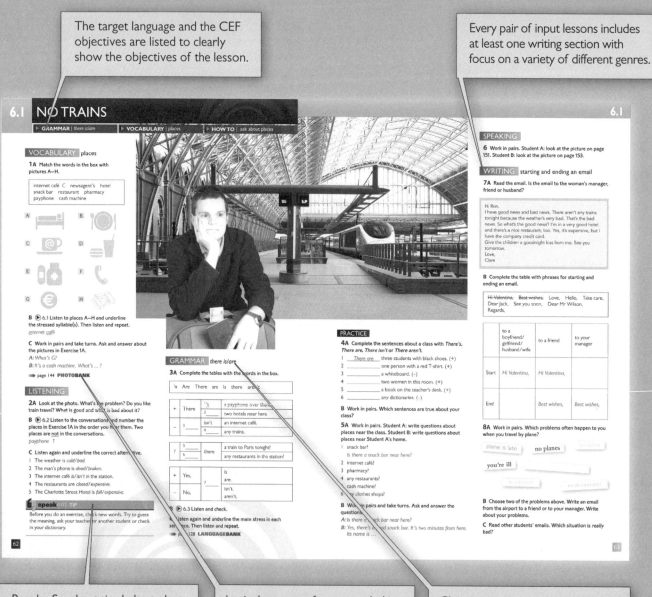

Regular Speakout tips help students to develop their study skills both inside and outside the classroom.

Lexical sets are often expanded in the full colour Photo bank at the back of the Students' Book.

Clear grammar presentations are followed by written and oral practice as well as pronunciation work.

INPUT LESSON 2

Lesson two continues to focus on grammar and vocabulary while extending and expanding the topic area. By the end of the second lesson students will have worked on all four skill areas.

> Lexical sets are introduced in context. Practice of new words often includes pronunciation work.

> All lessons include a focus on speaking where the emphasis is on communication and fluency building.

6.2 GETTING THERE

▶ **GRAMMAR** | a/an, some, a lot of, not any   ▶ **VOCABULARY** | transport   ▶ **HOW TO** | talk about transport

VOCABULARY transport

1A Write the transport words in the box under pictures A–H.

| bus   train   plane   taxi   underground |
| car   bike   motorbike |

A bus   B   C

D   E

F   G   H

B Work in pairs and answer the questions.
1 How do you come to class?
   By bus or sometimes I walk.
2 What's your favourite type of transport?
   Motorbike.
3 What type of transport do you *never* use?
   I never use a bike.

READING

2A Read the text. Which fact is not true?

B Write the name of the place or transport.
1 It doesn't have any stations. *Bhutan*
2 It's the number one place for bikes.
3 In London, they're usually black.
4 It's a noisy place to play.
5 Men don't use these.
6 They have two floors and stairs.

C Work in pairs and discuss. Which facts are surprising?
It's surprising that there are taxis for women. It's a good idea.

Transport facts...

More and more people are on the move. From Moscow to Beijing, and from Amsterdam to Thailand, we look at transport facts around the world.

There are 3 million cars in Moscow and 22 pink taxis. The pink taxis are for women and the drivers are women.

There are double-decker buses in the UK, Germany, Hong Kong and Singapore. There are double-decker trains in a lot of countries including Switzerland, Australia and the USA.

4.3 million people go by subway (underground) every day in New York City.

There aren't any trains in the country of Bhutan in Asia.

In Saudi Arabia some hotels have London taxis but they are white not black.

In China people often sit in the front seat of taxis.

People usually travel around Venice by car.

In Thailand, there's an airport with a golf course in it.

Amsterdam is the bike capital of the world. 40% of travel in this city is by bike.

64

GRAMMAR a/an, some, a lot of, not any

3A Look at the sentences. Match the words in bold with pictures A–D.
1 In Thailand, there's an airport with a golf course in it. B
2 There are double-decker trains in **a lot of** countries.
3 There aren't **any** trains in the country of Bhutan.
4 In Saudi Arabia **some** hotels have London taxis.

A   B

C   D

B Complete the table with 's, are, isn't or aren't.

+	There	___	a	train at four o'clock.
			some	buses this afternoon.
			a lot of	taxis.
–	There	___	an	airport here.
			any	cars in the centre.

C ▶ 6.4 Listen and check.

D Listen again and underline the stressed words. Then listen and repeat.

➠ page 128 **LANGUAGEBANK**

PRACTICE

4A Underline the correct alternative.
1 There's *a/an* airport.
2 There are *some/any* stations.
3 There aren't *a lot/any* taxis.
4 There are *a lot/some of* motorbikes.
5 There isn't *a/some* bus station.
6 There are *any/some* buses at night.
7 There aren't *some/any* problems with cars in the centre.
8 There are *any/a lot of* bikes.

B Work alone. Make the sentences true for your town/city or a town/city you know.

C Work in pairs and take turns to ask questions. Student A: you are a visitor to the town/city.
A: Is there an airport?
B: Yes, there are two airports.

6.2

SPEAKING

5A Work in pairs. Student A: turn to page 150. Student B: ask questions to complete the information for Venice and London.
B: Is there a train from the airport to Venice?
A: No, there isn't.

	Venice	London (Heathrow)
train / from the airport?		
underground?		
airport bus?		
other information?		

B Change roles. Student B: answer Student A's questions about Barcelona and Edinburgh.
A: Is there a train from the airport to Barcelona?
B: Yes, there is. It's three euros.

	Barcelona	Edinburgh
train / from the airport?	€3	no
underground?	yes but not from the airport	no
airport bus?	€5	£4
other information?	taxi, €30	taxi, £15

C What's the best way to go from the airport to the centre in these four cities?

> Each input spread has either a focus on listening or a focus on reading.

> Grammar and vocabulary sections often include a listening element to reinforce the new language.

> Every grammar section includes a reference to the Language bank with explanations and further practice.

13

FUNCTIONAL LESSON

The third lesson in each unit focuses on a particular function, situation or transaction as well as introducing important speaking and listening strategies.

The target language and the CEF objectives are listed to clearly show the objectives of the lesson.

Students learn a lexical set which is relevant to the function or situation.

Students learn important speaking and listening strategies which can be transferred to many situations.

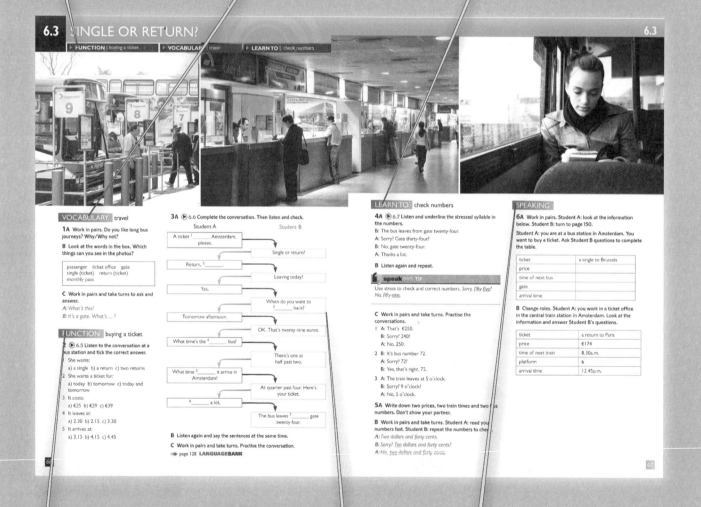

The functional language is learnt in context, often by listening to the language in use.

Conversation flow charts provide scaffolding that allows students to explore new language.

The lesson ends with a speaking activity which gives students the chance to practise the new language.

DVD LESSON

The fourth lesson in each unit is based around an extract from a real BBC programme. This acts as a springboard into freer communicative speaking and writing activities.

> A preview section gets students thinking about the topic of the extract and introduces key language.

> A series of different tasks helps students to understand and enjoy the programme.

> The Speakout task builds on the topic of the extract and provides extended speaking practice.

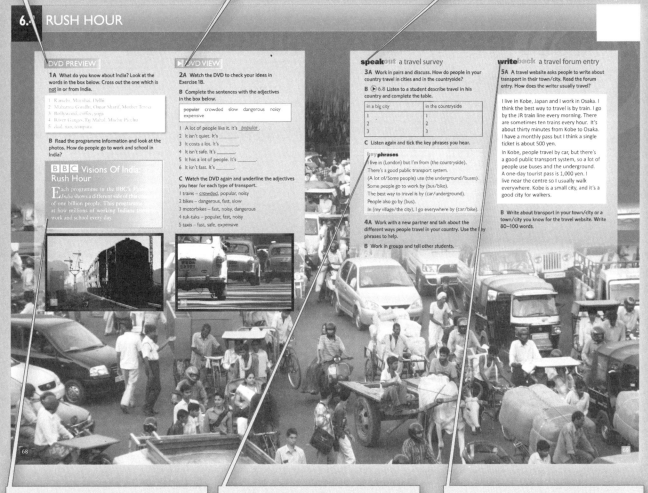

> A TV listing about the programme sets the context and helps students prepare to watch the clip.

> The key phrases box helps students to notice the key language for the speaking task and builds confidence.

> The Writeback task further extends the topic and provides communicative writing practice.

LOOKBACK AND REVIEW PAGES

Each unit ends with a Lookback page, which provides further practice and review of the key language covered in the unit. The review exercises are a mixture of communicative activities and games. The Lookback page also introduces the Video podcast, which features a range of real people talking about one of the topics in the unit.

There is also a review lesson after every other unit which provides further listening, reading, speaking and pronunciation practice and consolidates the language covered in the two preceding units.

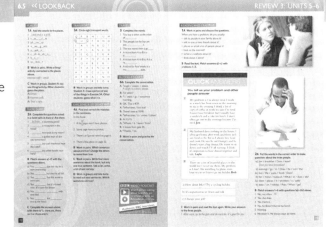

WORKBOOK

The Workbook contains a wide variety of practice and review exercises and covers all of the language areas studied in the unit. It also contains regular review sections as well as self-study tests to help students consolidate what they have learnt.

The Workbook features extensive practice of vocabulary, grammar, reading, writing and listening.

A variety of language practice activities consolidate the areas covered in the Students' Book.

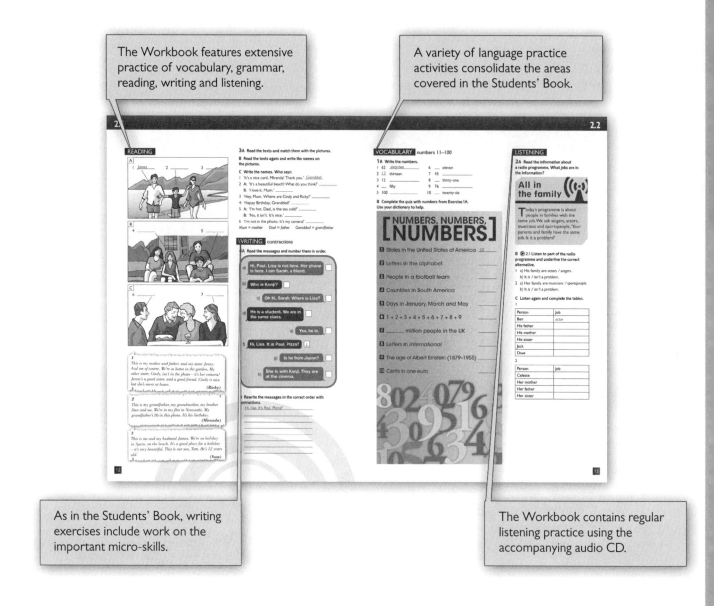

As in the Students' Book, writing exercises include work on the important micro-skills.

The Workbook contains regular listening practice using the accompanying audio CD.

MYSPEAKOUTLAB

MySpeakoutLab provides a fully blended and personalised learning environment that benefits both teachers and students. It offers:

- an interactive Workbook with hints, tips and automatic grade book.
- professionally written Unit Tests, Progress Tests, Mid-course and End of Course tests that can be assigned at the touch of a button.
- interactive Video podcast worksheets with an integrated video player so students can watch while they do the exercises.

ACTIVE TEACH

Speakout Active Teach contains everything you need to make the course come alive in your classroom.
It includes integrated whiteboard software which enables you to add notes and embed files.
It is also possible to save all of your work with the relevant page from the Students' Book.

An answer reveal function lets you show the answers to an exercise at the touch of a button.

All audio and video content is fully integrated and includes subtitles as well as printable scripts.

Shortcuts to the relevant pages of the Language bank and the Photo bank make navigation easy.

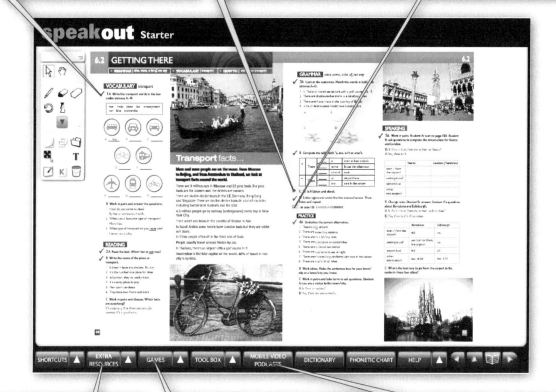

The extra resources section includes editable scripts, tests, the Video podcast worksheets and more.

The four grammar and vocabulary review games are perfect as warm ups or review activities.

Useful tools include a regular keyboard, a phonetic keyboard, a stopwatch and a scorecard.

WEBSITE

The Speakout website will offer information about the course as well as a bank of useful resources including:

- introductory videos by the authors of the course.
- sample materials.
- teaching tips.
- placement test.
- CEF mapping documents.
- Video podcasts for all published levels.

speakout is designed to satisfy both students and teachers on a number of different levels. It offers engaging topics with authentic BBC material to really bring them to life. At the same time it offers a robust and comprehensive focus on grammar, vocabulary, functions and pronunciation. As the name of the course might suggest, speaking activities are prominent, but that is not at the expense of the other core skills, which are developed systematically throughout.

With this balanced approach to topics, language development and skills work, our aim has been to create a course book full of 'lessons that really work' in practice. Below we will briefly explain our approach in each of these areas.

TOPICS AND CONTENT

In *Speakout* we have tried to choose topics that are relevant to students' lives. Where a topic area is covered in other ELT courses we have endeavoured to find a fresh angle on it. It is clear to us that authenticity is important to learners, and many texts come from the BBC's rich resources (audio, visual and print) as well as other real-world sources. At lower levels, we have sometimes adapted materials by adjusting the language to make it more manageable for students while trying to keep the tone as authentic as possible. We have also attempted to match the authentic feel of a text with an authentic interaction. Every unit contains a variety of rich and authentic input material including BBC Video podcasts (filmed on location in London, England) and DVD material, featuring some of the best the BBC has to offer.

GRAMMAR

Knowing how to recognise and use grammatical structures is central to our ability to communicate with each other. Although at first students can often get by with words and phrases, they increasingly need grammar to make themselves understood. Students also need to understand sentence formation when reading and listening and to be able to produce accurate grammar in professional and exam situations. We share students' belief that learning grammar is a core feature of learning a language and believe that a guided discovery approach, where students are challenged to notice new forms works best. At the same time learning is scaffolded so that students are supported at all times in a systematic way. Clear grammar presentations are followed by written and oral practice. There is also the chance to notice and practise pronunciation where appropriate.

In *Speakout* you will find:

- **Grammar in context** – We want to be sure that the grammar focus is clear and memorable for students. Grammar is almost always taken from the listening or reading texts, so that learners can see the language in action, and understand how and when it is used.

- **Noticing** – We involve students in the discovery of language patterns by asking them to identify aspects of meaning and form, and complete rules or tables.

- **Clear language reference** – As well as a summary of rules within the unit, there is also a Language bank which serves as a clear learning reference for the future.

- **Focus on use** – We ensure that there is plenty of practice, both form and meaning-based, in the Language bank to give students confidence in manipulating the new language. On the main input page we include personalised practice, which is designed to be genuinely communicative and to offer students the opportunity to say something about themselves or the topic. There is also regular recycling of new language in the Lookback review pages, and again the focus here is on moving learners towards communicative use of the language.

VOCABULARY

Developing a wide range of vocabulary is key to increasing communicative effectiveness; developing a knowledge of high-frequency collocations and fixed and semi-fixed phrases is key to increasing spoken fluency. An extensive understanding of words and phrases helps learners become more confident when reading and listening, and developing a range of vocabulary is important for effective writing. Equally vital is learner-training, equipping students with the skills to record, memorise and recall vocabulary for use.

In *Speakout* this is reflected in:

- **A prominent focus on vocabulary** – We include vocabulary in almost all lessons whether in a lexical set linked to a particular topic, as preparation for a speaking activity or to aid comprehension of a DVD clip or a listening or reading text. Where we want students to use the language actively, we encourage them to use the vocabulary to talk about their own lives or opinions. At lower levels, the Photo bank also extends the vocabulary taught in the lessons, using memorable photographs and graphics to support students' understanding.

- **Focus on 'chunks'** – As well as lexical sets, we also regularly focus on how words fit together with other words, often getting students to notice how words are used in a text and to focus on high-frequency 'chunks' such as verb-noun collocations or whole phrases.

- **Focus on vocabulary systems** – We give regular attention to word-building skills, a valuable tool in expanding vocabulary. At higher levels, the Vocabulary plus sections deal with systems such as affixation, multi-word verbs and compound words in greater depth.

- **Recycling and learner training** – Practice exercises ensure that vocabulary is encountered on a number of occasions: within the lessons, on the Lookback page, in subsequent lessons and in the Photo bank/Vocabulary bank at the back of the book. One of the main focuses of the *Speakout* tips – which look at all areas of language learning – is to highlight vocabulary learning strategies, aiming to build good study skills that will enable students to gain and retain new language.

FUNCTIONAL LANGUAGE

One thing that both teachers and learners appreciate is the need to manage communication in a wide variety of encounters, and to know what's appropriate to say in given situations. These can be transactional exchanges, where the main focus is on getting something done (buying something in a shop or phoning to make an enquiry), or interactional exchanges, where the main focus is on socialising with others (talking about the weekend, or responding appropriately to good news). As one learner commented to us, 'Grammar rules aren't enough – I need to know what to say.' Although it is possible to categorise 'functions' under 'lexical phrases', we believe it is useful for learners to focus on functional phrases separately from vocabulary or grammar.

The third lesson in every unit of *Speakout* looks at one such situation, and focuses on the functional language needed. Learners hear or see the language used in context and then practise it in mini-situations, in both a written and a spoken context. Each of these lessons also includes a Learn to section, which highlights and practises a useful strategy for dealing with both transactional and interactional exchanges, for example asking for clarification, showing interest, etc. Learners will find themselves not just more confident users of the language, but also more active listeners.

SPEAKING

The dynamism of most lessons depends on the success of the speaking tasks, whether the task is a short oral practice of new language, a discussion comparing information or opinions, a personal response to a reading text or a presentation where a student might speak uninterrupted for a minute or more. Students develop fluency when they are motivated to speak. For this to happen, engaging topics and tasks are essential, as is the sequencing of stages and task design. For longer tasks, students often need to prepare their ideas and language in a structured way. This all-important rehearsal time leads to more motivation and confidence as well as greater accuracy, fluency and complexity. Also, where appropriate, students need to hear a model before they speak, in order to have a realistic goal.

There are several strands to speaking in *Speakout*:

- **Communicative practice** – After introducing any new language (vocabulary, grammar or function) there are many opportunities in *Speakout* for students to use it in a variety of activities which focus on communication as well as accuracy. These include personalised exchanges, dialogues, flow-charts and role-plays.

- **Focus on fluency** – In every unit of *Speakout* we include opportunities for students to respond spontaneously. They might be asked to respond to a series of questions, to a DVD, a Video podcast or a text, or to take part in conversations, discussions and role-plays. These activities involve a variety of interactional formations such as pairs and groups.

- **Speaking strategies and sub-skills** – In the third lesson of each unit, students are encouraged to notice in a systematic way features which will help them improve their speaking. These include, for example, ways to manage a phone conversation, the use of mirror questions to ask for clarification, sentence starters to introduce an opinion and intonation to correct mistakes.

- **Extended speaking tasks** – In the *Speakout* DVD lesson, as well as in other speaking tasks throughout the course, students are encouraged to attempt more adventurous and extended use of language in tasks such as problem solving, developing a project or telling a story. These tasks go beyond discussion; they include rehearsal time, useful language and a concrete outcome.

LISTENING

For most users of English (or any language, for that matter), listening is the most frequently used skill. A learner who can speak well but not understand at least as well is unlikely to be a competent communicator or user of the language. We feel that listening can be developed effectively through well-structured materials. As with speaking, the choice of interesting topics and texts works hand in hand with carefully considered sequencing and task design. At the same time, listening texts can act as a springboard to stimulate discussion in class.

There are several strands to listening in *Speakout*:

- **Focus on authentic recordings** – In *Speakout*, we believe that it is motivating for all levels of learner to try to access and cope with authentic material. Each unit includes a DVD extract from a BBC documentary, drama or light entertainment programme as well as a podcast filmed on location with real people giving their opinions. At the higher levels you will also find unscripted audio texts and BBC radio extracts. All are invaluable in the way they expose learners to real language in use as well as different varieties of English. Where recordings, particularly at lower levels, are scripted, they aim to reflect the patterns of natural speech.

- **Focus on sub-skills and strategies** – Tasks across the recordings in each unit are designed with a number of sub-skills and strategies in mind. These include: listening for global meaning and more detail; scanning for specific information; becoming sensitised to possible misunderstandings; and noticing nuances of intonation and expression. We also help learners to listen actively by using strategies such as asking for repetition and paraphrasing.

- **As a context for new language** – We see listening as a key mode of input and *Speakout* includes many listening texts which contain target grammar, vocabulary or functions in their natural contexts. Learners are encouraged to notice this new language and how and where it occurs, often by using the audio scripts as a resource.

- **As a model for speaking** – In the third and fourth lessons of each unit the recordings serve as models for speaking tasks. These models reveal the ways in which speakers use specific language to structure their discourse, for example with regard to turn-taking, hesitating and checking for understanding. These recordings also serve as a goal for the learners' speaking.

READING

Reading is a priority for many students, whether it's for study, work or pleasure, and can be practised alone, anywhere and at any time. Learners who read regularly tend to have a richer, more varied vocabulary, and are often better writers, which in turn supports their oral communication skills. Nowadays, the internet has given students access to an extraordinary range of English language reading material, and the availability of English language newspapers, books and magazines is greater than ever before. The language learner who develops skill and confidence in reading in the classroom will be more motivated to read outside the classroom. Within the classroom reading texts can also introduce stimulating topics and act as springboards for class discussion.

There are several strands to reading in *Speakout*:

- **Focus on authentic texts** – As with *Speakout* listening materials, there is an emphasis on authenticity, and this is reflected in a number of ways. Many of the reading texts in *Speakout* are sourced from the BBC. Where texts have been adapted or graded, there is an attempt to maintain authenticity by remaining faithful to the text type in terms of content and style. We have chosen up-to-date, relevant texts to stimulate interest and motivate learners to read. The texts represent a variety of genres that correspond to the text types that learners will probably encounter in their everyday lives.

- **Focus on sub-skills and strategies** – In *Speakout* we strive to maintain authenticity in the way the readers interact with a text. We always give students a reason to read, and provide tasks which bring about or simulate authentic reading, including real-life tasks such as summarising, extracting specific information, reacting to an opinion or following an anecdote. We also focus on strategies for decoding texts, such as guessing the meaning of unknown vocabulary, understanding pronoun referencing and following discourse markers.

- **Noticing new language** – Noticing language in use is a key step towards the development of a rich vocabulary and greater all-round proficiency in a language, and this is most easily achieved through reading. In *Speakout*, reading texts often serve as valuable contexts for introducing grammar and vocabulary as well as discourse features.

- **As a model for writing** – In the writing sections, as well as the Writeback sections of the DVD spreads, the readings serve as models for students to refer to when they are writing, in terms of overall organisation as well as style and language content.

WRITING

In recent years the growth of email and the internet has led to a shift in the nature of the writing our students need to do. Email has also led to an increased informality in written English. However, many students need to develop their formal writing for professional and exam-taking purposes. It is therefore important to focus on a range of genres, from formal text types such as essays, letters and reports to informal genres such as blog entries and personal messages.

There are four strands to writing in *Speakout*:

- **Focus on genres** – In every unit at the four higher levels there is a section that focuses on a genre of writing, emails for example. We provide a model to show the conventions of the genre and, where appropriate, we highlight fixed phrases associated with it. We usually then ask the students to produce their own piece of writing. While there is always a written product, we also focus on the process of writing, including the relevant stages such as brainstorming, planning, and checking. At Starter and Elementary, we focus on more basic writing skills, including basic written sentence patterns, linking, punctuation and text organisation, in some cases linking this focus to a specific genre.

- **Focus on sub-skills and strategies** – While dealing with the genres, we include a section which focuses on a sub-skill or strategy that is generally applicable to all writing. Sub-skills include paragraphing, organising content and using linking words and pronouns, while strategies include activities like writing a first draft quickly, keeping your reader in mind and self-editing. We present the sub-skill by asking the students to notice the feature. We then provide an opportunity for the students to practise it.

- **Writeback** – At the end of every unit, following the DVD and final speaking task, we include a Writeback task. The idea is for students to develop fluency in their writing. While we always provide a model, the task is not tied to any particular grammatical structure. Instead the emphasis is on using writing to generate ideas and personal responses.

- **Writing as a classroom activity** – We believe that writing can be very usefully employed as an aid to speaking and as a reflective technique for responding to texts – akin to the practice of writing notes in the margins of books. It also provides a change of pace and focus in lessons. Activities such as short dictations, note-taking, brainstorming on paper and group story writing are all included in *Speakout*.

PRONUNCIATION

In recent years, attitudes towards pronunciation in many English language classrooms have moved towards a focus on intelligibility: if students' spoken language is understandable, then the pronunciation is good enough. We are aware, however, that many learners and teachers place great importance on developing pronunciation that is more than 'good enough', and that systematic attention to pronunciation in a lesson, however brief, can have a significant impact on developing learners' speech.

In *Speakout*, we have taken a practical, integrated approach to developing students' pronunciation, highlighting features that often cause problems in conjunction with a given area of grammar, particular vocabulary items and functional language. Where relevant to the level, a grammatical or functional language focus is followed by a focus on a feature of pronunciation, for example, the weak forms of auxiliary verbs or connected speech in certain functional exponents. Students are given the opportunity to listen to models of the pronunciation, notice the key feature and then practise it.

TEACHING STARTER LEARNERS

Starter can be the most rewarding level to teach; every lesson brings learners tangible advances in knowledge and skills, as they leave the lesson able to do or say something that an hour or two before was completely unknown to them. The particular challenges a teacher faces with starters require less in terms of knowledge of the language and more in terms of technique, in particular the ability to convey meaning of new language and instructions to people who may have heard little or no English in their lives.

It's sometimes said that there are no true starters in English among adult learners, because of the omnipresence of the language, but of course there are many who are beginning their study of English with no more than a handful of words and phrases and perhaps very little experience learning a language in a classroom. This point is perhaps one of the most important to keep in mind – that your starter students may find the context and routines of your classroom completely alien. Their expectations will be informed by their previous learning experiences, and may include a view of the teacher's role as authoritarian and directive. Routines and formats we take for granted, like checking an exercise in pairs, completing communicative activities with more attention to meaning than form, and working out grammar rules and meanings of words from context, may be new and even shocking to the starter learner. For this reason, considerable attention needs to be given to orienting starters to what's expected of them, to how to complete basic procedures, and most of all to taking initiative in indicating when they don't understand something. The nodding, smiling face of a starter may be hiding an utterly confused individual too afraid to show their disorientation, and it's vital that the teacher establishes a clear communication with students from the start, so that minutes and lessons don't pass where one or more students don't know what's going on.

Here are our Top Tips to help at this level:

- When planning your lessons, think through in detail how you will set up activities. It can be useful for starters to hear instructions in English and become familiar with some basic expressions, and that should be part of your routine. It's also important to invest time in demonstrating to students how an activity is supposed to be done. This is essentially learner training – training students how to function in a modern language classroom.

- Be realistic in your expectations of what starters can produce; while some starters can comfortably carry out speaking tasks in the Students' Book, some will be very reticent about saying anything at all. Aside from providing encouragement and support, often there is little you can do to hurry the pace of their learning.

- Review of vocabulary is important at any level, but at starter it is crucial. In part because the sound system of English is new, starters find retention of vocabulary extremely difficult. Try to work vocabulary review games and activities into your warmers, fillers and coolers.

- Whenever learners do written tasks, whether they're copying from the whiteboard or completing a task in their books, closely monitor what they write in their notebooks. It's common for starters to have serious difficulties with English spelling, and important that the record they go home with is accurate.

- If you have a monolingual group and speak the learners' mother tongue, consider doing so very selectively. It's useful for learners to hear English as much as possible, and careful planning of instructions can make them valuable listening practice. And the more you rely on their L1 to communicate, the more they will – and the greater difficulty they'll have becoming functional in English.

- If you have a multilingual group, consider providing extra support and/or homework for learners who are not able to rely on having similar words or grammar in their language or who have particular skills needs such as coping with a different script.

- If you're the kind of teacher who likes to adapt the Students' Book, consider limiting the extent to which you do this at starter. A first English course can be daunting for beginners, and the Students' Book can serve as a kind of anchor for them; and if they found a lesson completely overwhelming, it's much easier for them to go home and review the lesson if it came directly from the Students' Book.

- Be consistent about giving and checking homework, such as exercises in the workbook. A large proportion of learning – particularly retention – happens during self-study rather than during formal lessons.

- Finally, keep in mind that a language lesson may be an emotionally, very stressful experience for starters, more than at any other level. For this reason things that make each individual feel recognised and 'human' – encouragement, praise, the use of students' names, even a well-placed smile or eye contact (where culturally appropriate) – can go a long way towards students leaving a lesson feeling positive and motivated, and looking forward to the next one.

Antonia Clare, Frances Eales, Steve Oakes and JJ Wilson

TEACHER'S NOTES INDEX

OVERVIEW

1.1 WHERE ARE YOU FROM?

GRAMMAR | be: I/you

VOCABULARY | countries

HOW TO | introduce yourself

COMMON EUROPEAN FRAMEWORK

Ss can establish basic social contact by using the simplest everyday polite forms of greetings and introductions; can ask for or pass on personal details in written form.

1.2 ARRIVALS

GRAMMAR | be: he/she/it

VOCABULARY | jobs

HOW TO | ask questions about people

COMMON EUROPEAN FRAMEWORK

Ss can produce simple mainly isolated phrases about people and places.

1.3 HOW DO YOU SPELL ... ?

FUNCTION | giving personal information

VOCABULARY | the alphabet

LEARN TO | check spelling

COMMON EUROPEAN FRAMEWORK

Ss can spell their address, nationality and other personal details.

1.4 AROUND THE WORLD ◉ BBC DVD

speakout | you and your country

writeback | a personal introduction

COMMON EUROPEAN FRAMEWORK

Ss can describe what they do and where they live; can write simple phrases and sentences about themselves, where they live and what they do.

1.5 LOOKBACK

Communicative revision activities

▢ BBC VIDEO PODCAST

People talking about their names and where they come from.

WHERE ARE YOU FROM?

Introduction

Students practise introducing themselves, using be and the names of countries and towns/cities. They also practise listening and learn to use capital letters.

SUPPLEMENTARY MATERIALS

Resource bank p136 and p137

Warm up: have a map of the world available in the classroom, e.g. on a poster, a globe, on the internet.

Ex 6A: slips of paper for Ss to write chat messages.

Warm up

Use the world map to brainstorm the names of countries. Ask Ss to call out any countries whose names they know in English, and point to the relevant countries on the map as they are called out. Don't worry too much about correcting pronunciation at this stage, as this will be dealt with in the lesson. Alternatively, invite Ss to take turns coming to the map and pointing to countries for their classmates to name.

LISTENING

1A Direct Ss to the photo of the man and woman in photo A and encourage them to predict where they could be from, by pointing to each one and asking 'England? Spain?' etc. Establish that there are many possibilities. Gesture to show that Ss are going to listen to a recording, then write the numbers 1–4 on the board. Point to the four photos and demonstrate that you want Ss to write the letter A, B, C or D next to each number. Explain Ss should listen to the background noise to establish where the conversations are by using 'party' as an example: music, people laughing, glasses and plates being put down, etc. Play the recording and give Ss time to compare their answers before eliciting them.

Answers: 2 D 3 A 4 C

Teaching tip

Put Ss in pairs to compare their answers to a listening task. This helps to build their confidence before sharing their answers with the class, and encourages a cooperative, non-competitive atmosphere in the classroom. As you monitor this pairwork, you can also see whether Ss are struggling with some of the answers, and identify whether you need to play the recording again.

B Before playing the recording again, spend a few minutes helping Ss to familiarise themselves with the names on the chart (by writing or displaying a copy of it on the board). Point out/Elicit that Tom is male and Carmen, Cindy and Katie are female. Read out the names of the countries and cities, so that Ss recognise them when they hear them on the recording. Demonstrate that Ss need to match the names, countries and cities by drawing arrows between them, as in the example. Play the recording, then give Ss time to compare answers. Repeat the audio if necessary. Then check the answers with the class.

Answers: 2 Cindy–the USA–New York (N.B. Cindy says 'I'm from the US': point out to Ss that this is the same as 'the USA' but is commonly used in conversation.) 3 Tom–Australia–Melbourne 4 Katie–Ireland–Dublin

Unit 1 Recording 1

Conversation 1

A: Hello, I'm Simon.
B: Hi, I'm Carmen.
A: Nice to meet you.
B: Nice to meet you, too.
A: Where are you from?
B: I'm from Spain.
A: Oh, where in Spain?
B: From Madrid.

Conversation 2

A: Hello, I'm Dave.
B: Hi, I'm Cindy.
A: Nice to meet you.
B: Nice to meet you, too.
A: Where are you from?
B: I'm from the US.
A: Oh, where in the US?
B: From New York.

Conversation 3

A: Hi, I'm Sue.
B: Hello, I'm Tom.
A: Nice to meet you.
B: Nice to meet you, too.
A: Where are you from?
B: I'm from Australia
A: Oh. Are you from Sydney?
B: No, I'm not. I'm from Melbourne.

Conversation 4

A: Hi, I'm Martin.
B: Hi, I'm Katie.
A: Nice to meet you.
B: Nice to meet you, too.
A: Are you from Ireland?
B: Yes, I am.
A: Oh, where in Ireland?
B: From Dublin.

GRAMMAR   be: I/you

2A You may want to write or display copies of these tables on the board. Demonstrate *complete* by pointing to the first gap and eliciting from Ss that *are* is missing, then write it in. Also point out that *I'm* is short for *I am*, but that people always use *I'm* in conversation. Give Ss a minute or two to complete the tables: you could encourage them to consult the audio script if they wish.

Answers: Where *are* you from?/*Are* you from Sydney? (N.B. Remind Ss that the capital *A* is necessary because *are* is at the beginning of the question. You could also point out that the first question could have many answers, whereas the second has the answers *Yes* or *No*.) No, I'm not.

B Write the answer sentences on the board (without the underlining) and give Ss time to copy them into their notebooks. Before playing the recording, say *I'm Carmen* in two ways: *I'm Carmen* and *I'm Carmen* (you will need to exaggerate the stress to make sure that Ss hear the difference) and point out/elicit that the first way sounds more natural because the stress in on the important information, i.e. the person's name. Demonstrate underlining the stressed word in the sentence, then play the recording.

Answers: I'm <u>Carmen</u>. I'm from <u>Spain</u>.
<u>Where</u> are you <u>from</u>?
Are you from <u>Sydney</u>?
Yes, I <u>am</u>.
No, I'm <u>not</u>.

C Pause the recording after each sentence and gesture for Ss to repeat in chorus. You could then also ask a few individual Ss to repeat, taking the opportunity to correct any problems with word stress.

⟫ **LANGUAGEBANK** 1.1 p118–119

Give Ss a minute or two to look at the tables and point out the inversion of the subject and *be* in the questions form. Ss could do Ex 1.1A in class, then practise the complete conversation in pairs. They could do Ex 1.1B in class or for homework.

Answers:
A
2 I 3 Are 4 Am 5 not 6 aren't 7 I'm 8 're 9 'm
10 you're 11 you 12 I'm
B
2 Where are you from? 3 I'm from Italy. 4 Are you from Rome? 5 No, I'm not. 6 I'm from Venice.
7 Are you from Rome? 8 No, I'm not from Italy. 9 I'm from Barcelona, in Spain.

PRACTICE

3A Go through the example in conversation 1 with the class. You could also complete the second gap with the class as another example. Ss can then complete the conversations individually or work in pairs. If Ss ask about the meaning of *meet*, you could demonstrate this by acting out meeting a student for the first time; if they ask about *too*, you could indicate two Ss from the same country and say *You're from (Spain) … and you're from (Spain), too*.

B Play the recording for Ss to check their answers. You may want to write or display the conversations on the board in order to go through the answers with the class.

Answers: 1 2 'm 3 are 4 'm
2 1 'm 2 'm 3 are 4 'm 5 Are

C Put Ss in pairs to practise the conversations. Monitor and listen for examples of good language use and/or problems to deal with in feedback.

D Start by demonstrating this yourself with a *strong student*, or ask two *stronger Ss* to demonstrate. Then put Ss in pairs to practise. You could extend this by asking Ss to stand up and walk around, introducing themselves to the rest of the class.

VOCABULARY countries

4A You could start by asking Ss to cover the word box and see how many of the countries they can name from the maps of capital cities. They could do this in pairs, or as a whole class. Don't worry about correcting pronunciation: this will be covered in the next two stages. Give Ss time to write the numbers next to the names of countries in the box.

B Play the recording for Ss to check their answers.

> **Answers:** 2 China 3 Australia 4 Russia 5 Italy 6 England 7 Poland 8 USA 9 Saudi Arabia 10 Japan

C Demonstrate underlining the stressed syllable in *Brazil* on the board, pointing out that Ss need to underline the vowel – *a, e, i, o* or *u*. You may also want to show Ss how to use a stress 'box' on top of the stressed vowel. Before Ss listen again, they should write out the countries in the order that they appear on the recording, to make the underlining task more manageable.

> **Answers:** 2 Ch<u>i</u>na 3 Austr<u>a</u>lia 4 R<u>u</u>ssia 5 <u>I</u>taly 6 <u>E</u>ngland 7 P<u>o</u>land 8 <u>U</u>SA 9 S<u>au</u>di Ar<u>a</u>bia 10 J<u>a</u>pan (N.B. Ss are likely to find this one difficult to remember, because so many countries with two syllables have the stress on the first syllable.)

When you play the recording again for Ss to repeat in chorus, pause on the more difficult ones and invite individuals to repeat. This will give you a chance to correct pronunciation.

D Demonstrate this yourself with a *stronger student*, then put Ss into pairs. You could extend this activity by telling student A to say a country and student B to reply with the name of its capital city.

speakout TIP

You may want to suggest that Ss keep new vocabulary in a separate part of their notebook, and perhaps have pages for different topics, e.g. countries and cities. You could also show them how to keep a record of the stress pattern next to the word, using large and small circles, e.g. Br<u>a</u>zil oO.

⟹ PHOTOBANK p139

Ss match the countries with the flags, then in pairs complete the table with the correct countries.

Answers:
A
2 D 3 K 4 F 5 B 6 H 7 J 8 L 9 I 10 C 11 E 12 G
B
1 the USA 2 Argentina 3 Australia 4 Brazil 5 Canada 6 Egypt 7 Germany 8 Hungary 9 India 10 Italy 11 Korea 12 Mexico 13 Russia 14 Saudi Arabia 15 South Africa 16 Venezuela 17 China 18 Japan 19 Portugal 20 England 21 Ireland 22 Poland 23 Scotland 24 Spain 25 France 26 Greece 27 New Zealand

---

WRITING capital letters

5A To check that Ss understand *capital letter*, write *a* and *A*, *B* and *b* on the board and point to each one, asking 'Is this a capital letter?' Then go through the example and give Ss a few minutes to do the rest of the exercise. They can compare their answers with a partner before class feedback.

> **Answers:** b) <u>I</u>'m <u>A</u>li <u>M</u>ansour. c) <u>A</u>re you from <u>S</u>audi <u>A</u>rabia? d) <u>N</u>o, <u>I</u>'m from <u>E</u>ngland, from <u>L</u>ondon. e) <u>A</u>re you a student? f) <u>Y</u>es, <u>I</u> am.

B Go through the example with the class, checking the names in sentences a and b. Then give Ss a few minutes to match the rules. For *stronger classes*, ask Ss to cover the rules first, and give them a minute or two in pairs to think about and tell you why the capital letters are used in sentences a–f.

> **Answers:** 2 c), d) 3 d) 4 a), b), d), f) 5 a)–f)

Depending on your teaching context, you may want to point out that pronouns like *you, he, she*, etc. and normal nouns (e.g. *student, teacher*) only have a capital if they are at the beginning of a sentence.

C Start by asking two Ss to read out the online chat, and establish that there are no capital letters in the messages. Ask Ss to write out the messages in their notebooks with capitals where necessary. For feedback, you could invite different Ss to write the corrected messages on the board, and check that the others agree.

> **Answers:** 1 Hi, I'm Jeanette, and I'm a teacher in France. 2 Hi, I'm Makiko. I'm from Japan. Are you from Paris? 3 No, I'm from Lyon. Are you from Tokyo? 4 Yes, I am. I'm a student.

6A Give each student four slips of paper to write on. Ask them to write a message to their partner like the model in Ex 5C.

B Ss answer their partner's message and pass the answer back. They can then continue the chat, following the model.

SPEAKING

7A Demonstrate that Ss should write the country and city in their notebooks and keep them secret. Circulate and help with spelling and pronunciation as necessary. Ss could write more than one country and city, to give them more options in the following activity.

B Start by demonstrating the activity with the class: show Ss that you have written the name of a country and city on a folded slip of paper, then prompt them to ask *Where are you from?* then *Are you from … ?* until they guess the city. Put Ss into groups of 4–6 to take turns.

Homework ideas
- Ss exchange email addresses with someone they didn't work with during the lesson, then email messages to each other like the ones in Ex 5C.
- Ss find (e.g. three) small pictures of famous people to bring to the next lesson, and write the countries the people are from on the front of the pictures.
- Workbook Ex 1–5, p6–7

ARRIVALS

Introduction

Ss practise reading and talking about jobs, using the verb *be* and jobs vocabulary.

SUPPLEMENTARY MATERIALS

Resource bank p135

Ex 6 (optional extra activity): bring in a selection of photos of famous people, with their country of origin written on the picture (Ss should also bring in photos, c.f. homework idea from 1.1).

Project: bring in a large poster map of the world and small sticky labels for Ss to stick onto it.

Warm up

Elicit the word *teacher* by saying to Ss: *You're students. I'm a … ?* Write *teacher* on the board and the heading *Jobs* above it. Ask Ss for another example of a job in English and write it under the heading. Then tell Ss they have thirty seconds in pairs to think of any other jobs they know. After thirty seconds invite the pairs to share their ideas, and if they are correct, add them to the list on the board. Ss can later compare this list with the names of jobs they study in the lesson.

VOCABULARY jobs

1A Look at the example with the class, then give Ss a few minutes to write the names of the jobs. They can work in pairs or individually and compare answers with a partner.

B Play the recording for Ss to check their answers, and then play it again for them to underline the stressed syllable in each job. Point out that all the jobs apart from *engineer* have the stress on the first syllable, and that the *-er* and *-or* endings are 'weak' (you may want to show Ss the /ə/ sound at this point) and the 'r' sound is not pronounced. Then play the recording one more time for Ss to repeat, or simply say the names of the jobs yourself as the 'model'.

Watch out!

Ss may have trouble pronouncing *businessman/ businesswoman*: demonstrate that *business* only has two syllables: /ˈbɪznɪs/ and ask Ss to repeat this separately first. They may also need extra practice with *engineer* because of the unusual stress pattern, with the stress on the last syllable. You could use stress circles to help: ooO.

Answers: 1 teacher 2 waiter 3 doctor 4 singer 5 engineer 6 businessman/businesswoman 7 taxi driver 8 actor

2A Ask two pairs of Ss to read out the two conversations, and ask the class when they think we use *a* and when we use *an*. Then direct Ss to the rules and give them a minute or two to underline the alternatives. They can work in pairs or individually.

Answers: 1 an 2 a

B Demonstrate this activity yourself with a **strong student**, then put Ss in pairs to practise. You could extend the practice by asking Ss to include any other jobs from the list they made in the Warm up.

C Demonstrate by miming a job first, for Ss to ask questions. Put Ss in pairs or small groups to practise. Monitor the activity and make a note of any problems with the use of *a/an* or the pronunciation of jobs, to deal with in feedback.

➡ PHOTOBANK p139

Ss match the jobs with the photos, then in pairs complete the table.

Answers:
A
1 H 2 M 3 I 4 F 5 C 6 B 8 K 9 D 10 L 11 E 12 G 13 N 14 J
B
man: actor, waiter, businessman;
woman: businesswoman, waitress, actress, sportswoman

READING

3A Start by teaching *tourist, on holiday* and *happy*. You could do this by acting out a scenario where you are on holiday, sitting smiling and relaxing in a café with a cold drink, walking round taking photos and admiring the city, etc. Also teach *now*, perhaps by using a clock and contrasting the time now with an hour ago. Then focus Ss on the photos and establish that the people are in an airport: ask Ss the name of important airports in their country/countries. Give Ss a minute or two to look at the people and decide who is a tourist. Conduct brief feedback to see which person most Ss chose.

B Write *Who is a tourist?* on the board and tell Ss to read and answer the question.

Answer: Rosa Pérez López

C Direct Ss to the table (you may want to write or display a copy of it on the board) and make sure they understand the four types of information they need to find in the text, including *first time in London*. Do an example with the class, then give Ss about five minutes to complete the table and compare their answers with a partner.

Answers:

name	Ajay	Nicolas	Rosa	Gong Yue
job	computer engineer	actor/ waiter	doctor	student
where from?	India	France	Mexico	China
first time in London?	yes	no	yes	no

N.B. For Nicolas and Gong Yue it is not their first time in London because they work or study there. They could be at the airport to meet someone or because they are arriving back from a trip home.

Optional extra activities

1 Ask Ss to count the number of examples of *a* and *an* in the text and to check why, i.e. whether they're followed by a vowel or consonant. Answer: *a* = 8, *an* = 2

2 Ask Ss to underline all the examples of *in* + noun in the text (there are eight in total) and point out or elicit from Ss that here it is used with places, e.g. cities, countries, shops (*a café*). If Ss ask why *at* is used with *the University*, give examples such as *at school, at work, at the office* to show that we use *at* for places where we study or work. If your Ss are not studying in their hometown, they could practise telling the class: *I'm from (XX), but now I'm in (YY).*

GRAMMAR *be: he/she/it*

4A Start by reminding Ss of the *I* and *you* forms of *be,* which they have studied already. Establish that *he* is for male subjects, *she* is for female subjects, and *it* is for things. Write the four sentences on the board and give Ss a minute or two to identify the verb *be* then underline the examples on the board.

Answers: 2 She'<u>s</u> a doctor from Acapulco. (point out that *is* becomes *'s*) 3 It <u>isn't</u> my first time in England. (point out that *not* becomes *n't*) 4 <u>Is</u> it a good university? Yes, it <u>is</u>. (point out that in a *yes/no* question and an affirmative short answer we don't contract *is*)

B Give Ss a minute or two working individually to complete the tables. Monitor and check their accuracy.

Answers: isn't Is isn't 's (the question begins with a *Wh-* word, so it's possible to contract *is* to *'s*)

C Tell Ss to write the numbers 1–5 in their notebooks and explain that they need to write each sentence as they hear it. (N.B. Each sentence is said twice, the second time at normal speed.) Play the first example, pausing the recording to write the sentence on the board. For *weaker classes,* you may want to continue playing one sentence at a time and writing up the answer with the whole class; otherwise, play the rest of the sentences then give Ss time to compare what they've written with a partner.

Answers: 1 He's an actor. 2 She's a student. 3 Is he from India? 4 Is it your first time here? 5 Yes, it is.

Play the recording again. Each sentence is said slowly first, for Ss to hear how the words are linked together, then at natural speed, for Ss to repeat. You could ask Ss to repeat the sentence in chorus, then pause the recording and ask individuals to repeat. Help Ss to link words, e.g. *He's_an_actor, She's_a, Is_he* (N.B. the *h* in *he* is not pronounced), *Is_it, it_is.*

➡ **LANGUAGEBANK** 1.2 p118–119

Give Ss time to read through the summary. If you want to give Ss some extra practice in class, you could give half the class Ex 1.2A and the other half Ex 1.2B and provide keys for Ss to check their answers when they've finished. Then pair up Ss who have done different exercises and tell them to exchange answers.

Answers:
A
2 It's in Scotland. 3 He's from Switzerland.
4 Yes, she is. 5 No, it isn't. It's from South Korea.
6 It's in Brazil. 7 No, she isn't. She's from England.
8 No, it isn't. It's in Argentina.
B
2 Where's, from 3 Is, in 4 Where's 5 Is he a
6 Is she a 7 Is it 8 Where's

PRACTICE

5A Look at the example with the class, then Ss can work in pairs or individually to add *'s* in nine more places. You could run this as a race with Ss working in pairs to finish the exercise first. They can then read out their answers for the rest of the class to confirm or correct.

For *stronger classes* you could point out that we say we're in a place *for* a conference (also *for work, for a meeting, for a wedding*) but *on holiday* or *on business.*

Answers: Ellie Turner's from Montreal, Canada. She's a teacher at McGill. It's a big university in Montreal. She's in London for a conference.
Yong-Joon's from Korea. He's a taxi driver in Seoul, the capital. He's in London on holiday. He's happy to be here.
Pat's a businesswoman from Auckland, New Zealand. She's in London on business.

B Go through the example with the class, and remind Ss to think about where to add words like *a/an, in, from, on,* as well as *is/Is.* Ask Ss to write the questions in their notebooks, so they can use the prompts in their **Student's Book** for speaking practice later.

Answers: 2 Is she a doctor? 3 Is McGill University in London? 4 Is Yong-Joon in Japan? 5 Is he in London on holiday? 6 Is Auckland in New Zealand?

C Tell Ss to pay attention to the pronouns *he/she/it* as they match these questions and answers.

Answers: b) 5 c) 1 d) 4 e) 6 f) 2

D Before you put Ss in pairs to practise, you could say the questions for Ss to repeat in chorus, to give them a good model of the pronunciation. Tell Ss to cover the answers and use the prompts in Ex 5B to ask the questions. You could then extend the practice by asking Ss to write one more question about each person in Ex 5A to ask each other (e.g. *Is Ellie in London on holiday? Is Yong-Joon happy to be in London? Is Pat a tourist?*).

SPEAKING

6 Put Ss in pairs and direct A and B to the correct page, telling them not to show each other their information. Demonstrate what Ss have to do by drawing a simple sketch of a person's head and shoulders on the board, and eliciting some possible questions from Ss. Give Ss a few minutes to write their questions and circulate to help. Then tell them to ask their questions, starting with Student A. Monitor the activity and note down any examples of good language use, and any problem areas, so you can deal with these after the activity has finished.

Optional extra activity
Write the following words on the board: *an actor, a singer, a sportsman/sportswoman, a politician, a writer* and ask Ss to mime the jobs (to check that they understand them).

Hold up a picture of a famous person so that Ss can't see it, tell them it's someone famous and guide them to ask you questions to guess who it is, e.g. *Is it a man or woman? Where's he/she from? Is he/she (a singer)? Is he/she (a politician)?* Once you have done two or three examples, if Ss have brought their own photos of famous people, put them in groups to continue the activity.

Homework/Project ideas
• **Project:** if your Ss are from different countries, they write their names on sticky labels and stick them onto the correct part of the country on the world map poster. If your Ss are from the same country, they write the names of famous people on the sticky labels, and stick them onto the appropriate part of the world map. They can then add to the poster as the course goes on.
• **Workbook Ex 1–5, p8–9**

HOW DO YOU SPELL … ?

Introduction

Ss practise using the alphabet and learn to check spelling. They also practise listening and giving personal information.

SUPPLEMENTARY MATERIALS

Resource bank p138

Ex 1C (optional extra activity): Prepare a set of cards with the letters of the alphabet, large enough for the whole class to see when you hold them up, and small sets of alphabet cards for Ss to use in groups of 4–6.

Warm up

Use either of these warm up ideas if you think your Ss have some knowledge of the English alphabet. Don't worry about correcting Ss' pronunciation of the letters at this stage.

Either: Stand with Ss in a circle, say *A* and throw a ball or soft object to a *strong student*, who says *B*, throws the ball to another student, who says *C*, and so on until you reach the end of the alphabet. If a student doesn't know a letter, encourage the rest of the class to help, so that Ss pool their knowledge.

Or: Draw a line down the middle of the board and divide the class into two groups. Invite a student from each group to come and start the alphabet on the board, saying the first letter out loud as they write it, then tell them to run back to their group and pass the pen to a student who knows how to say and write the next letter, and so on. The aim is to be the first group to finish writing the alphabet on the board.

VOCABULARY   the alphabet

1A Before playing the recording, you could put Ss in pairs and give them time to go through the alphabet, putting a small tick ✓ by any letters they think they can pronounce, and a question mark *?* by any that they're not sure of. Play the recording once through for Ss to hear the pronunciation, then play it again for them to repeat.

B You may want to demonstrate to Ss that the letters are grouped according to their similar sounds, or you could let Ss work it out for themselves. Encourage Ss to work in pairs and help each other with this.

Answers: 1 A H J K 2 B C D E G P T V 3 F L M N S X
4 I Y 5 O 6 Q U W 7 R

C Play the recording twice for Ss to check their answers and repeat the groups of letters. Ss could then 'test' each other in pairs: student A says the number of a group of letters from 1B, student B says the letters in that group, e.g. Student A: *3* Student B: *F L M N S X*.

Optional extra activity

Using a large set of alphabet cards, hold up letters one at a time that spell a word (e.g. a job or the name of a country): the class calls out each letter as you hold it up, then the first person to work out the word you've spelled wins a point, and so on. You could then put Ss into groups of 4–6 with sets of small alphabet cards, to continue the activity. Ss could hold up letters that spell the name of another student in the group, then, once someone has worked out the name, the cards are passed to that student to spell another name, etc.

D Start by demonstrating the activity: tell Ss to listen and write the letters you say, then say *H–I* and *B–Y–E*. Ask a *strong student* to dictate back what they wrote down, then to spell a short word for you to write on the board. Then put Ss in pairs and direct them to their activities, and tell them to read out their letters for their partners to write down.

FUNCTION   giving personal information

2A Focus Ss on the photos and elicit some ideas about where the places are, e.g. office, gym, school. Tell Ss to write the numbers 1–3 in their notebooks, then play the first conversation and pause to check that Ss understand which photo it matches, before playing the other two conversations.

Answers: 1 C 2 A 3 B

B Direct Ss to the table and check that they understand what to listen for in each column: use one or two Ss' names to demonstrate *first name* and *family name*. Play the recording again, and give Ss time to compare answers with a partner before checking with the whole class.

Answers:

	First name	Family name	Room number
1	Frances	Taylor	379
2	Anabella	Almeida	124
3	Stefanie	Young	10

Unit 1 Recording 9
Conversation 1
A: Good evening. Can I help you?
B: My name's Taylor. Frances Taylor.
A: How do you spell that?
B: T-a-y-l-o-r.
A: T-a-y-l-o-r.
B: Yes.
A: And your first name?
B: It's Frances.
A: F-r-a-n-c … is it i-s?
B: No, e. E as in England. F-r-a-n-c-e-s.
A: Thanks. OK, here's your visitor's card.
    You're in television studio 379.
B: Thank you.
A: You're welcome.

Conversation 2
A: Can I help you?
B: Yes, I'm a student, a new student.
A: Welcome to the school. What's your family name?
B: Almeida.
A: How do you spell Almeida?
B: A-l-m-e-i-d-a.
A: And what's your first name?
B: Anabella.
A: OK, Anabella. Here's your student card.
B: Thank you. Oh, my name's wrong.
A: Oh, sorry. How do you spell it?
B: It's Anabella, A-n-a-b-e-l-l-a.
A: A-n-a-b-e-l-l-a.
B: That's right.
A: OK, Anabella. You're in room 124.
B: 124?
A: Yes.

Conversation 3

A: OK, what's your family name?

B: Young, Y-o-u-n-g.

A: And what's your first name?

B: Stefanie.

A: How do you spell that?

B: S-t-e-f-a-n-i-e.

A: Ah yes, for the fitness class in room ten.

B: That's right.

A: What's your phone number?

B: Er … it's oh five three two, four one nine.

A: And what's your email address?

B: It's stef at yahoo dot com.

A: OK, thank you.

3A Establish with Ss that this is an example of the type of form they might complete to join a club, a library, a class, etc. Then give Ss a minute or two to complete the form.

Answers: Family name Nationality Phone Email address

B Look at the example with the class, then Ss can work individually or in pairs to choose the correct alternatives and check in the audio script.

Answers: 2 spell 3 oh 4 at, dot

N.B. *oh* is used in British and American English. *Zero* is also possible, particularly in American English.

C Before playing the recording, you could model the two intonation patterns and ask Ss which they think sounds natural. Give Ss plenty of opportunity to practise the question with falling intonation.

Answer: b)

Teaching tip

The intonation usually falls on questions beginning with *wh-* words: you could show Ss that if you say the question with rising intonation, it sounds as if you are surprised or unsure. To help Ss to produce the falling intonation pattern, encourage them to emphasise the stressed word (*email*) and let their voices fall away after it.

▶ **LANGUAGEBANK** 1.3 p118–119

The **Language bank** has a summary of the questions and answers covered in Exs 2 and 3. If Ss ask you about *Argentinian* and *Italian*, point out that these are adjectives describing people from Argentina and Italy. Ss can do Ex 1.3 in class or for homework: if they do it in class, you could ask one or two pairs to act out the corrected dialogue.

Answers:

A: What's your first name?

B: Ana.

A: And what's your family name?

B: *It's* Fernandez.

A: What's *your* nationality?

B: I'm Italian.

A: And your *phone number*?

B: It's 0372 952 594.

A: What's *your* email address?

B: It's anastella247@hotmail.com.

A: How *do* you spell 'anastella'? With one 'n'?

B: Yes, one 'n' and two 'l's.

4A Ss can invent a phone number and email address if they don't want to give out their private details. Tell them not to show their partner the information, so they have to listen carefully for the information.

B Tell Ss to practise asking and answering, and to write down the information so their partners can check that it's accurate afterwards.

LEARN TO check spelling

5A Give Ss a moment to familiarise themselves with the four lines of dialogue and establish that they need to underline the individual letters that are stressed, not the words.

Answers: A: F-r-a-n-c … is it i-s? B: No, e. E as in England.

speakout TIP

Before Ss look at the tip, give them one or two more examples of how to use *as in* and a word, e.g. *b as in book, d as in doctor*. You could elicit some ideas for *Y* and *J*, then let Ss compare with the ideas in the tip. Give them a moment or two to think of words for *G, I* and *E* (e.g. *good, India, email*).

B Demonstrate the example with a *strong student*. You may want to give Ss time to go through the pairs of names and underline the letter that needs correcting before they start the practice in pairs.

SPEAKING

6 Ss can sit in groups of four to complete the table. Alternatively, they could stand up and walk round the room, finding three different Ss to talk to. Monitor the activity closely and note down examples of good language use and any problems with grammar, pronunciation, etc. to deal with in feedback.

Teaching tip

When monitoring a speaking activity, try to stand or sit near enough to the Ss to hear them, without making them feel self-conscious. Have a small notebook and pen handy so that you can write down examples of language from the lesson that a student uses well, as well as examples of mistakes. In feedback, write the good examples on the board and praise the Ss, then write the mistakes on the board and encourage Ss to correct them. Feedback like this helps Ss to see the benefit of this type of speaking activity. In smaller classes, make sure that it isn't possible to identify who said the examples, e.g. by varying the examples slightly while retaining the aspects you want to highlight.

Homework ideas

- Ss exchange phone numbers with two or three classmates that they didn't speak to in the lesson, and practise asking for and giving personal information on the phone.
- Ss make a list of 6–10 international words (c.f. lead-in lesson) and practise spelling them aloud.
- **Workbook** Ex 1–4, p10

AROUND THE WORLD

Introduction

Ss watch an extract from the BBC programme *Around the World* where people talk about their country, city or village, their job and the importance of English for them. Ss then learn and practise how to give a personal introduction in spoken and written form.

SUPPLEMENTARY MATERIALS

Warm up: A map of the world, e.g. a globe, a poster or on the internet.

Ex 1B: A picture of an ugly place, e.g. an industrial area.

Warm up

Using the world map, demonstrate that *around the world* means *in many places / parts of the world*. Divide the class into groups of 3–4 and play 'around the world': say the name of a country that begins with the letter *A*, then choose a group to say a country beginning with the letter *B*; they then choose the next group, who say a country beginning with the letter *C*, and so on. Groups get a point every time they can think of an appropriate country; if they can't, they have to say 'Pass'. The winning group is the one with the most points.

DVD PREVIEW

1A Lead in via a brief discussion of what Ss can see in the photos. This should give you an idea of how much of the vocabulary in Ex 1 is familiar to at least some of the Ss. Direct Ss to the word box and find examples of *city* in the photos with the class. Put Ss in pairs to do the rest of the words. In feedback, check the pronunciation of: <u>countryside, mountain, village</u> and <u>building</u>.

mountain, village, building
   /ɪ/   /ɪ//ɪ/   /ɪ//ɪ/

B You could point out to the Ss that, apart from *beautiful*, the other adjectives are pairs of opposites. You could check that Ss understand *beautiful* by using a picture of an industrial area, or something that is <u>not</u> beautiful. Go through the example with the class, then put Ss in pairs to continue.

Answers: new: city, village, building
big: city, mountain, river, building
small: city, river, village, building
beautiful: matches all the words
cold: city, sea, river, village
hot: city, village
N.B. With *cold* and *hot* it's more natural to say *the (city)'s hot* than *a (hot) city*, and *the sea's cold* rather than *a cold sea*, etc. The other adjectives are usually used in front of the nouns: *a small village, beautiful countryside*, etc. However, you may not feel it's necessary to address this yet.

2 Explain to the class that they're going to watch some people talking from different countries around the world. Ss could predict which countries by looking at the photos, then read the text to check. You may want to check the meaning of *important* by asking Ss what things are important to them, e.g. family, a job, to be happy, etc.

Answers: Finland, Oman, Chile, Malaysia, Canada

DVD VIEW

3A Demonstrate to Ss that they need to write a number from 1–5 next to each country when they see or hear about it on the DVD. Play the first part of the DVD and elicit that the first country is Chile, then play the rest of the DVD through.

Answers: 2 a 3 e 4 c 5 d

B and C Go through the example with the class then play the DVD again. Give Ss time to compare answers in pairs and help each other before checking with the whole class.

Answers: Canada: rivers, mountains, countryside
Oman: city, buildings, countryside, village
Finland: city, countryside
Malaysia: beach, sea, rivers

D Before putting Ss in pairs, teach *winter / summer sport* (e.g. mime skiing and playing golf) and *shop / office assistant* (mime someone on a till and someone doing filing). Give Ss 1–2 minutes to compare answers, then play the recording again.

Answers: 2 cold 3 waiter 4 student 5 village 6 winter
7 new 8 shop

Optional extra activities
1 Teach *favourite* (e.g. by telling Ss about your favourite chocolate, singer, actor, etc.), then put Ss in small groups to tell each other their favourite country from the DVD. Encourage them to give a reason, e.g. *X is my favourite because the buildings are beautiful.*

2 Personalise the topic by putting the following prompts on the board for Ss to complete about their country or a country they know:
   ... is a beautiful beach in ...
   ... is a new building in ...
   ... is an old city in ...
   ... is a small village in ...
   ... is a big river / mountain in ...
Ss compare their sentences in pairs or small groups.

DVD 1 Around the World

Pablo: Hello, or, ah, 'hola' from Chile. My name is Pablo, and I'm from Santiago. Santiago is a mix of old buildings and new buildings. My job – I'm a bus driver in Santiago. In my job I speak Spanish and English. The mountains in Chile are very beautiful. It's very cold, but I love it.

Eric: Hello, my name's Eric and I'm from British Columbia in Canada. I'm a waiter in a restaurant, a restaurant on a train. It's a good job; people are very nice, very friendly. I speak English and French in my job. Canada is beautiful – the rivers, the mountains – really beautiful. I love it here.

Mizna: 'Assalamu alaikum', that's hello in my country Oman. My name is Mizna, and I'm a student at university in Muscat. I speak English and Arabic at university. Muscat is a beautiful city with many big buildings, for example, the Grand Mosque. But I am not from Muscat. I am from a small village in the countryside. It's very hot in my village, but I love it.

Kustaa: Hello, or 'hei' from Finland. My name's Kustaa and I'm from Helsinki, the capital city of Finland. I'm a businessman in Helsinki. I speak English and Finnish in my work, and yes it's very, very cold here. The countryside around Helsinki is beautiful, and it's very good for sports – winter sports. I really love it here.

Aisha: Hi from Malaysia. I'm Aisha and I'm from Kuala Lumpur. KL is a big city with a lot of new buildings. I'm a shop assistant in a tourist shop. I speak English and Malay in my job. The countryside in Malaysia is beautiful – the beaches and the sea, and the rivers. It's very hot here. I love it.

speakout you and your country

4A Start by teaching the words *very* (e.g. by comparing something in the classroom that's small with something very small), and *centre* (e.g. ask for the name of a building/shop in the centre of the city where they're studying). Then tell Ss they're going to listen to a woman called Kaitlin answering questions 1–7 and give them time to read through the questions, so they know what information they're listening for. Establish that they only need to write short answers, e.g. two or three words, not full sentences. Play the recording, then give Ss a few minutes in pairs to check their answers.

Answers: 1 Dublin, Ireland 2 not big 3 old 4 tourist information assistant 5 centre of Dublin 6 yes 7 yes

B Give Ss a few moments to look at the **key phrases**. You may want to pause the recording after every couple of sentences, to give Ss time to tick the phrases.

Answers:
Hello or 'dia duit' from Ireland. ✓
I'm/My name is ✓ …
I'm a/an (teacher/engineer) in …
Dublin/Cannes is (a city/a town/a village) in…
It's/It isn't very (big/beautiful/hot/small/old/new). ✓
The countryside (in Ireland) is beautiful. ✓
I (really) love it (here).

Unit 1 Recording 12

Hello, or 'dia duit' from Ireland. My name's Kaitlin and I'm from Dublin, the capital city of Ireland. Dublin's a beautiful city. It isn't very big but it's very old. I'm a tourist information assistant, at the tourist information office in the centre of Dublin. So of course, English is important for my job. The countryside in Ireland is beautiful with mountains, rivers and the sea. The villages are old and beautiful. Goodbye, or 'slan' in Irish.

5A Tell Ss to write the numbers 1–7 in their notebooks, and to write full sentences for their answers. Check that Ss understand *town* (i.e. between a village and a city in terms of size). If your Ss are all from the same country, encourage them to comment on different parts of the country when talking about the countryside. Circulate and help, reminding Ss to use the key phrases. You could also encourage them to practise saying the answers, so they don't need to read them aloud from their notebooks.

B Before putting Ss in pairs you could give the whole class some practice in asking the seven questions, repeating in chorus and individually after your model. This will give you the opportunity to help Ss with pronunciation, especially the faking intonation on the *Wh-* questions. Ss then practise asking and answering, trying to refer to their books as little as possible. When Ss seem confident, you could invite several pairs to ask and answer their questions in front of the class. Finally, give Ss feedback on their use of language, both with praise for good examples and correction of common mistakes.

writeback a personal introduction

6A Ss should number the information from 1–7 in the order they find it in the blog. Give them time to compare answers with a partner before checking with the whole class. In feedback you could focus on the use of *with* in the text: when you say the name of your company (*I'm a businesswoman with Volkswagen*), for adding information about your city (*Berlin is a city with …*) and for adding information about what makes the countryside beautiful (*the countryside is beautiful, with mountains and …*).

Answers: b) d) e) f) h)

B Encourage Ss to write some notes first, using the example in Ex 6A to help, and also the **Key phrases** and the audio script, if they wish. Circulate and help with grammar, provide vocabulary that Ss need, etc. Once Ss have written their introduction, they can swap and read each other's work, perhaps suggesting additions and/or improvements.

Homework ideas
- Ss write a final version of their personal introduction.
- Workbook Ex 5, p10

LOOKBACK

SUPPLEMENTARY MATERIALS

Ex 3B: Prepare a list of jobs from the unit, including some from the Photo bank, if your Ss have studied them.

Ex 4B: Prepare a list of facts about famous people and places, to give to Ss who run out of ideas.

BE: I/YOU

1A Point out that the questions and answers are referring to sentences 1–6 in part B below. Go through the example, then give Ss 1–2 minutes to complete the sentences, working alone.

Answers: 2 'm 3 you 4 am 5 in 6 not 7 six 8 I

B Either go through the example or demonstrate the activity with the class: tell Ss you're thinking of one of the sentences and invite them to ask you questions until they guess the right one. Put Ss in pairs to continue.

COUNTRIES

2A Show Ss the example and point out that they have the first letter of each country to help them. Put Ss in pairs to write the countries. Once you've checked the answers, Ss could take turns to 'test' each other: Student A closes their book, Student B says names of cities and Student A responds with the correct countries.

Answers: 2 India 3 Russia 4 Saudi Arabia 5 China
6 Japan

B Ss work alone to write five more countries and a city from each. Circulate and help with spelling as necessary.

C Put Ss in pairs to say their cities and see if their partner can respond with the correct country in English. Monitor the activity to check Ss' pronunciation of the countries and deal with any problems in feedback.

JOBS

3A Ss could work in pairs and do this as a race, i.e. the first pair to finish wins five points, then further points are awarded to pairs around the class for correct spelling and pronunciation. Alternatively, this could be done as a competition in teams: write the gapped words on the board one at a time (Ss have books closed) and the first team to 'buzz' and answer correctly wins a point.

Answers: 1 waiter 2 taxi driver 3 engineer 4 doctor
5 actor 6 teacher 7 singer 8 businesswoman

B Put Ss in groups and tell them to choose any job from the unit, (including the **Photo bank** if Ss have studied it). Ss take turns to mime the job and answer *yes/no* questions from the other Ss in the group.

Alternative idea

Prepare a list of jobs, including ones from the Photo bank if appropriate. Divide the class into groups, then one member from each group comes to you and looks at the first job on the list. They run back to their group and draw or mime the job. When the group has worked out the job, another member comes to you, tells you their answer, then looks at the next job on the list, and so on.

BE: HE/SHE/IT

4A Say the first sentence from the exercise and see if Ss can correct it before they look at the example. Then give Ss time to correct the sentences, working alone or with a partner. Alternatively, you could run this as a competition (Ss have books closed), writing the sentences on the board (or for more of a challenge, simply reading out the sentences) for teams to 'buzz' and correct.

Answers: 2 Russia 3 France 4 Hong Kong 5 Russia
6 Japan 7 England 8 India 9 the USA 10 Australia

B Give Ss a few minutes to do this in pairs, and circulate to provide help with grammar, spelling, etc. You may want to have some facts about famous people and places available to give to Ss who run out of ideas. Both Ss in the pair should write down the three sentences, in case they are separated in the next stage of the activity.

C For this stage, you could put three pairs of Ss together into groups of six, or separate the pairs and put the Ss into new groups of 4–6.

Project idea

If your Ss started a world map project in lesson 1.2, sticking their names and/or the names of famous people onto a world map poster, they could add the people and places from Ex 4 to it, using small sticky labels.

THE ALPHABET

5A Ss work alone to correct the spelling of the words. They could also practise saying the spelling of the words to themselves before the next stage.

Answers: 2 television 3 camera 4 university 5 restaurant
6 email 7 football 8 chocolate 9 information 10 internet

B Put Ss in pairs and suggest that they ask about the spelling of words at random, rather than working through the words in numerical order. Monitor and be prepared to deal with any problems with the pronunciation of letters in feedback.

GIVING PERSONAL INFORMATION

6A Go through the example with the class, then give Ss time to write the other questions alone or with a partner.

Answers: 2 What's your family name?
3 Where are you from? 4 What's your phone number?
5 What's your email address?

B Ss work alone to make three changes to the information.

C You may want to demonstrate this first with a *strong student*, showing Ss that they can circle the three things on the card that their partner changes.

Homework ideas

- Ss need to bring two photos of their friends and family to the next lesson. They should also bring a photo of themselves when they were a baby/teenager.

OVERVIEW

FAMILY PHOTOS

Introduction

Students practise talking about their families, using *be* and family vocabulary. They also practise listening and learn to write contractions.

SUPPLEMENTARY MATERIALS

Resource bank p140

Warm up: bring in a photo of yourself as a teenager, and two photos of friends or brothers/sisters, also as teenagers.

Ex 1A: be prepared to draw a simple version of your family tree on the board.

Ex 6B: bring in two photos of your family and/or friends and be prepared to talk about them.

Warm up

Show Ss the three photos of yourself and two friends/brothers/sisters as teenagers but don't say which one is you. Put the photos on the board, number them 1, 2 and 3 and ask Ss *Which photo is me?* Get Ss to vote for the photo they think by putting their hands up, then finally reveal which one is you. If Ss have brought photos of themselves as babies/teenagers, collect them in so that they're anonymous, then mix them up and display them on the board or around the classroom. Ss work in pairs and guess who the photos belong to, saying *I think this is (Jorge)*, etc. Finally, Ss can reveal their identities, e.g. *No, it's not Jorge, it's me!*

VOCABULARY family

1A Illustrate the idea of *family* by drawing a very simple version of your family tree on the board, with your name somewhere on it, point to it and say *My family*. Then direct Ss to the family photos and elicit some ideas for photo A. Put Ss in pairs to help each other match the other photos to family members.

Answers: 1 D 2 C 3 F 4 E 5 A 6 B

Teaching tip

Putting Ss in pairs for a vocabulary matching activity encourages them to 'pool' their passive knowledge and 'teach' each other. Try to ensure that two weaker Ss are not paired together for this: put them with a stronger student to make a group of three, if necessary.

B Play the recording for Ss to check their answers. Then model the /ʌ/ sound, as in *but* and *cup*, for Ss to familiarise themselves with it before they listen to the recording again and underline four words with the sound. Play the recording again, pausing for Ss to repeat the words.

Answers: husband, son, mother, brothers
N.B. You may want to elicit/point out that the sound is often the letters 'o' and 'u'.

C Go through the examples with the whole class, then put Ss in pairs to complete the table.

Answers:

husband	wife
father	mother
son	daughter
brother	sister
parents	
children	

D Demonstrate the activity with a student, then put Ss in pairs. They could also 'reverse' the prompts, so A says the people, and B responds with the photo A–F. Monitor and deal with any pronunciation problems in feedback.

LISTENING

2A Tell Ss they're going to listen to two people talking about four of the photos. They need to write a letter from A–F next to the numbers 1–4. Play the recording, then give Ss a moment or two to compare their answers with a partner.

Answers: 1 A 2 E 3 D 4 C

B Direct Ss to the example and they need to write another name after *Margit*. Give them a moment or two to look at the other sentences, then play the recording again. Put Ss in pairs to check their answers.

Answers: 1 Margit and Erika 2 Tim 3 Erika 4 Flori
5 Johnny 6 Lewis

Unit 2 Recording 2

Conversation 1
B: Hi, Erika. Coffee?
A: No thanks.
B: Hey, photos. Let's see …
A: Yes, from the party.
B: The party?
A: Yes, my daughter's birthday. At the weekend.
B: Oh, great. Is this your family?
A: Yes, me, my husband, my two sons and my daughter.
B: And where are you?
A: We're at home in …

Conversation 2
B: Oh, and is this your mother?
A: Yes, this is my mum. And me, of course.
B: And the birthday cake.
A: Yes.
B: What's your mother's name?
A: Margit.
B: Margaret?
A: Well, yes, Margaret in English. Margit in Hungarian.
B: Are you Hungarian? You and your mother?
A: Yes.
B: You aren't English?
A: No, we aren't English!
B: Really, your English is *very* good!
A: Well thanks but …

Conversation 3
A: This is me and Tim.
B: Your husband.
A: Yeah.
B: Is he Hungarian too?
A: No, he's English.
B: I see. And what's his job?

A: He's a businessman.
B: A businessman. What business is he in?
A: The hotel and restaurant business.
B: Hmm …

Conversation 4
A: … and this is a photo of the children.
B: Oh, it's a great picture.
A: Yeah
B: And this is the birthday girl?
A: Yes, our daughter Florence. We call her Flori.
B: Ahhh. How old is she?
A: She's seven now.
B: And your sons …
A: Yes, Johnny and Lewis.
B: Are they students?
A: Yes. Johnny's at university.
B: So he's a student.
A: Yes, at the University of London.
B: And Lewis?
A: Lewis is at music school. He's a musician. Guitar, piano …
B: Really? That's great …

Optional extra activity
For practice of *yes/no* questions with *he/she*, ask Ss to work alone and write 4–6 questions (with the answer *Yes* or *No*) about the information in the recording (they can consult the recording script). Give them one or two of these examples:

Is Erika Hungarian?

Is Tim a waiter?

Is she married to a Frenchman?

Is Flori seven?

Is Johnny a musician?

Once Ss have written their questions, they work in pairs: Student A closes his/her book and answers Student B's questions, and vice versa (if the answer is *No*, they should give the correct information, e.g. *No, he isn't, he's a businessman*).

GRAMMAR *be: you/we/they*

3A Do the first answer with the class, then, while Ss are underlining the other verbs, write/display the sentences on the board so that Ss can come up and underline the verbs in feedback.

Answers:
1 A: Where <u>are</u> you? B: We<u>'re</u> at home.
2 A: <u>Are</u> they students? B: Yes. Johnny<u>'s</u> at university.
3 A: You <u>aren't</u> English? B: No, we <u>aren't</u> English.

B Before asking Ss to complete the table, make sure that they understand *we, you* (plural) and *they*. You could go through the table with the whole class, or give Ss a moment or two to work on it alone.

Answers: We/You/They *aren't* from Poland.
Are you/we/they in the right classroom?
Yes, you/we/they *are*.
Where *are* you from?

C Play the recording through once for Ss to familiarise themselves with the sound of the contractions, i.e. they sound like one word. When you play the recording again, encourage Ss to repeat all three examples of *you're, we're* and *they're* in each sentence.

D Tell Ss to write the numbers 1–6 in their notebooks and to write the six sentences they hear. You may need to repeat the recording if Ss seem to have difficulty with any of the sentences. When Ss have checked the answers, tell them to close their books (so they don't read aloud) and play the recording again for them to repeat the sentences.

Answers: 1 We're from England. 2 They're actors. 3 We're in Japan. 4 You're right. 5 We're in class. 6 They're here.

🠺 **LANGUAGEBANK** 2.1 p120–121

The **Language bank** reminds Ss that *you* can be used for one person or more than one. If you feel Ss need more consolidation of the difference between *we/you/they*, they could do Ex 2.1A in class.

Answers:
A
2 We're from France. 3 You're in the wrong room. 4 Are they Brazilian? 5 They're Louise and Kerri. 6 We're married. 7 They aren't in class. 8 A: Where are you? B: We're in class.
B
A: Hi, where are you from?
B: We're from California.
A: Are you from Los Angeles?
B: No, we're not. We're from San Francisco.
A: Are you Kathy and Chris?
B: No, they're in Room 205!

PRACTICE

4A Start by setting the context here: demonstrate that Student A is showing Student B two photos, and Student B is asking questions about them. Do number 1 with the class as an example, then give Ss a few minutes to complete the exercise.

Answers: 2 we aren't 3 We're 4 Are they 5 aren't 6 they 7 aren't 8 They're 9 Is 10 are

Optional extra activity
Ss work in pairs. Student A takes the role of one of the people in Ex 1 and 2, e.g. Johnny, Tim or Flori, and tells Student B about two of the photos in 1A. Student B asks questions about the people, e.g. *Are you brothers? Are they your parents? Is your father a doctor?* etc.

WRITING contractions

5A Write the example *They are my parents.* on the board, then rub out the *a* in *are* and write in the apostrophe, showing how the two words 'close up' together and look like one. Give Ss a few moments to do the other contractions.

Answers: 2 She's my daughter. 3 We aren't sisters. 4 Tom's my brother.

B You could go through the rules with the class, eliciting their ideas, or give Ss time to think about the rules and compare ideas with a partner.

Answers: 1 Use 2 Use
N.B. You could point out that it's only in more formal writing that Ss shouldn't use contractions.

C Focus Ss on the example and give them a few minutes to rewrite the text messages, working alone.

Answers: I'm at the airport but your brother *isn't* here. *What's* his mobile number? It *isn't* in my phone.
Hi, Tom. I'm sorry, I don't know. We're in an English class now.
Hi, Marianna. It's OK. Luca's here now. See you soon. T
N.B. If Ss ask you about the contraction in *don't*, explain that it means *do not*.

D Ss take turns to be Marianna or Tom, and read out their messages. You could extend this by underlining the following words/phrases in the messages and asking Ss to substitute different words/phrases: *airport, brother, mobile number, an English class, Luca.* Ss work in pairs to think of alternatives then read out the 'new' sequence of text messages to the class.

speakout TIP

Go through the sentences on the board with the class, reminding Ss that *She's married to X* means X is her husband. Tell Ss that we say *I'm married to (someone)*, or *I'm married*. If Ss ask about the difference between *in* and *at*, show them that we use *at* for a place or event (e.g. *airport, home, school, party, conference*), and *in* for countries, cities and rooms.

You could suggest that Ss build up a separate list of prepositions on a page in their notebooks, and start by copying the four examples here.

SPEAKING

6A If any Ss haven't brought in photos, they could look on their mobile phones for appropriate ones, or access some on the internet. Alternatively, they could draw rough sketches/ silhouettes of the people, or use the photos supplied in the Communication bank.

Give Ss time to write notes, reminding them that they can refer to the recording script for the listening in Ex 2, and the **Photo bank** p148 and 152 or previous lessons for jobs and nationalities. Circulate and help Ss with any language they need. Also suggest that they practise talking about the photos, using their notes, before the next stage where they talk to other Ss.

Teaching tip
For speaking activities where Ss have to give a talk/ present information, encouraging them to practise their talk before 'going public' (talking in front of other Ss) can help to build confidence, as well as making them sound more natural because they don't need to keep referring to their notes.

B If you've brought in some family photos, you could demonstrate what you want Ss to do, showing them that you are not referring to your notes and encouraging them to ask you questions at the end. Either put Ss in pairs or small groups to talk about the photos, or ask them to walk around the class and talk to different people. To finish, you could ask three or four Ss to hold up their photos and ask the rest of the class what information anyone remembers about them, e.g. *That's Suzanne. She's from France. She's a singer in the theatre.*

Homework ideas
- Ss exchange mobile numbers with two other Ss and arrange a time to have a 'text conversation', e.g. *I'm in/ at … Where are you? I'm in/at … with … Are you OK? Yes, I am.*, etc.
- Ss write two short paragraphs about the photos they presented in Ex 6.
- Workbook Ex 1–4, p11–12

A FAMILY BUSINESS

Introduction

Ss practise reading and talking about family businesses, using possessive adjectives and numbers.

SUPPLEMENTARY MATERIALS

Resource bank p139

Ex 3B: bring in a slip of paper with the names and ages of four of your family members or friends, and be prepared to tell Ss about them.

Warm up

Review the alphabet, family and jobs vocabulary. Ask the class *How do you spell 'mother'?* and write the word on the board as Ss call out the letters. Do the same with *manager*, then put Ss in pairs and tell them to take turns asking their partners how to spell words related to jobs and family. You may want to give Ss time to prepare their list of words first, referring to pages 10 and 18 of their **Student's Book**, and the **Photo bank** p139.

VOCABULARY numbers 11–100

1A Write the number *1* on the board and gesture to Ss to tell you the next number, and so on until you reach *10*. Then ask Ss what comes next, and if they start to call out *11, 12*, direct them to the numbers and words to continue writing the numbers from *12* onwards.

Answers: fifteen 15 nineteen 19 fourteen 14 twenty 20 sixteen 16 thirteen 13 eighteen 18 twelve 12 seventeen 17

B Play the recording for Ss to repeat the numbers, in chorus and individually. Make sure that Ss are stressing the second syllable in numbers *13* to *18*, e.g. *thirteen* oO.

C Demonstrate this by writing a number on the board and asking a student to say it. Then put Ss in pairs to continue, writing the numbers on a page of their notebooks.

2A Read through the first four numbers and tell Ss that the three missing numbers end in *-ty*. Give them a minute to write the numbers and check with a partner.

Answers: 70 seventy 80 eighty 90 ninety

B Play the recording for Ss to check their answers, then for them to repeat, making sure that they're stressing the first syllable in the numbers, e.g. *thirty* Oo.

C Tell Ss to write the numbers 1–8 in their notebooks and to listen and write eight numbers. Give Ss time to check their answers in pairs before checking with the class (or playing the recording again if they had difficulties).

Answers: 282, 312, 457, 593, 639, 728, 811

Watch out!

Ss may have trouble differentiating between 13/30, 14/40 and so on, both in listening and speaking. You could compare the two stress patterns: 13 – oO and 30 – Oo and give some brief practice where you dictate, e.g. *30, 40, 15, 16, 17, 80, 19* to Ss, then put them in pairs to dictate a selection of the numbers to each other.

3A Tell Ss to write the names and ages but not to show their answers to other Ss.

B Demonstrate the activity yourself first. Show Ss a slip of paper with four names and ages on it, tell them about one of the people and prompt them too ask you how old he/she is and how to spell his/her name. Then put Ss in pairs to ask and answer about their four people.

READING

4A Focus Ss on the first photo and say *Are they brothers and sister? What do you think?* Elicit one or two ideas from the class, then put Ss in pairs to continue.

B Tell Ss to read the text quickly, just to find the answers to 4A. Reassure them that they will have time to read the text again afterwards.

Answers: 1 brother and sister and her husband
2 husband and wife 3 husband, wife and two sons

C Before Ss read the text again, you could check the following vocabulary: *downtown* (in the business part of the city – mainly used in the USA), *friendly* (demonstrate someone being friendly), *fantastic* (very, very good), *shop* (verb meaning *go to the shops and buy things*), *perfect* (number 1), *stay* (time in a place). Direct Ss to the table and the information that is already filled in. Elicit where number 1 is (New York), then give Ss a few minutes to complete the table for 2 and 3.

Answers:

	Business	Where?	Good things
1	restaurant	New York	small, friendly and the food is fantastic
2	supermarket	Edinburgh	it's open 24/7
3	hotel	Paris	15 minutes from the city centre

Optional extra activity

Write the following phrases from the reading text on the board and ask Ss to complete them with information that is true about a place or places they know:

____ is in the centre of ____.

____ is open 24/7.

____ is only ____ minutes from the city centre.

____ is the perfect place for a coffee/a party/a holiday.

Put Ss in small groups to read out their phrases, then ask the groups to choose the best three to read out to the class.

GRAMMAR possessive adjectives

5A Start by telling Ss to cover the reading text. Then say *My name's …* and elicit the question *What's your name?*

Write *my* and *your* on the board and above them the title *possessive adjectives*. Direct Ss to the sentences and the example, and give them a few minutes to complete the sentences, working alone or in pairs. They can then uncover the text and check their answers.

Answers: 1 Her 2 its (point out that *its doors* means *the doors of the supermarket*) 3 their 4 My, our, your

B Focus Ss on the table and check that they understand the difference between *I* and *my*, e.g. *I'm a teacher. It's my job.* You may want to go through the table with the class, or give Ss a minute or two to complete it alone, then check their answers in **Language bank** 2.2.

Answers:

subject pronoun	possessive adjective	subject pronoun	possessive adjective
I	my	it	*its*
you	*your*	we	our
he	his	they	*their*
she	*her*		

⟹ LANGUAGEBANK 2.2 p120–121

Use the **Language bank** to highlight the difference between *its* and *it's*. Remind Ss that you don't add an -s to possessive adjectives for plural nouns, e.g. *your books*, not *yours books*.

If you feel that Ss need extra practice of possessive adjectives before moving on to Ex 6, give Ex 2.2A to one half of the class and Ex 2.2B to the other half. Give each half of the class an answer key to check their answers, then have pairs from one half read out the correct dialogues, so the Ss from the other half can complete those dialogues as they listen, and vice versa.

Answers:
A
1   A: Hi, my name's Gina. What's your name?
     B: Hi, I'm Brad.
2   A: Who's she?
     B: Oh, *her* name's Julia.
3   A: And who's the man with Julia?
     B: I don't know *his* name.
4   A: It's an American sport.
     B: What's *its* name?
     A: American football!
5   A: Mr and Mrs Black, what's *your* phone number?
     B: *Our* phone number's 2048 306 8420473.
6   A: This is a photo of the children.
     B: What are *their* names?
     A: Jake and Patsy.
B
Conversation 1   1 your   2 it   3 My   4 you   5 I
Conversation 2   6 She   7 her
Conversation 3   8 you   9 we   10 our   11 I

PRACTICE

6A Tell Ss that the sentences in this exercise are about one business, and to think about what the business is while they choose the correct answers.

Answers: 1 her 2 Her 3 his 4 Their 5 Its 6 Our 7 my

B Ss tell each other what they think the business is and why. They could also speculate about why Kasem isn't happy in his job.

Answers: It's a hotel. (receptionist, rooms)

7 Before Ss look at the text, direct them to the picture and ask them where they think Mama's salsa comes from, then tell them to read the text quickly to find out if they were right (It's from South America). Ss then complete the sentences, working alone or with a partner.

Answers: 2 its 3 Her 4 their 5 his 6 our

SPEAKING

8A Tell Ss that they're going to look at information about two more family businesses, but their information isn't complete. Put Ss into pairs of AA and BB (or groups of As and Bs) and direct the As to their incomplete texts on p148. Tell them to prepare questions to find the missing information in each gap, e.g. *Lucia is from _____. Question: Where's Lucia from?*

Monitor while Ss write their questions.

Answers:
How old is Julia?
What's his nationality?
Where's Julia from?
Where's their business?
What are their jobs?
What's their company called? (N.B. Encourage Ss to use this form instead of *What's their company's name?* which uses the possessive -s)
What's their family name?
What's their restaurant called? (See note above.)
Where's their restaurant?
Where are they from?

B Pair up Students A and B, and tell them to ask and answer their questions, and write the missing information in their texts. Remind them to ask about spelling if they're unsure. Monitor while they do this and take notes of any good use of question forms, possessive adjectives, etc. as well as any problem areas, to use for praise and correction in feedback.

Optional extra activity
Put Ss in pairs and tell them to invent a family business and be prepared to answer the following questions:
1   What's your business?
2   Where is it?
3   How old is it?
4   Who's the manager?
5   How many family members are in it, and what are their jobs?
6   What are the good things about it?

Circulate and help while Ss prepare the answers to the questions. Then put pairs of Ss into groups of four and tell them to ask and answer the questions about the business. They should also make a note of the other pair's answers, as they will need the information later. In feedback, ask Ss to report to the class about another pair's business, e.g. *It's a flower shop in London. It's two years old. The manager is Chantal and her mother is a shop assistant and her sister is the driver. The good things are: it's open on Sunday, and the flowers are always perfect.*

Homework ideas
• Ss write a short text about a family business, using one or more of the texts on p20–21 as a model. You may want to go through one of the texts in class, e.g. *Hotel de Coin* and show Ss where and how they can change the information to make it about their invented business.
• Workbook Ex 1–5, p13–14

LET'S HAVE A BREAK

Introduction

Ss practise making and responding to suggestions, using vocabulary related to feelings. They also practise listening.

SUPPLEMENTARY MATERIALS

Resource bank p141 and p142

Warm up: bring in a selection of pictures or short extracts of music to elicit 'happy' or 'sad'.

Warm up

Use music or pictures to introduce the idea of feelings: ask Ss *Are you OK? Are you happy?* then *What's the opposite of happy?* You could draw a happy and a sad face on the board. Then put Ss in pairs or small groups and pass round some pictures (e.g. of beautiful scenery, a cold winter's day) and/or play some short extracts of music (upbeat vs slow and sombre) and ask them to tell each other how they feel (happy or sad) after each one.

VOCABULARY feelings

1A Look at the example with the class, then Ss can work alone or with a partner on matching the rest of the adjectives. In feedback, make sure Ss understand the difference between *tired* (wanting to sleep) and *bored* (having nothing to do). Also, check the pronunciation of *hungry*, *thirsty*, *tired* and *bored* (the last two are pronounced as one syllable, not *tir-ed* or *bor-ed*).

Answers: A bored B hungry C tired D hot E thirsty F cold

B You could demonstrate this first, pointing to a picture, asking a student *What's the problem?* and prompting them to answer *I'm …* Then give Ss a minute or two to practise in pairs. You could also demonstrate that Ss can act out the feeling as they give their answer.

⟱ PHOTOBANK p140

If Ss are confident with the adjectives in Ex 1, direct them to the pictures on p140. Check the number of syllables in *interested* Ooo, *scared* O and *surprised* oO.

Answers:

A
1 D 2 H 3 C 4 G 5 A 6 E 7 B 8 F

B

+	–
happy	unhappy
well/fine	ill
interested	angry
	scared/afraid

surprised is fairly neutral

Optional extra activity

For extra practice of the feeling adjectives, including the ones from the **Photo bank** if Ss have studied them:

Put Ss in pairs, Student A mimes a feeling, Student B asks *Are you … ?* Student A replies *Yes, I am.* or *No, I'm not.* and Student B guesses again.

Listen to Ss' pronunciation of the adjectives during the practice and deal with any problems in feedback.

FUNCTION making suggestions

2A Start by directing Ss to the photos and asking them *Who are they?* and *Where are they?* to help Ss to predict the three situations in the recording.

Answers: 1 B 2 C 3 A

B Give Ss a few moments to read through the sentences. Play the first part of the recording for Ss to hear that the example (1a) is true, then play the rest of the recording for them to mark the other sentences.

Answers: 1a) T b) T 2a) F b) T 3a) T b) F

C You could correct these sentences with the whole class, or do 3b as an example, then give Ss time to do the other two alone or in pairs.

Answers: 1b) Café Lugo is an Italian café. 2a) It's their first meeting. 3b) They aren't hungry.

Unit 2 Recording 8

Conversation 1
A: Good class.
B: Yes.
A: I'm hungry.
B: Yeah, me too. Let's eat.
A: OK, where?
B: Erm … that Italian café? What's its name?
A: Lugo?
B: Yeah, let's go to Café Lugo.
A: OK. Good idea.

Conversation 2
A: Hello, are you Mr Tajima?
B: Yes.
A: I'm Lee Smith.
B: Oh, hello. Nice to meet you, Mr Smith.
A: Nice to meet you, too.
B: Erm … let's sit down. Coffee?
A: Yes, please.

Conversation 3
A: Let's have a break.
B: Good idea. I'm tired.
A: Me too.
B: … and hot.
A: Yeah. Let's stop.
B: Yeah, OK. Let's have a cola.
A: OK.

3A Direct Ss to the photos and establish that *have a break* is in the photos then let Ss find the other verbs in pairs.

Answers: A have a break, sit down, stop B go C have a coffee, sit down

Optional extra activity

To check that Ss understand the verbs (and to provide a little light relief), tell Ss to follow your instructions, but only if you start with *Please*. As an example, say to Ss, *Please stand up* (Ss stand), then *Sit down* (Ss should stay standing, because you didn't start the instruction with *Please*). Then continue the activity, using the verbs from the box, e.g. *Please sit down. Please have a coffee.*, go, eat, *Please eat a pizza.*, etc.

B Look at the example with the class and give Ss a few moments to read through the conversations before playing the recording.

> **Answers:** 2 A: Nice to meet you, too. B: Let's *sit down*. Coffee? A: Yes, please. 3 Let's *have a break*. B: Good idea. I'm tired. 4 A: Let's *stop*. B: Yeah, OK. Let's *have a cola*.

C Complete the rule with the class. You may want to clarify that *let's* means a good idea for *you and me* (i.e. not just for *you,* as in *Why don't you … ?*).

D Establish that Ss are only listening for the stressed words in the suggestions: *Let's …* Ss may wish to copy the five suggestions into their notebooks. In feedback, elicit/point out that the stress is on the 'information words' in the sentence, not on *Let's.*

> **Answers:** 2 Let's <u>sit down</u>. 3 Let's <u>have a break</u>. 4 Let's <u>stop</u>. 5 Let's <u>have a cola</u>.

⟫ LANGUAGEBANK 2.3 p120–121

The **Language bank** introduces the negative form, i.e. *Let's not …* which you may want to point out to *stronger classes.*

> **Answers:** 1 A: I'm very tired. B: OK, *let's* stop now. A: That's a good idea. B: And let's *have* a coffee. A: No, thanks, I'm not thirsty.
> 2 A: *I'm* hungry. B: *Me too.* A: *Let's* eat at the pizzeria. B: Good idea.

4A Look at the example with the class, then Ss can complete the conversations in pairs or alone.

> **Answers:** 2 too 3 Let 4 problem 5 's 6 break 7 Me 8 a

B Ss can start by reading the conversations aloud with their partners. Then they could choose one conversation to practise without reading from the book: tell them to write one-word prompts in their notebooks to help them remember the lines, e.g. *problem? – cold – inside – OK.*

LEARN TO respond to suggestions

5A Before playing the recording, demonstrate saying *Good idea* with interest and without interest. Play the first part of the recording for Ss to hear the example, then play dialogues 2–4.

> **Answers:** 2 – 3 – 4 +

Unit 2 Recording 10

1
A: Let's have a break.
B: Good idea.

2
A: Let's sit down.
B: OK.

3
A: Let's have a coffee.
B: OK.

4
A: Let's walk.
B: OK.

---

speakout TIP

Put the intonation arrow on the board and say *OK* in an interested way two or three times, for Ss to repeat. Then do the same with *Good idea,* showing Ss that the stress is on *idea* and that the intonation falls after that.

B Draw the two circles with + and – on the board, and do an example with one or two *strong students,* showing them that if they don't use a high enough pitch to show interest, you'll point to the – symbol.

SPEAKING

6A Tell Ss to write the complete conversations in their notebooks, so that they leave just the prompts in the **Students' Book,** for practice later.

> **Answers:** I'm hungry.
> Me, too.
> Let's eat.
> OK. Where?
> Let's go to …
> Good idea.

B Ss could read the conversation aloud the first time, then close their notebooks and use the prompts in Ex 6A, so that they sound more natural/spontaneous. Monitor and make a note of good use of grammar and intonation for praise in feedback, as well as any problems for correction.

7 Before Ss start their conversations they may need a few minutes to think of places to suggest for each adjective. Then put them in pairs to practise, or ask them to walk around and talk to at least two other Ss in the class.

Optional extra activity

To provide *stronger classes* with more language for Ex 7, give them a list of adjectives and activities to match, e.g.

A	B
bored	go to the cinema
tired	sit down
hungry	have a coffee or tea
hot	go inside
thirsty	eat
cold	get a taxi
	play tennis
	have a sandwich
	go to the park
	have a cold drink
	have a rest
	go to the beach

Homework ideas
• Workbook Ex 1–3, p15

ROYAL WEDDING

Introduction

Ss watch a BBC programme about the wedding of Prince William and Kate Middleton, with a focus on the people who attended the wedding. Ss then learn and practise how to speak and write about important people in their lives.

Warm up

Tell Ss to close their books. Teach *royal family* using a simple board picture of a king and queen wearing crowns and two children. Ask Ss to think of countries that have a royal family. Then teach *wedding* (a special day when a man and woman are husband and wife) and ask Ss to think of examples of royal weddings. If they mention William and Kate's wedding, ask them what they know about the British royal family, the names of some guests at the wedding, etc.

▶ DVD PREVIEW

1A Check that Ss know who Kate and William are, using their photos to help. Go through the example, then put Ss in pairs to discuss the rest. N.B. You may want to teach *grandparents* using a simple family tree on the board.

> **Answers:** Prince Charles is his father.
> Queen Elizabeth and Prince Philip are his grandparents.
> Pippa Middleton is her sister.
> Elton John is his friend.
> David and Victoria Beckham are his friends.

> **Culture notes**
> **Prince William** (born in 1982) and **Prince Harry** (born in 1984) are the sons of Prince Charles and Diana, Princess of Wales (died in 1997).
>
> **Elton John** (born in 1947) is an English singer-songwriter. He was a close friend of Diana, Princess of Wales.
>
> **David Beckham** (born in 1975) is an English footballer. **Victoria Beckham** (born in 1974) is an English singer and fashion designer.

B Direct Ss to the two questions and give them a minute or two to find the answers in the text. Vocabulary to check: *thousands, billions* (both used to emphasise the large numbers of people watching the wedding).

> **Answers:** Family and friends of William and Kate are at the royal wedding. It's at Westminster Abbey.

> **Culture note**
> Westminster Abbey is in the City of Westminster, in London. There have been sixteen royal weddings there. The funeral of Diana, Princess of Wales was also there.

▶ DVD VIEW

2A Tell Ss to watch and write the number next to the correct photo.

> **Answers:** 2 Elton John 3 Kate Middleton 4 Pippa Middleton 5 Prince William 6 Prince Harry 7 Queen Elizabeth and Prince Philip 8 Prince Charles

B Give Ss a minute or two to read through the sentences. They may already be able to find some of the mistakes. Check that Ss understand *ring* (point to an example in the class).

C Play the DVD for Ss to check their answers.

> **Answers:** 2 here 3 father 4 children 5 problem 6 day

DVD 2 Royal Wedding

It's London 2011. Today is the wedding of Prince William and Kate Middleton. Two billion people around the world watch it on TV. Thousands of people are in the streets of London. Victoria and David Beckham, friends of Prince William, are here.

Prime Minister David Cameron and his wife Samantha arrive at Westminster Abbey. The rich and famous are here including the singer Elton John, a great friend of Princess Diana.

Kate and her father go to Westminster Abbey. Her sister, Pippa Middleton arrives with children of friends and family. The Royal family arrive, first Prince William and his brother Harry.

Then their grandmother the Queen and grandfather Prince Philip. And their father Prince Charles and his wife Camilla. Kate arrives at the Abbey. Her sister Pippa meets her.

The big moment … and a problem with the ring. Kate and William are now husband and wife. Thousands of people in the streets celebrate the Royal Wedding.

The end of a big day for Kate and William.

> **Optional extra activity**
> Ss imagine what some of the people at the wedding are saying to each other. Pause the DVD just as each of the following people speak and either elicit from Ss or ask them to discuss with a partner and write down what the people say:
>
> David Beckham to a friend as he arrives
>
> David Cameron to his wife Samantha
>
> Kate to her father in the car
>
> William to the clergyman as they walk up the aisle
>
> Camilla to the Queen
>
> Pippa to Kate when she meets her at the car
>
> William to Kate in the carriage
>
> William to Kate on the balcony
>
> Ss could also act out some of their ideas for the class.

speakout five people in your life

3A Focus Ss on the title and elicit some ideas about who those people could be, e.g. a friend, a husband/mother/sister, a boss, etc. Tell Ss to start thinking about five people in their lives. Direct Ss to Jo and the five names around her, and to the people 1–5, including the example, *Duncan*. Tell Ss to listen and match names with people 2–5.

> **Answers:** 2 Wendy 3 Sarah 4 Rosa 5 Mark

B Give Ss a few moments to look at the **key phrases**. You may want to check the following vocabulary: *my best friend* (teach this as a 'fixed phrase' meaning 'my number one friend': it's a high frequency item and there's no need to deal with it as a superlative at this stage); *on the phone* (talking on the phone); *together* (demonstrate: *We're together in this classroom*).

Then play the recording again for Ss to tick the phrases. N.B. Demonstrate with an example on the board that Ss may only need to tick part of a phrase, or they may need to tick two alternatives within the same phrase.

Answers: OK, five people in my life. The first is …
Duncan's (my brother ✓/a very good friend).
We're on the phone a lot. ✓
I'm (a shop assistant /an office worker ✓) and Mark's my manager.
(She/He's ✓) very nice, very friendly.
Wendy is a (worker in my office/student in my class).
We're in a Spanish class together. ✓
We're good friends. ✓

Unit 2 Recording 11

OK, five people in my life. The first is Duncan. Duncan's my brother. He's thirty-one and he's a businessman. And Sarah … Sarah's a very good friend, my best friend really. She's from Scotland and she's a teacher. We are on the phone a lot! She's great. And this, this is Mark. I'm an office worker and Mark's my manager but he's very nice, very friendly. And Wendy is in my class. We're in a Spanish class together. Our teacher is Rosa. She's from Madrid in Spain and Wendy and I sit together in the class and now we're friends. The class is good … but our Spanish isn't very good!

C Tell Ss to draw the diagram in their notebooks, so they can write notes next to the names, etc. Give Ss time to write notes about each of the five people, i.e. who they are, where they're from, their job, something about their personality, etc. Circulate and help with ideas, as well as words and phrases that Ss need, and check that everyone has written notes about five people. As Ss finish writing their notes, encourage them to practise talking to themselves about the people to help build confidence.

D Put Ss in pairs and tell them to show each other their circles and ask/answer about the five people. For *stronger classes,* you could put Ss in small groups, so they have a bigger 'audience' to speak to. You could also tell the people listening to make notes about their classmates' five people and ask them to report back afterwards about some they found interesting, e.g. *Her best friend is her husband, but he's in the USA on business. They're on the phone a lot!*

writeback a description

4A Focus Ss on the three questions and give them a minute or two to find the answers in the text.

Answers: 1 Dennis, her brother and Ali, her mother
2 Pasqualo 3 Betsy

B Encourage Ss to use the text about Claudia as their model, with the following framework:

My name is ____. I'm (age) and I'm (job). Here are five people in my life:
(Name): She's/He's ____.
For each person they should mention some of the following:
friend/family relation
age
job
where she/he is
his/her personality (e.g. *nice, friendly, funny, kind*)

Circulate and help while Ss write their descriptions. You could then put Ss in pairs or small groups to read out their descriptions to each other.

Homework ideas
- Ss write the text *Five people in my life* from the point of view of Kate Middleton or another famous person they know about.

LOOKBACK

SUPPLEMENTARY MATERIALS

Ex 1A: be prepared to draw your family tree and ask Ss questions about it.

FAMILY

1A Start by checking that Ss understand how a family tree works. You could draw a simple version of your family tree on the board, then ask Ss about two or three people's relationship to you. Point to yourself and the person on the tree and ask Ss *Who's (X)?* and Ss answer *He's/She's your brother/ father/daughter/wife*, etc. Look at the example with the class, then Ss can work in pairs or alone to write the other names.

Answers: 2 Jim 3 Billy 4 Sue 5 Nas 6 Anne

B Demonstrate to Ss that it's possible to write more than one sentence about the same person, e.g. for Al: *My wife is Nas and my mother is Anne.* Circulate and help as Ss work alone on their sentences.

C Ask two *stronger Ss* to demonstrate this for the class, then put Ss in pairs to continue.

> **Optional extra activity**
> Ss draw their own family tree and write sentences as in Ex 1A. Then they swap notebooks with a partner, who writes the names of the people next to the sentences.

BE: YOU/WE/THEY

2A Tell Ss that A and B are looking at a photo of two people and talking about them. Ss complete the conversation alone, then check their answers in pairs. N.B. Remind Ss that if any of the missing words are at the beginning of a sentence, they must have a capital letter. Ask two Ss to read out the dialogue for the class to check their answers.

Answers: 2 They 3 are they 4 They,re 5 Are 6 we 7 Are 8 is (x2)

B Tell Ss to write two names and to think about where they're from, how they know them (school/university/work/ gym), if they're married or not, where they are now, etc.

C Demonstrate the activity by writing the names of two of your friends on the board and inviting Ss to ask you questions about them. As they do this, write up some prompts, to help them remember the questions without having to refer to their Students' Books:
Where … from?
… friends from … ?
… married?
Where … now?

Put Ss in pairs and give them a few minutes to ask and answer. In feedback, you could ask one or two Ss to report back about their partner's friends, e.g. *His/Her friends are … and … , they're from … ,* etc.

NUMBERS 11–100

3A Go through the example with the class, checking the pronunciation of *minus* and *plus* (and *equals*, if you decide to teach it, otherwise Ss can just say *is*). Ss write the other numbers, then read out their answers to the class.

Answers: 2 eighty-eight 3 ninety-seven 4 twenty-seven 5 sixty-eight

B Give Ss a minute or two to write in the numbers, and to think of how to say the answer to the sum in each case.

C Demonstrate number 1 with an example of your own, e.g. *What's 62 minus 20?* then put Ss in pairs to continue.

POSSESSIVE ADJECTIVES

4A Tell Ss there is one mistake in each sentence. They can work alone or in pairs to correct the mistakes.

Answers: 1 I'm Chinese and *my* name's Jun.
2 You're in Room 108 and Mr Watts is *your* teacher.
3 He's John. *His* family name's Wayford.
4 *Her* name's Vera and she's a singer.
5 We're students and *our* class is Room Ten.
6 *Their* names are Ahmed and Ali and they're from Egypt.

B Before Ss start the activity, you may want to give them the opportunity to check the spelling of each others' names and/or family names: encourage them to ask each other across the class, so other Ss can hear and make a note, e.g. *Excuse me, Pia, how do you spell your family name?* Tell Ss to try to use different content from the sentences in 4A, as long as it fits the pattern, e.g. *Mikel's from … and his best friend's …* Also make sure that Ss understand the idea of the false sentence by giving two examples about yourself, one true and one false, and asking Ss which one is false, e.g. *My name's … and I'm from …*

C Point out that Student B should wait until Student A has read out all their sentences before deciding which one is false. Monitor the pairwork and note down any good examples of language use as well as any problems for feedback.

FEELINGS

5A Start by eliciting the five vowels from the class and check that Ss can pronounce them accurately. Give them a minute or two to add the vowels to the words, then in feedback, ask Ss to tell you just the missing vowel(s) for each feeling.

Answers: 2 hungry 3 tired 4 cold 5 thirsty 6 bored

B If Ss have studied the feelings from the **Photo bank** p140, they could include some of these in the mime activity.

MAKING SUGGESTIONS

6A You could do the first line as an example with the class, then tell Ss to write out the lines of the conversation in their notebooks.

Answers: A: Let's go now. B: No, I'm tired. Let's sit down. A: OK, let's stop and have a break. B: Are you thirsty? A: Yes, I am. B: Let's go to a café. A: Good idea.

B Ss choose any key word that will help them remember the line. You could give them slips of paper to write the key words on, so they don't refer to their notebooks.

C Monitor the pairwork and in feedback be prepared to give Ss praise for good language use and to deal with any problems.

> **Optional extra activity**
> Tell Ss to write the key words on a slip of paper with some changes, so that the development of the conversation is different (e.g. *break / bored / cold? / yes / inside / hungry?/ yes / sandwich*). Then they pass the slip of paper to another pair, who reconstruct the conversation from the key words, either in writing first and then orally, or just orally (for *stronger students*).

REVIEW 1: UNITS 1–2

Introduction

The aim of the review units is for Ss to revise and practise the grammar, vocabulary and pronunciation from the previous two units, in a different context. The context for this review unit is a music festival.

READING AND GRAMMAR

1A Direct Ss to the picture and ask them one or two questions, e.g. *Who's she? Who's he? Where are they?* then put them in pairs to talk about their ideas. In feedback, establish that the people are at a *music festival* (you could give examples of other types of festivals, e.g. film/food/wine/comedy festival), and that *a fan* is someone who likes music a lot.

> **Culture notes**
> Attending music festivals is a popular summer weekend activity in many countries. The larger festivals last for several days and feature famous and less well-known bands playing at different times during the day. The festivals often take place in large open spaces, where there is room for people to camp, and there are food and drink stalls available on the site. Probably the best known festival in England is the Glastonbury festival, which takes place for five days in June.

B Focus Ss on the three messages in Ex 1B and establish that these are messages written by people at a festival. Tell Ss to read quickly, just to find the names. Reassure them that they will read the messages in more detail later. You may want to check the following words at this stage, or deal with them in Ex 1D: *a mix of, traditional, modern, concert.*

> **Answer key:** A Binny C Fifi D Sandra E Neil

C Show Ss how to find the information about the example (4). They could work in pairs to help each other with the rest.

> **Answers:** 217 room, Sandra
> 4439078442 phone, Jasmine
> 24 age, Binny
> 1 age, Fifi

D Put some prompts on the board and either spend a few minutes discussing them as a class, or put Ss in small groups to talk about them:
- *names of festivals, where?*
- *types of music – traditional/modern/rock/jazz/opera, etc?*
- *are they good?*
- *who's a music fan in the class?*
- *who's a fan of other festivals – food/wine/comedy, etc?*

2A Look at the example and elicit/point out that the questions are about the messages in Ex 1. Remind Ss that they need a capital letter if a word is at the beginning of a question. Give Ss a few minutes to complete the questions working alone.

> **Answers:** 2 Is 3 his 4 is/'s 5 her 6 Are 7 they 8 How
> 'it' is not used.

B Monitor this pairwork closely so that you can give Ss feedback on their pronunciation of the questions and use of grammar and vocabulary.

3 Establish that these messages are from different people who are also at the music festival.

> **Answers:** 2 re 3 is 4 isn't 5 are 6 Are 7 are 8 are

> **Optional extra activity**
> Write the following questions on the board for Ss to answer:
> *Is the group of students from Russia?*
> *Is it their first time at the festival?*
> *Is their hotel nice?*
> *Are Jeff and Robin in room 112?*
> *Is Arturo at the HJ Hotel?* (N.B. the answer here is 'I don't know')

LISTENING

4A Focus Ss on the name *Morelli* and ask them *Where's Morelli from?* Elicit the phrase *I think Morelli's from (Italy)* or *I think Morelli's (Italian)*, then put Ss in pairs to say what they think about the other names. Have a brief discussion with the whole class.

B Tell Ss to listen and write the nationality adjective next to each name. Play the recording, then give Ss time to compare their answers in pairs.

> **Answers:** Morelli – American Cho – Korean Fatimah – English Takahashi – Canadian Churchill – Australian Gonzales – Colombian

C Check that Ss know they only need to write the letter next to the name, not the whole word. Play the recording again and give Ss time to compare answers.

> **Answers:** 1 M 2 F 3 D

Review 1 Recording 1
Conversation 1
A: Hello, I'm Tony Morelli.
B: Hi, I'm Frank Cho.
A: Nice to meet you.
B: Nice to meet you, too. Is Morelli an Italian name?
A: Yes, it is, but I'm American.
B: I see.
A: And are you from China?
B: No, Cho is a Korean name. I'm from Korea. It's good music, yeah?
A: Yeah, it's good. The singer is my friend …
Conversation 2
A: Hi, I'm Fatimah.
B: Hello, my name's Terry. Terry Gonzales.
A: Nice to meet you.
B: And you. Is Fatimah your family name or your first name?
A: It's my first name. It's an Arabic name.
B: Where are you from?
A: My father's from Egypt, but I'm English. And you? Is Gonzales a Spanish name?
B: Yes, it is but I'm not from Spain, I'm from Colombia.
A: Oh, where in Colombia?
B: Bogotá.
A: Hey, I'm hungry.
B: Me too. Let's go and eat something.
A: Good idea. So, what … ?

Conversation 3

A: Brad Churchill, nice to meet you.

B: Sue Takahashi. Nice to meet you, too.

A: Your English is very good!

B: Thanks, but I'm from Canada.

A: Oh, I'm sorry. But Takahashi is a Japanese name.

B: Yes, my family is from Japan, but I'm Canadian.

A: Ah. Yes, my name's Churchill, very English! But I'm Australian, from Sydney.

B: Oh, I know Sydney.

A: Really? Hey, let's go and have a coffee.

B: OK, yeah I …

SPEAKING

5 Give Students A time to find their table and tell Ss not to show their partner the information. Establish that they must ask questions to get the information they need to complete the table and give them a few minutes to think about the questions. Circulate and help (you may need to check the meaning and pronunciation of *nurse* with Students A, so they can explain it to Students B when the time comes). Tell the pairs to start asking and writing down the information, and monitor and make a note of anything you need to deal with in feedback.

6A Focus Ss on the example and tell them to complete the circles with information about three people, writing the information in random order. Point out that the information (ages, jobs, etc.) should be mixed up, so that partners will need to ask questions to find out which information refers to each person

While Ss are writing their notes, write information about three members of your family on the board.

B Start by demonstrating the activity with the class, inviting different Ss to ask you questions and answering *Yes …* or *No …* . Ss could do the activity in pairs or small groups.

SOUNDS /æ/ AND /ə/

7A Direct Ss to the pictures and point out that the symbols represent the sounds. Play the recording for Ss to listen to the sounds and the words. You may also want to show Ss how the shape of the mouth is different for the two sounds: open, like a big smile for /æ/, and relaxed, nearly closed for /ə/. Play the recording again for Ss to repeat.

B Point out that Ss need to look at the underlined syllable when they decide which group to put the words in. Pause the recording if necessary to give Ss time to write.

Answers: /æ/ t<u>a</u>xi, <u>a</u>ctor, n<u>a</u>tionality, underst<u>a</u>nd, h<u>a</u>ppy
/ə/ teach<u>er</u>, doct<u>or</u>, <u>E</u>ngland, c<u>o</u>mput<u>er</u>, daught<u>er</u> (N.B. *actor* and *understand* could also be in this group)

8A and B Put Ss in groups of 3–4 to help each other with these words. Tell them to practise saying the words aloud to each other, so they can hear which syllable has the sound in it.

Answers:
/ə/ Br<u>a</u>zil, childr<u>e</u>n, sev<u>e</u>n, int<u>e</u>rnet, tel<u>e</u>vision, Indi<u>a</u>
/æ/ c<u>a</u>mera, f<u>a</u>mily, <u>a</u>ctress, b<u>a</u>nk, c<u>a</u>pitals, m<u>a</u>nager

Optional extra activity

To give Ss more practice in distinguishing between the sounds /æ/ and /ə/, write the following words from the review unit on the board, and ask Ss to divide them into two groups. There is one word which doesn't belong in either group.

Scotland	*fan*	*festival*	*cats*
Jasmine	*concert*	*black*	*brother*

Answers:
/ə/ Scotl<u>a</u>nd, festiv<u>a</u>l, c<u>o</u>ncert, broth<u>er</u>
/æ/ f<u>a</u>n, c<u>a</u>ts, bl<u>a</u>ck, J<u>a</u>smine

Homework ideas
• Workbook Ex 1–6, p16–17

OVERVIEW

WHAT'S THIS?

Introduction

Students practise talking about objects, using *this, that, these* and *those*. They also practise listening and learn to ask the name for things in English.

SUPPLEMENTARY MATERIALS

Resource bank p144

Warm up: bring in some objects or pictures of objects for a memory game.

Warm up

Memory game:

Put a selection of objects (6–8) that Ss know in English on a desk where they can all be seen, or display pictures of the objects on the board. Give Ss a minute to memorise the objects, then cover/remove the objects and put Ss in pairs to make a list of all the ones they remember. You could award points for the number of words each pair remembered and for accurate spelling.

Suggested objects: a book, a pen, a phone, a DVD, a photo, a passport, a camera, a dictionary, a calendar.

VOCABULARY objects

1A Direct Ss to the photos and elicit the names of some of the objects from the class, e.g. *keys, phone, computer, chair.* Then put Ss in pairs to help each other and underline any words in the box which are not in the photos. If any words are unfamiliar, you could use simple board drawings (*picture, business card, clock*) and mime (*printer*) to show the meaning. Help Ss with pronunciation by modelling the words for them to listen and repeat.

> **Answers:** *picture, printer, clocks* and *business cards* are not in the photos

> #### Teaching tip
> To help Ss with the pronunciation of words with more than two syllables, ask them first to listen and count the number of syllables in the word, then to listen again and underline the stressed syllable and finally to listen and repeat, e.g. *com–pu–ter (3 syllables) comp<u>u</u>ter*.

B To check *singular* and *plural*, use classroom objects such as *a pen/pens*. Establish that they should write S next to *picture*, then give them a moment or two to mark the other words.

> **Answers:** S – picture, computer, printer, desk, chair, lamp
> P – keys, clocks, business cards, boxes

C When Ss have practised saying the plural words, you could ask them which sound (/s/ or /z/) the following words from Ex 1A have: *desks (/s/), lamps (/s/), chairs (/z/), printers (/z/), pictures (/z/), computers (/z/).*

> #### Teaching tip
> A simple rule is that the plural sound is /s/ if the word ends in the following unvoiced consonant sounds: /f/ /k/ /p/ /t/ /θ/.

▸ **PHOTOBANK** p140

Ss could work on these exercises in class or for homework: Ex 1 introduces twelve more 'everyday' objects and Ex 2 deals with the spelling of plurals and irregular plurals. Bear in mind that the speaking practice in Ex 5 involves Ss asking each other for the names of common objects in English, so you may not want to pre-empt this.

Answers:
1A
1 H 2 C 3 K 4 A 5 D 6 L
7 J 8 E 9 G 10 F 11 B 12 I
2A
+ -s pencils, bags, mouses, notebooks, credit cards, tables, newspapers, cups
+ -es watches, glasses
+ -ies dictionaries, diaries
B
B boys C girl D girls E man F men G woman H women I child J children

LISTENING

2A Direct Ss back to photos A–D and tell them to order them 1–4 as they listen to the conversations.

Answers: 1 B 2 C 3 A 4 D

B Before Ss listen to the recording again, check the pronunciation of all the names.

Answers: Mr Fletcher (conversation 2), Denise (conversation 3)

C Give Ss a few minutes to complete the conversations and check their answers.

Answers: 1 D 2 B 3 A 4 C

UNIT 3 Recording 2

Conversation 1
A: Congratulations, Sam, and welcome to the company.
B: Thank you, Mr Stanford.
A: Bill.
B: Thank you … Bill.
A: These are your keys.
B: My keys?
A: Yes, keys to the building and the office. And the company car.
B: Great, thanks.

Conversation 2
A: Hey, Anne. What's that?
B: This is my new phone, my work phone.
A: Nice.
C: Ahem.
B: Yeah, some great games. Look at this, Jill.
A: Oooh …
B: And music.
A: Wow, great.
C: AHEM!
B: And here's a video of my baby.
C: Sorry, ladies. Lovely phone, but is this a coffee break?
A: Oh, sorry Mr Fletcher. Hmm … Good idea. Let's have a break!

Conversation 3
A: Thanks, Janet.
B: No problem. What's in this box? It's very heavy.
A: It's my new printer.
B: And what's in those boxes?
A: Oh, these small boxes are my office things. Oh, be careful!
B: Oh, no. Denise, I'm so sorry.
A: Oh, no. My new printer.
B: I'm so sorry …

Conversation 4
A: … and come in here. This is my home office.
B: OK. And is that your new computer?
A: Yeah, it is.
B: Nice. Is it good?
A: Yeah.
B: Expensive?
A: Erm … yeah.

GRAMMAR *this/that/these/those*

3A Look at photo A with the class and elicit the examples: *this box, those boxes*. Give Ss a minute or two to circle the other examples and compare their answers with a partner.

Answers: A What's in <u>this</u> box? And what's in <u>those</u> boxes? B <u>These</u> are your keys. C What's <u>that</u>? <u>This</u> is my new phone. D <u>This</u> is my home office. And is <u>that</u> your new computer?

B and C You could look at these rules with the whole class, or give Ss a minute or two to complete the exercises in pairs first.

Answers: B 2 these 3 that 4 those
C this/that + is these/those + are

D This exercise focuses on the difference between the short /i/ sound in *this* and the longer /ɪ/ sound in *these*. Write the four pairs of words on the board and pause the recording, asking Ss to tell you which word to tick in each pair and then to repeat. You could then ask individual Ss at random to say one of the three words (*this/these/those*) and you point to the word you hear, then put Ss in pairs to do the same.

Answers: 1 this 2 these 3 those 4 these

Optional extra activity
Tell Ss to look back at photos A–D and practise the conversations. Then ask them to change some of the objects and practise the conversations again, e.g.
A *It's my new (chair).*
B *These are your (business cards).*
C *This is my new (desk).*
D *And is that your new (clock)?*

▐▶ **LANGUAGEBANK** 3.1 p122–123

If you feel Ss need more practice of *this/that/these/those*, give half the class Ex 3.1A and the other half Ex 3.1B. Give them each an answer key, then they can pair up with a student from the other half of the class and talk each other through the answers to the exercises.

Answers:
A
2 that 3 this 4 those 5 that 6 that
B
Conversation 1
A: These are our photos of Thailand.
B: Is this your hotel?
A: Yes, it is. And *these* are our friends, Sanan and Chai.
Conversation 2
A: What's *that* over there?
B: It's Red Square. And this is your hotel here.
A: Thank you.
Conversation 3
A: What are *these* in English?
B: They're 'coins'. *This* one here is a pound coin.
Conversation 4
A: Who are *those* people over there?
B: That's my brother, Juan and his friends.
Conversation 5
A: Where are those students from?
B: They're from Bogotá, in Colombia.
A: And *that* student?
B: She isn't a student. She's our teacher!

PRACTICE

4A Start by setting the context here: demonstrate that A is showing Miki around the school, first taking her to the students' room, then the classroom. Ss can complete the conversations in pairs or working alone. Remind them to use a capital letter if *this/that/these/those* is at the beginning of a sentence.

Answers: 2 those 3 This 4 that 5 that 6 This 7 these 8 That

B Put Ss in groups of three. Once they've read through the conversations together, encourage them to be less reliant on the written word, e.g. by:

• reading a line and making an action to go with it (pointing to friends 'over there', etc);

• looking at a line, then looking up and saying it, still making the action;

• trying to practise the conversations without looking and not worrying about being 100 percent accurate.

speakout TIP

You could act out introducing 'Tina' and 'Dr Meyer' to each other, using two Ss. Then Ss could practise introducing the people sitting on their left and right to each other. Alternatively, they could walk round the class in pairs, introducing their partners to other Ss (they may also want to invent new identities for this).

SPEAKING

5A Put Ss in pairs and check that they understand they should choose six objects in total. Ss could also refer to the **Photo bank** to find words.

B Circulate and help, checking that Ss can pronounce the words they find. You could give them a minute or two to practise saying the words aloud to each other, before moving on to the next stage.

C Before putting Ss in groups, model the four questions below for them to listen and repeat. Elicit/point out that the stress is on *this/that/these/those* and that the intonation falls at the end of the question:

What's this/that in English? ↘

What are these/those in English? ↘

You could also encourage Ss to extend the conversations by asking for repetition and about spelling:

Sorry, could you say that again?

OK, how do you spell that?

Put two pairs of Ss together to make groups of four and give them time to ask and answer about all the objects. In feedback, you could ask two or three Ss what new words they learnt in the activity.

Homework ideas

• Set up the following as a way for Ss to learn the names of objects at home:

Tell Ss to write the names of objects (e.g. *table, chair, clock, picture*) on sticky notes and to stick them on the objects at home. Every time they see the label, they should practise saying the word. When they think they've learnt the word, they can remove the label and write a new one for another object, and so on.

• **Workbook** Ex 1–4, p19–20

WHOSE SHOES?

Introduction

Ss practise reading about famous people's possessions and practise talking about clothes and colours, using the possessive 's. Ss also learn to use the linkers and/but in writing.

SUPPLEMENTARY MATERIALS

Resource bank p143 and p145

Warm up: a box to put objects in.

Ex 7B and 7C: bring in photos of Gisele Bündchen, Luol Deng, Penelope Cruz and Miroslav Klose.

Warm up

Revise names of objects, this, these and your. Collect an object from each student, e.g. a phone, a pen, a set of keys, etc. Put all the objects in a box, including something of yours, then redistribute the objects so all Ss have something belonging to someone else. Demonstrate that Ss should walk round asking Is this/Are these your …(s)? and answering Yes, it is/they are or No, it isn't/they aren't. The activity ends when all the objects have been handed back to their owners.

READING

1A Before Ss look at the photos, check the following vocabulary: mus<u>eu</u>m (give one or two examples of local museums that Ss will know); f<u>a</u>mous (use two or three photos of famous people, then check Ss' understanding by pointing to a student and asking Is he/she famous?) and objects/things (remind Ss of some objects from the previous lesson and tell them that here things means the same as objects). Tell Ss to cover the text with their notebooks and direct them to the photos. Establish that the museum has famous things in it.

B Look at photos 1–6 with the class and elicit/give the name of each object: a glove, glasses, a dress, a guitar, shoes, a tennis racquet. Make sure that Ss can pronounce the names of the objects. Put Ss in pairs to match the objects with the famous people. You could then ask one or two pairs for some of their ideas, but don't confirm any answers yet.

C Tell Ss to read the text quickly, just to check their ideas. At this stage they shouldn't worry about unfamiliar vocabulary.

Teaching tip

It's important for Ss to realise that they can read a simple text and find key pieces of information or understand the general idea of the text, without needing to understand every word in it. When Ss have a simple task to do, such as the one in Ex 1C, discourage them from looking up unfamiliar vocabulary in their dictionaries. It should also help to build confidence when they see that they can complete the task in spite of the unfamiliar vocabulary.

D Focus Ss on the task and check that they understand singers, films, clothes. Give them a few minutes to find the examples (they could circle them in the text) then compare answers with a partner.

Answers: two names of films: *The Seven Year Itch*, *Love Me Tender*
two singers: Michael Jackson, Elvis Presley
two clothes: a glove, a dress
two sports people: Usain Bolt, Venus Williams
two nationalities: English, Jamaican

Culture notes

Michael Jackson (1958–2009), an American singer, dancer and musician. His 1982 album *Thriller* was the best-selling album of all time.

Daniel Radcliffe (1989–) started playing Harry Potter when he was 11 and made more than £60 million from the Harry Potter films.

Marilyn Monroe (1926–1962), an American actress, singer and model.

Elvis Presley (1935–1977), an American singer from Mississippi.

Usain Bolt (1986–) runs in the 100 metres and 200 metres.

Venus Williams (1980–), first became world number one in women's tennis in 2002.

2A Tell Ss to think about things from famous sportspeople, actors, singers, politicians or characters in films. Some other suggestions for international items:

Johnny Depp's hat (from *Pirates of the Caribbean*); Ghandi's glasses or sandals; Bono's sunglasses; Muhammed Ali's boxing gloves; a famous footballer's T-shirt; Tiger Wood's cap

B Before you put Ss into groups, you could teach them some phrases for discussing which item to choose, e.g. *I think that's a good idea; I think that's the best idea; What do you think?* N.B. Ss have already seen *best* (in *best friend*), meaning 'number one'.

Put pairs together into groups of four or six, and tell them to choose one object. Ask a student from each group to tell the class their decision.

GRAMMAR possessive 's

3A Focus Ss on the example and give them a minute or two to add the apostrophes.

B Ask Ss to repeat in chorus and individually, so you can check that they're pronouncing the 's clearly. Highlight the pronunciation of *Williams's*.

Answers: 2 These are Usain Bolt's gold running shoes.
3 This is Michael Jackson's glove. 4 This is Venus Williams's tennis racquet.

C You could go through this on the board with the class.

Answer: 's

LANGUAGEBANK 3.2 p122–123

Use the **Language bank** to highlight the difference between 's for possession and 's for the contracted form of *is*. Point out where the 's goes if the object belongs to two people. For some basic practice before Ex 4, you could use Ex 3.2A (also reviews family vocabulary) and/or Ex 3.2B in class.

Answers:
A
2 Ellen is Mark and Sarah's (Sarah and Mark's) mother. 3 Mark is Sarah's brother. 4 Sarah is Mark's sister. 5 Mark is Jon and Ellen's (Ellen and Jon's) son. 6 Sarah is Jon and Ellen's (Ellen and Jon's) daughter. 7 Ellen is Jon's wife.
8 Jon and Ellen are Mark and Sarah's (Sarah and Mark's) parents.
B
2 I'm Josh's friend. 3 Are you Emily's sister? 4 Eric's family name's White. 5 These are Bella and David's children. 6 Rex's phone number is 396 294.

PRACTICE

4A Go through the example with the class, reminding Ss that *Is* and *Are* need a capital letter, then give them a minute or two to complete the other questions.

> **Answers:** 2 Is that Yasmin's chair? 3 Are those the teacher's shoes? 4 Is this Carolyn's phone? 5 Are these James's pens?

B Demonstrate how Ss can change the questions to make them about things in their own classroom.

C Ss could point at the relevant items in the room, or the pairs could walk round the classroom as they ask and answer.

> **Alternative idea**
> Put Ss in pairs and ask them to swap an object with each other, either something they're wearing, or something on their desk. Ask the rest of the class to look at each pair in turn, and try to guess which items they've swapped.

VOCABULARY clothes and colours

5A You could start by eliciting the names of the items of clothing you're wearing to see how much Ss already know. Then direct them to the words and the pictures. Ss can work in pairs. As you go through the answers, check Ss' pronunciation, especially of the vowel sounds in *sweater* and *shirt*. Also point out that *trousers* are always plural.

> **Answers:** A trousers B jacket C shirt D hat E sweater F T-shirt

B Refer Ss to the famous people and the pictures of clothes. You could elicit ideas from the class before putting Ss into pairs.

C Tell Ss to write the numbers 1–6 in their notebooks, so they can write the correct answers as they listen. Also tell them not to worry about the colours at this stage.

> **Answers:** 1 Elvis Presley's trousers. 2 Marilyn Monroe's jacket. 3 Michael Jackson's shirt. 4 Venus Williams's hat. 5 Harry Potter's sweater. 6 Usain Bolt's T-shirt.

D You could tell Ss to write the colours under the pictures, in front of the name of the clothes, so they get used to the idea of putting an adjective in front of a noun.

> **Answers:** 1 white trousers 2 black jacket 3 red shirt 4 blue hat 5 brown sweater 6 yellow T-shirt

Unit 3 Recording 5

A: These are Elvis Presley's white trousers from a concert in Nashville.

B: I'm sure you know this from photos of Marilyn Monroe. It's her black jacket.

C: This is very famous. It's Michael Jackson's red shirt from the 1990s.

D: This is from a tennis match in Mexico in 2009. It's Venus Williams's blue hat. It's the winner's hat.

E: This is a typical schoolboy sweater, so you probably know it's Harry Potter's brown sweater.

F: That's Usain Bolt's yellow T-shirt. It's his T-shirt for running.

> ➠ **PHOTOBANK** p141
>
> If you feel that there are too many items in Ex 1 for Ss to learn at one time, you could suggest that they choose 4–6 items to learn, according to what they wear most often. If Ss do Ex 2 in class, you could teach them the question *What's your favourite colour?* and get them to ask and answer around the class.
>
> > **Answers:** 1 A handbag B dress C sweater D socks E suit F coat G T-shirt H trainers I jacket J trousers K jeans L shoes M shirt N hat O gloves P tie Q boots R glasses S skirt
> > 2 A orange B brown C red D white E green F purple G pink H yellow I black J blue

6A You could demonstrate this activity first, giving one true and one false example about people in the class and asking Ss to say *True* or *False*. Ss work alone on their four sentences.

B You could tell Ss that Student B should turn their back to the rest of the class while Student A is reading out their sentences, so they have to try to remember the information about their classmates' clothes.

WRITING linkers *and, but*

7A You could write the three sentences on the board and go through them with the class, establishing that *but* is used to join two pieces of information where the second one tells us something unexpected.

> **Answers:** 1 and 2 and 3 but

B If you've brought in photos of the famous people in Ex 7B and Ex 7C, show them to the class and elicit any information they know about them. You could go through these sentences with the whole class or give Ss time to work on them alone first.

> **Answers:** 1 These are Gisele Bündchen's sunglasses and hat. Her name is German *but* she's Brazilian.
> 2 This is basketball player Luol Deng's red shirt. Deng isn't from Britain *but* he's in the British basketball team *and* he's in an American team: the Chicago Bulls.

C Tell Ss they need to change or add some words in these sentences.

> **Answers:** 1 This is actress Penelope Cruz's hat. Cruz is from Spain but she's in American films.
> 2 This is football player Miroslav Klose's shirt. Klose is from Poland but his nationality is German and he's in the German national team.

SPEAKING

8 Direct Ss to their pictures and tell them not to show each other. Establish that they both have a picture of the same people at a party but there are six differences between the clothes in the pictures. Take the part of Student A and use a *stronger* Student B to demonstrate the activity. Then monitor as Ss do the activity and note examples of good language use and any problems for praise and correction in feedback.

> **Homework ideas**
> • Ss research two or three famous people and famous things belonging to them and write sentences about them, following the pattern in Ex 7C.
> • Workbook Ex 1–6, p21–22

A COFFEE, PLEASE

Introduction

Ss practise ordering in a café, using food and drink vocabulary. They also practise listening and learn to say prices.

SUPPLEMENTARY MATERIALS

Resource bank p146

Ex 3A: take in pictures to help you teach the vocabulary that is likely to be new in the orders.

Ex 5B (optional extra activity): bring in a set of ten blank slips of paper or card for each pair of Ss.

Warm up

Put the headings *food* and *drink* on the board, then put Ss in pairs and give them one minute to write down all the names of food and drink they can think of. Then compile two lists on the board of their ideas. Possible words: *coffee, tea, beer, chocolate, pizza, pasta, salad, burger, sandwich, fish and chips.*

VOCABULARY food and drink

1A Focus Ss on the photo and elicit some ideas from the class.

B You may want to read the first sentence with the class and elicit the first country (England), before giving Ss time to read the rest of the information.

Answers: England, China, Venezuela, the Czech Republic

C Check that Ss understand *different:* (demonstrate with three books or pens, two that are exactly the same, and one that is a different colour) and ask Ss: *What's different about his book/pen?* Tell Ss to read the information again and discuss the questions. For question 2, ask Ss to give simple reasons why they think a certain café is good.

Answers: 1 The cafés are full of rock and roll memorabilia. (*are full of* here means *they have a lot of*)

Culture notes
The Hard Rock Café was founded by two Americans and opened in London in 1971. The collection of rock and roll memorabilia started in 1979, with the gift of Eric Clapton's guitar. In total there are more than 70,000 items. There are 150 Hard Rock cafés and hotels around the world, and the largest is in Orlando, Florida, where there is a pink Cadillac that belonged to Elvis.

2A Tell Ss that the pictures are of food and drink that you order in a café, and focus them on the example.

Answers: 2 – F 3 – C 4 – A 5 – B 6 – E

B Tell Ss to check by asking each other *What's (B)? A tea and a mineral water*, etc. To help Ss say the orders naturally, you could model them at natural speed for Ss to repeat, showing them that items of food and drink are stressed and the other words are 'squashed' in between them.

C You could start by setting the scene in a café, demonstrating that you are a waiter and inviting a student to come and be a customer. Ask Ss what the waiter says to elicit *Can I help you?* then indicate that the customer should order something from Ex 2A. As you mime handing over the order, elicit or give *Here you are.* Tell Ss to look at their pictures in Ex 2A but cover the words. Put them in pairs to practise the dialogue. Ss take turns to be the waiter/waitress or the customer.

FUNCTION ordering in a café

3A Before you play the recording, give Ss time to read through the orders and check any unfamiliar vocabulary, e.g. *white coffee* (with milk: elicit that the opposite is *black coffee*), *sugar* (mime putting a spoonful of sugar in a cup of coffee and stirring it), *espresso* and *cappuccino* (mime using a coffee machine), *egg* (draw a picture), *white bread* (a picture, elicit/ teach that the opposite of *white* here is *brown*), *sparkling* (a picture showing the bubbles in the water, a glass of *still water* to show the opposite). Tell Ss to cross out any words that are wrong and write the correct ones above them. Play the recording. Give Ss time to compare their answers and play the recording again if necessary.

Answers: 1 1 *black* coffee with sugar 2 2 espresso coffees 3 1 egg sandwich (*brown* bread), 1 chocolate cake, 1 *mineral water* 4 1 sparkling mineral water

B Look at the example with the class, then give Ss a minute or two to go through the rest of the dialogue.

Answers: b) W c) W d) C e) C f) W g) C

C You could find the first line (d) with the class, then put the Ss in pairs to put the rest in order. Play the recording for Ss to check.

Answers: 1 d) 2 c) 3 g) 4 b) 5 e) 6 a) 7 f)

Unit 3 Recording 6
Conversation 1
A: Can I have a coffee, please?
B: With milk?
A: No thanks. Black.
B: Sugar?
A: Yes, please. One.
B: One black coffee with sugar! That's five euros.
Conversation 2
A: Can I have two coffees, please?
B: Espresso or cappuccino?
A; Oh, espresso, please.
B; Anything else?
A: No thanks. How much is that?
B: That's four euros fifty.
Conversation 3
A: Hi.
B: Hi. Can I have an egg sandwich, please?
A: White or brown bread?
B: Oh, brown bread, please.
A: Anything else?
B: Yeah, can I have one of those cakes?
A: These ones?
B: No, the chocolate ones.
A: Anything to drink?
B: Yes, a mineral water, please. How much is that?
A: That's two euros for the sandwich, one for the cake and one for the mineral water. That's four euros.
B: Here you are.
Conversation 4
A: Can I have a mineral water, please?
B: Still or sparkling?
A: Sparkling, please.
B: Anything else?
A: No, thank you. How much is that?
B: That's two euros.

4A Give Ss time to read through the table, then elicit the missing words from the class.

Answers:

Can I have	a	mineral water, please?
	two	coffees, *please?*
Still	*or*	sparkling?
Espresso		cappuccino?

B Remind Ss that the arrows show if the voice is going up or down. Play the recording several times if necessary, for them to hear the pattern and repeat.

Answer: 2

Teaching tip

A rising intonation pattern, as on *still* here, often shows that the speaker hasn't finished. In contrast, a falling intonation suggests finality.

C Demonstrate this with one or two Ss first, prompting them to ask you the question. For *stronger classes* you could ask Ss to suggest other choices, e.g. *black/white (coffee)*.

5A Tell Ss to write the completed conversation in their notebooks, so they can refer back to the prompts in their Student's book for speaking practice later. Ss can work in pairs, or work alone and compare answers with a partner.

Answers: A: Can I have a coffee, please? B: With milk? A: Yes, please. B: Anything else? A: Yes, can I have a mineral water? B: Still or sparkling? A: Still, please. B: Anything else? A: No thank you. How much is that? B: That's four euros.

B Before you put Ss in pairs, help them with pronunciation of the conversation by saying each line at natural speed for them to repeat in chorus. In the first line focus on the weak form of *Can* /kən/ and the linking between *Can* and *I*. Give Ss time to practise the conversation twice, so they both say the customer's and the waiter's lines. For *stronger classes,* encourage Ss to change three or four words in the prompts, e.g. *coffee, still, four*. Monitor and note down common problem areas, so you can decide whether to do extra practice from the **Language bank** in class.

Optional extra activity
To help Ss to move away from the prompts and gain confidence, give each pair a set of ten blank slips of paper or card, and ask them to write the prompt for a line of the conversation on each of them. Ss then put the prompts in front of them in the correct order as they practise the conversation.

⇒ LANGUAGEBANK 3.3 p122–123

Ss could do Ex 3.3 in class if they are making mistakes with the word order, etc. of phrases in the conversation.

Answers: A: Can I help you? B: Yes, can I *have* an egg sandwich, please? A: White *or* brown bread? B: Brown, please. A: Anything *else?* B: Yes, *can* I have two coffees, please? A: Espresso or cappuccino? B: One espresso and *one* cappuccino. A: OK, *that's* six fifty.

LEARN TO say prices

6A Get Ss to read through the prices and tell them to number the prices in the order they hear them.

Answers: 2 3.00 3 2.50 4 5.20 5 10 6 12.75

B Play the recording for Ss to listen and repeat. Then put Ss in pairs. Tell them to take turns pointing to a price and saying it.

Unit 3 Recording 9

one euro fifty
three euros
two euros fifty
five twenty
ten euros
twelve seventy-five

speakout TIP

To give Ss more examples of this, write prices on the board, and ask then to say them in both ways. They could also practise the same prices with *dollar(s)* and *pound(s)*. N.B. Point out that if the price is a 'round' number, e.g. $2 you do need the name: *two dollars*.

C Ss could write all four prices in their country's money, or four different currencies.

D Demonstrate this by saying four prices for Ss to write, then checking them by asking four Ss to come and write them on the board.

SPEAKING

7 You could put Ss into groups of As and Bs to prepare this role-play. Circulate and help with vocabulary and pronunciation.

As: The waiters need to think about the options they can offer the customer for coffee or tea, cola, mineral water, sandwich. They also need to practise saying the prices.

Bs: The customers need to think about what type of coffee/tea/sandwich/cake they want. They also need to think about what they can get for two people with their money.

Pair up As and Bs and give them time to practise. You could then move Ss around the classroom, so they're working with different partners, and practise the role-play again. You may want to ask two or three pairs to act out their role-play for the class.

Homework ideas
• Ss go to their favourite café and make some notes about the food and drink on the menu and the prices. Then they write some sentences about the café.
• Workbook Ex 1–5, p23

THE MARKET

Introduction

Ss watch a BBC extract about a man's first day as a salesman in an Istanbul market. Ss then learn and practise how to buy items in a market, and write a paragraph about a market they know.

SUPPLEMENTARY MATERIALS

Ex 4C: for *stronger classes*, prepare a vocabulary sheet with simple labelled pictures of jewellery and pottery (see notes for suggestions).

Ex 5B: bring in some photos and information (e.g. from the internet) about some famous markets, e.g. Camden or Portobello Road in London.

Warm up

Direct Ss to the photo and put them in small groups to answer the following questions about it:

What's in the photo?

What country is it?

Is it a good market?

Where is a good market in your country/city?

▶ DVD PREVIEW

1A Look at the example with the class and check the pronunciation of *spices*. Put Ss in pairs to help each other match as many words as they can. As you check the answers, help Ss with the pronunciation of *clothes*, *jewellery* and *leather*.

Answers: 2 C 3 A 4 D 5 F 6 B

B Ask for some ideas from the class, e.g. food, drink, toys for children, pictures, books, old things (antiques), things for your house.

2 Read out the two questions to the class and tell Ss to read quickly and find the answers. Vocabulary to check: *TV presenter* (give an example), *carpet seller* (a person who sells carpets), *a salesman* (a man who sells things).

Answers: He's in Istanbul, at the Grand Bazaar.
He's a carpet seller.

▶ DVD VIEW

3A Direct Ss back to the photos in Ex 1A and tell them to look for any of the objects. You may want to play the DVD without sound the first time, so Ss don't get distracted by trying to understand the dialogue. Otherwise, reassure Ss that they'll watch the extract again.

Answers: spices, carpets, jewellery, pottery, leather wallets and bags

B Before playing the DVD again, give Ss time to read through the sentences and check the following vocabulary: *thousand, old/new, silk* (if possible, take in something/a picture of something made of silk), *real* (here used to emphasise how good the carpet is. Another example is *a real friend*), *a nightmare* (a big problem, e.g. *Traffic/Parking in my city's a nightmare!*), *a sale* (act out selling something), *a special price, a discount* (draw a price ticket with $500 crossed out and $350 written above it). Give Ss a few minutes to compare and check answers with a partner.

Answers: 1 second 2 thousand 3 learn 4 new 5 real 6 a nightmare 7 Eight 8 friendly 9 sale 10 discount

C You could also ask Ss if they think it's an easy or difficult job and put some prompts on the board: *opening time? street market cold? no sales? people not friendly?* Don't worry about correcting Ss' mistakes in a discussion like this, it's more important to encourage them to try to say whatever they can.

DVD 3 The Market

F=Francesco da Mosto H=Harkan Nayveen
M1=1st man M2=2nd man M3=3rd man S=Seller W=Woman

F: My second day in Istanbul, and it's seven o'clock in the morning – opening time at the Grand Bazaar.
There are four thousand shops here, selling jewellery, pottery, spices, carpets, leather, and of course – Turkish Delight. Lost!
I'm meeting carpet seller, Harkan Nayveen.

H: Francesco, how are you?

F: Very well.

H: It's good to see you.

F: So I'm here to learn.

H: Yes.

F: I have to tell you that really I don't know anything about carpets.

H: Yeah, no?

F: I'm totally in your hands.

H: Yeah, no problem, no problem.
This is new. This looks old but it is not old. This is pure silk carpet.

F: Wow.

H: This is a real art. Like Turkish Picasso.

F: Hello, hello, would you like to to have a look at some carpets sir? Carpets with silk, Turkish silk …

M1: No thanks.

F: No.
Ah would you like to buy a carpet?

M2: What?

F: Carpet, ah, 'tappeto'. It's nice, really, come.
Just have a look, you don't have to buy it.

M3: Don't buy carpets.

F: You don't like carpets, you have carpets at home?

M3: No.

F: No carpets?

M3: No carpets.

S: It's not that easy, not that easy.

F: Yeah, it's a nightmare, a nightmare.
This is Turkish silk, it's very good, it's big.

W: Three hundred dollars.

F: Ah, eight hundred.

W: No. Six …

F: So, six.

W: No, five, five hundred – no, no.

F: Five hundred and fifty, five hundred and fifty.

H: Francesco, you are doing very good, and are you from America?

W: Yes.

H: Americans are good.

W: Yes, they are.

H: They are friendly. As you see you can stop and talk to Americans.

F: OK five hundred, five hundred, OK, five hundred.

W: Alright.

F: OK, so …

H: Let me, let me help. It is his first sale. He is doing very good, so we will give you a special discount, five hundred dollars …

F: And it's good.

speakout in a market

4A You could set the scene by asking Ss which of the objects in Ex 1A the conversation is about, and play the recording once through (answer: a lamp). Then direct Ss to the sentences and tell them to correct the false sentences. Play the recording again.

> **Answers:** 2 F The seller's first price is 200. 3 T 4 F The final price is 100.

B Give Ss a few moments to look at the **key phrases**. You may want to check the following vocabulary: *have a look* (= 'look'); *this/that one* (you could demonstrate that *one* replaces *lamp*, so the speaker doesn't keep repeating it, and give one or two more examples, e.g. *How much is that carpet? This one? Yes.*); *expensive* (you could contrast this with *cheap*).

Then play the recording again for Ss to tick the phrases. N.B. You may also want to highlight *the (blue) one* from the recording, showing Ss that they can put in a different adjective, (e.g. a colour, *big/small*), to help to identify the object.

> **Answers:** Excuse me.
> Where is (this/that)(lamp/carpet) from?
> Where are (these/those ✓)(lamps ✓/carpets) from?
> Can I have a look? ✓
> This one? ✓
> No, that one. ✓
> How much (is it ✓/are they)?
> That's expensive.
> For you, a special (discount ✓/price).

Unit 3 Recording 10

A: Excuse me.
B: Yes.
A: Where are those lamps from?
B: They're from Turkey.
A: Can I have a look?
B: Yes. This one?
A: No, that one. The blue one.
B: It's very nice.
A: How much is it?
B: It's two hundred.
A: That's expensive. Hmm. Fifty.
B: One hundred and fifty.
A: Seventy-five.
B: For you, a special discount. Only one hundred.
A: OK. One hundred.
B: It's a very good price.

C Ss should take turns at being the seller and the customer. Give them a minute or two to agree on an item and think about the price they're willing to pay/accept. For *weaker classes* you could suggest that Ss choose an item of clothing for this role-play, so they can review some of the items from lesson 3.2. For *stronger classes*, you could provide a vocabulary sheet with simple labelled pictures of items of jewellery (e.g. *ring, bracelet, necklace, earrings*) or pottery (e.g. *plate, cup, bowl, jug*) so that Ss are more challenged. Monitor the role-plays and make a note of good language use and problem areas for praise and correction in feedback. You could also ask two or three pairs to perform their role-plays for the class.

writeback a description

5A You could start by asking Ss where they might see this kind of text, e.g. in a guide book or on a tourist information website. Ask different Ss to read out the questions to the class, then give Ss a few minutes to read and answer the questions.

> **Answers:** 1 Covent Garden market 2 It's in the centre of London. 3 Yes, it is. 4 It's good for jewellery, clothes, pictures, small shops and cafés.

B You could start by giving Ss some alternative ways of answering the questions, e.g.

Q2 *It's in the centre of …/It's near …*

Q3 *It's open on weekdays/at weekends.*

Q4 *It's a good market for visitors/local people.*

You could also take in some photos and information (e.g. from the internet) about famous markets in different countries to give Ss ideas. Circulate and help with vocabulary, etc. as Ss write their information. When Ss have finished writing, you could:

- put their information on the wall so they can walk round and read each other's work;
- put Ss in groups to read out their information to each other;
- (in a smaller class) ask each student to read out their information to the class.

You could finish by asking the class to vote on the most interesting market.

> **Homework ideas**
> - Ss review all the new vocabulary items they've studied in this lesson and choose five that they think will be most useful to remember. They write a short dialogue in a market that includes all five items.

LOOKBACK

OBJECTS

1 You could run this as a team game (Ss have their books closed). Display one word at a time: team members 'buzz' to answer, then call out just the missing vowels. The team wins a point for each correct vowel in the word, then when the word is complete, an extra point if they can pronounce the word correctly.

Answers: 2 computer 3 desk 4 chair 5 printer
6 business card 7 clock 8 box 9 lamp 10 picture

THIS/THAT/THESE/THOSE

2A To familiarise Ss with the content of the conversation before they complete the gaps, give them a minute or two to read through it and answer these questions: *Who's Carlos?* (Jan's husband) *Who's Maria?* (Jan's friend) *Who are Ana and Paolo?* (Jan and Carlos's children) Then put Ss in pairs to complete the conversation.

Answers: 2 this 3 these 4 this 5 this 6 that 7 those

B Put Ss in groups of five and tell them to practise the conversation two or three times, changing roles each time. Then you could ask Ss to write one or two key words from each person's line in their notebooks, to act as prompts so they can close their **Students' Books** and practise the conversation again.

C You could give Ss slips of paper to write the new information on, then pass the slips to their partner. When they have their new 'identity', give them a few moments alone to practise talking about it, e.g. spelling their name, saying where they're from and what their job is.

D Put Ss in groups of six, and establish that when one person is introducing their partner, the other four should participate and ask questions, e.g.:

A: *This is (Soraya).*

B: *Hello. Nice to meet you.*

C: *Nice to meet you, too.*

D: *That's a nice name. How do you spell it?* etc.

Monitor the group work and note down examples of good language use and any problem areas for praise and correction.

POSSESSIVE 'S

3A Go through the objects in pictures 1–6 and check the pronunciation of *telescope Ooo* and *basketball Ooo*. Check that Ss know who the people are.

Answers: 2 Bill Gates's computer 3 Picasso's brush
4 Galileo's telescope 5 Michael Jordan's basketball
6 Mozart's piano

Culture notes

William Shakespeare (1564–1616) an English poet and playwright. He wrote thirty-eight plays and they are performed more than the plays of any other playwright.

Bill Gates (1955–) American co-founder of Microsoft.

Pablo Picasso (1881–1973) a Spanish painter and sculptor. He co-founded the Cubist movement.

Michael Jordan (1963–) an American basketball player, considered the greatest basketball player of all time.

Galileo Galilei (1564–1642) an Italian scientist, astronomer and mathematician. He is often called 'the father of modern science'.

Wolfgang Amadeus Mozart (1756–1791) a German classical composer. He started composing at the age five and composed more than 600 works.

B Demonstrate this first, naming a student in the class as in the example, then invite the other Ss to ask you three questions. Put Ss in pairs to continue.

CLOTHES AND COLOURS

4A You could unjumble the first word as an example with the class. Ss can work in pairs, or work alone and compare answers with a partner.

Answers: 1 dress 2 black 3 blue 4 shirt 5 jacket
6 yellow 7 trousers 8 brown

B Point out that Ss should not let their partner see the words as they are writing them.

C Demonstrate this with a student, then put Ss in pairs.

FOOD AND DRINK

5 You could run this as a team game. Display the wordsnake on the board: team members 'buzz' when they find a word, then they must spell it aloud correctly in order to win a point for their team.

Answers: coffee cake tea mineral water sandwich cola

ORDERING IN A CAFÉ

6A Look at the example with the class, then tell Ss to write out the lines of the conversation in their notebooks.

Answers: 2 Can I have an egg sandwich, please?
3 White or brown bread? 4 White, please.
5 Anything else? 6 Yes, can I have a mineral water?
7 Still or sparkling? 8 Sparkling, please. How much is that?
9 That's $5.90. 10 Here you are.

B Ss practise once by referring to the conversation they've written in their notebooks, then close their notebooks and practise using the prompts in their **Students' Books**.

Optional extra activity
Ss change four things in the conversation and practise it again. Then they act out their conversations for the rest of the class, who note down the four things that are different.

7A You could also encourage Ss to add more choices to the list, e.g. *black/____ coffee, brown/____ bread, large/____ cola.*

Answers: 2 espresso, latte 3 sparkling 4 dollars, pounds

B Demonstrate this by saying *Coffee or … ?* and gesturing for the class to finish the question in chorus. Remind Ss about the rising, then falling intonation pattern.

OVERVIEW

WHAT'S DIFFERENT?

Introduction

Ss practise listening and talking about people's lifestyles, using the present simple and verb phrases. They also learn to use *and/because* in writing.

SUPPLEMENTARY MATERIALS

Resource bank p147 and p148

Warm up: prepare sets of cards for each group of Ss (4–6 Ss per group) with items of vocabulary (see notes below).

Warm up

Vocabulary review in groups:

Prepare sets of cards with the following items of vocabulary: *a phone, a cola, a coffee, homework, an office, a house, a shop, a flat, a café, a taxi, university, parents, a brother, sport, clothes, a week, an evening.*

Divide Ss into groups of 4–6 and place the cards face down in a pile in the centre of each group. Demonstrate that Ss should take turns to pick a card (without showing the rest of the group) and mime, draw or give a very short verbal clue for the word on it. The first student in the group to guess the word gets the card, and picks up the next one. The winner is the student with the most cards when the pile is finished. N.B. If a student doesn't know the word on the card, he/she puts it at the bottom and takes another one. Clarify any words that are left at the end, e.g. *an evening, a week, a flat.*

VOCABULARY verb phrases

1A Before Ss start this exercise, you may want to check what a verb is. Say *I'm a teacher. I'm from (country)* and write these on the board. Then mime drinking a coffee and looking contented, say *I like coffee* and write this on the board. Then ask Ss to identify the verb in each phrase: *Where's the verb?* Focus Ss on the example and say *I like coffee and I like clothes and I like football* to show that the same verb matches all the nouns. Give Ss a few minutes to complete the word webs and compare answers with a partner.

Answers: 2 have (show, e.g. by mime, that *have a phone/a brother* indicates possession, whereas *have a cola* indicates consumption) 3 work (highlight the use of *in* with places) 4 drive (highlight the use of *to* to show destination) 5 study (you could check *ten hours a week* with a page from a diary showing two hours of study every morning from Monday to Friday) 6 live (highlight the use of *in* for places and *with* for people) 7 go (highlight the use of *to* to show destination) 8 do (highlight the possessive adjective with *homework*)

B Put Ss in pairs and direct them to the photos of things from the USA.

Answers: have a cola, do sport, live in a house, drive a car, like football

Optional extra activities

1 Ss work in pairs and add one more word to each word web. They should be able to do this with vocabulary from previous lessons, apart from *do* – you may need to give them *business* or *the shopping*.

Examples: *like chocolate, have a sandwich, work in a shop, drive a bus, study French/at school, live in (country), go inside, do the shopping/business.*

2 Ss 'test' each other on the verb phrases, e.g.

A: *ten hours a week*

B: *study ten hours a week*

C Demonstrate this with a student, taking the part of Student A. Ss should be familiar with *Me too*. Tell them that *I don't* is the negative answer, but leave the grammatical analysis of this for later in the lesson. Tell Ss to take turns as A and B, and give them a few minutes to practise.

speakout TIP

Explain to Ss that learning verb phrases will help them to speak more in English and sound fluent more quickly. You could suggest that Ss keep separate pages in their notebooks for some of the more common verbs, e.g. *have, go, do*, so they can keep adding phrases as the course goes on.

➧ PHOTOBANK p142

Ss could work on these exercises at various stages of this lesson, e.g. after Ex 4 or after Ex 8, to give them more choice of verb phrases to use in the writing and speaking activities, or you could set them for homework.

Answers:
A B read C listen D play E cost F watch G write H want
B b) be c) listen d) read e) watch f) play g) cost h) write

LISTENING

2A Tell Ss they're going to listen to people talking on a radio programme called *The USA Today*. Give them a moment or two to read the information and answer the question. Check *the same* and *different* by using objects in the classroom, e.g. two **Student's Books** – *the same*, two notebooks – *different*.

Answer: No, the people are from different countries. N.B. You may want to ask Ss if they think people will say life in the USA is the same or different, i.e. to predict from their background knowledge.

B Show Ss that *houses* is number 1, and check that they're listening for three more topics, to be numbered 2–4.

Answers: 2 students 3 cars 4 friends

C Give Ss a minute or two to read the sentences before you play the recording again. Then get Ss to check their answers in pairs.

Answers: 1 houses 2 evenings 3 drive 4 the same

UNIT 4 Recording 1

A: Excuse me. Do you have a moment?

B: Yes?

A: You aren't American?

B: No, no, I'm from Japan. I'm on holiday here.

A: OK. So, my question is: what's different for you about life here?

B: Erm … well, here people live in houses … they live in big houses. I'm from Tokyo, and we live in flats, small flats. So that's very different.

A: … and so for you, what's different about life here?

C: Erm … well I study at university here. And it's very different from my country because here in the United States, the students have jobs. They work in the evenings, maybe ten hours a week.

A: And you? Do you work?

C: Me? No, I don't. I don't have time. And in my country students don't work, they only study.

D: What's different here? Erm … oh yeah, people drive everywhere. I mean, they drive two hundred metres to the shops.

A: Do you have a car?

D: Yes, I do, but I don't drive to the shops. Not two hundred metres! I walk.

A: And where are you from?

D: I'm from England.

E: I think it's not so different. I'm from Italy and my American friends are not so different from me. Er … we like sport … we like clothes … We er … we go to the cinema, restaurants, have a coffee …

A: So you like the same things.

E: Yeah, the same … not different.

GRAMMAR present simple: *I/you/we/they*

3A and B Write the sentences on the board and ask Ss to tell you which words to underline. Check that the present simple refers to *all the time*, not just *now*. N.B. If Ss ask why *he/she/it* are missing, tell them they're different and that they'll study them in the next lesson.

Answers: 2 They <u>work</u> in the evenings. 3 You <u>like</u> the same things. 4 I <u>don't drive</u> to the shops. I/You/We/They *don't* live in a house. (Elicit/Point out that *don't = do not* and that we use contractions in speaking.)

➧ LANGUAGEBANK 4.1 p124–125

The **Language bank** summarises the affirmative, negative and question forms. Practice Ex 4.1A is similar in format to Ex 4 below, but practises *you/we/they*: you may want to set it for homework or ask Ss to do it after Ex 4.

Answers:
A 2 like 3 don't have 4 don't drive 5 write 6 live 7 eat 8 don't know

PRACTICE

4A Go through the example with the class, then give Ss a minute or two to complete the sentences. As you check the answers, write the completed sentences on the board so you can demonstrate the next stage.

Answers: 2 have 3 don't have 4 study 5 don't work

B Demonstrate this first by ticking the sentences that are true for you, then making changes to the others to make them true. Give Ss time to work on their sentences, then put them in pairs to compare their answers.

WRITING *and, because*

5A Focus Ss on the question and tell them to read the blog and see how many things are the same for them. Demonstrate that they should put a tick (✓) in the margin when they find something the same. Ss can discuss their answers in pairs or with the whole class.

B Write the two sentences on the board and ask Ss for the missing words. Elicit/point out that *because* answers the question *Why?*

Ask Ss to find two more examples of *because* in the blog.

e.g. *I drive to the shops. Why? Because they're five kilometres from my house.*

I walk to work. Why? Because I don't have a car.

> **Answers:** 1 and 2 because

C Ss work alone on the sentences, then compare answers with a partner and check with the class.

> **Answers:** 1 because 2 and 3 and 4 because

6A You could give Ss some prompts to help them structure the blog entry, e.g.

I'm from …

I live in …

I work for (company)/in (place)…

I study …

I drive/don't drive to … because …

I'm often … because …

Circulate and help with vocabulary, spelling, etc. while Ss write their entries.

B Tell Ss to swap their entries with a partner and write S or D in the margin to indicate what is the same or different for them. In feedback, ask two or three pairs to give an example of what is the same for them, e.g. *We live with our parents.*

GRAMMAR *present simple questions*

7A Give Ss a few minutes to look at the tables and think about the answers, then elicit the complete questions and answers and write them on the board. Demonstrate to Ss that when the question begins with *Do*, the answer is either *Yes* or *No*, and that when *What* or *Where* is added in front of *do*, the question is 'open', i.e. there are many possible answers.

> **Answers:**
>
> | Do | you | have | a car? |
> |---|---|---|---|
> | Yes, I *do.* | | No, I *don't.* | |
>
> | Where | *do* | you | live? |
> | What | | | study? |

B Play the first line of the recording for Ss at least twice, and show with your hand that the intonation rises. Then play the rest of the recording for Ss to circle the correct arrows. You could then play each line again, pausing for Ss to repeat.

> **Answers:** 2 ↘ 3 ↗ 4 ↘ 5 ↘

C Ss practise the conversation twice, taking turns at reading A and B's lines.

⟹ **LANGUAGEBANK** 4.1 p124–125

Refer Ss to the **Language bank** for a summary of the question forms and practice of the plural forms *you, we, they.*

> **Answers:** B 2 Do you and Jack live together? 3 Do you work in an office? 4 Do you have a black sweater? 5 Do your parents understand Spanish? 6 Do you walk to work?
>
> C 2 No, we don't. 3 Yes, I do. 4 No, I don't. 5 Yes, they do. 6 No, I don't.
>
> D 2 Where do you work? 3 When do we have a break? 4 How do you spell George? 5 What do they like?

PRACTICE

8A When you've checked Ss' answers to this exercise, you could model each question with rising intonation for them to repeat to prepare them for the next stage. You could also highlight the way that *Do* and *you* are 'squashed together' at natural speed and give Ss a chance to practise this.

> **Answers:** 2 Do you like American films? 3 Do you have a dictionary? 4 Do you like cola? 5 What sports do you like? 6 Where do you live?

B Remind Ss to answer *Yes, I do./No, I don't. And you?* When they've asked all the questions, you could tell them to change one word in each question (i.e. *cats, American, dictionary, cola, sport, live*), and ask/answer again.

SPEAKING

9A Monitor this carefully: if Ss want to use verbs after *like/don't like* (e.g. *I like play football*) you could tell them individually that they need to say *playing* (this is dealt with later in the book). Similarly, if any Ss add *-s* to an uncountable noun (e.g. *I like musics*), tell them that some words don't have a plural, without addressing the issue of countability.

> **Optional extra activity**
>
> If Ss have studied the verb phrases in the Photo bank, they could use them to write another three sentences about themselves, e.g. *I play tennis at the weekend, I want a new phone*, etc. and add these to the sentences from 9A.

B You may want to put Ss into new pairs for this. Tell Ss to ask each other questions about their sentences from 9A, and to make a note of any answers that are the same. Use the example to show Ss how to use *both: We both like Chinese food.*

> **Watch out!**
>
> Ss may say *We both don't like (cola)*. Point out that *both* is only for positive answers, so they should just say *We don't like (cola).*

C Ask each pair to report back to the class, and if there is anything that's the same for all the Ss, you could demonstrate *We all like …*

> **Homework ideas**
> - Ss imagine that they're living in the USA (or another country) and write a short paragraph about what is the same or different for them.
> - Ss work on the exercises about verb phrases in the **Photo bank** and write eight sentences which are true about themselves.
> - Workbook Ex 1–6, p24–25

DOUBLE LIVES

Introduction

Ss practise reading about people and their avatars, and practise talking about people's lives, using the present simple (he/she/it), days of the week and time phrases.

SUPPLEMENTARY MATERIALS

Resource bank p149

Warm up: prepare a list of 12–15 verb phrases from lesson 4.1 and the **photo bank**, e.g. *have a coffee, work in an office, go to a café, do your homework, play the guitar*, etc.

Warm up

Revise verb phrases:

Either: Put Ss into groups of 4–6. One student from each group comes to you and you show them one of the verb phrases on your list. The student runs back to their group and mimes the verb phrase. When another student guesses it, they run to you and say the phrase and if correct, you show them another to mime to their group, etc.

Or: Put Ss into two or three teams. Write the second part of a verb phrase on the board (e.g. *an email, a coffee, the guitar, football, to work, a lot, a flat, ten hours a week*) and ask Ss to think of a verb to complete it. The first person to 'buzz' from a team must say the complete verb phrase to win a point for their team, e.g. *write an email*. Other teams can win bonus points if they can think of different verbs to complete the phrase correctly, e.g. *read an email*.

READING

Culture note

An avatar is a digital identity that you create for yourself as your representative on the internet. The avatar can be two-dimensional, e.g. as an icon in an internet forum, or three-dimensional, e.g. in a video game or virtual world. The 'Second Life' referred to in the texts is an online virtual world that has more than 20 million registered users.

1A Tell Ss to cover the texts, then focus them on the four photos and check that everyone understands the term *avatar*. After eliciting some initial comments about the appearance of Rebecca, José and their avatars, put Ss in pairs to discuss the questions, or discuss them with the whole class. Vocabulary to check: *a tree house* (simple board drawing), *a band* (examples of bands that Ss will know).

B Divide the class in half and tell one half that they're all Student A, and the other half are all Student B. Students As read only Rebecca's text and Students Bs read only José's. Ss find the answers to the questions they discussed in 1A.

C Ss check their answers in pairs. Reassure them that at this stage they don't know all the answers.

Answers:
Student A: 1 Rebecca works in a bank. 2 LittleMe sings in a band. 3 LittleMe drives a sports car. 5 LittleMe lives in a tree house. 6 Rex05 plays guitar in a band.
Student B: 4 José speaks Spanish. 6 Rex05 plays guitar in a band. 2 LittleMe sings in a band. 3 Rex05 drives a sports car.

2A Ss now need to work with a partner from the other half of the class. Move Ss around so that As and Bs are sitting together and give them time to prepare their questions.

Answers: 2 What's your job? 3 Do you drive? 4 What do you do in the evening? 5 What do you do at the weekend? 6 What's your avatar's name?

B Ss take turns asking and answering the questions, in their role as Rebecca or José. By the end of this, 'Rebecca' and 'José' should discover that their avatars are boyfriend and girlfriend.

Then Ss look for three differences that are the same for both Rebecca and José.

Answers: In their real life they don't drive, they live in a small flat, they watch TV.
In their Second Life they live in a big flat, they drive a sports car, they're in a band.

C Ss could discuss this in small groups.

Possible answers: Rebecca and Jose aren't a good couple because she doesn't like sport and he watches football on TV.
LittleMe and Rex05 are a good couple because they both like music.

Optional extra activity

Highlight the following pattern from Rebecca's text:

My flat's/I live (twenty minutes/two hours) from (Madrid/the beach) by (bus/car/train) and ask Ss to write two or three sentences that are true about where they live.

GRAMMAR present simple: *he/she/it*

3A Give Ss a minute or two to look at the sentences, then write them on the board and underline the verbs.

Answers: 1 Rebecca <u>lives</u> in London.
2 She <u>has</u> a small flat. (N.B. if Ss ask why this isn't *haves*, explain that some verbs are irregular.)
3 She <u>doesn't have</u> a car.

B Give Ss a few minutes to complete the table. They can work alone or with a partner. When you check the answers, elicit/point out that *doesn't* is the contracted form of *does not* and that you use it in speaking. Also highlight that in the negative form, there is no *-s* on the verb.

Answers:

+	He	works	in a supermarket.
	She	watches	TV every night.
	It	costs	a lot of money.
	He	has	a small flat.
–	He	*doesn't* know	her name.
	She	*doesn't* have	a house.
	It		

C Go through the rules on the board with the class.

Answers: 1 -s 2 has 3 -es

4A Tell Ss they will hear eight verbs in the *he/she/it* form. Play the recording, pausing if necessary for Ss to write each verb.

Answers: lives, works, teaches, goes, talks, watches, costs, does

B Tell Ss to write /ɪz/ next to the two verbs and play the recording again. Then ask Ss to listen and repeat.

Answers: teaches, watches

Optional extra activity

Ss read look through the texts on p42 and make a list of all the verbs in the *he/she/it* form (affirmative) that they haven't seen in Ex 3 and 4. Answers: (as) says, likes, wants, drives, plays, cycles, speaks, phones, emails, sings.

Then Ss draw two columns in their notebooks with /s/ and /z/ at the top of each. As you read out the ten verbs from the text, they copy them into the correct column, according to the sound of the final -s. N.B. The same rule for the pronunciation of -s applies as for plurals: c.f. unit 3.1.

Answers:
/s/ likes wants speaks
/z/ says drives plays cycles phones emails sings

➡ LANGUAGE BANK 4.2 p124–125

Use the **Language bank** to highlight the spelling rules for the third person -s. Ss could do Ex 4.2A and 4.2B in two groups: Students As do Ex A and Students Bs do Ex B. Give them a key to check their answers, then they pair up with someone from the other group and go through the answers to both exercises.

Answers:
A
2 doesn't email, phones 3 drives, walks 4 works, doesn't like 5 has, he doesn't like 6 understands, doesn't speak
B
Conversation 1
A: My wife, Kalila, *is* a teacher.
B: Near here?
A: Yes, she *has* a job at City School. She *teaches* Arabic.
B: Is it a good place to work?
A: Yes, but she *doesn't* like the travel every day.
Conversation 2
A: My son Jaime *studies* engineering at Madrid University.
B: Oh, my daughter *goes* there. She likes it a lot.
A: Yes, Jaime *says* it's good too.

PRACTICE

5A You could start by asking Ss to read the paragraph quickly and decide who has a good life, Dean or NeoStar. Then give them a few minutes to complete the text and check their answers with a partner.

Answers: 1 lives 2 live 3 work 4 doesn't have 5 has 6 knows 7 goes 8 don't know 9 don't go 10 costs 11 likes 12 don't like

B Ss can either work together to write sentences about both Dean and NeoStar (remembering to change Dean's information into the third person), or Student A writes about Dean and Student B writes about NeoStar (in this case you can ask weaker Ss to be Student B, because the sentences about him are already in the third person). When Ss have written as much as they can remember, check the sentences with the whole class.

SPEAKING

6 Once Ss have found their page and activity, tell them to find another Student A or B to work with (so As and Bs are sitting together). Give them a few minutes to look at their pictures. With *weaker classes*, review verb phrases first. Use a *strong student* to demonstrate the example with you. Ss then return to their original partners so they're in AB pairs and say their sentences about the pictures. Monitor carefully so that you can give Ss feedback on language use after the activity.

VOCABULARY days; time phrases

7A Ss could work in pairs to number the days of the week, saying them aloud as they do so.

Answers: 2 Tuesday 3 Wednesday 4 Thursday 5 Friday 6 Saturday 7 Sunday

B Before Ss listen and repeat, you could ask them to choose which of the following stress patterns the days have:

Ooo   oO   Oo   ooO

Answers: Saturday = Ooo, the other days = Oo

8A You may want to tell Ss to look for examples of the time phrases in the text on p42, either before or after they do this exercise. N.B. If Ss ask you about *Saturday mornings* (from José's text) tell them that *on* is always used with the name of the day.

Answers: 2 at 3 in 4 on

B Give Ss a minute or two to underline the alternatives, then compare answers.

Answers: 1 every 2 in 3 on 4 at 5 every

C Demonstrate how to change sentence 1 in different ways, e.g.
I have tea every morning.
I have coffee every afternoon.
Put Ss in pairs to read out their sentences and compare answers. Then tell Ss to be prepared to tell the class things about their partner, e.g. *Sasha meets her friends on Saturdays and she studies English every evening.*

Optional extra activity

Ss invent their own avatar and write a short text about him/her. You could give them some prompts, e.g. *My avatar is (name). He/She lives in … with … He/She has … He/She works … In the evening, he/she … At the weekend, he/she …* then collect in the texts and redistribute them. Ss then read out the text they have and the class guesses whose avatar it is.

Homework ideas

• If you don't have time in class, Ss could write about their avatar (optional extra activity above) and bring the text to the next class.
• Workbook Ex 1–6, p26–27

WHAT TIME IS IT?

Introduction

Ss practise telling the time, using vocabulary related to events. They also practise listening and learn to check times.

SUPPLEMENTARY MATERIALS

Resource bank p150

Ex 3A (optional extra activity): take in a toy clock with hands that Ss can move (you could make this from cardboard).

Warm up

Review numbers from 1–100 by doing some counting activities. Ss count in multiples of two, e.g. *two, four, six,* etc. and *one, three, five,* etc. then in multiples of five, e.g. *five ten, fifteen,* etc. They could do this around the class, or in groups of 4–6. Rather than going around in order, give Ss a ball or soft object: the first student says a number, e.g. *five,* then throws the ball to the person they choose to say the next number, and so on.

VOCABULARY events

1A Direct Ss to the pictures and put them in pairs to find six of the events from the box. As you check the answers with the class, elicit verbs associated with the events, e.g. *see a play/film/match, go to a party/lesson/match/concert, have a lesson/party.* You could also elicit some activities that people do at the events, e.g. *listen to music, dance* (a party, a concert), *study, listen, read, write* (a lesson). Check also the pronunciation and the plural form of the events: *films, parties, plays, concerts, matches, festivals, lessons.*

Answers:
A play B match C lesson D party E film F concert
festival is not in the pictures

B Ask two Ss to demonstrate, using the example, then put Ss in pairs to practise. For *stronger classes,* you could encourage Ss to extend the conversations by asking for a reason, e.g.

A: I don't like concerts, but I like plays.

B: Why?

A: Because I like the actors.

FUNCTION telling the time

2A Play the first conversation for Ss to check the example, then play the rest of the recording.

Answers: 2 lesson 3 film 4 match 5 party 6 concert

B Tell Ss to write the numbers as words, e.g. *two* then play the recording again. Ss can compare answers in pairs, and/or check their answers in the audio script. Draw seven 'clock faces' on the board, and as you go through the answers, ask Ss to come up and draw the clock hands in the correct position on each clock face.

Answers: 1 four 2 three 3 nine, ten 4 two 5 eleven
6 seven

Unit 4 Recording 5

Conversation 1
A: Excuse me. What time is it?
B: It's four o'clock.
A: Thank you. Oh, and do you know … where's the music festival?
B: You go down here and …

Conversation 2
A: Hi, Lisa.
B: Hi, Manuel. Come and sit down.
A: It's time for class.
B: What time's the lesson?
A: At half past three. New time.
B: Oh, no. We're late.
A: Yeah, let's go.

Conversation 3
A: Excuse me. What time is the film?
B: At quarter to nine and half past ten.
A: Oh, that's late. Is there an early one?
B: Hmmm … yeah, at quarter past six.

Conversation 4
A: The World Cup Final is on TV tomorrow!
B: What time's the match?
A: Erm … at quarter past two.
B: Quarter past two. Thanks.

Conversation 5
A: We're late again.
B: No, we're not. It's a party. It's OK to be late.
A: What time is it now?
B: It's quarter to eleven.
A: Quarter to *eleven*?
B: It's OK …

Conversation 6
B: What time's the concert?
A: At quarter past seven.
B: Sorry? When?
A: Quarter past seven.
B: Quarter past seven. Thanks.

LANGUAGEBANK 4.3 p124–125

Use the **Language bank** to clarify the difference between *What time is it? It's (two o'clock)* and *What time's the (concert)? It's at (two o'clock).* Ss could do Ex 4.3 in class or for homework.

Answers: 1 five o'clock 2 quarter past six
3 half past nine 4 quarter to nine 5 quarter to five
6 half past twelve 7 eleven o'clock 8 quarter past seven

3A Focus Ss on the four positions of the hands on the clock (A–D), then play the recording for them to listen and repeat.

Unit 4 Recording 6

ten o'clock

quarter past ten

half past ten

quarter to eleven

Optional extra activity

Take in a large toy clock with moveable hands. Pass the clock to a student, who sets the time, then chooses another student and asks *What time is it?* If that student answers correctly, the clock is passed to them to set the time, and so on.

B Demonstrate an example with a student, then put Ss in pairs to practise.

⟫ PHOTOBANK p142

Ss practise writing times to match the photos.

Answers: A five past eight B ten past ten C twenty past three D twenty-five past one E twenty-five to ten F twenty to four G ten to two H five to twelve

Optional extra activities

1 Use the times in Ex 3B for Ss to practise the difference between *What time is it?* and *What time's the (event)?* Student A points to a time and asks either *What time is it?* or *What time's the (party/film/lesson/match/play/concert/festival)?* Student B answers either *It's (7.30)* or *It's at (7.30)*.

2 For *stronger classes*, you could introduce *five, ten, twenty, twenty-five past/to* and ask Ss in pairs to take turns and write a time for their partner to say, e.g.
A: (writes 9.20) *What time is it?*
B: *It's twenty past nine.*

LEARN TO check times

4A You could write the conversation on the board and ask Ss which words to underline.

Answers: A: <u>Sorry?</u> <u>When?</u> A: <u>Quarter past seven.</u> Thanks.

B Ss could look at the arrows and try to predict how to say the two words. Then either play the recording again or model the intonation yourself, giving Ss a few opportunities to repeat.

Teaching tip

A fall-rise intonation pattern is often used to show uncertainty. It sounds more polite than a rise, which can sound rather abrupt. To help Ss copy the pattern, say each word slowly, exaggerating the high start and the following fall and rise.

speakout TIP

Refer Ss to the final line of the dialogue in Ex 4A, where A says *Quarter past seven. Thanks.* Show them that the intonation falls on these two sentences, because the speaker is sure of what they're saying.

C Ask two Ss to demonstrate the example dialogue for the class, encouraging them to exaggerate their intonation. Point out that Student B shouldn't look at the exercise while checking and writing the time. Put Ss in pairs to practise.

SPEAKING

5A and B Give Student Bs time to find their page and activity, and tell Ss not to look at each other's information. You could elicit *Let's go to a … on …* by saying *I want to go to a festival with (student's name): what can I say?* Then direct the class to the example dialogue and act it out with a student, taking the part of B yourself, so you can demonstrate writing the event and time into the correct space in the diary. Tell Ss to ask and answer until all the spaces are complete. Monitor carefully and take note of good language use and any problem areas for praise and correction later.

Optional extra activity

Ss invent their own weekend diary, writing two events and times for each day. Encourage them to be creative and write more than one word for each event, e.g. *music/food festival, Lina's party, dancing lesson, tennis match,* etc. Then they either work in groups, or walk round the class, talking to different people and asking them to the events. Remind them to note down the name of the student who agrees to go to each event with them. In feedback, Ss can report back on what they've got in their diaries, e.g. *Saturday, 4.30, a jazz concert with Alicia,* etc.

Homework ideas
• Workbook Ex 1–4, p28

RIVERS

Introduction

Ss watch an extract from the BBC series *Human Planet* about a man who crosses the Mekong River every day to catch fish for his family. Ss then learn and practise how to talk and write about their favourite season.

SUPPLEMENTARY MATERIALS

Ex 1A: bring in/download pictures of a river, falls/waterfall, a fish, a bridge, or be prepared to draw simple sketches of these on the board.

Ex 4A (alternative approach): bring in a soft ball or other object for Ss to throw to each other.

Warm up

Tell Ss to close their books and put the title *Rivers* on the board, then check that Ss understand by giving an example of a river in the country where they're studying. Then write the sentence *The River Thames goes through London* and put Ss in pairs to think of more examples of famous rivers and which countries/cities they go through. After a few minutes, invite Ss to share their ideas with the class.

▶ DVD PREVIEW

1A Start by using pictures to illustrate the meaning of *falls/waterfall, river, fish, bridge* and *boat*. Direct Ss to the photos to identify any of the words.

B Demonstrate *cross* (go from one side to the other) e.g. by crossing the classroom. Direct Ss to the map and elicit the answers to the two questions.

Answers: The Mekong River crosses Thailand, Laos, Cambodia and Vietnam.
The Khone Falls are in Laos.

C Go through the example, checking that Ss understand *wet* and *dry* by miming washing your hands (*they're wet*) and drying them with a towel (*now they're dry*). Put Ss in pairs and encourage them to help each other with the meaning of the adjectives and to use a dictionary for any they're not sure of. When you go through the answers, check Ss' understanding, e.g. by asking: *If a fish is very cold and hard, is it fresh or frozen? Is it safe or dangerous to walk in (a park) at midnight?* (Pointing to the sum 2+2=?) *Is this difficult or easy? Are we alive or dead?*

2 Before Ss read the information, check *the four seasons* (spring, summer, autumn, winter), the months that correspond to each season and *rainy season*. Give Ss a few minutes to find the answers to the questions.

Answers: Good things: they give us fresh water, food and ways to go from place to place.
Bad things: life on a river is sometimes difficult and dangerous.
The man is Sam Niang.

▶ DVD VIEW

3A Give Ss a minute or two to read through the alternatives, then play the DVD. You may want to play it without sound the first time, so Ss can concentrate on the man's actions.

Answers: A man crosses a bridge and catches two fish.

B Before playing the DVD again, give Ss time to read through the sentences and think about the alternatives: they may already be able to predict some of the answers. When Ss have watched the DVD, give them a few minutes to compare and check answers with a partner.

Answers: 1 The world is a place of extremes: hot and *cold*, wet and *dry*.
2 In winter, the dry season, the Falls *aren't* very big, but in summer, the *rainy* season, they're very dangerous.
3 He crosses the river on a *simple* bridge. It's very, very *dangerous*. A man falls and he's *dead*.
4 Sam Niang fishes. He catches his family's *dinner*.
5 Tomorrow is a *new* day and Sam Niang will go back to the *river* to catch fish for his family again.

C Check that Ss understand the adjectives by miming them yourself in random order and asking Ss to identify which adjective you're miming. You could replay the DVD without sound from the point where Sam starts to cross the bridge to the end, and ask Ss how he feels at different stages, i.e. *afraid* when he's crossing the bridge, *hungry* when he sees the fish, *tired* as he crosses the bridge again, *happy* when his son meets him and when he has dinner with his family.

DVD 4 Rivers

The world is a place of extremes: hot and cold, wet and dry. Only one animal lives in all of these places, man. This is the Human Planet.

Rivers are alive.

They change with the four seasons. Rivers give us many things – fresh water, food, and ways to go from place to place. A river gives, and a river takes. Sometimes it has too much water, sometimes it's frozen, and sometimes it's dead.

Life on a river is sometimes difficult and dangerous.

The Khone Falls are on the Mekong River. In winter, the dry season, the Falls aren't very big, but in summer, the rainy season, they're very dangerous.

The Falls are good for fishing. For Sam Niang the Falls are important. He has a wife and six children. Sam Niang goes fishing every day.

He crosses the river on a simple bridge. It is very, very dangerous. A man falls and he's dead. The river gives fish, gives life, but it can also take a man's life.

Sam Niang fishes. He catches his family's dinner.

He crosses the bridge again, with the fish. His son comes to meet him. Today, Sam Niang's family has a dinner of fresh fish. Tomorrow is a new day and Sam Niang will go back to the river to catch fish for his family again.

speakout a favourite season

4A Ask Ss for the names of the seasons and write them on the board. Then write the four topics on the board and elicit an example for each one, e.g. *winter: holidays – Christmas; clothes – jacket; activities – go for a walk; weather – cold*. Give Ss a few minutes to decide on their favourite season and make notes about the topics, working alone. Remind Ss to use the **Photo bank** to help them with vocabulary, as well as asking you and their classmates.

Alternative approach

Play a word association game to generate ideas. You'll need a soft ball or other object for Ss to throw to each other. Write the four topics (holidays, clothes, activities, weather) on the board. Tell Ss to stand in a circle (including you) then say the name of a season and throw the ball to a student, prompting them to say the first thing they think of, e.g. *summer – T-shirt*. This student then throws the ball to someone else, and so on. After a few Ss have thrown the ball, call out the name of another season and tell them to continue. If Ss have difficulty thinking of a word or phrase, point to the topics on the board.

B Direct Ss back to the topics in Ex 4A and tell them to tick the ones the person talks about.

Answers: holidays, activities, weather

C Give Ss a few moments to look at the **key phrases**. Then play the recording again for them to tick the phrases. As you check the answers, you could elicit some alternative ways of completing the phrases, e.g. *I like it because it's my birthday in (month); I don't like autumn because it's wet; my favourite holiday is in spring,* etc.

Answers: My favourite season is (spring/summer/autumn ✓/winter)
I like it because it's … ✓
It's a beautiful season.
I don't like the (summer ✓/winter) because I don't like (very hot ✓/very cold) weather.
My favourite holiday is in autumn. ✓
(The/My family ✓/Friends) come(s) together for (a big dinner ✓/a party).

Unit 4 Recording 8

My favourite season is autumn. I like it because it's not too hot and not too cold. I don't like the summer or the winter because I don't like very hot or very cold weather. In autumn, the trees are beautiful … all red and yellow. At the weekend, I walk with my family in the mountains. My favourite holiday is in autumn. It's Thanksgiving, and it's in November. The family comes together for a big dinner. I also like autumn because it's the start of the school year. I know some people don't like school, but I'm a teacher and I like it!

5A Put Ss in pairs to 'rehearse' their talk: encourage them to make suggestions to each other for improvements, e.g. if something is unclear or difficult to understand. Circulate and help where necessary.

B Put Ss in groups of four or five. Tell them to make a note of the question they want to ask while they're listening. When each student finishes speaking, the others in the group ask their questions. In feedback you could ask a few Ss to tell the class one surprising/interesting thing they found out from the activity.

writeback a forum reply

6A You could start by asking Ss if they ask questions or write replies on forums, and if they think it's easy to do that in English. Direct them to the questions and give them a few minutes to find the answers.

Answers: 1 winter 2 Because she loves cold mornings and the frozen countryside, the beautiful trees and roads. 3 Travelling is difficult.

B Tell Ss to use the example in Ex 6A as a model for their reply, e.g.:

My favourite season is ____.

I like it because ____ and ____.

I know that (X) is sometimes difficult/a problem, and/but ____.

I also like ____ because I ____.

When Ss have finished writing you could collect in their replies and redistribute them so that each student has someone else's reply. Ss then take turns to read out the replies to the class and the other Ss guess who wrote them.

Homework ideas

- Ss read some questions and replies on an English forum. You could suggest some forums on particular topics.

LOOKBACK

SUPPLEMENTARY MATERIALS

Ex 4 (optional extra activity): prepare 'Find someone who …' handout for each student (see notes).

VERB PHRASES

1A Point out that sometimes a phrase is not correct because there's a small word (like *in* or *to*) missing. Ss can work in pairs and check their answers with the class.

Answers: 2 ~~the city~~ 3 ~~university~~ 4 ~~hungry~~ 5 ~~a flat~~
6 ~~bored~~ 7 ~~work~~ 8 ~~tennis~~

B Direct Ss to the example and point out that they can change what comes after the verbs. Circulate and help as Ss write their sentences.

C Put Ss in pairs and tell them that while Student A reads his/her sentences, Student B should think of a 'follow up' question to ask about Student A and his/her friend, and vice versa.

PRESENT SIMPLE *I/YOU/WE/THEY*

2A You could draw the table on the board, and demonstrate how the three columns link together to make the beginning of the example question. Tell Ss to write a minimum of four questions. *Stronger classes* could write eight questions, one for each verb.

B Before you put Ss in pairs, focus on the questions beginning *Do your friends … ?* and *Do the other students in the class … ?* and establish that they may not know the answer. Tell Ss to say *I don't know/I'm not sure/I think so/I don't think so.*

You could follow up by asking different pairs to check their ideas about the other Ss in the class, e.g.

Ss: *We think the other students in the class watch TV every day.*

Ss: *That's true!*

Ss: *That's not true!* etc.

PRESENT SIMPLE *HE/SHE/IT*

3A Go through the example and tell Ss to write the sentences in their notebooks.

Answers: 2 She lives in a flat. 3 He doesn't like hamburgers. 4 She has a brother. 5 He doesn't like shopping. 6 She does sport at the weekend.

B Tell Ss that it doesn't matter if they don't know whether the information is true about the other Ss, because they'll have a chance to check later.

C Ss can check the information either by asking across the class, or by walking around and asking the relevant Ss.

DAYS; TIME PHRASES

4A You could run this as a spelling game in teams (Ss close their books first). Write the first two letters of a day on the board (go through the days at random, rather than in order), and the first student to 'buzz' spells the rest of the word. If all the letters are correct they win two points for their team, but they lose points for wrong letters and hesitation.

Answers: Tuesday, Thursday, Friday, Saturday, Sunday

B Look at the example first, then Ss can work alone or in pairs on the rest.

Answers: 2 d) 3 a) 4 f) 5 b) 6 e)

C Check that Ss know they need to write six sentences. Circulate and help with vocabulary while Ss write their sentences.

D You could demonstrate this with an example of your own and encourage the class to guess when you do the activity.

Optional extra activity

'Find someone who …'

Prepare the handout below and give one to each student. Ss work in pairs to complete the gaps with their own ideas. Then the pairs separate and walk round the class, asking other Ss *Do you … ?* until someone answers *Yes* and they write that person's name next to the question. They continue until they have a name next to each question. Ss then return to their partners and compare the answers they found. Then they can report back to the class, e.g. *Mica and Franca drive to work every day.*

Find someone who …

drives _____ every ____ .

plays _____ at the weekend.

listens _____ in the ____ .

watches _____ every ____ .

wants _____ .

reads _____ in the ____ .

goes _____ at the weekend.

writes _____ every ____ .

EVENTS

5A You could run this as a team game (Ss close their books). Write each gapped word on the board: team members 'buzz' and tell you only the missing vowels. They win a point for each correct vowel.

Answers: 2 concert 3 lesson 4 party 5 play 6 festival
7 match

Alternative idea

To provide more challenge, write blanks for the whole word, e.g. for *concert*: __ __ __ __ __ __ __ .

Ss from the teams 'buzz' and call out any letter they think may be in the word. If the letter is in the word, write it in the correct place and give the team a point; if it isn't in the word, give the team a penalty point. The winning team is the one with the fewest penalty points at the end.

B Go through the example with the Ss and put them in pairs.

TELLING THE TIME

6A Give Ss a few minutes to write the times, working alone.

Answers: 2 Half past twelve. 3 Quarter past seven.
4 Three o'clock. 5 Quarter to four. 6 Quarter past eleven.

B Demonstrate that Ss should write any times, apart from the ones in Ex 6A. Tell them not to show their partner the times.

C Demonstrate the activity with a student, taking the part of Student A yourself, so that you can show Ss how to stress the incorrect numbers.

REVIEW 2: UNITS 3–4

Introduction

The aim of the review units is for Ss to revise and practise the grammar, vocabulary and pronunciation from the previous two units, in a different context. The context for this review unit is favourites.

SUPPLEMENTARY MATERIALS

Ex 4C: be prepared to talk about your favourite categories.

Ex 5C (optional extra activity): prepare a matching handout to review verb + noun combinations (see notes).

LISTENING AND GRAMMAR

1A Start by checking *favourites*, i.e. the things you like the most, and another word for *bookmarks* on the computer, for saving links to websites. Then check *icon* (a small sign or picture, e.g. on a computer or phone screen) and put Ss in pairs to match the words to the icons A–F. As you check the answers with the class, elicit two or three examples for each icon, e.g. *People* – friend, sister, boss; *Clothes* – dress, jacket, shoes; *Cafés* – names of local cafés that Ss know, and so on.

> **Answers:** A places B people C websites D clothes
> E films

B Demonstrate the example with a student, then put Ss in pairs. Tell them to give an example from each icon at least twice.

2A Tell Ss to write the list of icons from Ex 1A in their notebooks and write a number from 1–6 next to each one when they hear them. You could play the first part of the recording and tell Ss to say 'Stop!' when they hear the woman mention the first icon (People). Then play the rest of the recording. Vocabulary to check: *meet* (e.g. *I meet my friends at the café*), *traveller* (someone who travels a lot), *ice cream* (simple board drawing), *love* (e.g. *I love ice cream*).

> **Answers:** 1 people 2 places 3 clothes 4 websites 5 cafés
> 6 films

B Play the first part of the recording again for Ss to hear the three people mentioned, then play the rest of the recording. Give Ss time to compare their answers in pairs before checking with the class.

> **Answers:** Cafés 1 Clothes 1 Films 2 Places 3 Websites 1

3A Go through the example with the class, then give Ss a few minutes to complete the sentences, working alone. Then they can compare their answers in pairs before checking with the whole class.

> **Answers:** 2 William says Alicia is beautiful.
> 3 Beth knows Keith from university.
> 4 Beth and Monique aren't friends.
> 5 Beth has a red party dress.
> 6 She likes the BBC website.
> 7 She goes to the Gelatino Café every day.

B Ss can either check the recording script or you could play the recording again. Ask Ss what the corrected sentence should be.

> **Answer:** Sentence 7 is false. Correct answer: *She doesn't go to the Gelatino Café a lot.*

Review 2 Recording 1

A: So if I press this …
B: Beth, who's that?
A: These are my favourite people.
B: That woman. She's beautiful.
A: William! That's my sister Alicia. Watch it!
B: Your sister? Oh … who's that then?
A: That's Keith. He's a good friend from university.
B: Do you meet a lot now?
A: No, but we email each other every day.
B: And this?
A: Monique, from work.
B: Are you friends?
A: Not really. But I like her a lot.
B: And if I press this … Oh, look!
A: Yeah, Paris …
B: … Cairo … and the Great Wall of China. Big traveller!
A: Yeah, then here …
B: Hey, nice dress.
A: You know that dress. My black party dress.
B: Yeah, I like that dress. Oh, you like the BBC.
A: Yeah, the website's great for the news.
B: Let's look at … What's this? Ice cream?
A: Yeah, from the Gelatino Café. I love it. But I don't go there a lot.
B: And what's this?
A: Johnny Depp.
B: Is he one of your favourite people?
A: No, but *Pirates of the Caribbean* is one of my favourite films.
B: And here's another film. *Pirates of the Caribbean II*. Johnny Depp again and here's…
A: OK, that's enough …

SPEAKING

4A You could draw the table on the board and demonstrate choosing three categories for yourself, pointing out that Ss need to choose categories where they can think of the names of several things or people to include.

B Tell Ss that for most categories they simply need to write a name, e.g. *Erica, Bar Italia, Prague, the King's Speech*, etc. For *music*, they could write the name of a band or a type of music, and for *animals* the name of a pet or a type of animal. For *clothes* they need to write the items, e.g. *black jacket*. Tell them that they also need to be able to explain why each thing/person is a favourite.

C Demonstrate this by choosing a student to ask you about your favourites. Ss can then walk around the class and talk to (three or four) different people. Monitor the activity carefully and note down examples of good language use and any problem areas for praise and correction later. In feedback you could ask Ss if they found anyone who had the same favourite as one of theirs, e.g. *Yes, Monica. We both like Tino's Café because the chocolate cake is very good!*

> **Alternative idea**
> Ss write one sentence in their notebooks about each favourite item from the table, but don't write the name.
>
> In pairs, Student A shows Student B their favourites and reads one of their sentences. Student B guesses which favourite item the sentence is about, e.g.
> A: It has very good Greek food.
> B: *Sofie's?*
> A: Yes!

READING AND GRAMMAR

5A You could elicit/remind Ss that Alicia is Beth's sister and Keith is her friend from university. Tell Ss to read the texts quickly, just to find out what their jobs are. Vocabulary to check: *alone* (contrast simple board drawings of person standing in a group, and person standing alone), *difficult* (mime trying to do a difficult sum), *a typical day* (usual, like every day), *welcome* (act out welcoming a student), *check* (act out checking someone's name on a list).

Answers: Keith is a taxi driver.
Alicia is a hotel receptionist.

B Go through the example with the class then give Ss a few minutes to find the answers.

Answers: 2 K 3 A 4 A 5 A 6 K

C Ss could work in pairs to write the questions, or work alone and compare answers in pairs.

Answers: 2 Do you work in an office? 3 Do you speak on the phone (a lot)? 4 Do you use a computer in your job? 5 Do you work in the evenings? 6 Do you drive a lot in your job?

Optional extra activity
Review some of the verb + noun combinations from the texts, so that Ss can use them in Ex 5D and Ex 6. Prepare the following matching activity on a handout or on sets of cards (one set per pair of Ss):

1 work	4 welcome	a) people	d) people's names
2 answer	5 check	b) alone	e) around the city
3 get	6 drive	c) tired	f) the phone

When Ss have matched the verbs and nouns, they could fold the handout in half or turn over some of the cards so they can only see half of the combination, then try to remember the whole phrase.

Answers: 1 b) 2 f) 3 c) 4 a) 5 d) 6 e)

D Focus Ss on the example. You could then do another example comparing your day to Keith's and Alicia's. If Ss don't work, they could invent a job, or talk about their parents' or friends' jobs, or you could give them a job. When Ss have finished, ask two or three pairs to tell the class their answers.

SPEAKING

6A Put Ss in groups of three or four. Tell them to write their list of jobs on a large piece of paper that everyone in the group can see.

B Elicit/Remind Ss of some of the questions they could ask (only *yes/no* questions), e.g.
Do you work alone/at night/in an office? Do you answer the phone? Do you take people's money? Do you get very tired? Do you have special clothes? Do you like your job?

When a student thinks they've guessed the job, they ask *Are you a … ?* Monitor the activity carefully so you can give Ss feedback on their use of vocabulary and pronunciation.

SOUNDS /s/ AND /z/

7A Direct Ss to the pictures and point out that the symbols represent the sounds. Play the recording for Ss to listen to the sounds and the words. You may also want to show Ss that they need to 'use their voice' to make /z/: if they put their hands over their ears and make /z/ they should hear their voice in their heads, whereas with the sound /s/ there is no voice. Play the recording again for Ss to repeat.

B You may want to ask Ss to predict which group the words belong to before they listen.

Answers: /s/ s̲andwich, s̲port, thi̲s̲
/z/ ha̲s̲, euro̲s̲, drive̲s̲

8A Go through the example with the class, then put Ss in pairs to complete the exercise.

Answers: 2 Tom's 3 trousers 4 it's 5 bags 6 likes

B Pause the recording if necessary while Ss are checking their answers.

C You may want to go through these rules with the whole class, or with *stronger classes,* give Ss the opportunity to work out the rules in pairs.

Answers: 1 /s/ 2 /s/ 3 /z/

9A You could go through the first sentence with the class, as an example.

Answers: 1 My s̲on live̲s̲ near the s̲ea and the mountain̲s̲.
2 The lamp̲s̲ and the clock̲s̲ are in the room̲s̲ near the bed̲s̲.
3 Can I have s̲ix egg̲s̲, plea̲s̲e?
4 S̲ue email̲s̲ her parent̲s̲ on S̲unday̲s̲.

B Encourage Ss in pairs to read the sentences aloud to each other, so they can hear how the 's' is pronounced.

Answers:
1 My s̲on live̲s̲ near the s̲ea and the mountain̲s̲.
  /s/ /z/   /s/   /z/
2 The lamp̲s̲ and the clock̲s̲ are in the room̲s̲ near the bed̲s̲.
        /s/   /s/   /z/   /z/
3 Can I have s̲ix egg̲s̲, plea̲s̲e?
              /s/ /z/ /z/
4 S̲ue email̲s̲ her parent̲s̲ on S̲unday̲s̲.
 /s/   /z/   /s/ /s/   /z/

C You may want to pause the recording for Ss to repeat the sentences in shorter 'chunks'.

Homework ideas
• Ss write two sentences about one favourite from each category in Ex 4, beginning: *One of my favourite (places) is … I like/love it because …*
• Workbook Ex 1–5, p29–30

OVERVIEW

5.1 BAD HABITS

GRAMMAR | present simple questions

VOCABULARY | daily routines

HOW TO | describe people's routines

COMMON EUROPEAN FRAMEWORK

Ss can ask and answer questions about other people's habits; can understand and extract the essential information from short recorded passages dealing with everyday matters that are delivered slowly and clearly.

5.2 SUPERMAN AND SUPERMODEL

GRAMMAR | adverbs of frequency

VOCABULARY | food

HOW TO | talk about what you eat

COMMON EUROPEAN FRAMEWORK

Ss can understand very short, simple texts, picking up familiar names, words and basic phrases and re-reading as required; can use the most frequently occurring connectors to link simple sentences in order to describe something as a simple list of points.

5.3 WHEN DOES IT OPEN?

FUNCTION | asking for information

VOCABULARY | hotel services

LEARN TO | show interest

COMMON EUROPEAN FRAMEWORK

Ss can communicate in simple and routine tasks requiring a simple and direct exchange of information.

5.4 DOCTOR WHO ⊙ BBC DVD

speakout | desert island food

writeback | a forum entry

COMMON EUROPEAN FRAMEWORK

Ss can identify the main points of TV items where the visual supports the commentary; can give a short, rehearsed, basic presentation on a familiar subject.

5.5 LOOKBACK

Communicative revision activities

BBC VIDEO PODCAST

People talking about their weekend routines.

BAD HABITS

Introduction

Ss practise listening and talking about daily routines and things that drive them crazy, using present simple questions and related vocabulary.

SUPPLEMENTARY MATERIALS

Resource bank p152

Ex 6: be prepared to answer questions about a friend or family member.

Warm up

Review days of the week and verb phrases. Prompt a student to ask you what your favourite day of the week is and why, e.g.

S: *What's your favourite day of the week?*

T: *Thursday.*

S: *Why?*

T: *Because I go to my dance class in the evening.*

Put Ss in pairs or small groups to ask and answer about their favourite day of the week. Ask a few Ss to report back to the class about their partners, e.g. *Kirsten's favourite day is … because she …*

VOCABULARY daily routines

1A Tell Ss to write the numbers 1–7 in their notebooks. Play the first sound and check that Ss understand *get up* by asking a student to act it out. Then play the rest of the recording: you may want to stop after each sound for Ss to confer in pairs about which verb it matches. When you've checked the answers, Ss could work in pairs, taking turns to say a verb for their partner to act out.

Answers: 2 have breakfast 3 go to work 4 have lunch 5 get home 6 have dinner 7 go to bed

B Direct Ss to the example and put them in pairs to practise asking and answering.

Optional extra activity

Ss imagine that they have a job where the daily routine is different from their own (they could look at the **Photo bank** p139 for ideas) and answer their partner's questions about their routine. Their partner has to guess the job.

⟼ PHOTOBANK p142–143

For *Daily routines: Movement verbs* you may want to clarify *go to work* vs *come home* by acting them out, showing that *come* means move towards a place, when the person speaking is in that place. For *Daily routines: Verb phrases* give Ss an opportunity to practise 'testing' each other on the phrases in pairs, as in Ex 1B.

Answers: Daily routines: Movement verbs 1D 2 B 3 C 4 A Daily routines: Verb phrases 2 go 3 get 4 leave 5 make 6 start/finish

LISTENING

speakout TIP

Give Ss a few minutes to write seven true sentences. Suggest that they keep them somewhere (at home, in their bag, in the car) where they'll see them every day. Point out that they could do this with any items of vocabulary that they want to remember: choose about six items to put into sentences (e.g. about themselves or people they know) and practise repeating them every day. They could do this with some of the verb phrases from the **Photo bank**.

2A Direct Ss to the photos and ask them which person is angry and why.

Possible answers: The woman in photo A, because the man doesn't listen to her.

B Before you play the recording give Ss a few moments to read through the alternatives and check *neighbour* (someone who lives next to or near you).

Answers: 1 daughter 2 boyfriend 3 his neighbour

C Go through the example with the class and give Ss a few moments to read the sentences, then play the recording again.

Answers: Sentence 5 is true. 2 Clara doesn't talk to her parents. 3 Julio doesn't listen to Paula. 4 Paula talks about her problems. 6 Wayne doesn't get up at eight o'clock. OR Wayne gets up at five o'clock.

D You could start by giving an example of a problem you have, e.g. with a neighbour or friend (show Ss that they don't need to talk about things that are too 'close to home' if they don't want to), then put Ss in pairs to discuss. If appropriate, invite Ss to report back to the class about their partner.

Unit 5 Recording 2

Conversation 1

A: How's the family?
B: Fine. Well, you remember Clara?
A: Clara, your daughter? Yes, how old is she now?
B: She's seventeen.
A: She isn't at school?
B: No.
A: Does she have a job?
B: No, she doesn't. That's the problem.
A: So what does she do all day?
B: Well, she listens to her music and … and she sleeps a lot.
A: What time does she get up?
B: I don't know because I'm at work. At the weekend she gets up at eleven.
A: Does she want a job?
B: I don't know. She doesn't talk much.
A: What do you mean?
B: Well, for example, in the evenings, we have dinner together. But Clara just sits there and listens to her music. Or she answers her phone and talks to her friends, but not to her family. It drives me crazy.
A: Does she … ?

Conversation 2

A: Hi, Paula.
B: Hi. What's the problem? You look bad.
A: It's Julio.
B: Julio?
A: Yeah. Well, he doesn't listen to me.
B: What do you mean?
A: Well, I talk about my problems and he just checks his text messages or watches TV.
B: Does he talk to you?
A: Yeah … well, no … he says 'Mmmm'.
B: 'Mmmm'! What does that mean?
A: It means he doesn't really listen.
B: Oh, my boyfriend is exactly the same.

Conversation 3

A: Hey, Wayne. What's up? You look tired.
B: Yeah. No sleep.
A: What's the problem?
B: Neighbours. Problem neighbours. Or just one, the man in the flat upstairs.
A: Why? Does he play loud music? Big parties?
B: No, he doesn't. The problem is he works at night. He goes to work at six in the evening. I get home and I see him go to work every night.
A: What's his job?
B: He sells coffee in a snack bar at the train station.
A: And when does he get home?
B: About half past four. And then he watches television for two or three hours.
A: So when does he go to bed?
B: Oh, about six or seven.
A: And what time do you get up?
B: Huh! Now I get up at five. It's impossible to sleep. So I listen to music, drink coffee then I go to work around eight.
A: And when do you go to bed?
B: Late. Midnight or 1 a.m.
A: Ooh, four hours' sleep. Not good.

GRAMMAR present simple questions: *he/she/it*

3A Give Ss a minute or two to compete the tables, while you copy them onto the board. As you check the answers you could point out that the questions are the same in form as those for *you/we/they*, but with *does/doesn't* instead of *do/don't*.

Watch out!

If Ss want to say *What does it mean<u>s</u>? What time does she get<u>s</u> up?* etc., point out that the third person *-s* is on *doe<u>s</u>*, so it isn't necessary at the end of the verb.

Answers:

What		it	mean?
What time	*does*	she	get up?
When		he	go to bed?

	Does	she	have a job?
		he	play loud music?
Yes, he/she *does*.		No, he/she *doesn't*.	

B Give Ss time to familiarise themselves with the phonemic script and listen to the pronunciation before you ask them to repeat the questions.

Teaching tip

To help Ss to see why auxiliary verbs like *do/does* are pronounced like this, write the following on the board:

What / mean?

When / go to bed?

have / job?

Elicit/point out that these words carry the meaning of the question, so they are stressed: the other 'helping' words are not stressed, so they become 'squashed' together.

➡ LANGUAGEBANK 5.1 p126–127

You could set Ex 5.1.A, B and C in class: half the class does Ex 5.1A and the other half does Ex 5.1B (Ss check their answers against a key) then for Ex 5.1C, Ss match the questions and answers across the class. Ss could do Ex 5.1D for homework or in pairs in class.

Answers: A 2 Does Stefan speak Chinese?
3 Does Katia have children? 4 Does your brother like his job? 5 Does your cat have a name? 6 Does this word mean 'very big'?
B b does c doesn't d does e doesn't f does
C 2 e 3 a 4 d 5 f 6 c
D 2 does he work 3 does Cristina get home 4 does she have dinner 5 does 'late' mean 6 does the lesson start

---

PRACTICE

4 Go through the example with the class, and remind Ss that *does* is used in short answers as well as questions. Ss can check their answers in pairs and practise reading the conversations, paying attention to the pronunciation of *does he/she/it*.

Answers:
1 A: What time *does* Mike come home in the evenings?
B: At about eight o'clock.
A: So, *does* he play with the children?
B: No, he doesn't. They go to bed at seven.
B: And *does* he work at the weekends?
A: Yeah, he *does*, or he goes out and plays tennis!
2 A: Ana, *does* your sister phone you on your birthday?
B: No, she doesn't.
A: When *does* she phone you?
B: On <u>her</u> birthday because she wants money!
A: Really! So *does* it drive you crazy?
B: Yes, it *does*.

5A Focus Ss on the example, then give them a few minutes to complete the questions, working in pairs or alone.

Answers: 2 Does she do 3 Does he have 4 Does she study 5 Does your teacher read 6 Do you listen 7 Does your sister watch 8 Does he go

B Do the first example for the class, using the name of one of the Ss. Encourage Ss to use a different name for each question.

C Demonstrate the example, using a student as A and taking the role of B yourself. Tell Ss to make a note of the answers and give them a few minutes to ask and answer. Choose a few Ss to tell the rest of the class what they found out about different people.

SPEAKING

6A You may want to demonstrate this activity by choosing a person to answer about yourself and inviting different Ss to ask you the ten questions. This will also allow you to check vocabulary, e.g. *all the time, for hours, copy, loud, fast*. When Ss have asked all the questions, they can agree as a class how many of the habits you have.

B Put Ss in pairs and monitor carefully so that you can give Ss feedback on their language use. When they've finished, Ss could count how many of the habits their two people have in common. Finally, you could have a class vote on the number one habit that drives people crazy.

Optional extra activities

1 Ss could add two or three habits to the list. They could look back at the audio script for Ex 2 and use some of the habits mentioned, e.g. *checks his/her text messages all the time; watches TV all the time; gets up very late/early; gets home late.*

2 Encourage Ss to listen 'actively' when their partner is talking about their habits, by saying e.g. *Oh no!/Really?/ That's bad./My ___ is exactly the same.*

Homework ideas

- Ss think of two people in their lives (friends, family, neighbours, people at work/school, etc.) and write a few sentences about their daily routines, using vocabulary from the Photo bank as well as Ex 1, e.g. *My brother gets up at ____ . He doesn't have breakfast. He leaves home at ____ and goes swimming before work.*
- Workbook Ex 1–4, p32–33

SUPERMAN AND SUPERMODEL

Introduction

Ss practise reading and talking about people's eating habits, using food vocabulary and adverbs of frequency. They also learn to use linkers in writing.

SUPPLEMENTARY MATERIALS

Resource bank p151 and p153

Ex 5B: be prepared to demonstrate this activity.

Warm up

Put Ss in pairs (with their books closed). Give the pairs one minute to write a list of as many names of food and drink as they can think of. Then tell the pairs to choose five or six words and write them on a separate slip of paper, leaving out all the vowels (Ss should be familiar with this kind of vocabulary activity from the **Lookback** pages). Each pair then passes their slip of paper to the pair on their left, who have to fill in the missing vowels.

VOCABULARY food

1A You could start by telling Ss to cover the words and see how many of the food items they can name, either working together as a class or in pairs. Then give them a few minutes to match the words and pictures, working alone.

Answers: 2A 3J 4C 5G 6B 7L 8I 9H 10D 11E 12 F

B Ss could work in pairs, saying the words to each other and counting the syllables. Tell Ss the maximum number of syllables is three: if they query this with *vegetables*, point out that the second e is squashed between *veg* and *tab* because of the stress pattern (which is the same as *cereal*: Ooo).

Answers: 2 steak 1 3 chicken 2 4 chips 1 5 fish 1 6 fruit 1 7 vegetables 3 8 bread 1 9 cereal 3 10 eggs 1 11 cheese 1 12 sugar 2

C When Ss have practised repeating the words after the recording, they could 'test' each other in pairs: Student A says a letter and Student B responds with the name of the food.

2 You could demonstrate this on the board, putting a tick or cross next to food items that you like/dislike.

Put Ss in pairs and tell them that the aim is to find how many types of food they both like. When Ss have finished asking and answering, ask several pairs what food they both like. If you have time to ask all the pairs, find out which food is the most popular in the class.

➡ PHOTOBANK p143

If Ss seem confident with the vocabulary from Ex 1, they could do the **Photo bank** exercise in class, so that they have more food and drink items to use in the activities later in the lesson. To help Ss process these vocabulary items:

1 They choose the five items that they like best and tell their partner;

2 They work in pairs and decide which items are healthy and which unhealthy.

Answers: 1 A 2 B 3 F 4 J 5 Q 6 D 7 R 8 U 9 C 10 O 11 I 12 S 13 N 14 P 15 L 16 E 17 G 18 M 19 K 20 H 21 T

READING

3A Tell Ss to look at the names and the photos, but not the texts. Give them a few minutes to think about the food the people eat, then they can tell the class, e.g. *We think Michael Phelps eats a lot of steak.*

Culture note
Michael Phelps (1985–) is an American swimmer who won eight Olympic medals at Athens in 2004, and eight (all gold) at Beijing in 2008.

Heidi Klum (1973–) is a German model, actress, television host, businesswoman, fashion designer, television producer and occasional singer.

B Tell Ss to read through questions 1–6 before they start reading the texts. Ss can compare answers in pairs before checking with the whole class.

Culture note
French toast is bread which is dipped in beaten egg, then fried in oil or butter.

Teaching tip
It's important for Ss to read the questions first, so they know what they're looking for when they start reading the text. In this way they have a clear purpose for reading. The same applies to listening activities.

Answers: 2 H 3 H 4 MH 5 M 6 M

C Give Ss a few minutes to read the texts again. In feedback, ask them to justify their answer, e.g. *It isn't Michael because he eats pizza and he doesn't eat a lot of fruit and vegetables. It's Heidi because she eats fruit and vegetables and she doesn't eat chips.*

Answer: Heidi

D You could start by giving an example about yourself, e.g. *My diet is similar to Michael's because I eat a lot of pasta, but it's also similar to Heidi's because I eat fruit and vegetables.* Ss can discuss in pairs or in small groups, then report back to the class.

Optional extra activity
Focus on the following phrases from the Michael Phelps text: *a piece/two pieces of …, a plate of …, a whole …*

Ask Ss to decide which of the following food items can combine with each of the phrases: *pasta, cake, vegetables, chips, pizza.*

Answers:
a piece/two pieces of cake, pizza
a plate of pasta, chips, vegetables
a whole cake, pizza

GRAMMAR adverbs of frequency

4A You could find the first example with the class (*usually* in the Michael Phelps text) then give Ss a few minutes to underline the rest, and check their answers in pairs. Tell Ss to think about the meaning of the words but not to worry about their exact meaning for the moment.

Answers: Michael Phelps text: usually, always, not often Heidi Klum text: never, usually, often, not often, sometimes, never

B Put the following sentence from the Heidi Klum text on the board:

I sometimes eat fish, maybe two or three times a week.

Show Ss that *two or three times a week* helps them to guess the meaning of *sometimes*.

Also point out that the chart will help them with the meaning of the adverbs. Put *sometimes* next to *40%* on the line, and give Ss time to add the others, working in pairs or alone.

> **Answers:** 100% always 80% usually 60% often
> 10% not often 0% never

C When Ss have underlined the stress, elicit/point out that the stress in on the first syllable for all of them. Also highlight that *usually* has three syllables: Ooo (not four).

> **Answers:** <u>u</u>sually, <u>of</u>ten, <u>some</u>times, not <u>of</u>ten

D For *weaker classes,* write the sentences and the rules on the board and go through the rules with the whole class. Otherwise, give Ss a few minutes to discuss the rules first.

> **Answers:** 1 The adverb goes *after* the verb *be.*
> 2 The adverb goes *before* other verbs.

➡️ **LANGUAGEBANK** 5.2 p126–127

The **Language bank** gives Ss more examples of the adverbs in sentences and highlights the fact that *not usually* is possible as well as *not often*. If you feel that your Ss need more basic practice with the position and meaning of adverbs, Ss could do Ex 5.2A and B in class. Otherwise they could do them for homework.

> **Answers:**
> A
> 2 My mother usually phones me on Monday evenings.
> 3 He's often tired in the mornings.
> 4 We always have a drink after work on Fridays.
> 5 Do you usually walk to work?
> 6 I'm not usually at home in the afternoons.
> 7 Classes are sometimes on Saturdays.
> 8 I don't often watch TV.
> B
> B: Er, no, doctor. I *never eat* vegetables and I *don't often eat* fruit.
> A: What about meat and fish?
> B: Well, I *sometimes eat* fish, maybe once or twice a week and I *often eat* chicken. I like steak so I *always eat* steak for lunch and I *usually have* it with chips.

PRACTICE

5A Go through the example with the class, then give Ss a few minutes to put the sentences in order.

> **Answers:** 2 I never eat sweets. 3 I'm never hungry.
> 4 I often eat chicken. 5 I'm usually home for dinner.
> 6 I don't often eat fruit. 7 I sometimes have vegetables for lunch. 8 I always eat steak on Sundays.

B Demonstrate the activity yourself first: tick the sentences that are true for you, and change the others to make them true. Show Ss that they can change the adverb or any other part of the sentence, e.g.

I always have fish on Fridays. OR

I usually have pizza on Fridays. OR

I usually have fish on Mondays.

SPEAKING

6A Write the first sentence from the questionnaire on the board, then ask a student if they have a coffee before breakfast, and depending on how they answer, write the appropriate letter in the circle. Give Ss a few minutes to complete the questionnaire individually.

B Ask two Ss to demonstrate the activity, using their own answers to the first question. Remind Ss to try to find two things the same, then give them time to go through all the questions. Monitor carefully and note down examples of good language use and problem areas for praise and correction. When Ss have finished, ask any pairs who found two (or more) things the same to tell the class about them.

WRITING linkers to sequence

7A As they read the description, Ss could put a tick next to anything that is the same for them and a cross next to anything different. They can discuss their answers in pairs, e.g. *I get up at six, too, but I don't read emails or listen to the radio.*

B Direct Ss to the example *first* in the text, then give them a minute or two to find the other three. To help Ss see the need for linkers to show the sequence of events in the text, you could read it without the four linkers and elicit/point out that it sounds as if all the activities happen at the same time.

> **Answers:** 2 then 3 after that 4 finally

C Ss read through the text again to find the linker without a comma after it.

> **Answer:** then

8A Ask Ss to write their descriptions on a separate piece of paper, so they can be passed round or displayed around the room. Tell Ss to use at least four adverbs of frequency, as well as the linkers. Circulate and help Ss while they write their descriptions if necessary.

B The descriptions can either be passed around the class, or displayed for Ss to walk round and read.

> **Optional extra activity**
> Each student writes one thing which is not true in their description. The rest of the class has to guess what it is.

> **Homework ideas**
> • Ss write two short paragraphs: one about someone they know who has good eating habits, and one about someone with bad eating habits, e.g. *My best friend's eating habits are very good. He always has a big breakfast, with cereal and fruit. He usually eats a lot of … and … He doesn't often eat … and he never eats …*
> • Workbook Ex 1–5, p34–35

WHEN DOES IT OPEN?

Introduction

Ss practise asking for information about hotel services. They also practise listening and learn to show interest.

SUPPLEMENTARY MATERIALS

Resource bank p154

Warm up

Either: lead in to the topic via a discussion about hotels. Put the following prompts on the board for Ss to discuss in small groups or as a class:

Do you like big or small hotels?
Do you like old fashioned or modern hotels?
Do you like hotels in the city centre or in the countryside?

Or: review telling the time. Tell Ss you are going to read some questions. Using the board, demonstrate that they should write the answers in a different order from the questions, so it's not obvious which answer matches which question. Read out the following questions:

What time do you …
get up from Monday to Friday?
have lunch from Monday to Friday?
go to work or school?, etc.

Then Ss show each other their answers and try to guess which questions they relate to, e.g.

A: *(looking at 9.30a.m.) Do you get up at 9.30 at the weekend?*
B: *No, I don't.*
A: *Do you go to work at 9.30?*
B: *Yes, I do!*

VOCABULARY hotel services

1A Direct Ss to the photos and elicit some ideas about what the places are, then give Ss a minute or two to look at the services in the box. Check *gift shop* (a place that sells small things to give as presents) and *guided tour* (a trip round a city, building, etc. with someone who tells people about the place).

Answers: A gym B guided tour C gift shop D hairdresser's

B Ss could match the services and activities in pairs or alone.

Answers: 2 money exchange 3 hairdresser's 4 gym
5 café 6 swimming pool 7 gift shop 8 guided tour

Optional extra activity

Ss practise using the names of the services and activities. Student A covers the box in Ex 1A and looks at the services in Ex 1B. Student B looks at the box in Ex 1A and covers the services in Ex 1B.

A: *I want to get a haircut.*

B: *Go to the hairdresser's.*

Then A and B swap roles.

N.B. Point out that we say *go on a guided tour*.

C Put Ss in pairs and demonstrate how to discuss the question, using a **strong student**:

S: *I think a gym is important.*

T: *I don't. I think a gift shop is important.*

Tell Ss to try to agree on two important services to tell the rest of the class at the end.

FUNCTION asking for information

2A Focus Ss on the pictures and explain that they are services in a hotel. You could play the first part of the recording for Ss to hear the example, then play the rest of the recording for them to write the other three services.

Answers: 2 restaurant (breakfast) 3 hairdresser's
4 guided tour

B Tell Ss to read through the woman's notes about opening times and the price of the guided tour. Using the board, demonstrate that Ss should correct the information by crossing out the mistakes and writing the correct answers above. Play the recording again.

Answers: gym: 6a.m.–~~9p.m.~~ *10p.m.* closes: 12–1
breakfast: 6.30–9.00 – in ~~café~~ *restaurant*. hairdresser's: 10–6;
Tuesdays to ~~8p.m~~ *9p.m.*; closes Mondays. guided tour:
9a.m. and ~~2p.m.~~ *3p.m.* ~~€50~~ *€15*.

3A Ss could work in pairs and help each other to complete as many of the sentences as they can. Either play the recording again for them to check, or direct them to the audio script.

Answers: 2 opens 3 time 4 to 5 Do 6 every 7 does
8 leaves 9 cost 10 It

B Remind Ss that we usually stress the words that carry the meaning of the sentence or phrase. You could demonstrate this when you go through the answers by only writing the stressed words on the board and pointing out that the questions and answers can still be understood, e.g.

When – gym – open? opens – 6a.m. – 10p.m.
time – breakfast? etc.

When Ss repeat the questions and answers, encourage them to copy the falling intonation on the *Wh-* questions. You could help by doing an exaggerated model yourself so that Ss can hear the movement.

Answers: 2 It <u>opens</u> from <u>6a.m.</u> to <u>10p.m.</u> 3 What <u>time</u>
is <u>breakfast</u>? 4 From <u>half</u> past <u>six</u> to <u>nine</u> o'<u>clock</u>. 5 Do you
have a <u>hairdresser's</u> in the <u>hotel</u>? 6 Yes, it <u>opens</u> every <u>day</u>
except <u>Monday</u>. 7 <u>When</u> does the <u>tour leave</u>? 8 It <u>leaves</u>
at <u>9a.m.</u> and at <u>3p.m.</u> 9 How <u>much</u> does it <u>cost</u>? 10 It costs
<u>fifteen euros</u>.

➠ LANGUAGEBANK 5.3 p126–127

You could use the tables in the **Language bank** to give Ss some question and answer practice across the class.
A: *When does the café open?* B: *It opens at nine.*
C: *How much is it?* D: *It's twenty euros.*

Ss could do Ex 5.3 in class, then you could use the completed dialogue to give them some speaking practice in pairs before moving on to the prompted dialogue in Ex 4A.

Answers:
A: Excuse *me?*
B: Can I help you?
A: Yes, *what* time is dinner?
B: From seven *to* half past ten.
A: And *do* you have a swimming pool?
B: Yes, it opens every day *except* Sunday.
A: When does *it* open?
B: It *opens* at seven in the morning.
A: When *does* it close?
B: *It* closes at nine in the evening.

Unit 5 Recording 6

A: Excuse me?

B: Yes, can I help you?

A: I have a reservation for tonight.

B: And your name?

A: Shannon.

B: Ah, yes. Miss Shannon. A single for two nights.

A: That's right.

B: I'm sorry, but your room isn't ready yet.

A: Oh, am I early? What time is check-in?

B: 2p.m. usually. Your room is almost ready. Please have a seat.

A: Thank you. I have one question.

B: Yes?

A: When does the gym open?

B: It opens from 6a.m. to 10p.m., except lunchtime. It closes from twelve to one.

A: Lovely. Oh, just one more question. What time is breakfast?

B: From half past six to nine o'clock.

A: And where is it?

B: In the restaurant, over there.

A: Thank you.

A: Excuse me?

B: Yes?

A: Me again. I have one more question.

B: Sure.

A: Do you have a hairdresser's in the hotel?

B: Yes, it opens every day except Monday.

A: And today's Monday.

B: Yes, I'm sorry. But it opens tomorrow.

A: That's good.

B: From ten to six. Actually, I'm wrong. On Tuesdays it closes at nine o'clock in the evening.

A: That's great, thank you.

B: Excuse me, madam.

A: Yes?

B: Your room's ready now. Here's your key card. Room 538 on the fifth floor.

A: Wonderful, thank you.

B: You're welcome. Enjoy your stay.

A: Oh, but I have one more question.

B: Yes?

A: I want to go on a guided tour of the old town. Do you know a good one?

B: Ah, yes. We do a tour from the hotel.

A: Oh good. When does the tour leave?

B: It leaves at 9a.m. and at 3p.m.

A: How much does it cost?

B: It costs fifteen euros.

A: Great. Thank you.

B: Any more questions I can help you with?

A: No, thank you. Oh, just one …

4A Ss write the full conversation in their notebooks, or for *stronger classes*, Ss could complete it orally, without notes.

> **Answers:** A: When does the gift shop open?
> B: It opens from 10a.m. to 8p.m.
> A: Is the swimming pool open all day?
> B: Yes, it opens from 6a.m. to 9p.m. But it closes from 12p.m. to 1p.m.
> A: How much does the guided tour cost for children?
> B: It's free for children.
> A: When does it leave?
> B: It leaves at 10a.m.

B If Ss have written the full conversation, ask them to use the prompts for practice, rather than reading aloud. You could encourage *stronger students* to substitute some of the services in the conversation, e.g. *money exchange* for *gift shop, hairdresser's* for *swimming pool, haircut* for *guided tour.*

LEARN TO show interest

5A Play the first extract from the recording so that Ss hear how the word *Lovely* is used. Then play the rest of the recording and check answers at the end.

> **Answers:** 2 That's good. 3 That's great. 4 Wonderful.
> 5 Oh, good. 6 Great.

speakout TIP

Before Ss read the speakout tip you could ask them why they think the woman says *Lovely, Great,* etc. Have a brief discussion with the class about what they say in their language(s).

B Play the recording and when Ss have answered the question, ask them to demonstrate how the person sounds interested, i.e. because they speak with a higher pitch and more movement in their voice. It's worth pointing out to Ss that they may often need to speak with a higher pitch in English than they would in their own language.

> **Answer:** person 2 is interested.

C Ss take turns to say words or phrases from the box in Ex 5A, trying to sound interested or not interested.

SPEAKING

6A Focus Ss on the example question then put them in pairs to write the others. Circulate and help while Ss do this, and encourage them to practise asking their questions, paying attention to polite intonation.

> **Possible questions:** What time does the Café Slavia open? How much does a coffee cost?
> What time does the hotel café open? ·
> When does the guided tour leave? How much does it cost?
> What time is the opera? Where is it? How much does it cost?

B Move Ss around so they're working with new partners. Direct Student B to their information sheet on page 150 and give them a few moments to look through it. Tell Student A to start asking their questions and remind them to write the answers in their notebooks. Monitor the pairwork carefully and note down examples of good language use and any problems for praise and correction in feedback.

C Direct Student A to their information on p153 and give them a few moments to look through it. Tell Student B to ask their questions and make a note of the answers.

D Students check their partner's notes against their information sheet.

> ### Homework ideas
> - Ss research a hotel (in their country/city or one they've heard of in another country) on the internet and write a short paragraph with the information they've found.
> - Workbook Ex1–3, p36

DOCTOR WHO

Introduction

Ss watch an extract from an episode of *Doctor Who*, the BBC science fiction programme. Ss then learn and practise how to talk about food to take to a desert island and write a forum entry about food.

Warm up

Review food vocabulary. Tell Ss to close their books and to write the items that you read out in their notebooks, in random order. Read out the following, giving Ss time to write between each one:

- one food that's good for you;
- one food that's bad for you;
- one food that you like to eat in winter when it's cold;
- one food that you like to eat in summer when it's hot;
- one that you like to eat in the cinema;
- one that you like to eat in a restaurant;

Then tell Ss to swap notebooks and look at their partner's answers, then check what they mean by asking questions, e.g.
A: (looking at the word *ice cream*) *Do you like to eat ice cream in summer when it's hot?*
B: *No, I like to eat ice cream in the cinema.*

▶ DVD PREVIEW

1A You could start by directing Ss to the photos and asking them which things they can name (e.g. Big Ben). Then direct them to the words in the box and give them a minute or two to match the photos, working in pairs or alone.

Answers: A The O2 Stadium B beans C fish fingers
D Big Ben E custard

Culture notes

The London Eye is a 135-metre tall giant Ferris wheel (a rotating upright wheel with passenger cars) situated on the South Bank of the River Thames, in London. It is the tallest Ferris wheel in Europe, and the most popular paid tourist attraction in the UK, visited by over 3.5 million people every year.

Big Ben is the nickname for the great bell of the clock at the north end of the Palace of Westminster in London and is generally extended to refer to the clock or the clock tower as well. It is the largest four-faced chiming clock and the third-tallest free-standing clock tower in the world.

Fish fingers are a processed food made using a white fish such as cod, which have been breaded or battered. They are commonly available in the frozen food section of supermarkets, and on children's menus in family-oriented restaurants. They can be baked in the oven, grilled or fried.

Custard is based on a cooked mixture of milk or cream and egg yolk. Depending on how much egg or thickener is used, custard varies from a thin pouring sauce to a thick pastry cream.

The O2 is a large entertainment district on the Greenwich peninsula in South East London, including an indoor arena, a music club, a Cineworld cinema, an exhibition space, piazzas, bars and restaurants.

(Baked) beans are pre-cooked, tinned white beans in a tomato sauce. They are a popular, inexpensive convenience food, often part of a *full English breakfast*.

B Give Ss a minute or two to read the questions, then direct them to the text to find the answers.

Answers: 1 He's an alien from space.
2 The Tardis 3 He's hungry but he doesn't know what food he likes.

Culture notes

Doctor Who is about the adventures of an alien known as the Doctor, who explores the universe in a time machine called the TARDIS which flies through time and space. He and his companions meet a variety of enemies while working to save civilisations, help people and right wrongs.

The programme (which started in 1963) is listed in Guinness World Records as the longest-running science fiction television show in the world. It has been recognised for its imaginative stories, special effects and pioneering use of electronic music. The show is a significant part of British popular culture in the UK, and elsewhere it has become a cult television favourite. The Doctor has been played by eleven actors. The change from one actor to another is written into the plot of the show as regeneration, whereby the character of the Doctor takes on a new body and, to some extent, a new personality.

▶ DVD VIEW

2A Tell Ss to put a tick next to the items as they see them. Alternatively, you could ask them to number the items in the order they appear: *the TARDIS, the O2 Stadium, Doctor Who, The London Eye, Big Ben, an English house, beans, fish fingers, custard.*

Answer: *a banana* is not in the DVD

B Give Ss time to read through the sentences. Then elicit some predictions of the answers before you play the DVD again.

Answers: 1 Can I have an *apple*? All I can think about … *apples*. I love *apples*. 2 No, no, no, I love *yoghurt*. *Yoghurt's* my favourite. Give me *yoghurt*. 3 Ah. You see? *Beans*. *Beans* are evil. Bad, bad *beans*. 4 A: I've got some *carrots*.
B: *Carrots?* Are you insane? No, wait, hang on, I know what I need, I need, I need, I need …, fish fingers and *custard*.

C Play the DVD again for Ss to underline the adjectives. Point out that more than one adjective may be mentioned for some of the types of transport.

Possible answers: 1 afraid D (at the start), G (in the garden) 2 unhappy D (with the food) 3 surprised G
4 bored N 5 happy D (with the fish fingers and custard)
6 angry D (with the beans) 7 tired G (it's after her bedtime)

Optional extra activity

Ask Ss what they think of the combination of fish fingers and custard. Then give them a few minutes to think about any unusual combinations of food that they or their friends/family members like, and put them in pairs to tell their partners.

DVD 5 Doctor Who

D=The Doctor G=Girl

D: Can I have an apple? All I can think about … apples. I love apples.
That's disgusting, what is that?

G: An apple.

D: Apples are rubbish. I hate apples.

G: You said you loved them.

D: No, no, no, I love yoghurt. Yoghurt's my favourite. Give me yoghurt.
Ah. You see? Beans.
Beans are evil. Bad, bad beans.
Bread and butter. Now you're talking.
And stay out!

G: I've got some carrots.

D: Carrots? Are you insane? No wait, hang on, I know what I need, I need, I need, I need …, fish fingers and custard.

speakout desert island food

3A Introduce the idea of a desert island with a simple board sketch and elicit some ideas about life there, e.g. the weather, where to live, things to do, other things on the island such as plants, animals, rivers, etc. Give Ss a few minutes to write their list of food and drink.

B Ss write down the food and drink as they listen to the recording. They could check answers in pairs.

Answers: bananas apples ice cream pasta (with cheese) cereal milk English tea

C Give Ss a few moments to look at the **Key phrases** then play the recording again for them to tick the phrases they hear. After you've checked the answers, give Ss some pronunciation practice by modelling the phrases for them to repeat.

Answers: What's on your list? ✓
Number (one ✓/two/three) on my list is … ✓
It's important to have …
I really like …
It's (good/bad ✓) for you …
What about drinks? ✓
Do you really like … ? ✓
Me too. ✓
Really? ✓
I don't like (it/fruit/eggs).
I like (it/fruit/eggs) too.

Unit 5 Recording 10

A: What's on your list?
B: Well, number one on my list is fruit.
A: Fruit? Why fruit?
B: It's good for you.
A: Do you really like it?
B: I like bananas and apples.
A: Bananas and apples. That's two things.
B: OK, fine. One is bananas and two is apples.
A: And what's number three on your list?
B: Number three is ice cream. I love ice cream.
A: Me too. It's on my list.
B: Maybe it's bad for you, but …
A: Ice cream and fruit. That's OK.
B: Yeah, with fruit, it's good.
A: And number four?
B: Pasta with cheese.

A: Mmm … that's two …
B: No, I think it's one. I eat pasta every day. With butter, with cheese …
A: Yeah.
B: And number five is cereal.
A: Really? Do you really like cereal?
B: I do, yes.
A: What about drinks?
B: Milk for my cereal.
A: Yes. And what other drink do you have?
B: I have tea. English tea.
A: Of course. Me too.

4A Give Ss a few minutes working alone to review the list they made in Ex 3A and think about how to incorporate some of the Key phrases into their talk. Circulate and help. Then put Ss in pairs to talk about their lists, and encourage the listeners to use the appropriate **Key phrases** (Me too, Really? I like X too.) to keep the conversation going. At the end direct Ss to the audio script to see how these phrases are used in practice.

B Put Ss in groups of four or five. Monitor the group work closely and make notes of any good language use and problem areas for praise and correction later.

Alternative approach
Tell Ss that they need to discuss the best five food types and two drinks to take, and to agree on one list between them. Then ask each group to report back to the class and justify the choices on their list.

writeback a forum entry

5A Give Ss a few minutes to read the entry and compare the list to their own, then put them in pairs/small groups to discuss the questions.

B Ss could work in pairs and help each other think of reasons for including the items on their lists. Circulate and help with vocabulary. When Ss have finished writing, they could walk round the classroom and read each other's lists, and tell each other which reason for including an item in the list they thought was the best.

Homework ideas
• Ss write a short paragraph describing a simple dish from their country.
(X) is a dish from (region) in my country.
It has (ingredients) in it.
You (cook it in the oven/cook it on the grill/you don't cook it).
You have it for (breakfast/lunch/dinner/a snack).
(It's very good/It's not very good) for you because it has (X) in it.
(I make it/(X) makes it for me/I usually eat it in a restaurant/café).

LOOKBACK

DAILY ROUTINES

1A You could run this as a team competition (Ss have their books closed). Write up or display one phrase at a time and the first team member to 'buzz' and tell you the missing vowels wins a point for their team. If they make a mistake with any vowels, the other team can try for a bonus point.

> **Alternative idea**
> To provide more challenge, write blanks for the whole phrase, e.g. for 'get up': _ _ _ _ _
> Ss from the teams 'buzz' and call out any letter they think may be in the phrase. If the letter is in the phrase, write it in the correct place and give the team a point; if it isn't in the phrase, give the team a penalty point. The winning team is the one with the fewest penalty points at the end.

> **Answers:** 1 go to bed 2 have breakfast 3 get up
> 4 get home 5 go to work 6 have lunch 7 have dinner

B Make sure Ss cover the verbs before they start.

> **Optional extra activity**
> Ss work in pairs and think of reasons why the order might be different for some people or on some days, e.g.
> *have breakfast, get up – if you have breakfast in bed on a special day, e.g. Mother's Day;*
> *get up, go to work – you get up late and don't have time, you have breakfast at work;*
> *have breakfast, don't go to work – you work at home;*
> *have dinner, go to work – you work at night.*

PRESENT SIMPLE: QUESTIONS

2A Give Ss a few minutes to complete the questions, working alone.

> **Answers:** 2 Does she like coffee or tea? 3 What time does he go to work? 4 What does she have for lunch?
> 5 Does he have a car? 6 When does she get home? 7 Does she study at the weekend? 8 Does he phone you every day?

B Demonstrate this by taking the role of B and prompting Ss to ask questions. Point out that Student A will need to change *he* to *she* and vice versa, depending on whether the person is male or female. For *stronger classes,* encourage Ss to think of some more questions of their own, e.g.
What does he/she do in the evening?
When does he/she go to bed?
What does he/she do at the weekend?

FOOD

3A You could run this as a race, with Ss working in pairs. The first pair to write out all the words and bring them to you wins, as long as all the words are spelled correctly.

> **Answers:** 2 cereal 3 bread 4 sugar 5 chips
> 6 steak 7 chicken 8 fruit 9 cheese 10 pasta
> 11 fish 12 vegetables

B Tell Ss not to show their three circles to their partner. Remind them that there are more food words in the **Photo bank** p143: they could choose any of these to put in the circles.

C You could demonstrate this by saying a food and inviting Ss to guess whether you like/don't like or don't eat it. You could teach *I'm allergic to it* and/or *It's bad for me* as reasons for not eating something. Put Ss in pairs to take turns to say a food item and to guess the reaction.

ADVERBS OF FREQUENCY

4A Ss could start by finding the sentence that is correct. Then remind them that they need to think about the word order, i.e. the position of the adverb, in most of the sentences.

> **Answers:** 1 We always speak English together ~~always~~ in class. 2 I usually do my homework. (CORRECT)
> 3 I'm never late ~~never~~ for English lessons. 4 I ~~not~~ don't often watch English videos. 5 My English teacher often says ~~often~~ 'Good!' 6 I never read an online English newspaper ~~never~~.

B You could demonstrate this by changing a sentence and making it true for you.

HOTEL SERVICES

5 You could run this as a race. Give Ss a minute or two in pairs to circle the words. The first pair to finish put their hands up, then spell out each word for the class. If they make a mistake with spelling, another pair can try to spell all the words, and so on.

> **Answers:** 2 café 3 gift shop 4 swimming pool 5 money exchange 6 guided tour 7 restaurant 8 hairdresser's

> **Optional extra activity**
> Ss write four or five sentences about how often they use hotel services when they stay in a hotel, either alone or with their family, partner, etc.
> e.g. *I sometimes go to the gym.*
>   *We often go to the café for lunch.*
>   *My children usually go to the swimming pool.*
> Ss work in pairs and tell each other their sentences.

ASKING FOR INFORMATION

6A Give Ss a few minutes to complete the questions, working alone.

> **Answers:** 1 What time does the gym close?
> 2 When does the café open? 3 When does the gift shop open on Mondays? 4 When does the swimming pool open and close?

B Point out that Ss decide on the times for themselves.

C Remind Ss about the falling intonation on *Wh-* questions. You may want to give them some repetition practice with the questions before you put them in pairs.

> **Optional extra activity**
> Divide Ss in to two groups: hotel receptionists and customers. Tell the hotel receptionists to write their own timetable of hotel services, as in Ex 6A. Tell the customers to write three hotel services that are important to them. Then tell the customers to go and visit at least three hotels and ask about the services. Finally, the customers decide which is the best hotel for them and tell the rest of the class in feedback.

OVERVIEW

NO TRAINS

Introduction

Students practise listening and talking about travel and places, using *there is/are* and related vocabulary. They also practise starting and ending an email.

SUPPLEMENTARY MATERIALS

Resource bank p157

Ex 1C (optional extra activity): prepare a matching activity.

Ex 8B (alternative approach): prepare a gap fill of an email.

Warm up

Focus on the unit theme of *journeys*. Establish that a *journey* is when you go from one place to another, and elicit some ideas from Ss about where and why people go on journeys, e.g. go to work or school/university, go to another city to visit someone, on holiday or on business, etc. For *stronger classes* you could also direct Ss to the photos at the bottom of p61 and ask them what they think of the types of journey they can see there.

VOCABULARY | places

1A For *stronger classes*, Ss could cover the words and, working in pairs, see how many of the pictures they can name.

> **Culture note**
> Instead of *pharmacy*, Ss may have heard or seen the word *chemist's*, which is common in British English.

> **Answers:** newsagent's H hotel A snack bar D restaurant B pharmacy E payphone F cash machine G

B Before you play the recording, give Ss an opportunity to count the number of syllables in each word. They could also predict where the stress is, then listen to check. You may also want to point out that *hotel* is the only word with an unusual stress pattern: all the other nouns have the stress on the first syllable (or first word if they are compound nouns like *snack, bar,* or *cash machine*).

> **Answers:** <u>news</u>agent's ho<u>tel</u> <u>snack</u> bar <u>res</u>taurant <u>phar</u>macy <u>pay</u>phone <u>cash</u> machine

C Ss should cover the words in Ex 1A to do this activity.

> **Optional extra activity**
> Prepare an activity like the one below: Ss match activities that people do with the places. Then they practise asking and answering in pairs:
>
> *What do people do at a … ?*
>
> *They …*
>
> | A | B |
> |---|---|
> | snack bar | check emails |
> | payphone | have dinner |
> | pharmacy | buy a newspaper |
> | hotel | get money |
> | restaurant | buy medicine |
> | internet café | make a call |
> | cash machine | have a sandwich |
> | newsagent's | relax |

➠ **PHOTOBANK** p144

Several of the places in the **Photo bank** should be familiar to Ss from previous units, e.g. *school*, *supermarket*, *gym*, *cinema*. Ss could match the names of the places to the photos for homework, or at some stage before Ex 5, so they have the option of using the place names in the practice activity. It would also be useful to highlight the stress on the words of more than one syllable.

Answers: Places: 1 O 2 H 3 J 4 F 5 B 6 A 7 C 8 N 9 P 10 L 11 D 12 G 13 K 14 I 15 M 16 E
Places: Signs: 1 I 2 C 3 D 4 E 5 B 6 J 7 A 8 H 9 G 10 F

LISTENING

2A Focus Ss on the photo and have a brief discussion about where the man is, what his problem is, etc. Then give Ss a minute or two to think of good and bad things about train travel. Use this context to teach *bad weather*, i.e. trains are slow or sometimes stop if the weather is bad. Ss may also try to express ideas such as *crowded, expensive, fast*: you could teach these words if they come up, although they are dealt with systematically in lesson 6.4.

Possible answers: good: fast, comfortable, safe
bad: sometimes expensive, noisy, crowded, sometimes slow

B Refer Ss back to Ex 1A and tell them to write the numbers either next to the pictures or next to the words.

Answers: 2 internet café 3 restaurant 4 snack bar
5 cash machine 6 hotel
newsagent's and *pharmacy* are not in the conversations

C Before you play the recording again, give Ss time to look through the alternatives in pairs and encourage them to help each other with unfamiliar words or try to guess their meaning by looking at the other words around them. If they can't guess, they should look in their dictionaries or check with you. Check that everyone understands *dead* (no battery power) vs *broken* and *full* (no free rooms).

Answers: 1 bad 2 dead 3 isn't 4 closed 5 expensive

speakout TIP

Remind Ss about the strategies they used to guess/find out the meaning of unfamiliar words in Ex 2C, and give them a few moments to read the tip.

Unit 6 Recording 2

A: Excuse me … ?
B: Sorry, I'm in a hurry.
A: Excuse me?
C: Yes?
A: Is there a train to Paris tonight?
C: No, sorry, there aren't any trains tonight. It's the weather. It's very bad.
A: Not any trains? Not one?
C: No, not tonight. Maybe tomorrow. They …

D: Hello? Pete, where are you?
A: Hi, I'm here in London, in the station, but there aren't any trains and … Oh, no … Excuse me, is there a payphone near here? My phone's dead.
E: Yes, there's a payphone over there.
A: Thanks. Oh, and is there an internet café?

E: Erm … I don't think so. No, there isn't an internet café. Not in the station but there's one in Judd Street.
A: Judd Street. Thanks.

F: Can I help you?
A: Yes. Are there any restaurants in the station?
F: Yes, there are … but … what's the time?
A: Half past eleven.
F: Ah, they're closed now, but there's a snack bar over there. That's open.
A: And is there a cash machine here?
F: Yes, over there.
A: Thanks. And hotels?
F: There are two hotels near here. The Charlotte Street Hotel … that's about two hundred and fifty pounds a night.
A: Two hundred and fifty pounds? That's expensive.
F: And there's the Ridgemount, that's about eighty pounds.
A: Where's that?
F: It's here on the map.
A: OK … thank you for your help.

GRAMMAR *there is/are*

3A Go through the example with the class, and use the classroom to elicit one or two more examples with *there's a*, e.g. *There's a mobile phone on the desk./There's a jacket on the chair.* Elicit/point out that *'s* is the contracted form of *is*. Then give Ss time to complete the tables. They could work in pairs and help each other to do this.

B You may need to pause the recording as Ss check their answers.

Watch out!

Ss may try to say *There isn't any trains.* Tell them that *any* is used only with plural nouns (uncountable nouns are not dealt with at this level).

Answers:

There	¹'s	a payphone over there.
	²are	two hotels near here.
³There	isn't	an internet café.
	⁴aren't	any trains.

⁵Is		a train to Paris tonight?
	there	
⁶Are		any restaurants in the station?

+			is	
	Yes,	⁷there	are.	
−	No,		isn't.	
			aren't.	

C You could do the first sentence with the class as an example, pointing out that the stress is on the words that carry the important information. You may also want to highlight and give Ss the opportunity to practise the linking between *there* and the verb *be*, e.g. *there's a, there are, there isn't, there aren't any, is there a, are there any*

Optional extra activity

Ss find and underline all the examples of *there is/are* (including questions and short answers) in the recording script of the conversations in Ex 2. There are 14 examples.

⟹ LANGUAGEBANK 6.1 p128–129

The **Language bank** reminds Ss to use *any* in the question form and negative with plural nouns. It also shows them that the question is formed simply by inverting the order of *there* and *is/are*. Ss could do Ex 6.1A in class, then for further practice they could show each other the contents of their own bags/pockets and make sentences following the pattern of the exercise, e.g. *There are car keys, so you have a car. There's a gym membership card, so I think you go to the gym.*

Answers: A 2 There's a cinema ticket
3 There a business card (for a bank)/There's a bank business card 4 There aren't any (car) keys 5 There's a (wedding) ring 6 There are glasses 7 There's a picture/photo of a cat 8 There aren't any pictures/photos of children
B 2 isn't 3 there's 4 are 5 there 6 are 7 Are 8 aren't 9 are 10 is 11 there 12 is

PRACTICE

4A Tell Ss that the sentences are about an imaginary class, not theirs. Point out that they need to make the sentences positive or negative according to the symbol at the end.

Answers: 2 There's 3 There isn't 4 There are 5 There's 6 There aren't

B Once Ss have ticked the sentences that are true about their class, they could change the others to make them true. In this case they will need either to change the form of *there is/are* or to change other words in the sentence, e.g. *There are six students with black shoes. There isn't a person with a red T-shirt.* Pairs could then write three more sentences of their own about their class.

5A Go through the example and make sure that A and B know where they're writing their questions about. If you feel it would generate more discussion, you could change the locations, e.g. to the city centre, Student A's office, etc. You could also encourage Ss to add questions about two or three of the places in the **Photo bank**, p144.

B Encourage Ss to recommend places, as in the example, perhaps expanding on why the place is good, or to criticise places, e.g. *Yes, there's a restaurant near my home. Its name is (X) but it isn't very good and it's expensive.*

SPEAKING

6 Give Ss time to find their pictures and to think about/write the questions they're going to ask to find the differences. For *weaker classes* you may want to group As and Bs together for this stage, to help each other prepare questions and practise describing their picture, then put Ss into AB pairs to start the activity. Monitor carefully and make notes of any good language use and problem areas for feedback. Tell Ss to circle the differences they find, then they can report back to the class afterwards, e.g. *There's a French restaurant in my picture, but in (X's) picture there's a Chinese restaurant.*

Answers:

Student A's picture	Student B's picture
French restaurant	Chinese restaurant
newsagent's	internet café
pharmacy is closed	pharmacy is open
one payphone	two payphones
man and woman	two women

WRITING starting and ending an email

7A Tell Ss to read the email quickly and decide who it's to. Suggest that they underline words/phrases that help them decide, e.g. *Hi, the children, Love* (also the fact that she mentions the company credit card so it's unlikely to be to her manager). Also check that Ss understand where the woman is and why (she's in a hotel because the weather's very bad and there aren't any trains).

B Tell Ss to copy the table into their notebooks, and point out that some phrases go in more than one place. Ss can help each other in pairs or work alone.

Answers:

	to a boyfriend/ girlfriend/ husband/wife	to a friend	to your manager
Start	Hi Valentina, Hello,	Hi Valentina, Dear Jack,	Dear Mr Wilson, Dear Jack,
End	Love, Take care, See you soon,	Best wishes, Love, Take care, See you soon,	Best wishes, Regards,

8A Give Ss a minute or two to discuss the problems: they're all possible but the one that happens most often is probably *the plane is late.*

B Once Ss have chosen their two problems, tell them to use the email in Ex 7A as a 'model' to follow. Encourage them to start by writing a few notes as a first draft, then to write the email itself. While they're doing this, circulate and help with grammar, punctuation and vocabulary.

Alternative approach
Weaker classes may need more support with their emails.

Either: Elicit a basic framework onto the board, showing Ss the alternatives that they could use.

Or: Prepare a gap fill of an email for Ss to complete with their own ideas.

C You could put Ss in groups of four to swap and read each other's emails. Then ask a few Ss to report back on the worst situation in their group.

Homework ideas
• Ss write an email from the airport to another person (Ex 8A), i.e. if they wrote to their friend in class, they write to their manager, and vice versa.
• Workbook Ex 1–5, p37–38

GETTING THERE

Introduction

Ss practise reading and talking about transport and getting around town, using *a/an, some, a lot of, not any* and related vocabulary.

SUPPLEMENTARY MATERIALS

Resource bank p155 and p156

Ex 3A (alternative approach): bring in paper cups and sweets/nuts.

Warm up

Review vocabulary related to places and transport from the previous lesson. Write the following words on slips of paper (one set per group of 5–6 Ss): *hotel, pharmacy, train, internet café, snack bar, airport, newsagent's, pay phone, plane, cash machine, station* (you may also want to add three or four places from the **Photo bank**, p144).

In their groups, Ss take turns to pick up a slip of paper and mime, draw or give a verbal clue for the word, for the rest of the group to guess. The first person to guess the word keeps the slip of paper and the winner is the student with most slips of paper at the end.

VOCABULARY transport

1A You could start by telling Ss to cover the words and see how many of the types of transport they can name, either working together as a class or in pairs. Then give them a few minutes to match the words and pictures, working alone. Check the pronunciation of *underground* Ooo and *motorbike* Ooo.

Culture note
Synonyms for *underground* are *metro* and *subway*. The London Underground is also known as 'the tube'.

Answers: B taxi C car D bike (more formally, *bicycle*)
E underground F plane G train H motorbike

B Tell Ss to use *by* with all the types of transport (*by car, by bus*, etc.), but point out that they should say *I walk/I come on foot* if they don't use transport. Give Ss a few minutes to discuss the questions and ask some of the pairs to report back about things they found in common, e.g. *We both come to class by bus. Our favourite type of transport is a train.*

READING

2A You could start by using the photos to generate a brief discussion to lead in to the text, e.g. *What type of transport is in the photo? Which cities use this type of transport a lot?* Tell Ss to read the text through to the end and decide which fact is obviously not true.

Answer: Not true: People usually travel around Venice by car.

B Look at the example with the class. Ss can work alone and compare answers in pairs.

Answers: 2 Amsterdam 3 taxis 4 a golf course in an airport in Thailand 5 pink taxis in Moscow 6 double-decker buses and trains

Culture notes
The red **double-decker bus**, which has been in London since the 1950s, is a symbol of Britain.

Bhutan is a small landlocked country in the Himalayas. It has a strong sense of culture and tradition, and had no phones until 1960, and no TV until 1999.

The **London taxi**, or 'black cab' was introduced in the late 1950s. They're now available in a number of countries including the USA, South Africa, Bahrain, Cyprus, Singapore and Saudi Arabia.

Amsterdam has been voted the most bike-friendly city in the world, and the bicycle is part of the city's way of life and culture. The city is suited to bikes because it's not very big, and it's almost flat. 75 percent of people over twelve in Amsterdam own a bike, and there are bike paths and bike racks everywhere in the city.

The **golf course** is in Bangkok's Don Mueang International airport. It's between two runways, and golfers are stopped by a red light when a plane is landing.

In **Venice** people either travel on foot (it's only an hour from one end of the city to the other) or in water buses and water taxis (and sometimes gondolas).

C Put Ss in pairs and encourage them to say what they think about the surprising facts, as in the example.

GRAMMAR *a/an, some, a lot of, not any*

3A Focus Ss on the pictures and ask about C and D: *Is it a small number? Is it a large number?* Then give Ss time to match the sentences, working in pairs to help each other.

Answers: 1 B 2 D 3 A 4 C

Alternative approach
Use real objects, e.g. four paper cups and small sweets or nuts to demonstrate the meaning of *a/an, some, a lot of, not any*.

In the four cups put a sweet, a small number of sweets, a large number of sweets and no sweets. As you do this ask Ss *How many sweets are in the cup?* and elicit/give the answer, checking the difference between *some* and *a lot of* by asking *Do you know the exact number?* (No.) *Is it a large number? Is it a small number?*

You could add an element of fun by turning the cups upside down with their contents underneath, then moving them around quickly and asking Ss if they can remember how many sweets are under each cup.

You can then use Ex 3 to consolidate and give Ss a record of the language.

B Ss can work alone and check answers in pairs.

Answers:

+	There	's	a	train at four o'clock.
		are	some	buses this afternoon.
		are	a lot of	taxis.
−	There	isn't	an	airport here.
		aren't	any	cars in the centre.

C Play the recording for Ss to check their answers.

D You could play the first sentence and underline the stress on the board as an example with the class. Then pause after each sentence for Ss to discuss which words to underline. Finally, play the recording again for Ss to repeat.

Answers: There's a <u>train</u> at <u>four</u> o'<u>clock</u>.
There are some <u>buses</u> this after<u>noon</u>.
There are a <u>lot</u> of <u>taxis</u>.
There <u>isn't</u> an <u>airport</u> here.
There <u>aren't</u> any <u>cars</u> in the <u>centre</u>.

⇒ **LANGUAGEBANK** 6.2 p128–129

The **Language bank** highlights the fact that *no* is possible instead of *not any*, e.g. *there are no buses/there aren't any buses*. For practice of the language in a different context from transport, Ss could do Ex 6.2A and B in class or for homework.

Answers:
A
2 There are some 3 There isn't a 4 There's an
5 There are a lot of 6 There aren't any
B
1 Students don't have a lot of money. 2 A book usually has a lot of pages. 3 Some people don't have a home.
4 Ben has a sister but he doesn't have any brothers.
5 Our school has a lot of students. 6 Some people have a lot of children.

PRACTICE

4A Ss could work on this alone or in pairs.

Answers: 2 some 3 any 4 a lot 5 a 6 some 7 any
8 a lot of

B If Ss are from the same town/city, tell them to make the sentences true for a town/city they know, so that in the next stage, their partner won't already know the answers to the questions and the communication will be more realistic. They should also make notes so they can give more information about their answers, e.g. *There's an airport, it's fifteen minutes from the city centre. It's very big.*

C Demonstrate this by inviting two or three Ss to ask you questions about a town/city you know. Remind Ss to extend their answers and give more information. You could suggest that Ss ask the questions in random order, so their partner can't predict which answer they need to give and has to listen more carefully.

Optional extra activities

1 Ss write three positive and three negative sentences about their town/city, using *there is/are* and *a/an, some, a lot of, not any*, then they compare their sentences in small groups. If they're from the same town/city, they can agree or disagree with each other's sentences, and if they're from different towns/cities, they can find things in common. N.B. encourage Ss to include some places from the **Photo bank**, e.g. *In all our cities there's a good hospital.*

2 Put Ss small groups and tell them to write down the names of five towns/cities that they all know, using *there is/are* and *a/an, some, a lot of, not any*. Encourage Ss to include some places from the **Photo bank**, e.g. *In this city there are a lot of parks, and there's a zoo.* Each student then writes three sentences about one of the towns/cities and reads them out to the group without mentioning the name of the town/city. The other Ss try to guess which one they're describing.

SPEAKING

Culture notes
Venice's Marco Polo airport (named after the Venetian traveller) is eight kilometres north of the city.

London's Heathrow airport is the busiest of London's five airports and the third busiest in the world. It's used by ninety airlines, travelling to 170 destinations. It's twenty-two kilometres west of the city centre.

Barcelona's El Prat airport is the second largest in Spain after Madrid's Barajas airport. It's twelve kilometres south west of the city centre.

Edinburgh airport is the busiest in Scotland and the sixth busiest in the UK. It's nine kilometres west of the city.

5A Give Ss A time to find their page and give all the Ss a few minutes to look through their information. While they're doing this, draw the table for Venice on the board. Go through the table, eliciting the questions, e.g. *Is there a train/an underground/an airport bus from the airport? What other information do you have?* Show Ss that they should make a note of their answers in the table. Monitor the pairwork carefully and make notes on good language use and any problem areas for feedback. N.B. You may want to highlight and correct any common errors with the class before Ss move on to part B, so they can avoid repeating their mistakes.

B Ss change roles so that Student A is asking the questions and Student B is answering. Monitor and be prepared to give Ss praise for improvements made since the previous stage.

C Tell Ss to look at all their information with their partners and decide on the best way in each case.

Possible answers: These will depend on Ss' preferences, but in terms of price:
Venice – the airport bus
Heathrow – the underground
Barcelona – the train
Edinburgh – the airport bus

Homework ideas
• Ss write an email to a friend who is coming to visit their town/city, giving them information about getting to their house from the airport/station. You could give them some phrases to use, e.g.

Hi ____ ,

I'm sorry but I'm at work/school on (Friday). There's a (train) from the airport, it costs (X), or there's a (taxi).

Have a good trip, see you soon.

• **Workbook** Ex 1–5, p39–40

SINGLE OR RETURN?

Introduction

Ss practise buying a ticket at a bus station, using travel vocabulary. They also practise listening skills and learn to check numbers.

SUPPLEMENTARY MATERIALS

Resource bank p158

Ex 6 (optional extra activity): collect some local bus and train timetables or print them from the internet.

Warm up

Review the transport vocabulary from Ex 1 in lesson 6.2. Put Ss in pairs and tell them to write one positive thing and one negative thing about each of the eight types of transport, without mentioning the name, e.g. *It's cheap. It's sometimes cold (bike).* Put the pairs into groups of four or six. Then they take it in turns to read out their clues and the other Ss try to guess the type of transport.

VOCABULARY travel

1A Introduce the idea of long bus journeys, i.e. from city to city, rather than within the city. Put Ss in pairs to discuss why they like/don't like long bus journeys. You could write some prompts on the board to help, e.g. *see/countryside, meet/people, slow, read/book, uncomfortable, be/ill,* etc. Ask a few pairs to report back to the class on their ideas. You could also ask Ss what they think it's a good idea to take with them on long bus journeys, e.g. *a good book, music, water, some snacks,* etc.

B Tell Ss to cover the words in the box. Direct them to the pictures and ask them where it is and what they can see there, e.g. *bus station, people, buses,* etc. Then direct them to the box and ask them to find the items in the picture, working alone or in pairs. As you go through the answers, check the stress on *passenger* Ooo, *ticket office* Oo Oo, *return* oO, *monthly pass* Oo O. Also check the meaning of *gate* in this context (the place where you go to get your bus).

Answers: passenger, ticket office, gate

C Ss should cover the words in the box while they point to the items in the picture and 'test' their partners.

FUNCTION buying a ticket

Optional extra activity

Tell Ss they're going to buy a ticket for a bus journey and ask them to suggest some places they could go to, and which day/time they want to go. Elicit some ideas about what they could say at the ticket office and how the person at the ticket office could answer. Put Ss in pairs to act out the conversation using any ideas/language they have. You could ask a few pairs who do well to act out their conversation for the class. Then when Ss listen to the recording, they can compare what they hear to their performance, and notice useful language which will help them to improve their conversation next time.

2 Give Ss time to read through the questions and all the options in the answers, so they understand what they are listening for.

Answers: 1 b 2 c 3 b 4 a 5 b

3A Tell Ss that there is one word missing from each gap and they can use the words around the gap to help them guess what's missing. Check the meaning of *leave*: in this context it means *go*. Also point out that in B's line *there's one at half past two* 'one' means 'a bus' and is used to avoid repeating 'bus'. They can help each other in pairs or work alone. Play the recording for Ss to check their answers.

Answers: 1 to 2 please 3 come 4 next 5 does 6 Thanks 7 from

Unit 6 Recording 6

A: A ticket to Amsterdam, please.
B: Single or return?
A: Return, please.
B: Leaving today?
A: Yes.
B: When do you want to come back?
A: Tomorrow afternoon.
B: OK. That's twenty-nine euros.
A: What time's the next bus?
B: There's one at half past two.
A: What time does it arrive in Amsterdam?
B: At quarter past four. Here's your ticket.
A: Thanks a lot.
B: The bus leaves from gate twenty-four.

B The idea here is that Ss repeat as soon as the voice on the recording starts, rather than waiting for each sentence to finish before they repeat it. The result may sound rather strange at first, as Ss are unlikely to be in chorus, but it encourages them to mimic natural stress and intonation patterns. You may need to try the technique a couple of times with the class for it to be really effective.

C When Ss have practised the conversation once, encourage them to go through it again, this time looking up from the page as they say their lines. When they have more confidence, tell them to cover their side of the conversation and practise again.

Optional extra activity

Write the following words on the board:

No, tomorrow.   *on Sunday afternoon*   *twelve B*
quarter past ten   *forty*   *Madrid (x2)*   *quarter to two*

Ss find the correct place for the words in the dialogue in Ex 3A, and practise it again. Then they can substitute their own ideas in the same places.

▐▶ **LANGUAGEBANK** 6.3 p128–129

You could use the tables in the **Language bank** for Ss to practise making questions and answers, choosing from the alternatives. Ss could do Ex 6.3 in class, then you could use the completed dialogue to give them some speaking practice in pairs, especially if they were not very confident with the dialogue practice in Ex 3.

> **Answers:** A: Two *singles* to Glasgow, please.
> B: For today?
> A: Sorry, no, for *tomorrow*.
> B: When *do* you want to go?
> A: At about nine o'clock in the morning.
> B: OK, that's seven pounds fifty.
> A: What time's the bus?
> B: There's one at quarter to nine.
> A: When does *it* arrive in Glasgow?
> B: At half past nine.
> A: Thanks *a* lot.

LEARN TO check numbers

4A Give Ss a moment or two to read the four lines of dialogue before you play the recording.

> **Answers:**
> B: The bus leaves from gate twenty-<u>four</u>.
> A: Sorry? Gate <u>thirty</u>-four?
> B: No, gate <u>twenty</u>-four.
> A: Thanks a lot.
> N.B. It's usual to stress the second part of numbers over twelve, e.g. *thir<u>teen</u>, twenty-<u>five</u>, thirty-<u>seven</u>, forty-<u>nine</u>*, etc. The first part is only stressed when there is uncertainty, as in the last two examples.

B You may need to let Ss repeat this a couple of times. You could divide the class in half, with one side repeating A's part, and the other B's, then swapping roles and playing the recording again.

> **Teaching tip**
> Ss can sometimes struggle to make the stressed syllable 'stand out' enough. To help them with this, demonstrate that they need to speak more loudly and raise the pitch of their voice on that syllable. Use your hand to show the pitch moving up on *twen* and quickly down on *ty-four*.

speakout TIP
You could ask Ss whether they use stress like this in their own language(s), and if not, what they would do to check or correct this kind of information.

C Ss could prepare by reading through the conversations silently first and underlining the syllables that need to be stressed in each case. Monitor carefully while they practise the conversations and give some feedback on their use of stress.

5A Point out that Ss can write the prices in any currency they know.

B If appropriate to your Ss, you could suggest that they mumble or say the numbers indistinctly as well as fast, so there's a real reason for their partner to check. This will also add an element of fun to the activity.

SPEAKING

6A Before you start the activity, elicit/teach the word *platform* and also the questions related to *gate/platform*. For *stronger classes* you could elicit/teach *What gate does the bus leave from?* and *What platform does the train leave from?* Otherwise, simply *What's the gate/platform number?*

Then give Student B time to find p150 and look through their information. You may also want to give Ss time to prepare and practise their questions before you put them into pairs.

B Monitor the pairwork carefully and note down examples of good language use and any problems for praise and correction in feedback.

> **Optional extra activity**
> Take in some local train and bus timetables or print them from the internet. Give half the class the train timetables and the other half the bus timetables. Ss think about where they want to go in the local area, then pair up with someone from the other half of the class and practise buying a ticket.

> **Homework ideas**
> • Ss write an email with real instructions for someone travelling to their city or around their city, e.g. *The bus leaves from King's Cross. It's number 72. A single ticket costs £2.50. It leaves at 8.30a.m.,* etc.
> • **Workbook** Ex 1–4, p41

RUSH HOUR

Introduction

Ss watch a BBC extract with people talking about travelling in India in the rush hour. Ss then learn and practise how to do a travel survey, and write a travel forum entry about transport in their town/city.

SUPPLEMENTARY MATERIALS

Ex 1A: bring in/download a large map of India.

Ex 1B: bring in/download pictures of a tuk-tuk, a rickshaw and a lorry.

Ex 2C (optional extra activity): prepare a handout for practice of the adjectives.

Warm up

Tell Ss to close their books and write the title *Rush Hour* on the board. Establish that it's the time (usually twice a day, and longer than an hour) when a lot of traffic is on the roads because people are going to or coming home from work, school, etc. Give Ss the example of rush hour in London: 7.30–10.00a.m. and 4.30–7.00p.m., and write the following questions on the board to discuss:
When is rush hour in your country?
Do you travel in rush hour?
How do you travel?
Is it easy or difficult? Why?

▶ DVD PREVIEW

1A Tell Ss to keep their books closed and show them a map of India, or draw one on the board. Prompt Ss to tell the class what they know about India, i.e. names of cities, language(s), religions, famous food, drink, people, places, etc.

Possible answers:
cities: Mumbai, Calcutta, Delhi
languages: official language – Hindi (English is the second official language)
religions: Hinduism, Buddhism, Sikhism
food: curry, rice, spices
drink: India is famous for producing and drinking tea
people: Gandhi, Mother Teresa
places: Taj Mahal
Put Ss in pairs to do the quiz.

Answers: 1 Karachi is in Pakistan
2 Omar Sharif is Egyptian
3 Coffee is mainly grown in Brazil and Colombia
4 Machu Picchu is in Peru
5 Tempura is a Japanese style of cooking

Culture notes

Gandhi (2 October 1869–30 January 1948) was the political leader of India during the Indian independence movement. He led India to independence and he also inspired non-violent movements for civil rights across the world. His birthday, 2 October, is a national holiday in India and the International Day of Non-Violence.

Mother Teresa (26 August 1910–5 September 1997), was a Catholic nun of Albanian ethnicity and Indian citizenship, who founded the Missionaries of Charity in Calcutta, India in 1950. Following her death she was beatified by Pope John Paul II and given the title Blessed Teresa of Calcutta.

Bollywood refers to the Hindi-language film industry based in Mumbai (formerly Bombay). It is the largest film producer in India and one of the largest film production centres in the world.

Yoga originated in ancient India and is a physical, mental and spiritual discipline. The word is associated with meditative practices in Hinduism and Buddhism.

The Ganges is the most sacred river to Hindus and millions of Indians who live along its course depend on it for their daily needs.

The Taj Mahal is a mausoleum in Agra. It was built by Emperor Shah Jahan in memory of his third wife and is regarded as one of the eight wonders of the world.

Daal is a thick soup or stew made from lentils and spices.

Naan is a flat bread which is baked in a hot clay oven.

B Give Ss a minute or two to read the text, then direct them to the photo. Ask Ss what they can see and use the photo and any other pictures you've brought in to teach *rickshaw, tuk-tuk, lorry* and *accident*. Make a list of the types of transport Ss think people use on the board.

▶ DVD VIEW

2A Ss check the ideas they predicted in Ex 1B.

Answer: People go to work and school by train, bike, rickshaw, motorbike, tuk-tuk, bus and taxi.

B Ss can complete the sentences alone or in pairs. Check the pronunciation of the following adjectives: *expensive* oOo, *dangerous* Ooo, *crowded* Oo.

Answers: 2 noisy 3 expensive 4 dangerous 5 crowded 6 slow

C Play the DVD again for Ss to underline the adjectives. Point out that more than one adjective may be mentioned for some of the types of transport.

Answers: 2 bikes – slow 3 motorbikes – fast, dangerous 4 tuk-tuks – popular, noisy 5 taxis – fast, safe, expensive

Optional extra activity

Give Ss the opportunity to personalise the adjectives from the DVD and relate them to their own lives.

Write the following on the board or put them on a handout and tell Ss to work alone to write their answers:

Write the name of these places in your town/city:

A noisy street.

An expensive restaurant.

A park that is dangerous at night.

A road with slow traffic in the rush hour.

A bar that is always crowded.

A popular clothes shop.

A quiet place to relax.

A safe place for children.

Put Ss in pairs or small groups to compare answers: if they're from the same town/city they can see if they agree, if they're from different towns/cities, they'll need to give some information about what/where the place is.

DVD 6 Rush Hour

V=Voice-over B=Boy M=Man W=Woman

V: India, it's a country of millions of different people, colours and sounds. Every morning in India millions of people travel to work or to school.

B: I get up every morning at five o'clock and go to school by train. I like it because I can see a lot of places and people from the train. There are a lot of people on the train. It's very crowded.

V: The Indian train system is over a hundred years old. It goes to hundreds of places in India, and it's a very popular way to travel. On the roads people and animals walk everywhere. Hundreds of people use bikes and rickshaws.

M: I live in Delhi, and I go to work by bike every day. There are a lot of bikes on the road. It's sometimes very slow.

V: A motorbike is a good way to travel around. You often see three or four people from a family on one motorbike.

M: Motorbikes are great, they're fast, but they're often dangerous. There are sometimes bad accidents with lorries and motorbikes.

V: And then there are tuk-tuks. Tuks-tuks are very popular, but they are also very noisy. Finally, taxis go everywhere in the cities.

W: I travel to Mumbai on business a lot. In Mumbai, I usually travel by taxi. It's fast and it's safe, but taxis are expensive.

V: For a visitor the different types of transport and the millions of people can be too much, but it's all part of the many faces of India.

speakout a travel survey

3A Tell Ss to work in pairs, and remind them to use *by* with forms of transport, but to say *on foot* or *I walk* if they don't use transport. Also point out that people often say *I drive* instead of *I go by car*. Circulate and help Ss with any vocabulary they need.

B Tell Ss to complete the table with one or two word answers. Play the recording and give them a moment to compare answers in pairs.

Answers:

in a big city	in the countryside
1 *by underground*	1 *by car*
2 *by bus*	2 *by bus*
3 *by bike*	3 *by bike*

C Give Ss a few moments to look at the **Key phrases**. Check that Ss understand *public transport system* (bus and train services for everyone to use). Then play the recording again for Ss to tick the phrases.

Answers: I live in (London) but I'm from (the countryside). ✓
There's a good public transport system. ✓
(A lot of/Some people) use (the underground/buses). ✓
Some people go to work by (bus/bike). ✓
The best way to travel is by (car/underground). ✓
People also go by (bus).
In (my village/the city), I go everywhere by (car/bike). ✓

Unit 6 Recording 8

I live in London but I'm from the countryside. British people love their cars, but it's expensive to drive in London. There's a good public transport system and a lot of people use the underground or buses. Some people go to work by bike but I don't. I think bikes are dangerous in the city. The best way to travel is by underground, but it's very crowded in the mornings. In the countryside, a lot of people drive, of course, or they use buses. In my village I go everywhere by bike.

4A Give Ss a few minutes working alone to write some notes about their country. If Ss are from the same town/city, suggest that they talk about a family member or friend who lives somewhere different, i.e. smaller/bigger, where there isn't an underground, etc. Circulate and help, and encourage Ss to practise saying some of their sentences for you to check. Put Ss in pairs to talk about their ideas.

B Put Ss in groups of 4–6 to take turns to talk about travel in their country. Tell the listeners to write one question that they want the speaker to answer when they've finished, e.g. *Why do a lot of people go by bike? Why is by car the best way to travel?*

writeback a travel forum entry

5A Give Ss a few minutes to read and answer the question.

Answer: He usually goes to work by train and in Kobe he usually walks.

B Tell Ss to use the entry about Kobe and Osaka as their 'model', and to include information about: where they live/work, the best way to travel and reason why, what different types of transport there are, the cost of tickets, etc. Circulate and help with vocabulary, etc. as Ss write their information.

Homework ideas

- Ss review all the new vocabulary items they've studied in this lesson and choose five that they think will be most useful to remember. They write a short paragraph about transport in India that includes all five words.

LOOKBACK

PLACES

1A You could run this as a team competition (Ss have their books closed). Write up or display one phrase at a time and the first team member to 'buzz' and tell you the missing vowels wins a point for their team. If they make a mistake with any vowels, the other team can try for a bonus point.

Answers: 2 restaurant 3 pharmacy 4 newsagent's
5 payphone 6 cash machine 7 hotel 8 snack bar

Alternative idea
To provide more challenge, put Ss in pairs and direct them to the 'places' vocabulary on page 62. Tell them to jumble the letters of each word (c.f. Ex 3A p60) and write them on a piece of paper. They then pass the paper to the next pair, who have to put the letters in order.

B Point out that Ss can't use a thing which is already in the word, e.g. for *cash machine*, they can't write *cash*, but they could write *money, euros*, etc. Circulate and help. Possible ideas for Ss who are struggling: payphone – *credit card, cash, talk*; newsagent's – *magazine, newspaper, pen*; pharmacy – *aspirin, medicine*; hotel – *shower, bed*; snack bar – *sandwich, coffee, burger*.

C Put Ss into groups of 4–6 to guess the places from each other's clues.

THERE IS/ARE

2A Ss could complete the questions in pairs, or working alone. As you check the answers, you could take the opportunity to give Ss pronunciation practice, modelling the questions with polite intonation for them to repeat.

Answers: 2 Is there 3 Are there 4 Is there 5 Are there
6 Are there

B Tell Ss to match the answers to the questions by using the vocabulary to help them.

Answers: a 4 b 6 c 1 d 2 e 3 f 5

C Ss complete the answers alone, then compare answers with a partner. Then they can practise the dialogues.

Answers: a there aren't b there are c there is d there is
e there aren't, There's/is f there aren't, there's/is

Optional extra activity
In pairs, Ss change the answers that begin with *Yes* to *No* and vice versa, and change the rest of the information in each answer so that it makes sense, e.g. *Is there a guided tour of the city tomorrow? Yes there is, it leaves at 9.30a.m.*
Each pair then acts out two or three of their new dialogues for the rest of the class.

TRANSPORT

3A You could run this as a race, with Ss working in pairs. The first pair to circle all the words and bring them to you wins.

Answers:

B You could demonstrate this first, showing Ss that their picture doesn't need to be very sophisticated.

A/AN, SOME, A LOT OF, NOT ANY

4A Establish that the sentences are referring to the Students' Book. You could go through the mistakes with the whole class.

Answers: 2 Some *pages* have six photos. 3 There's *a* Spanish word on page 6. 4 There's *a* blue glove on page 32.

B Give Ss enough time to look through the book (later units as well as earlier ones) and find the correct information.

Answers: 1 Some pages don't have photos.
2 True 3 True ('libro' is Spanish and Italian for 'book')
4 There's a yellow glove on page 32.

C If Ss need some help with ideas for this, you could give them some prompts on the board:

There's a picture of a famous person/place on page …

There are some pictures of food/clothes on page …

The title of lesson (4.2) is …

Circulate and help Ss to write their sentences.

D When Ss have finished this group work, they could report back to the class about any true facts about the book that they found surprising.

TRAVEL

5 You could run this as a race. Give Ss a minute or two in pairs to complete the words. The first pair to finish put their hands up, then spell out each word for the class. If they make a mistake with spelling, another pair can try to spell all the words, and so on.

Answers: 1 office 2 passengers 3 gate 4 single 5 return
6 monthly

BUYING A TICKET

6A Go through the example, pointing out that Ss need to add one or two words to each line. Give Ss a few minutes to complete the sentences, working alone.

Answers: 2 I want to go tomorrow morning. 3 What time's the first bus? 4 What time does it arrive in Lisbon? 5 Where does it leave from? 6 Thanks a lot.

B When Ss have practised the conversation once or twice using the prompts, encourage them to look up from the page and try to remember as much of their lines as they can.

REVIEW 3: UNITS 5–6

Introduction

The aim of the review units is for Ss to revise and practise the grammar, vocabulary and pronunciation from the previous two units in a different context. The context for this review unit is problems.

SUPPLEMENTARY MATERIALS

Ex 1A: take in some examples of 'agony aunt' pages from a magazine or website.

Ex 5A (optional extra activity): prepare prompts on cards (see notes).

READING AND GRAMMAR

1A Start by brainstorming some examples of problems, e.g. that you might read about in the 'agony aunt' page of a magazine or website (you could take in some examples of these). You could put some categories on the board and ask Ss to think of one or two problems for each category, e.g. *work, family, money, relationships, health*. Then put Ss in pairs to talk about the question. You could encourage them to report back to the class afterwards, using adverbs of frequency, e.g. *I sometimes talk to one or two friends about it; I often think about it alone.*

B You could suggest that Ss cover the answers while they read the problems and first think about the answer they would give to each person, then match the answers to the problems and see if any of their own ideas were similar.

Answers: 1 c) 2 b) 3 a)

C Ss can start by comparing the ideas they thought of in 1B, then help each other to write their answers. Invite a few pairs to read out their answers and ask the class to decide which is the best one for each problem.

2A Point out that there are two questions for each of the three people in the text in Ex 1, so that Ss can refer back to the content.

Answers: b Does he go out in the evenings?
2a Does Layla buy the food?
b What does her husband do at home?
3a Is there a problem with planes?
b When does Rob go on holiday?

B For *stronger classes*, you could ask Ss to cover Ex 2B and write their own answers to the questions first, then they can compare the two versions. Ss could also practise asking and answering the questions in pairs.

Answers: 1a) 4 2a) 2 2b) 5 3a) 3 3b) 6

Optional extra activity

Working in pairs, Ss invent two more problems and write about them on two pieces of paper (two or three sentences each), putting their names at the end of the problem, as in the texts in Ex 1B. Circulate and help while Ss are doing this, then collect in the problems and redistribute them so that all the pairs have two new problems to read about. Then they write their answers and send them back to the pair who wrote them. Some of the pairs can then read out their problems and the answers they got to the class, and say what they think of the answers.

LISTENING AND GRAMMAR

3A You could play the first conversation for Ss to confirm that it's in a snack bar. Then play the rest of the recording.

Answers: 2 newsagent's 3 cash machine 4 internet café 5 pharmacy

B Before you play the recording again, give Ss a minute or two to read through the alternatives. Vocabulary to check: *ill* versus *well*.

Answers: 1 another coffee 2 doesn't have/doesn't buy 3 doesn't have money/She 4 three/goes to another computer 5 ill/doesn't buy

Review 3 Recording 1

Conversation 1
A: Excuse me.
B: Yeah.
A: There's a problem with my coffee. It's cold.
B: Oh, sorry. Let me get you another one.
A: Thanks.

Conversation 2
A: Do you have *The New York Times*?
B: Sorry, we don't. We usually have it, but not today.
A: Oh. Well, do you have any other newspapers in English?
B: We have *The Times*.
A: That's a British paper, yeah?
B: That's right.
A: Hmm, no thanks. I really want an American paper.

Conversation 3
A: OK, let's get some money out.
B: What's the problem?
A: It says there isn't any money in the machine.
B: Oh, no.
A: Maybe it's because it's a bank holiday. Look, I have some money. Let's go to Salvatore's café. It isn't expensive.

Conversation 4
A: Excuse me.
B: Is there a problem?
A: Yes, I'm in number three and the computer's broken.
B: Let me see. Ah, yes, there's a problem. Please try number five.

Conversation 5
A: Can I help you?
B: Yes, I'm not very well. I'm very hot and I'm tired all the time. Do you have something to help?
A: These are good. Go home and go to bed.
B: How much are they?
A: Five euros.
B: Five euros. Hmm, no thank you.

SPEAKING

4A Put Ss in pairs and give them a few minutes to choose a conversation and practise it.

B Demonstrate this by playing the first conversation while Ss follow it in the audio script. Ask them to call out 'Stop!' when they want to suggest a keyword: if the rest of the class agrees, write the keyword on the board and continue until you have a list of 6–8 words for the conversation. Tell Ss to choose a different conversation and write keywords. Circulate and help.

C Monitor this practice carefully so you can give Ss feedback on their language use.

5A Go through the example with the class, then give Ss time to choose a place and think of a problem.

> **Optional extra activity**
> Give Ss the following prompts on cards to pick up and look at if they need help (either one set of cards for Ss to come and choose from at the front of the class, or one set of cards per pair):
> - *1 café*
>   *2 customer, waiter*
>   *3 you have chicken soup, you want vegetable soup*
> - *1 newsagent's*
>   *2 customer, shop assistant*
>   *3 you want cola; they have it, but it's a big bottle (you want a small bottle)*
> - *1 pharmacy*
>   *2 customer, assistant*
>   *3 you're ill; you don't have money*
> - *1 cash machine in a bank*
>   *2 customer, bank assistant*
>   *3 your card is stuck in the machine*
> - *1 snack bar*
>   *2 customer, waiter*
>   *3 you have a sandwich with white bread, you want brown bread*

B Encourage Ss to practise their conversation two or three times, asking you for help with any words/phrases they're not sure of, so that they feel confident to act out their conversation in a group.

C Ss could work in groups of six, or in a smaller class, act out their conversations in front of the whole class. The other Ss guess the place, and say why they think it's that place. Make notes of some good examples of language use so you can give Ss praise when they've finished.

SOUNDS: /ð/ AND /θ/

6A Direct Ss to the pictures and point out that the symbols represent the sounds. Play the recording for Ss to listen to the sounds and the words. You could also show Ss that to make the two sounds, their tongue needs to touch the bottom of their top teeth (demonstrate that if their tongue touches the roof of the mouth instead, the sounds produced will be /s/ and /z/).

B You may want to ask Ss to predict which group the words belong to before they listen.

> **Answers:** /ð/ father, with, these, together
> /θ/ monthly, thirsty, think, thirteen

C You could pause the recording after each group of words, and ask individual Ss to repeat them, rather than Ss repeating in chorus. This will give you more opportunity to correct their pronunciation of the 'target' sounds.

7A Tell Ss they will hear each word twice on the recording, but only one has the correct pronunciation. You could do the first word as an example with the class.

> **Answers:** 1 a 2 a 3 b 4 b 5 b 6 a 7 a 8 b 9 a 10 b

B Give Ss time to practise saying the sentences several times. This should be kept light-hearted.

C You could set this up as a race and see which pair finishes first. Then they can demonstrate saying the sentences fast for the whole class.

> **Homework ideas**
> - Ss email three or four other Ss from the class with an invented problem, and answer each other's problems. Then they choose the answer they think is best and email that person to tell them.
> - **Workbook** Ex 1–4, p42–43

OVERVIEW

7.1 WHERE WERE YOU?
GRAMMAR | past simple: *was/were*
VOCABULARY | dates
HOW TO | talk about where you were

COMMON EUROPEAN FRAMEWORK
Ss can ask and answer questions about themselves and other people, and where they were; can indicate time by such phrases as last Friday, in November, 15th October.

7.2 RECORD BREAKERS
GRAMMAR | past simple: regular verbs
VOCABULARY | actions
HOW TO | talk about the past

COMMON EUROPEAN FRAMEWORK
Ss can get an idea of the content of simpler informational material and short simple stories, especially if there is visual support; can produce simple phrases about people and past activities.

7.3 HOW WAS IT?
FUNCTION | giving opinions
VOCABULARY | adjectives
LEARN TO | show feelings

COMMON EUROPEAN FRAMEWORK
Ss can perform and respond to basic language functions, such as expressing opinions.

7.4 THE CHILEAN MINERS BBC DVD
speakout | a history quiz
writeback | a history quiz

COMMON EUROPEAN FRAMEWORK
Ss can exchange relevant information and give their opinions on practical problems; can write short simple questions with numbers and dates.

7.5 LOOKBACK
Communicative revision activities

BBC VIDEO PODCAST
People talking about their birthdays.

WHERE WERE YOU?

Introduction

Students practise listening and talking about where they were at certain times, using *was/were*, dates and related vocabulary. They also review punctuation in an email.

SUPPLEMENTARY MATERIALS

Resource bank p160

Warm up

Review verb + noun collocations. Write the following verbs on the board:

go, be, listen to, watch, play, have

Put Ss in pairs and give them two minutes to write down two nouns that go with each verb.

Possible answers: go to work, to a party; be a student, at home; listen to music, to the radio; watch TV, a film; play tennis, football; have a shower, a sandwich.

Go through their answers and add the nouns to the board. If Ss don't think of the following nouns, write them on one side of the board and ask which verbs they go with: *the sunrise (watch), bed (go to), on a beach (be), at home (be), fireworks (watch), in hospital (be).*

LISTENING

1A Write the date 31/12 on the board and ask Ss for another way to say that day (New Year/New Year's Eve). Focus Ss on the photos and ask them if they usually celebrate like this at New Year. Then put them in pairs to compare what they do at New Year with the photos. Ask one or two pairs for their answers.

B Give Ss a moment or two to look at the places. You could play speaker 1 for Ss to check the example.

Answers:
Speaker 2 – at a concert
Speaker 3 – at work
Speaker 4 – on a beach
Speaker 5 – in hospital

C Use the example to establish that the speakers may talk about more than one of the subjects. Encourage Ss to compare their answers in pairs.

Answers: a) 5 b) 4 c) 3 d) 2 e) 4 f) 5 g) 3 h) 5

UNIT 7 Recording 1

1

I was at home with my parents and my brother and sister. There was a family party, but nothing really special. There were fireworks on TV … but I think I was asleep at midnight. I don't really remember.

2

We were in Miami, Florida, at a concert. There was great music – the Gipsy Kings and some other local bands. It was great.

3

I was at work in London. I work at a club, and of course it was a very big night for us. The money was good. Everybody was happy, crazy. There were fantastic fireworks over the River Thames.

4

I was on a beach in Fiji with my friends. There was a beautiful sunrise. We were the first people to see the start of the year 2000. And we weren't alone – there were hundreds of people on the beach with us. It was a beautiful morning, very peaceful …

5

I was in hospital. I was born on January 1st, 2000. My mother says there was a party. Maybe it was for the New Year … or was the party for me?

GRAMMAR past simple: was/were

2A Tell Ss that the sentences come from the recording in Ex 1 and ask them if they're about the present or the past. You could write today's date on the board and elicit *present*, then write two or three past dates, including 31/12/2000 and elicit *past*. You could then go through the sentences on the board with the class, or give Ss a minute or two to work on them alone first.

Answers: 1 was 2 were 3 weren't 4 Was

B Ss could complete the table in pairs, then check with the rest of the class.

Answers:

I He/She/It	was wasn't	at home. in Beijing. tired.
You/We/They	were weren't	

Was Were	he you	here? in class?
Yes,	he we	was. were.
No,	he we	wasn't. weren't.

3A Tell Ss to underline one word in each sentence. Point out that the main stress is always on the word carrying the important information.

Answers: 1 I was at <u>home</u>. 2 We were <u>tired</u>. 3 She was in <u>class</u>. 4 They were <u>here</u>.

B If Ss have trouble pronouncing the weak forms, tell them to practise saying /wəz/ for *was* and /wə/ for *were*.

LANGUAGEBANK 7.1 p130–131

Give Ss a few minutes to read through the summary of the form of *was/were*. Ss could do Ex 7.1A and B in class if you feel they need some basic practice of the form before moving on to the more sophisticated practice in Ex 4.

Answers: A 2 isn't, was 3 weren't, 're/are 4 were, aren't 5 wasn't, 's/is 6 're/are, weren't
B 2 Was the film good? Yes, it was. 3 Were your brothers and sisters nice to you? Yes, they were. 4 Were you cold in Scotland? No, I wasn't./No, we weren't.
5 Were you and Emma at the party? No, we weren't.
6 Was there a gift shop in the hotel? Yes, there was.

PRACTICE

4A Before Ss start the exercise, check *birthday* and *public holiday* (a special day when people don't go to work and shops don't usually open).

Answers: 2 Were 3 Was, was, Were 4 was, were, was

B Establish that a)–d) are the answers to 1–4 in Ex 4A. Check *mountain*, *River Thames* and *Christmas*.

Culture notes

The **River Thames** is the longest river in England. It's best known because it flows through central London, but it also flows alongside several other towns and cities, including Oxford, Reading, Henley-on-Thames, Windsor, Kingston upon Thames and Richmond.

Christmas is a holiday, usually celebrated on December 25th to commemorate the birth of Jesus.

Answers: a wasn't, were b weren't, were c was, wasn't d was, were, weren't, were

Optional extra activity

Highlight the examples of *on* and *at* in the sentences in Ex 4A and B, so that Ss can use them in the next stage. Give Ss a few minutes to find and underline them, then group them together on the board:

at New Year, a concert, a party, (X's) house

on (X's) birthday, a mountain, a boat, a river, holiday

Then elicit from the class any other examples they know, e.g.

at work, home, a restaurant, the cinema, the theatre, a club

on a beach, business

C You may want to give Ss time to think about/make notes on their answers first. However, discourage them from writing full sentence answers, to avoid reading aloud and keep spontaneity. You could also model rhythm and intonation of questions 1–4 for Ss to repeat in chorus, before they start asking each other in pairs. Monitor carefully so you can give feedback on Ss' use of language, especially *was/were*, etc. and their intonation in the questions.

speakout TIP

Establish that there's no difference in the meaning of the three questions, but that they all invite the other person to continue speaking, so the conversation can keep going.

VOCABULARY dates

5A Check *months* by asking Ss what month you are in now.

Answers: 2 February 3 March 4 April 5 May 6 June
7 July 8 August 9 September 10 October 11 November
12 December

B As Ss listen and check, they could underline the stress on each month with more than one syllable:
<u>Ja</u>nuary, <u>Fe</u>bruary, <u>A</u>pril, <u>Ju</u>ly, Au<u>gust</u>, Sep<u>tem</u>ber, Oc<u>to</u>ber, No<u>vem</u>ber, De<u>cem</u>ber

C Ss should cover Ex 5A while they do this.

6A Ss can either draw lines or write the number next to the word it matches. You could say the numbers for Ss to repeat, reminding them to touch the bottom of their top teeth with their tongue to pronounce the final *-th* in *fourth, fifth, fifteenth, twentieth*.

Answers: 2nd second 3rd third 4th fourth 5th fifth
15th fifteenth 20th twentieth 21st twenty-first

Optional extra activity
Put Ss in pairs to practise asking and answering:
A: *What's the (fourth) month?*
B: *(April)*, etc.

B Give Ss a few moments to read through the dates before you play the recording.

Answers: October 15th 2
April 16th 5
August 8th 6
September 21st 4
March 25th 3

C This is a common way of saying dates and is simpler for Ss at this level than *the first of December*, etc.

7A Establish that the dates could be birthdays, public holidays, anniversaries, etc. and give Ss a few minutes to think about and write their dates. Circulate and help as necessary. Then Ss dictate their dates to their partners.

B Write a date that is important for you on the board, and invite a student to ask you about it, eliciting the question *Why is … the … important?*

➡ PHOTOBANK p145

Use these phrases to give Ss practise of years and time phrases.

Answers:
Dates: Years 1 E 2 A 3 H 4 C 5 D 6 G 7 B 8 F
Dates: Time phrases 1 e) 2 c) 3 g) 4 a) 5 h) 6 b)
7 d) 8 f)

SPEAKING

8A Point out that the order starts with the most recent. Ss can work alone and compare answers with a partner.

Answers: 2 on Saturday afternoon 3 last Friday
4 last month

B Demonstrate this by inviting different Ss to ask you the five questions. Then put Ss in pairs to practise.

Optional extra activity
Ss change the time phrases in Ex 8A and practise asking and answering with a new partner, e.g.
last (Wednesday)
last (week)
yesterday (morning)
this time last (month)
on (Sunday) afternoon

WRITING punctuation review

9A Look at the example with the class and elicit when a comma is used (to divide up a sentence and make it easier to read). Then put Ss in pairs and ask them to match the punctuation marks and explain when they are used.

Answers: 2 full stop b – at the end of a sentence
3 exclamation mark a – after a word, phrase or sentence to show emotion, e.g. you're surprised, excited, amused, angry
4 question mark c – at the end of a question
5 capital letter d – at the beginning of a sentence and names of people, places and special days

B Give Ss a minute or two to read the email and find the answers.

Answers: Jane is at the Olympic Games. Paola is in Italy.

C Ss can work on this in pairs, or work alone and compare answers in pairs when they've finished.

Answers: 1, (it's a convention to use a comma after 'Hi'
or 'Dear' at the beginning of a letter or email, although the next sentence starts with a capital letter)
2 ?
3 .
4 .
5 .
6 ?
7 . or ! (the exclamation mark shows that the person is excited about their news)
8 ,
9 . or ! (see note for 7)
10 . or ! (see note for 7)
11 .
12 ,
Capital letters: Paola, Matt, Olympic Games, Italy, Jane

10A Ss could write their email in pairs to help each other with ideas. Tell them to follow the shape of the email in Ex 9B (and to put XXXX instead of the name of the place). Circulate and help as required.

B Either put Ss into groups of six to swap and read their emails, or display the emails round the classroom and give Ss time to walk round and read them.

Homework ideas
• Ss write another email like the one in Ex 9B, from a different place. They can swap emails with their partner in the next lesson and guess the place.
• Workbook Ex 1–5, p45–46

RECORD BREAKERS

Introduction

Ss practise reading about people breaking records. They also practise talking about past activities, using vocabulary to describe actions and the past simple of regular verbs.

SUPPLEMENTARY MATERIALS

Resource bank p159

Ex 4B (optional extra activity): prepare a set of cards to display and move around on the board (see notes).

Warm up

Direct Ss to photos A–D and put the following questions on the board for them to discuss in pairs or small groups:
Where is the person/Where are the people?
Who is he or she/Who are they? Famous or 'ordinary'?
When is it? Now or in the past?

Encourage Ss to justify their answers as they tell the rest of the class their ideas in feedback.

VOCABULARY actions

1A Give Ss a moment or two to read through the actions, then play the first part of the recording, for them to hear the example: *start*. When you go through the answers, check the pronunciation of *laugh* and *arrive*.

Answers: 2 move home 3 cry 4 talk 5 arrive 6 wait
7 dance 8 play tennis 9 laugh 10 walk

B You could demonstrate this by acting out one of the verbs yourself for Ss to guess. Tell Ss to take turns to act out and guess the actions.

READING

2A Look at photos A–D one at a time with the class and elicit the actions.

Answers: A walk B dance C play tennis D talk

B Remind Ss that the title of the lesson is *Record breakers* and establish what happens when someone breaks a record, e.g. someone runs 100m in 10 seconds, then another person runs 100m in 9.58 seconds and breaks the record. Tell Ss to read the headlines and imagine what record the person is/people are breaking. Check *marathon* (an activity that lasts a long time and needs a lot of energy, patience, etc.) and *match* (like *game*: an organised sports event between two people or teams). Then tell Ss to read the four texts quickly and match the headlines. You could give them a time limit of a minute to encourage them to read just enough to decide on the headline, without worrying about unfamiliar vocabulary.

Answers: 1 Woman walks round world 2 Dance marathon 3 Non-stop tennis match 4 Man talks for six days

C Look at the example with the class and give Ss a minute or two to find the relevant information in the first text. When they've found all the names, they can compare answers in pairs.

Answers: 2 Ffyona Campbell 3 Carlo (Santelli) 4 Errol Muzawazi 5 Edith Boudreaux

D Before Ss read the texts again, you could check the following vocabulary: *ballroom* (a very large room for dancing); *childhood* (the time in your life when you are a child); *democracy* (everyone votes to elect the government); *audience member* (someone who watches and/or listens to a concert, play, etc.). Give Ss a few minutes to find and correct the mistakes in the notes. In feedback, ask Ss to read out the correct numbers like this: *It was 5,152 hours, not 5,512 hours; it was 48 minutes, not 44 minutes*, etc.

Answers: dancing: 5,152 hours and 48 minutes
walking: 32,000 kilometres
talking: 121 hours
playing tennis: 38 hours, 2 minutes, 9 seconds

Optional extra activity

Ask Ss to discuss in pairs which record breaker story they like best, and why. Then invite Ss to share their answers with the class.

Teaching tip

You can make a text memorable for Ss by asking for a personal response to it, if the subject matter lends itself to this, e.g. *What surprised you? Do you agree with the writer?*

GRAMMAR past simple: regular verbs

3A Tell Ss to write the past form next to the verb, as in the example, and to copy the spelling carefully. Give them several minutes to find the past forms, and to check their answers with a partner.

Answers: 2 danced 3 moved 4 cried 5 laughed 6 walked
7 arrived 8 stopped 9 talked 10 listened 11 waited
12 played

B Either go through the table on the board with the whole class, or put Ss in pairs to work out the rules. Make sure they understand *vowel, consonant, add, change, double* (demonstrate these with examples on the board).

Answers:

	Spelling	Examples
1 most verbs	add -ed	*started, laughed, walked, talked, listened, waited, played*
2 verbs ending in -e	add -d	*danced, arrived, moved*
3 verbs ending in consonant + -y	change to -ied	*cried*
4 most verbs ending in consonant + vowel + consonant	double the final letter, then add -ed	*stopped*

C Point out/Elicit that the verb doesn't have -ed or -d on the end in the negative because *didn't* already tells us it's a past form.

Answer: didn't

4A You could model the examples for Ss to repeat, so they can feel and hear the difference between the three endings.

> **Answers:** /t/ laughed, walked, stopped, talked (the verbs end with an unvoiced consonant)
> /d/ cried, arrived, listened, played (the verbs end with a voiced consonant)
> /ɪd/ waited (the verbs end with t or d)

B Ss listen to the three groups and repeat after each group.

▶ **LANGUAGEBANK** 7.2 p130–131

The **Language bank** reminds Ss that the past simple from is the same for all persons (I/you/he/she/it/we/they). It also highlights when the past simple is used, i.e. for past events at a point in time, or over a period of time in the past. Ss could do Ex 7.2 A and B in class or for homework.

> **Answers:**
> A
> 2 Last weekend my father played tennis. 3 Last year Francisco worked in a shop. 4 Last night the baby cried all night. 5 In 2009 my parents moved to Barcelona.
> 6 Yesterday the train stopped for half an hour.
> B
> 2 I didn't watch TV last night. I studied for three hours.
> 3 Noriko emailed me yesterday but she didn't phone.
> 4 The film didn't start until eight and it finished at eleven.
> 5 James wanted to see the concert but he arrived an hour late.
> 6 I repeated the instructions because the students didn't understand.

Optional extra activity
Highlight the use of *for, in* and *about* in the 'record breakers' texts.

Make a set of cards large enough to display and move around on the board, with the following words on each:
for, in, about, thirteen hours, 1991, Tangiers, wait, talk, ask, be happy

Alternatively you could prepare small sets of cards, one for each pair of Ss.

Ask Ss to tell you which combinations are possible with *in, for* and *about*, then direct them back to the texts to confirm their ideas.

Answers:
for thirteen hours, wait for (him)
in 1991, in Tangiers
talk about (sth), *ask about* (sth), *be happy about* (sth)
Ss could practise the combinations by writing sentences about a topic, e.g. studying English:
I studied English for … last week.
I started English classes in …
Yesterday I asked the teacher about …
In class we often talk about …
Last week my teacher was/wasn't happy about (my homework/test result).
I was late for class on … because I waited for (my friend/the bus).

Other topics: a sport or free time activity

PRACTICE

5A Before Ss start this, check *when he was a boy* (from about 4–12 years old) and *the whole time* (all the time). Ss work alone then compare answers in pairs.

> **Answers:** 1 lived, moved 2 waited, didn't arrive
> 3 cooked, liked 4 walked, closed 5 asked, didn't understand
> 6 watched, cried

B You could ask two Ss to demonstrate the activity for the class first. Then when Ss change roles and it's Student A's turn to read out the sentences, suggest that they read them in random order.

> **Optional extra activity**
> Ss go through the sentences again, but this time they complete the second part of the sentences with their own ideas, e.g. *He lived here when he was a boy, but he didn't like it/he moved to the city.*

SPEAKING

6A Start by telling Ss to write the name of a friend or family member where the asterisks are. Give Ss a few minutes to write their sentences in their notebooks. Circulate and help as required.

B You could demonstrate this by reading out one false and one true sentence of your own for Ss to guess. Put Ss in groups of four or five to do this. Monitor and note down examples of good language use and problems areas for praise and correction in feedback.

> **Optional extra activity**
> Ss choose one of the people from the 'record breakers' texts and imagine that it's the day after they broke the record. In pairs, they tell each other what they did and ask each other how they feel about it now, and why. Ss then report back to the class about what their partner said.

> **Homework ideas**
> • Ss write their diary for the last week, including at least two sentences about each day, e.g. *On Monday morning I … In the evening I …* You could warn them that some verbs are irregular and that they should check the past form of any verb they use in their dictionaries.
> • **Workbook** Ex 1–4, p47–48

HOW WAS IT?

Introduction

Ss practise giving opinions, using positive and negative adjectives. They also practise listening and learn to show feelings.

SUPPLEMENTARY MATERIALS

Resource bank p161 and p162

Warm up

Review adjectives to describe feelings. Divide the class into two teams, then bring one member of each team to the front of the class and sit them with their backs to the board. Tell the teams to look at the word you write on the board and help their team member to guess what it is: they can do this by giving verbal clues or by miming. When one of the people with their back to the board calls out the word, they win a point for their team, and the next member from each team comes up to guess the next word, and so on.

Adjectives: *happy, cold, tired, hungry, ill, angry, surprised, unhappy, thirsty, well, scared, bored, interested* (leave out the last two if you feel your Ss will get confused between *bored/boring* and *interested/interesting*).

You could then direct Ss to the photos and ask them about the people's feelings, e.g. *the women in the cinema are happy.*

VOCABULARY adjectives

1A Go through the examples with the class, then put Ss in pairs to help each other with the meanings of the adjectives. Encourage Ss to discuss the meaning together first, before consulting their dictionaries. As you go through the answers, if Ss ask about the difference between *boring/bored* and *interesting/interested* (*bored* and *interesting* were introduced in unit 2), give them examples to show that *bored/interested* are for feelings, whereas *boring/interesting* describe places and things, e.g. *The Taj Mahal is interesting. The lesson was boring.*

Teaching tip

Ss can benefit from using an English to English dictionary, even at very low levels. Although it's challenging for them to understand an explanation in English, it will expose them to more English and be more memorable for them.

Answers:

+	–	+/–
great	awful	OK
fantastic	not very good	
interesting	boring	

B Tell Ss to mark the plus and minus signs next to the words in the table, and encourage them to help each other. When checking the answers, to avoid Ss making mistakes by saying *very delicious,* etc. you could write on the board:

delicious = very good ✓ ~~*very delicious*~~

Then check by asking *Is it OK to say 'very delicious'?* (*No*)

Answers: 1 great, fantastic, interesting 2 terrible, awful 3 delicious

C You may want to give Ss a chance to predict where the stress goes, before you play the recording.

Answers: terrible, delicious, OK, awful, great, fantastic, not very good, boring, interesting (N.B. This is usually pronounced with three syllables: Ooo)

2A You could give Ss some ideas for these names:

person: an actor, a singer, a politician

place: a city, a country, a shop, a café, a street

thing: a sport/game, a type of food, a drink, a book/magazine/newspaper, a type of music

B You could demonstrate this by saying the name of something yourself and pointing out that Ss should close their books while they're trying to guess (this will be more challenging because they'll have to remember the adjectives). Ss could report back at the end of this activity about something they have in common, e.g. *We both think R&B is great.*

➡ PHOTOBANK p145

There are nine more adjectives with their opposites in the **Photo bank**. Ss could do the exercises at this stage of the lesson, before the speaking practice (Ex 6) or for homework.

Answers:
A
2 I 3 A 4 F 5 C 6 D 7 G 8 H 9 B
B
1 far – near 2 soft – hard 3 heavy – light 4 dark – light
5 long – short 6 full – empty 7 expensive – cheap
8 noisy – quiet 9 fast – slow

FUNCTION giving opinions

3A Start by asking Ss which three situations are shown in the photos (a restaurant meal, a concert, a film). You may want to stop after the first conversation to check the example.

Answers: 2 R 3 C 4 P

B Give Ss a few moments to look through the phrases before you play the recording again. Then Ss can compare answers in pairs before checking with the class.

Answers: 2 d 3 h 4 e 5 b 6 c 7 f 8 a

Unit 7 Recording 9
Conversation 1
A: Hey, let's go!
B: What?
A: Let's go!
B: Why?
A: The film. It's terrible.
B: Really? I think it's great!
A: Oh, come on. Let's just go.
B: No, let's stay. Here, have a sweet.
A: Thanks a lot.
Conversation 2
A: How was your steak?
B: Delicious, just right. I really liked it. How was your chicken?
A: Urgh, I didn't like it. It wasn't very good.
B: Oh, well here's the ice cream. Thank you. Mmm, this is good.
A: Yes, this is nice.
Conversation 3
A: Hi.
B: Hi. How was the concert?
A: Fantastic! I loved it! The band was fantastic and the singer … she was great!
B: Oh, yeah, she is good.
A: So, are you free tomorrow?

Conversation 4

A: Hi, Mary. How are you?
B: Fine, thanks and you?
A: I'm OK. Um, were you at Warren's party last night?
B: Yeah.
A: How was it?
B: It was all right …
A: But … ?
B: Mmm. Well, it was boring – there weren't a lot of people there.
A: Ah.
B: So where were you?
A: Ah, well. I was at Alan's party.
B: Alan's party?
A: Yeah, uh, sorry …
B: Oh. How was it?
A: Er … it was very good.

4A You could do the first question with the class as an example. Ss work alone or in pairs on the rest of the questions and answers.

Answers: 1A: How was your steak? B: Delicious, just right.
2A: How was your chicken? B: It wasn't very good.
3A: How was the concert? B: The band was fantastic.
4A: How was the party? B: It was boring.

B Elicit/Remind Ss that we usually stress the words that carry the meaning of the sentence or phrase. Give them a minute or two in pairs to decide on the stressed words.

Answers: How was your steak? How was your chicken? How was the concert? How was the party?

C When Ss repeat the questions, encourage them to start with a high pitch (to show interest), and to use the weak form /wz/ for *was*. To help them to do this, you could start by modelling and asking them to repeat *How – steak? How –chicken?* etc., then add in *was your/was the* without changing the rhythm, so the unstressed words are 'squashed in' between the stressed ones.

D Point out that Ss need to stress the adjective in the answer, and that *was* is still pronounced /wz/ as in the question. Monitor the practice, so you can give Ss feedback on their pronunciation afterwards.

⇒ **LANGUAGEBANK** 7.3 p130–131

Ss could do Ex 7.3 in class or for homework.

Answers:
Conversation 1
A: Hi, Sally. *How* ~~Who~~ was the film?
B: It was *fantastic/very good* ~~delicious~~, really great.
A: Who was in it?
B: Tom Hanks.
A: How *was* ~~is~~ he?
B: He was fantastic.
Conversation 2
A: *How* ~~Who~~'s the chicken?
B: It's *not* very good – really awful.
A: Oh, I'm sorry.
B: How about your steak?
A: I'~~m~~ think it's OK.
B: And this restaurant is very expensive.
A: Yes, it is!

LEARN TO show feelings

5A Play the first conversation and check that Ss can hear that the voice is high. As you check the answers, ask Ss what difference the high or low voice makes to the opinion (i.e. positive versus negative).

Answers: 1 H 2 L 3 H 4 L

speakout TIP

Read the speakout tip with the class, and demonstrate the difference between the two intonation patterns. You could use you hand to show that the positive intonation starts much higher than the negative one.

B Demonstrate this by inviting one or two Ss to ask you a question and answering with high or low intonation. In each case, ask Ss whether you sounded positive or negative. Then Ss can give each other feedback on their intonation while they practise this in pairs.

Teaching tip

An effective way of giving Ss feedback on their intonation is for them to record themselves. You could encourage them to use their mobile phones to record themselves, then play back the recording and comment on each other's intonation.

SPEAKING

6A Start by eliciting some names of films that are showing currently, and the names of the main actors in them. Give Ss a few minutes to write out the sentences in their notebooks, or for *stronger classes*, Ss could work in pairs and say the lines. To check the answers, you could either elicit the lines and model them for Ss to repeat (if your Ss aren't very confident) or you could give Ss the complete dialogue as a key for them to check their answers against. N.B. You may want to highlight the use of *at* with *party* and *cinema*.

Answers: A: Where were you last night?
B: I was at Kelly's party. A: How was it? B: It wasn't very good. I didn't like it. A: Why not? B: The people were boring and the music was awful. Where were you?
A: I was at the cinema. B: Which film was it?
A: (name of film) B: How was it? A: It was great! I really liked it. B: Who was in it? A: (name of actor or actress). He/She was very good.

B Ss could work with new partners to role-play the conversation. Encourage them to look up from the page as much as possible, so they can concentrate on their intonation, rather than reading the prompts.

C Start by eliciting some names of restaurants and bands/ singers. Tell Ss to practise the conversation once with the prompts, changing them as necessary, then to close their books and try to remember as much as they can. Monitor and note down examples of good language use and problem areas, for praise and correction afterwards.

Homework ideas
• Ss write an email to a friend, telling them about something they did at the weekend and giving their opinion on it. They can finish the email by asking about their friend's weekend.
• **Workbook** Ex 1–3, p49

THE CHILEAN MINERS

Introduction

Ss watch a BBC extract from a news programme about the rescue of thirty-three miners from a mine in Copiapó, Chile, in 2010. Ss then learn and practise how to discuss the order of events in history and write questions for a history quiz.

SUPPLEMENTARY MATERIALS

Ex 4B: take in reference material about events in history, e.g. printed out from an internet search, or in reference books.

Warm up

Use the photo on p81 to lead in to the topic with the class. Ask Ss who the men are and where they work (miners, a mine). Then put Ss in pairs to discuss:

Is it a good job? Why/Why not?

Is it easy or difficult? Why?

What about a miner's wife and family?

In feedback on the discussion, elicit *dangerous* and *accident* (these words have been introduced in lesson 6.4), then ask if Ss know any examples of accidents in mines.

DVD PREVIEW

1A Look at the example and elicit/point out that *drill* is a noun and a verb. Put Ss in pairs to help each other, and use their dictionaries (preferably English–English) to check the vocabulary if necessary.

As you go through the answers, you could check the meaning and pronunciation of the following words, underlining the stressed syllables and asking questions that test whether Ss understand the meaning:

tunnel – *where else do you see a tunnel? (On a road or railway)*
microphone – *which other people use microphones? (singers, politicians)*
surface – *touch the surface of your desk*
accident – *when do you sometimes see accidents? (On a road, e.g. two cars, a car and a bike)*

Answers: miner C tunnel B microphone G note F
underground D surface E accident H

B Before Ss look at the sentences, elicit any information they know about the story. Then tell them to cover the text in Ex 1C and work in pairs on the sentences (you could display the sentences on the board for Ss to focus on, and avoid having them look at the text).

C Start by reading the title with the Ss and elicit/explain what a *rescue* is (to get someone out of a dangerous place or situation). Ss read the text and tick or adjust their answers in Ex 1B.

Answers: The programme information answers questions 1–6: 1 2010 2 an accident 3 33 4 17 5 a note 6 weeks

DVD VIEW

2A Remind Ss that they're looking for the answers to questions 7 and 8 from Ex 1B.

Answers: 7 at night (it was 11.20p.m.) 8 boss

B Check that Ss understand the words in the box and the following words from the sentences: *shelter* (the place where the miners stayed to keep out of danger), *healthy* (not ill), *positive* (not sad, confident). Ss complete the sentences in pairs or alone.

C Play the DVD again for Ss to check their answers.

Answers: 2 well 3 worked 4 families 5 rescue 6 minutes
7 travelled 8 days

Optional extra activity

Ss work in pairs and prepare a role-play between a rescued miner and a news reporter. You could give some prompts for possible questions for the interviewer, e.g.

Tell us about your life in the shelter.

Was it (difficult/boring)? Why?

Tell us about your feelings in the first days/after (four) weeks/when the rescue started.

How do you feel now?

Give Ss time to prepare and practise the role-play, providing help with vocabulary and grammar as required. Then invite a few pairs to act out their role-play for the class.

DVD 7 The Chilean Miners

2010, near Copiapó, Chile. The San José Mine. Thirty-three men. Sixty-nine days. This is their story.

August the fifth, 2010. It was two o'clock in the afternoon. Thirty-three miners were underground, seven hundred metres underground. There was a bad accident in the mine. Were the men dead or alive?

Workers started to drill down. They listened to microphones, but nothing.

August the twenty-second, 2010, day seventeen.

Finally, there was a note. It was from the miners; 'We are well in the shelter, the thirty-three.' The men were safe. The rescue wasn't easy, the drills worked day and night.

The miners worked to keep healthy and positive. The miners' families watched and waited. The world watched with them.

October the twelfth, 2010, day sixty-eight.

The tunnel was finished. The rescue started. It was eighteen minutes from the mine to the surface.

At twenty past eleven at night, the first man arrived to meet his family and friends.

Then, one by one, the miners travelled to the surface.

October the thirteenth, 2010, day sixty-nine.

Twenty-four hours later, the last man arrived. He was the boss, Luis Urzúa. After sixty-nine days, the miners were free.

speakout a history quiz

3A Start by checking that Ss can say the years on the timeline correctly, i.e. *nineteen eighty-six, two thousand and four,* etc. Also check that Ss are familiar with the four events to some degree. Give Ss time to discuss all four events and mark them on the timeline. You could suggest that Ss record themselves doing this (e.g. on their mobile phones), so they can later (e.g. after Ex 3C) listen and compare what they said with the people in the recording.

Culture notes

Michael Jackson (see notes for lesson 3.2), the 'King of Pop', died while preparing for a concert series *This Is It*.

Google is an American company best known for its search engine. It was founded by Larry Page and Sergey Brin.

The **Asian tsunami** killed over 230,000 people in fourteen countries (the worst affected was Indonesia). Some of the waves were nearly thirty metres high and the earthquake lasted nearly ten minutes.

The **Chernobyl nuclear accident** happened in Ukraine (at the time part of the USSR) in a plant near the city of Prypiat. An explosion released a large amount of radiation into the atmosphere, and spread over much of Western USSR and Europe.

B When Ss have listened to the recording, you could find out how many pairs got all four answers right.

Answers: a Michael Jackson died 2009 b Google started 1996 c Asian tsunami 2004 d Chernobyl nuclear accident 1986

C Give Ss a few moments to read the **Key phrases**. Check that Ss understand *It was before my time* (before I was born). Then play the recording again for Ss to tick the phrases.

Answers: Which was first? ✓
I think (Chernobyl ✓/the Asian tsunami ✓) was (first ✓/ next ✓).
Yes, I agree. ✓
I don't know./I'm not sure.
No, (Google) was before (the Asian tsunami). ✓
No, (it) was after (the Asian tsunami).
Which date? ✓
It was before my time.
I remember it well.
Let's check the answers. ✓
We were (right ✓/wrong ✓) about (three answers ✓/ Google. ✓)

Optional extra activity

To give Ss some practice of the **Key phrases** before they start doing the history quiz, make a copy (large enough to display on the board) of the phrases with gaps, e.g.

Which was ____?
I think (Chernobyl/the Asian tsunami) was (first/____).
Yes, I ____.
I don't ____./I'm not ____.
No, (Google) was ____ (the Asian tsunami).
No, (it) was ____ (the Asian tsunami).
Which ____?
It was before my ____.
I remember it ____.
Let's ____ the answers.
We were (right/____) about (three answers/Google).

Tell Ss to close their books and elicit the complete phrases from the class, one at a time, prompting the class to repeat the phrase in chorus and/or individually.

D Put Ss in small groups of three or four and direct them to the quiz. Remind them to use the **Key phrases**, both for doing the quiz and for checking their answers. Monitor and note down examples of good language use (especially of the **key phrases**) and any problem areas for praise and correction afterwards. Invite groups to report back to the class about which dates they got right/wrong.

Unit 7 Recording 11

A: OK, so which was first?
B: I think Chernobyl was first.
A: Yes, I agree. But which date? 1986 or 1991?
B: I think it was 1986.
A: OK let's put that. So, what was next?
B: I think Google started.
A: I'm not sure. Maybe the Asian tsunami?
B: No, Google was before the Asian tsunami.
A: OK. Which date?
B: Erm … 1991, I think.
A: OK. 1991.
B: And I think the Asian tsunami was next, in 2004. I remember it well. It was in December at the end of the year.
A: OK, so that's 2004. And Michael Jackson?
B: He died in 2009, I think.
A: 2009. Right, let's check the answers.
A: OK, we were right about three answers. The Chernobyl nuclear accident was in 1986, the Asian tsunami was in 2004 and Michael Jackson died in 2009.
B: But we were wrong about Google?
A: Yes. Google didn't start in 1991. It started in 1996.

writeback a history quiz

4A You could go through the quiz with the whole class (e.g. divided into two or three teams), or put Ss in pairs to discuss it. Then check the answers at the bottom of the page.

B Direct Ss back to the quiz in Ex 4A and focus on the beginning of the questions, i.e. *When were … ? Which … was … ? Why was … ?* Elicit some other possibilities, e.g. *Who was … ? Where was … ? What was … ?* N.B. Ss can only write questions with *was/were*: try to direct them away from making questions in the past with any other verbs. Ss could research their questions on the internet if there is access in class, or on their phones. Otherwise, you could bring in some material, either printed from the internet (e.g. via a search such as: *important historical events in the 20th century*), or from reference books.

Ss work on their questions alone or in pairs. Circulate and help as required, especially with the word order in the questions.

Homework ideas

• Ss write a quiz with five questions. If they're from the same country, they research and write questions about different countries. If they're from different countries, they research and write questions about their own country. Ss can swap quizzes in the next lesson.

LOOKBACK

PAST SIMPLE: *WAS/WERE*

1A Tell Ss they need to write the name of another student next to each statement 1–8. Give them a few minutes to write the questions in their notebooks: point out that all the questions should use the positive form of the verb, even when they want a negative answer.

> **Answers:** 2 Were you tired this morning? 3 Were you in the town/city centre at the weekend? 4 Were you here in the last class? 5 Were you in a café before class? 6 Were you on a train at eight o'clock this morning? 7 Were you late for something yesterday? 8 Were you ill yesterday?

B Demonstrate how the activity works by inviting three Ss to ask you the first three questions. Answer *No, I wasn't* to 1 and 2 and *Yes, I was* to 3, and ask Ss where they should write your name (i.e. next to number 3, but not 1 or 2). Point out that Ss should write the names of the people they find on the left of the statements in Ex 1A. Put Ss in groups of six or, preferably, ask Ss to stand up and walk around asking their questions: in this way they will talk to more people and have more chance of getting an answer to all their questions. Encourage Ss to give reasons for their answers, e.g.
Were you here in the last class?
No, I wasn't, because I was at the dentist.
When Ss have finished, ask some of them to tell the class what they found out.

DATES

2A You could ask a student to come and write the date on the board and ask the rest of the class to check it.

B You could do the first date (for *yesterday*) with the class, as an example. Then give Ss a few minutes to write the other dates, working alone.

C Demonstrate this by asking a student to say one of the time phrases, and choose another student to say the appropriate date. Then put Ss in pairs to continue.

D Give Ss time to write their dates, then repeat Ex 2C. For *stronger classes* you could ask Ss to do this orally, without writing their list of dates first.

ACTIONS

3A You could run this as a competition in teams. Write or display the words on the board, one at a time. When a team member guesses a word, they put up their hand or 'buzz' to answer, then they have to both say the word and spell it correctly to win a point.

> **Answers:** 2 talk 3 dance 4 arrive 5 laugh 6 cry 7 start 8 walk

B Look at the example with the class, then give Ss a few minutes to complete the sentences, working alone.

> **Answers:** 2 arrive 3 starts 4 talks 5 walk 6 dance 7 cry 8 wait

C Demonstrate this by telling Ss one sentence which is true for you and changing another to make it true. For *stronger classes,* tell Ss to change the sentences orally, rather than writing them out in full.

PAST SIMPLE: REGULAR VERBS

4A Start by eliciting the three ways of making the past of regular verbs: add -*ed*, add -*d*, change -*y* to -*ied*. When you go though the answers, check Ss' pronunciation of the past forms, i.e. watched /t/, waited /ɪd/, phoned /d/.

> **Answers:** 2 waited 3 phoned 4 asked 5 laughed 6 played 7 cried 8 studied 9 stopped 10 danced

B You may want to give Ss some repetition practice of *when was the last time you … ?* and make sure that they're using the weak form /wz/. Go through the example or demonstrate the activity yourself, showing Ss that they should explain what happened, as well as saying when. N.B. If Ss haven't done the action, they can answer: *Never.*

ADJECTIVES

5A You could run this as a race in pairs. The first pair to finish put their hands up, then read the word and the missing vowels only, e.g. *terrible: e, i, e.* If they make a mistake, another pair can take over, and so on.

> **Answers:** 1 terrible 2 delicious 3 interesting 4 awful 5 fantastic 6 boring 7 great 8 all right 9 not very good 10 OK

B Point out that Ss can either agree with each other and use adjectives with a similar meaning (as in the example) or disagree, e.g.
A: *The concert was terrible!*
B: *Oh no, I think it was great!*

GIVING OPINIONS

6A Give Ss a few minutes to number the sentences, working alone.

> **Answers:**
> A: Why not? 3
> B: Because the food was terrible. And the film? 4
> A: It was great. 5
> B. How was it for Anne? 6
> A: She thinks it was all right. 7

B Give Ss time to practise the conversation once or twice (swapping roles), then put the following prompts on the board. Then ask Ss to close their books and practise the conversation again, using the prompts:
restaurant?
good X
?
food/terrible. film?
great
Anne?
all right

OVERVIEW

NICE PLACE TO MEET

Introduction

Students practise reading and talking about meeting people for the first time, using past simple irregular verbs and prepositions of place.

SUPPLEMENTARY MATERIALS

Resource bank p163 and p165

Warm up

Review names of places. Ask Ss to close their books and draw two columns in their notebooks, with a + and – sign at the top of each. Tell Ss to write the words that you dictate (see below) under the + or – column, depending on whether they have positive or negative feelings about the place: *café, cinema, supermarket, bank, gym, hospital, hotel, market, airport, school, park, club, zoo, station.*

Then put Ss in pairs or small groups to compare answers and explain why they wrote the words in the + or – column, e.g. *airport is in the positive column because I think of holidays.*

READING

1A Establish that Ss are thinking about the first meeting with a new friend and elicit an example from the class before putting Ss into pairs.

> **Possible answers:** at a party, at a café, at a friend's house, at school/university/an evening class, at work, at the gym, on holiday.

B You could use the photos to lead into the text. For each photo, ask Ss what the place is (teach *rope bridge* in the first photo), and whether it's somewhere you usually meet a new friend. Then tell Ss to read the stories and number them 1–4, starting with 1 for the most unusual. Ss can then discuss their choices in pairs or with the whole class.

C Tell Ss to cover the text before doing this exercise. They could work in pairs and help each other to find and correct the mistakes.

D Ss read the text to confirm the correct information, then check again in pairs. N.B. If individual Ss ask you about any of the irregular past forms in the text while they're reading, tell them it's a verb in the past and encourage them to guess which verb it is. Reassure them that you are going to study these verbs next.

> **Answers:** 1 The bridge was in Northern ~~Scotland.~~ *Ireland* 2 Cynthia and Anne were on the bridge for ~~an hour.~~ *half an hour* 3 The taxi driver worked in ~~London.~~ *New York City* 4 Darnell worked at a ~~shop.~~ *club* 5 Jon was in a ~~train~~ accident. *car* 6 Jon was in hospital for a ~~month.~~ *week* 7 Someone took Alison's ~~passport.~~ *money* 8 The waitress said, 'Do you need ~~money?'~~ *help*

GRAMMAR: past simple: irregular verbs

2A You could use the first story in the text to show Ss the difference between regular and irregular verbs. First, ask them to underline the examples of *were* in the text (there are three examples), then to underline the regular verbs (*walked* x 2, *helped*), then to find two more past verbs (*met* and *came*); elicit the present forms of these verbs (*meet* and *come*). Establish that irregular verbs do not add *-ed* in the past, but their form changes in different ways. Remind Ss that, like regular verbs, the past form is the same for all persons. Give Ss a few minutes to find the irregular verbs in the text and compare answers in pairs and/or with the whole class. Check *become* by using a timeline:

you meet ➜ *you talk* ➜ *you like the person* ➜ *you become friends*

Answers: 2 came 3 took 4 thought 5 became 6 broke 7 went 8 had 9 sat 10 said

B Encourage Ss to repeat the present and past forms together to help them remember the combination. You could also put Ss in pairs to 'test' each other on the past or present form, e.g.

Student A: *take*   Student B: *took*
Student B: *broke*   Student A: *break*

C Give Ss a minute or two to find the example in the text (it's in Alison's story). Establish that, as with regular verbs, *didn't* indicates the past, so the main verb stays in its present form.

speakout TIP

Before Ss read the speakout tip, you could ask them how they can find the past of an irregular verb and establish that any good dictionary will have this information. Give Ss a minute to read the speakout tip and emphasise the importance of keeping good records of past forms in their notebooks, so they can refer back to them and try to use them whenever possible. You could suggest that they keep a separate section of their notebooks for verbs and their past forms, and give them a few minutes to record the five verbs given: *drive – drove, know – knew, stay (reg), see – saw, give – gave.*

Optional extra activity

Ask Ss to find three ways of saying 'be very good friends' in the text:

be/become friends for life

be/become great friends

be/become (instant) best friends

Ss can make a note of these to use in the speaking practice (Ex 6).

⏩ LANGUAGEBANK 8.1 p132–133

Give Ss a few minutes to look at the summary and examples. You could use Ex 8.1A for basic practice in manipulating the positive and negative past forms of some common irregular verbs. Ex 8.1B is another story about an unusual place to meet: when Ss have completed the story and checked their answers, they could work in pairs and take turns to close their books and try to remember as much of the story as they can.

Answers:
A 2 take 3 say 4 thought 5 became 6 sat
B 2 went 3 became 4 saw 5 didn't have 6 had
7 broke 8 gave 9 ate 10 had 11 drove

PRACTICE

3A Tell Ss to read the stories quickly and decide which two people from the *Unusual Stories* text are speaking.

Answers: Darnell and Claudia

B Give Ss a few minutes to complete the stories, working alone. As you go through the answers in feedback, check spelling and pronunciation of the past verb forms.

Answers: 2 finished 3 didn't want 4 stopped 5 drove 6 thought 7 became 8 worked 9 saw 10 went 11 said 12 didn't have 13 didn't know 14 gave

C Demonstrate how to change things in a story, e.g.
In the 1980s, I was a singer at a theatre in New York.
I worked as a waitress at a café in 2009.

Give Ss a couple of minutes to change things in their stories.

D You could demonstrate this by starting to tell story 1 as in the example above, and indicate that Ss should say *Stop!* and correct you.

Optional extra activity

Refer Ss to the story in the **Language bank** Ex 8.1B, about how a man met his wife, Manuela. In pairs, Ss rewrite the story from the point of view of Manuela. Tell them they can invent any extra information they need, e.g. *One Saturday afternoon in 2008 I was on a mountain in Scotland. I lived near the mountain and I often walked there …*

Two or three pairs then read out their stories and see what's similar/different about them.

VOCABULARY prepositions of place

4A You could go through these sentences with the whole class, referring Ss back to the photo on page 84 for *on a bridge,* and reminding them that we use *in* for towns, cities and countries. You could also explain that we say *at work, at school* for places we go to regularly. See more on *at* vs *in* below.

Answers: 1 on   2 in   3 at

B Give Ss time to look carefully at the word webs and help each other decide on the correct preposition. If Ss ask whether it's also possible to say *in Dublin airport,* you could demonstrate, e.g. by drawing a box with sides and a person inside it, that with some places (also *station, café, restaurant, office*) we use *in* if we think of the space as three-dimensional, but we use *at* if we think of the place as a point, as we would a point on a map.

Answers: 1 at   2 in   3 on

Optional extra activity

Ss look back through the *Unusual Stories* text to find other examples of *at* and *in* and add them to the word webs.

Answers:

at night, at a club, at 4a.m.

in the centre, in New York, in the 1990s, in hospital, in a car accident, in my room

N.B. *club* and *hospital* are further examples of places that can be used with *at* or *in*, depending on how you think of them.

5A Ss work on the sentences alone, then compare answers in pairs.

Answers: 2 I met one of my friends *on* the internet. 3 I went *on* holiday with a friend last year.   4 I met a great friend *in* my English class last month.   5 I was *at* a friend's party on Saturday.   6 I had lunch with a friend *in* the city centre yesterday.

B Demonstrate this by making one of the sentences true about you. Give Ss time to tick and/or change the sentences, then put them in pairs to read out and compare sentences.

⫸ PHOTOBANK p146

Use these exercises to give Ss further practice of the prepositions *in, on, at,* as well as *under* and *over.* Ss could do these for homework.

Answers:

A

A in   B on   C on   D at   E over   F under

B

1 The cat's ~~over~~ on the table.   2 There's a man ~~in~~ *under* a car.   3 There's a plane ~~at~~ *over* the sea.   4 There are two elephants ~~over~~ *in* a river.   5 I live ~~on~~ *at* number sixty-six. 6 Rome is ~~in~~ *on* the River Tiber.

SPEAKING

6A Give Ss time to prepare their timetable and to make notes about how they met each person (e.g. what they did, what they said, etc.) and why they liked them. Encourage them to look back at the stories in Ex 1 and 3 for ideas.

B Put Ss into groups of four to six and invite a stronger student in each group to start talking about their timeline. Encourage the listeners to ask questions at the end. Monitor the practice and make notes of good language use and any problem areas for praise and correction afterwards.

N.B. For the next lesson, ask Ss to bring some photos from their last holiday: these could be photos downloaded from the internet of the place(s) they went to or their own personal photos. They could also bring a map which shows the location of the place(s) they went to.

Homework ideas

• Ss write three stories about their three friends from the timeline in Ex 6. In the next lesson, you can collect in the stories and redistribute them so that each student has someone else's stories. They read the stories and guess who the writer is.

• Workbook Ex 1–6, p50–51

GOOD AND BAD

Introduction

Ss practise listening to people talking about good and bad holidays. They practise talking about holidays, using vocabulary related to holiday activities and past simple questions. They also learn how to use *so* and *because* in writing.

SUPPLEMENTARY MATERIALS

Resource bank p164

Ex 6B: bring in some photos from your last holiday and a map of where you went.

Warm up

Lead in to the topic of holidays.

Tell Ss to close their books and put the following questions on the board: *When was the last time you went on holiday? Was it a good holiday? Why/Why not?*

Prompt Ss to ask you the questions and in your answer include an explanation of when and where you went and why it was/ wasn't a good holiday. Then put Ss in pairs to do the same.

VOCABULARY holiday activities

1A Before Ss start the activity, check *local* Oo (from the place or area) and the pronunciation of *building* (the *u* is not pronounced). Ss can work alone or with a partner to match the verbs and nouns. As you go through the answers, you could ask Ss for examples of the local food from their area.

Answers: 2 d) 3 a) 4 b) 5 g) 6 h) 7 e) 8 f)

B Give Ss a minute or two to discuss the pictures.

Answers: eat the local food, see old buildings, meet the local people, go camping

C Demonstrate this with a **strong student**, showing the class that they should take turns to be A and B, so they both get practice in saying the complete phrases. When Ss have finished, check the past forms of all the verbs. Then Ss can repeat the activity, this time adding a pronoun in front of the verb, e.g.
A: *old buildings.* B: *I saw old buildings.*

D Give Ss a few moments to read the example, then put them in pairs to ask and answer. Afterwards, ask two or three Ss to report back about their partner.

LISTENING

2A Give Ss a few minutes to read through the list and decide on their order. Tell them to be prepared to justify their choices.

B You could demonstrate this by telling Ss which holiday you put first/last and indicating that they should ask you why, then justify your choice. Put Ss in pairs to compare and justify their choices. They could then report back about any choices in common, e.g. *We both put a holiday in Sydney for number one.*

3A Tell Ss that they'll hear different people talking about the holidays in Ex 2A, and that they should just listen for whether each holiday was good or bad.

Answers: a) G b) B c) B d) G e) G

B Give Ss time to read through the sentences and check *lose/ lost* (mime searching for something in your pockets/bag) and *lunch* vs *dinner* (midday vs evening meal). Also remind Ss that *get to/got to = arrive(d) in*. Ss can work in pairs to help each

other remember the correct information before listening again to check whether they were right.

Answers: 2 television 3 passport 4 food 5 got 6 dinner 7 Chinese 8 spoke

Unit 8 Recording 2

A: Welcome to *Good and Bad*. This week we talk about holidays – good ones and bad ones. Our hotline is 123 2222. And here's our first caller. Hello, Ken?

B: Hi.

A: So, tell us about your two holidays.

B: Yeah, well my family went camping in Canada when I was twelve. We had one tent for six people, and we didn't have water or electricity.

A: Oh, right. Did you like it?

B: Yes, I did. It was … fantastic. No TV, no internet … we cooked on a fire and played games.

A: Sounds great. And your other holiday?

B: Last year I went to Sydney with my girlfriend. I lost my passport on the first day.

A: Sorry to hear that.

B: But Sydney was beautiful. We saw some interesting buildings and lovely museums … but then I ate some bad food … fish … and I was very ill.

A: Ow. So that was a bad holiday. But as you say Sydney's a beautiful city.

B: Yes, it is.

A: OK, Ken. Thank you for calling. Next caller, Clare? Are you there?

C: Yeah, hello.

A: Hi. Tell us about your holidays.

B: Well, last year we went to France.

A: Oh, where did you go?

B: We went to Paris, but … there was a problem with the plane. We waited for ten hours at the airport. Then they said there weren't any seats on the next plane. Or the next plane.

A: Oh, no! What did you do?

B: We went by train! We had five hours in Paris then we came home.

A: By plane?

B: No, by train. We had dinner on the train. Expensive sandwiches.

A: So that wasn't very good. How about your other holiday? The good one?

C: Ah yes, it was in China. I was there for two months. I was alone, so I met a lot of local people. They were very nice.

A: Did you speak English with them?

C: No, I didn't. I spoke a little Chinese and they liked that.

A: Great. Thanks, Clare. And next we have Dan. Hi, Dan.

D: Hi.

A: Is your first holiday good or bad?

D: Good – really good. I went to Peru. It was a walking holiday and it was wonderful.

A: Why was that?

D: Well I went with a friend and we …

Optional extra activity

Write the following phrases on the board:

____ on a fire	____ five hours in Paris
____ lovely museums	____ games
____ for ten hours at the airport	____ very ill

Ss complete the phrases with the past form of the appropriate verbs (*cooked, saw, waited, had, played, was*) and check their answers in the audio script. Then they tell each other when they last did any of these things on holiday.

GRAMMAR past simple: questions

4A Play the recording once for Ss to listen to the questions and answers, then again for them to complete the table. Point out that *did* always comes before the pronoun, and that in a *Wh-* question, the *wh-* word comes before *did*.

Answers:

Questions and short answers						
Did	you	like	it?	Yes,	I	*did.*
		speak	English?	No,		*didn't.*
Wh- questions						
Where	*did*	you	go?			
What			do?			

B Play the recording again and ask Ss how the speaker says *Did you … ?* Highlight the way that the final *-d* and initial *y-* merge together and make a 'j' sound, then model this for Ss to repeat. Play the recording again for them to repeat the complete questions (paying attention to their intonation) and answers.

➡ **LANGUAGEBANK** 8.2 p132–133

Give Ss a few minutes to read the **Language bank** and look at the examples of *Wh-* questions. Highlight that the question form is the same for regular and irregular verbs. You could use Ex 8.2A for some basic question and answer practice with irregular verbs and Ex 8.2B to review *Wh-* question words.

Answers:
A
2 A: Did, meet B: didn't, met 3 A: Did, dance B: did, danced 4 A: Did, see B: didn't, saw
5 A: Did, write B: did, wrote 6 A: Did, have B: did, had
B
2 Where did you go? 3 What did you eat? 4 What did you drink? 5 What did you see? 6 When/What time did you come home?

PRACTICE

5A You could do the first question as an example with the class, then tell Ss to write the questions in their notebooks.

Answers: 1 Did you go on holiday last summer? 2 Did you have good weather on holiday? 3 Did you eat in a restaurant yesterday? 4 Did you meet your friends last night? 5 Did you speak English yesterday? 6 Did you have breakfast this morning?

B Tell Ss to write the completed answers next to the relevant questions in their notebooks.

Answers: 2 Yes, we did. It was very hot. 3 No, I didn't. I ate at home yesterday. 4 No, I didn't. I met my friends last weekend. 5 Yes, I did. I spoke English with my teacher. 6 Yes, we did. We had toast and coffee.

C Give Ss a few minutes to think about their answers to the questions. You could direct them to Ex 1A on weather vocabulary in the **Photo bank** at this point, so they can use the vocabulary to answer about the weather on holiday. Before Ss start asking and answering in pairs, you could put prompts on the board for the questions in Ex 5A and use them to give Ss pronunciation practice, with a focus on intonation and the linking in *Did you … ?* e.g. *go / holiday / summer ?*

➡ **PHOTOBANK** p146

Use these exercises to help Ss learn to talk about the weather. Give Ss a few minutes to go through Ex 1A. Check answers, then put Ss in pairs for Ex 1B.

Answers: A 1 D 3 E 4 C 5 A 6 B

SPEAKING

6A N.B. If Ss have brought in photos, a map, etc. from a holiday, they should refer to them while they make notes for this speaking activity, and think about when to incorporate them, e.g. use the map to show where they went, use the photos to show who they went with, the weather, what they did. Show them the example of notes for question one and give them time to prepare their own, asking their partners or you for help with vocabulary, etc. as needed.

B You could demonstrate by inviting Ss to ask you about a good holiday that you had, and show them your map and photos as you answer their questions. Then put Ss in groups of four to do the same. Monitor carefully and make notes of good language use and any problem areas for praise and correction afterwards.

WRITING so and *because*

7A Start by eliciting some ideas from Ss about mistakes people make when they plan/book a holiday, e.g. they go in the summer holidays, the hotel is expensive, etc. Then give Ss a minute or two to match the decision to the mistake. In the meantime, write sentences 1–3 on the board.

Answers: 1 c 2 a 3 b

B Underline *so* and *because* in the sentences on the board and establish that *because* answers the question *why?*

C Write the two sentences on the board and go through the answers with the class. Point out that *so = that's why* (it gives the reason).

8A Ss work on this exercise alone before comparing answers.

Answers: 1 Our plane was at eleven *so* we got to the airport at quarter past ten. 2 I didn't book a hotel *because* I didn't have time. 3 We went to New Zealand in July *because* we have school holidays in the summer. 4 We didn't find any mineral water *so* we drank the local water.

B Look at the example with the class and elicit a possible ending, e.g. *so we missed our flight.* If Ss need some help with ideas for situations 2–4, put the following prompts on the board:
sleep / car / hotels / full
July / winter / New Zealand / weather / cold
ill / water / bad

Homework ideas
• **Workbook Ex 1–5, p52–53**

WHERE'S THE FRUIT?

Introduction

Ss practise listening to and giving directions using prepositions of place. They also learn to use examples.

SUPPLEMENTARY MATERIALS

Resource bank p166

Ex 6 (optional extra activity): prepare cards for students A and B (see notes).

Warm up

Review the names of things you can buy in a supermarket. Say *I went to the supermarket and I bought (bread)* then indicate that the student sitting nearest you should continue by saying *I went to the supermarket and I bought bread and (cheese)*. They choose another student to continue, who has to remember the two things already mentioned and add one more, and so on. If a student can't remember everything, they say *Pass* and choose another student to continue. To make the activity more challenging, say the items in alphabetical order. N.B. Avoid using *some (bread)* because Ss haven't studied uncountable nouns.

VOCABULARY prepositions

1A Look at the example with the class, then put Ss in pairs to match the other prepositions to the pictures. As you go through the answers, check the stress on <u>opposite, be<u>tween</u></u>, be<u>hind</u> and <u>next</u> to. Also check the difference between *in front of* and *opposite*: the two things/people are facing each other if they are *opposite*.

Answers: on the left of A, in front of E, near D, behind F, between G, next to C, opposite H

B N.B. For picture H, point out that Ss need to say *Where is the ball? It's opposite the box.*

Alternative approach

Tell Ss to close their books. Use objects on your desk to show Ss the eight prepositions in Ex 1A. One at a time, position the objects and ask: *Where's the (key)?* eliciting the preposition from the Ss if possible. Ss can then open their books and do Ex 1A.

Then put Ss in pairs to practise with their own objects on their desks: Student A gives an instruction and Student B moves the objects into the correct position, and so on.

2A Check *window* and *noticeboard* before Ss read through the sentences. They can tick the sentences that are true, then check with a partner.

B Change one sentence with the class as an example, e.g. *There are windows opposite the door.* Ss work in pairs on the other sentences. They could also add one or two sentences of their own and read these out to the class.

Optional extra activity

In groups, each student draws a simple picture showing the location of two or three items, e.g. a cat, a chair, a book. Then they whisper a sentence describing the picture to the person next to them, etc. until it gets back to the original student – they then see if the sentence that came back to them is the same as in the picture.

FUNCTION giving directions

3A Direct Ss to the photo and ask them what the man's problem is (e.g. *he forgot his shopping list/he doesn't know where things are in the supermarket*). Give Ss time to read through the types of food and check *cereal* (e.g. cornflakes) and *snacks* (small amounts of food you eat between meals, at a party, at the cinema, etc.). Point out that while they listen to the recording Ss just need to write the numbers 2 and 3 next to the appropriate food.

Answers: bread 2 cakes 3

B Establish that Ss need to write a letter for a section of the supermarket next to each food. Also point out (using the diagram or a simple board drawing) that *opposite* is used to describe two sections that are across the aisle from each other. Play the recording again.

Answers: bread e cereal d cakes a

Unit 8 Recording 4

Conversation 1

A: Excuse me, where's the fruit?
B: Do you see the vegetables over there?
A: Vegetables? What are they?
B: Vegetables … you know, tomatoes, potatoes, carrots.
A: Oh, vegetables.
B: Yeah. Vegetables
A: OK … vegetables.
B: The fruit's behind the vegetables.
A: Sorry?
B: You see the vegetables? They're in front of the fruit. Over there.
A: Let me check. The fruit's behind the vegetables.
B: Yes, that's right.
A: Oh, OK. Thanks.
B: No problem.

Conversation 2

A: Excuse me, where's the bread?
B: Er … Do you see the snacks?
A: Snacks? I don't know 'snacks'.
B: Snacks, for example, chocolate, nuts and crisps.
A: Oh, I understand.
B: The bread is on the right of the snacks.
A: Can I check? On the right of the snacks?
B: Yes. Opposite the fruit.
A: Thank you.
B: You're welcome.

Conversation 3

A: Excuse me, where are the cakes?
B: I think they're near the snacks.
A: Near the snacks. Which way?
B: I'm not sure. I know the cereal is opposite the snacks …
A: Cereal? What's that?
B: Cereal. Like Corn Flakes.
A: Er … ?
B: Erm, for breakfast. You have it with milk.
A: Oh, OK.
B: Yes, so the cereal is opposite the snacks.
A: OK, and the cakes?
B: I think they're on the right of the cereal.
A: On the right. Thank you.
B: No problem. Or maybe …
A: Thank you!

Optional extra activity
Use the diagram for further practice of the prepositions. Tell Ss to write the names of each type of food in the correct section, and to allocate sections b and c to meat and fish. Then Ss work in pairs and take turns asking and answering *Where's the … ?/Where are the … ? It's (behind) the …/They're (next to) the …* For more challenge, tell the person answering that they need to give at least two prepositions for each type of food, e.g. *Where's the cereal? It's opposite the drinks, and in front of the cakes.*

4A Ss could complete the conversation in pairs or working alone. For *stronger classes*, you could tell Ss to cover the words in the box and try to complete the gaps with their own ideas. N.B. At this level, treat *Let me check* as a fixed phrase.

Answers: 2 where 3 Do 4 see 5 over 6 of 7 Let 8 behind

B Before putting Ss in pairs, you could model the lines of the conversation for them to repeat in chorus, focusing on stress and polite intonation. When Ss have practised the conversation once or twice reading from the book, encourage them to try to remember as much as they can or to write one or two word prompts for each line, then tell them to close their **Student's Books** and practise again.

> **⯈ LANGUAGEBANK** 8.3 p132–133
> Give Ss time to read through the summary, including *Can I check?* as an alternative to *Let me check*. You could use Ex 8.3 for further conversation practice in pairs.
>
> **Answers:** A: Excuse me, where ~~is~~ are the sweets?
> B: ~~Are~~ Do you see the newspapers over there?
> A: Where?
> B: Over there, near ~~of~~ the snacks.
> A: Oh, yes.
> B: Well, the sweets are next to the newspapers, on the right.
> A: Can I check? They're on the left of the newspapers.
> B: No, they're on the right.
> A: Ah, yes. Thanks a lot.
> B: No problem.

LEARN TO use examples
5A Before you play the recording, give Ss time to read the conversations and try to predict the missing words.

Answers: 1 What 2 know 3 example 4 that 5 Like

Unit 8 Recording 5
1
A: Vegetables? What are they?
B: Vegetables … you know, tomatoes, potatoes, carrots.
A: Oh, vegetables.
2
B: Do you see the snacks?
A: Snacks? I don't know 'snacks'.
B: Snacks, for example, chocolate, nuts and crisps.
A: Oh, I understand.
3
A: Cereal? What's that?
B: Cereal. Like Corn Flakes.

speakout TIP
Before Ss read the speakout tip, ask them to look through the three conversations and find three ways of giving examples. Then they can read the tip to check. You could also play the recording for Ss to repeat the three ways of giving examples, and point out that there is a pause after *you know* and *for example*, so their intonation should rise on *know* and *example*. After *like* there is no pause.

B Ss could practise the conversations twice, so they take turns to be A and B.

C You could demonstrate this with a **strong student** taking the part of A. Check that Ss understand *dairy*.

SPEAKING
6A Give Ss a few minutes to decide where to put the types of food and to think about how to explain where they are in relation to the other sections.

B Do an example with the class first, showing Ss that they shouldn't show their diagram to their partner, and making sure that they realise where they're standing, so they can use *behind* and *in front of* accurately. Monitor carefully, making notes of any good language use and any problem areas for praise and correction afterwards.

Optional extra activity
Put Ss in pairs and explain that Student A is a visitor to Student B's city/town (i.e. the city/town where Ss are studying). Student A wants to buy some things and asks Student B who explains where to find them in the town, e.g.
A: *Excuse me, I want to buy (pens).*
B: *OK, go to (name of shop). It's in (name) street, (next to/opposite/near) …*
Tell Student B that if they don't understand what Student A wants, they should ask for examples.
Give Student A the following on a card/slip of paper:
You want to buy …
… jewellery (rings, earrings, bracelets).
… stationery (paper, pens, pencils).
Then Student B is the visitor, with the following on a card/slip of paper:
You want to buy …
… toiletries (soap, toothpaste, deodorant).
… furniture (tables, chairs, beds).

Homework ideas
- Ss have a friend staying with them who has offered to go to the supermarket for them. They write a note to leave on the kitchen table for their friend, telling them five things they need, and where to find them in the supermarket. Check that Ss know *aisle*, e.g. *it's in the second aisle/the biscuits and snacks aisle.*
- Workbook Ex1–3, p54

GUIDED TOUR

Introduction

Ss watch an extract from the BBC comedy show *Little Britain*, about people on holiday in Spain and their rude tour guide. Ss then learn and practise how to tell and write a story about a bad holiday.

SUPPLEMENTARY MATERIALS

Ex 4C (optional extra activity): make a copy of the **key phrases** to display on the board with the past verb forms removed.

Ex 6 (alternative approach): make copies of the story divided into five parts (see notes).

Warm up

Review some common verb + noun collocations. Tell Ss to write each of the following verbs inside a circle, with three 'branches' from each circle, for them to add nouns/phrases: *take, have, stay, go.*

Read out the following nouns and phrases for Ss to write next to the correct verb: *a photo, fun, dinner, home, in bed, a tour, a good time, at home, a bus/train, out in the evening, in a hotel, on holiday.*

Give Ss a few minutes to compare answers in pairs, and check their spelling.

Answers: *take: a photo, a tour, a bus/train*

have: fun, dinner, a good time

stay: in bed, at home, in a hotel

go: home, out in the evening, on holiday

DVD PREVIEW

1A Give Ss a few minutes to tick the appropriate sentences and tell them to be prepared to justify their answers using *because*, e.g. *On holidays, I always read about the place because I want to see all the important things.*

B Put Ss in pairs and encourage them to ask each other follow-up questions, e.g.

A: *I always relax and do nothing because that's the meaning of 'holiday' for me!*

B: *Where do you relax?*

A: *On the beach or by the pool.*

2 Ask four Ss to read the questions aloud to the class and check that Ss understand *funny* (demonstrate by laughing), *tour guide* (or *rep*, short for *representative*, which is how Carol describes herself in the extract), *episode* (a TV programme that is part of a series). Then direct Ss to the text: when they've decided if the sentences are true or false they can compare answers in pairs.

Answers: 1 T – it's a *comedy.* 2 F – a man (David Walliams) plays Carol. 3 F – she's rude 4 T

Culture notes

Little Britain is a sketch show which features exaggerated parodies of British people in various situations familiar to the British. A narrator comments on the sketches in a way which suggests that the programme is a guide – for non-British people – to the ways of life of different classes in British society.

Majorca is a very popular tourist destination for the British because of its good weather and cheap prices, and because there are a lot of British people there, British products are readily available – it's like a sunny version of Britain.

▷ DVD VIEW

3A Ss use the text to help them decide which photo is Carol.

B Ss watch to confirm which photo is Carol. You could also ask them if they find the extract funny, and why/why not? (For example, Carol's facial expression, her voice, her bad pronunciation of Spanish).

Answer: Carol is on the right.

C Give Ss time to read through the phrases before you play the extract again. They can compare answers in pairs and/or with the whole class.

Answers: a) 5 b) 3 c) 6 e) 2 f) 4 g) 7

D Give Ss a minute or two to think of ideas in pairs, then discuss them with the whole class. Possible ideas: they take a taxi to the hotel, they walk, they hitch a lift from someone on the road, they complain to the tour company.

Optional extra activity

Ss work in groups of three and role-play the conversation between the couple from the DVD extract and the tour company manager. They explain what happened, and the manager apologises and offers some kind of compensation. Give Ss time to prepare the conversation, and help with vocabulary as necessary. The groups then act out their conversation for the class.

DVD 8 Guided Tour

N=Narrator M=Man W=Woman C=Carol

N: Spain is very popular for tourists from Britain. Here in Majorca Carol Beer is the friendly tour guide for Sunsearchers Holidays.

M: Sunsearchers, ah, this must be us, dear.

W: Morning.

M: Morning.

C: Hello, my name is Carol. I am your rep. Welcome to Spain. If you look to your left, you'll see Spain. If you look to your right, you'll see Spain. Now I'm here to make sure your holiday is fun, fun, fun. Fun. Any questions or problems, come to me.

M: Excuse me. … Excuse me.

C: Yes, old man?

M: Sorry, sorry, ah, my wife's feeling rather nauseous. Do you think it would be possible just to stop the coach for a moment so she can get out and get some air?

C: 'Gonzalez, ¿puedes parar el bus?'

M: Thank you. Thank you, excuse me. OK, alright.

C: 'Gonzalez, vamos.'

M: OK, yeah? It must be something you had on the plane or …

W: My stomach!

M: … Hey, hey, hey, hey! Hey, hey! It's alright.

speakout a bad holiday story

4A You could write on the board: *The man had a bad holiday because …* and tell Ss to think of as many reasons as they can, in pairs. Remind them that they can use *so, because* and linkers such as *first, then* and *the first day/night, the next day/night*. At the end, ask some pairs to tell the class their ideas.

> **Possible answers:** The man had a bad holiday because …
> first, he missed the plane.
> it rained so he stayed in the hotel and he was bored.
> he didn't sleep because the hotel room was noisy.
> and the hotel restaurant was expensive.

B Tell Ss to look at the pictures while they listen and find the difference.

> **Answer:** Picture 3 – the man didn't watch TV. He read a book.

C Give Ss a few moments to read the **Key phrases**. Check that Ss understand *dirty*. Then play the recording again for Ss to tick the phrases.

> **Answers:** I missed my (plane ✓/train/bus).
> I arrived (in Honolulu) one (hour/day ✓/week) late.
> I lost my (passport/money/bags).
> It rained for (the first three days ✓/all week).
> I stayed in (my hotel room ✓/the café) (all day).
> The hotel was (noisy ✓/expensive/dirty).
> The food was (bad/expensive ✓).
> I was very happy to go home. ✓

> **Optional extra activity**
> To give Ss some practice of the **Key phrases** before they make their own version of the story, make a copy (large enough to display on the board) of the phrases with the past verb forms removed, e.g.
>
> I ____ my (plane/train/bus).
> I ____ one (hour/day/week) late.
> I ____ my (passport/money/bags)., etc.
>
> Tell Ss to close their books and elicit the complete phrases from the class, one at a time, prompting the class to repeat the phrase in chorus and/or individually.

5A Elicit one or two examples from the class of how they could change the story, e.g. *First, I missed my train, so I waited for six hours in the station and took another train,* etc. When Ss have decided on the changes, they should practise telling the story until they can remember it with the photos in front of them but without looking at the **Key phrases** (tell them to cover the **Key phrases** when they're ready).

B Move each student along one place in the class, so they're working with a new partner. Encourage them to sound interested while they're listening to their partner's story, e.g. by saying *Oh no! Really? That's awful!* etc. When both Ss have told their story, they should note down the differences, then two or three pairs report back to the class. Monitor the practice closely and be prepared to give praise for good language use and deal with any problem areas afterwards.

Unit 8 Recording 6

This is my bad holiday story. Last year I went to Hawaii on holiday. First, I missed my plane, so I took another plane. I arrived in Honolulu one day late. The weather was very bad, and it rained for the first three days. I stayed in my hotel room and read a book. The hotel was noisy because my room was next to the road. There was a restaurant, but the food was expensive, and it wasn't very good. I was there for two weeks, and I was very happy to go home.

---

writeback a holiday story

6A When Ss have underlined the six positive things, ask them why it's a bad holiday story, not a good one (because the writer missed the train to Edinburgh and stayed the night in the station, then became ill and stayed in bed for five days.)

> **Answers:** 1 The food was great 2 the waiter was very nice 3 the weather was good 4 the place was beautiful 5 Our hotel was lovely 6 the people were friendly

B Remind Ss to use the example story as a model. If Ss don't have a story to tell of their own, they could start by working in pairs and brainstorming ideas for an invented story, noting down positive things as well as the negative things that made it a bad holiday. Circulate and help with vocabulary while Ss write their stories.

> **Alternative approach**
> Help Ss to analyse the way the example story is organised (see below). Divide the story into five parts and either display these on the board or give Ss copies to work on in pairs, then write the five titles on the board (on the right below) for them to match to the parts of the story.
>
> | | |
> |---|---|
> | Last year we went to Edinburgh on holiday, and I didn't have a good time. | Introduction |
> | We took a boat from Dublin to Holyhead in Wales, and then a train to Edinburgh. | Description of journey |
> | In Holyhead, we were hungry, so we went to a restaurant in the station. The food was great and the waiter was very nice, but we were there for too long and we missed our train. There were no other trains that day, so we stayed in the station. | A problem on the journey |
> | The next day, we arrived in Edinburgh. We were very tired but the weather was good and the place was beautiful. We were happy – for one hour! | A positive start to the holiday |
> | Our hotel was lovely and the people were friendly, but then I became ill and I was in bed for five days. We were there for one week. It was a very long week. | Explanation of why the holiday was bad |

C Either put Ss in groups of four to read each other's stories, or display the stories round the class so that Ss can walk round and read them. Ss can then vote on the worst story in their group or in the whole class.

> **Homework ideas**
> • Ss either write a final draft of the story they wrote in class, making improvements, corrections, etc., or they write another bad holiday story.

LOOKBACK

PAST SIMPLE: IRREGULAR VERBS

1A Go through the example with the class, then give Ss time to complete the sentences and compare answers in pairs.

> **Answers:** 2 Two students came to class late for this lesson. 3 I thought English was difficult, but it's easy. 4 I went home by train last night. 5 I didn't sit here last lesson. 6 I didn't have breakfast at home. 7 I saw the teacher in a supermarket yesterday.

B Demonstrate how Ss can change any part of the sentence, e.g.
I met my sister in a café yesterday.
I met a friend at the gym yesterday.
I met a friend in a café on Saturday.
I didn't meet a friend in a café yesterday.

C You could encourage Student A to read their sentences in random order, so Student B has to listen carefully to find their equivalent sentence. For **stronger classes**, Ss could also report back on what they found in common, e.g. *We both met a friend in a café on Saturday.* N.B. If the answer is negative, Ss can simply say: *We didn't meet a friend in a café,* or you could introduce the phrase: *Neither of us (met a friend in a café yesterday).*

PREPOSITIONS OF PLACE

2A Tell Ss to circle all the examples of *in, on* or *at* as they complete the sentences.

> **Answers:** 1 home, work 2 car, bike 3 holiday, Bangkok 4 class, street

B Go through the example with the class and point out that Ss can write any sentences they want but they must start with the words in bold and the sentences must contain two examples of *in, on* or *at.*

C Ss read out their sentences to each other and comment on anything that is similar/different, e.g. *Really? Me too./Really? I'm surprised.*

HOLIDAY ACTIVITIES

3A You could run this as a competition in teams. Write or display the words on the board, one at a time. When a team member guesses a word, they put up their hand to answer and say the missing vowels only. They win a point for each correct vowel and continue until they make a mistake (and another team can continue) or finish the phrase.

> **Alternative idea**
> Run the activity as a team game, but for each phrase just write the correct number of dashes on the board. Teams guess one missing letter at a time, winning a point for each correct letter and losing a point if the letter isn't in the phrase.

> **Answers:** 2 speak English 3 see old buildings 4 drink the local water 5 eat the local food 6 be ill 7 have a good time 8 meet the local people

B Put Ss in pairs or small groups to discuss these questions.

PAST SIMPLE: QUESTIONS

4A Start by eliciting how to make questions in the past, i.e. *Did* + subject + verb/*Wh-* + *did* + subject + verb. Ss work alone then compare answers in pairs.

> **Answers:** 2 What did you *do*? 3 *Did you meet* any friends? 4 Where did you *go*? 5 a) Did you buy anything? (correct) b) What *did* you buy? 6 a) *Did you* see a film at the cinema or on TV? b) What *was* it?

B Before Ss start asking and answering, remind them how to make short answers in the past, i.e. *Yes* + subject + *did*/*No* + subject + *didn't*. When Ss have finished, they could ask other Ss in the class about their partners, e.g. *Maria, did Sonja have a good weekend? Yes, she did.* Etc.

> **Optional extra activity**
> Review the weather vocabulary from the **Photo bank**.
>
> Write the following on six slips of paper and give them to six Ss:
> *It was windy./It was hot and sunny./It was cold./It was cloudy./It rained./It snowed.*
>
> Ss mime their weather for the rest of the class who try to guess the answer.
>
> Then put Ss in pairs to ask each other the following questions about their country/countries (point out that *last* means *the last time*):
> *When was it last hot and sunny?*
> *When was it last cold?*
> *When was it last cloudy?*
> *When was it last windy?*
> *When did it last rain?*
> *When did it last snow?*

PREPOSITIONS

5A You could run this as a race in pairs or as a competition in teams. To win points, Ss need to say the word and spell it correctly.

> **Answers:** 1 right 2 between 3 next 4 left 5 behind 6 front

B When Ss have found the mistakes, they write three sentences to describe where the things are in the picture.

> **Answers:** In the picture:
> The tree is between the shop and the <u>road</u>.
> The man is behind the <u>shop</u>.
> The woman is in front of the <u>house</u>.

GIVING DIRECTIONS

6A Give Ss a few minutes to put the words in the correct places in the sentences, working alone.

> **Answers:** A: Excuse me, where are the vegetables?
> B: Do you see the fruit over *there*? A: Where?
> B: Over there, *near* the magazines. A: Yes, I see it.
> B: Well, the vegetables are *next* to the fruit. On the left.
> A: Let me check that. They're on the left *of* the fruit.
> B: Right. A: On *the* right? B: No, you were right. On the *left*. A: I see. Thank you. B: *No* problem.

B Give Ss time to practise the conversation once or twice (swapping roles), then tell them to replace *vegetables, fruit* and *magazines* with different supermarket sections, and practise the conversation again.

REVIEW 4: UNITS 7–8

Introduction

The aim of the review units is for Ss to revise and practise the grammar, vocabulary and pronunciation from the previous two units in a different context. The context for this review unit is a murder mystery story.

READING AND GRAMMAR

Warm up

Use the pictures (tell Ss to cover the rest of the page) to check the following vocabulary: *a hotel, play tennis, listen to the radio, a cleaner, a body/a dead person, kill someone.* Then put Ss in pairs and tell them to think of a story that connects all these things. Give them a few minutes to make notes (reminding them to use the past to tell the story), then put the pairs together into groups of four to tell each other their stories. Invite one pair from each group to tell the rest of the class their story.

1A Give Ss a few moments to skim the article.

Answer: Someone killed him./He died.

Optional extra activity
Write/display the following questions on the board for Ss to answer as they read the text again:
1 Where is the hotel? (Edinburgh)
2 What did Rose Green do? (She found the body.)
3 Was Jim Black rich? (Yes, very rich.)
4 Did he die in the hotel? (No, behind it.)
5 When did he die? (Between ten o'clock and midnight.)
6 Who's Carla? (Jim's wife)
7 Who's Mike Brown? (Jim's business partner.)

B Establish that the police *interview* Mike and Carla, and take their *statements.* Elicit some examples of questions they might ask (e.g. *Where were you between … and … ?*) then give Ss a few minutes to complete the questions, working alone.

Answers: 2 Did you see Jim yesterday afternoon?
3 Did you have dinner with Jim and Carla?
4 What time did you go to your room?
5 Where were you between ten o'clock and midnight?

C Check that Ss understand *witness* (someone who sees a crime or tells what they know about a crime – in this case the latter). Tell Ss to find the answers to the questions in the statement and answer them as if they are Mike.

Answers: 1 Yes, we were. 2 Yes, I did. 3 Yes, I did.
4 At ten o'clock. 5 In my room.

Optional extra activity
Ss role-play the interview between a police officer and Mike Brown. They could add one or two extra questions of their own, e.g. *Did you talk to Jim at dinner? What time did you go to bed?*

2A Give Ss a few minutes to complete the statement, working alone.

Answers: 2 were 3 weren't 4 didn't like 5 played
6 walked 7 went 8 wrote 9 came 10 didn't talk 11 met
12 had 13 wanted 14 was

B Give Ss time to find the differences on their own.

Answers: 1 Mike: Jim Black was a good friend
Carla: they weren't friends. Mike didn't like Jim.
2 Mike: At half past three, we went to our rooms in the hotel. Carla: Jim came back at six.
They also both say that the other person killed Jim.

C Ss could discuss what reasons each person possibly had for killing Jim, and who they think did it at this stage. Possible reasons: Carla wanted his money; Carla thought he had another woman; Mike wanted his part of the business; Jim discovered that Mike took money from the business and Mike wanted to 'silence' him; Mike and Carla were in love and planned to kill Jim together.

LISTENING AND GRAMMAR

3A Draw a clock face on the board and briefly review how to tell the time: *o'clock, quarter past, half past, quarter to,* also *ten to/ten past.* Give Ss time to read through the information in the table before you play the recording. Ss can compare answers in pairs.

Answers: 1b 3.30 2 10.00 3 10.50 4a 10.00 4b 10.15
5 10.30

B Before you play the recording again, give Ss a minute or two to read through the statements. As you check the answers, elicit any differences between what these witnesses said and Mike and Carla's statements, e.g. Carla said she danced with Jim at 10.50, but the waiter says she danced with one of the men from 9.30–10.00, before Mike left the restaurant; the guest says the radio was on in Jim and Carla's room at the time Carla said she danced with Jim.

Answers: 2 T 3 F 4 F 5 T

C Ss could discuss this as a class. The most likely answer is that it was Carla, in a man's clothes.

Review 4 Recording 1
1
My name's Sara. I'm the receptionist in the hotel. Mr Black and Mr Brown went out yesterday afternoon at a quarter to two. They came back together … at about half past three, and they went to their rooms.
2
My name's Alan. I'm a waiter in the hotel restaurant. I was in the restaurant last night. There were two men and a woman in the restaurant all evening. One man and the woman danced for about half an hour – from half past nine to ten o'clock. They all left at ten o'clock.
3
I'm a guest in the hotel. My room is on the right of Mr and Mrs Black's room. Their radio was on last night from about ten to eleven. It was very noisy!
4
I'm the night receptionist. Mr Black went out at ten o'clock. He said he wanted to take a walk. Then at a quarter past ten, another man went out. I didn't see him very well. Maybe it was Mr Brown. I don't know.
5
My name's Mary White. I'm a guest in the hotel. I came back from the town at about half past ten. I saw a woman in front of the hotel. She had men's clothes: a man's jacket, a man's trousers and a man's hat. I was surprised, you know. A woman in a man's clothes. Was there a party or something?

7–8 TEACHER'S NOTES

SPEAKING

4A The idea of this role-play is that Students A and B provide an alibi for each other by saying they were together somewhere else at the time of a robbery. The 'police' try to find differences between their stories, to prove that one (or both) of them was the robber. Put Ss into groups of four and direct Students A and B to p150 and tell them to read the information and start preparing their answers. If possible, they should go out of the room to prepare their part of the role-play, but if this isn't practical, divide the classroom and ask all the As and Bs to move to one side so that they can't hear the other people in their group. Tell Ss C and D from each group that they're the police, and give them a few minutes to read the information and put the four questions in order.

Answers: 1 What time did you arrive at the restaurant? 2 What was the restaurant's name? 3 What did you eat? 4 How much did it cost?

B You could give the police some prompts to help them to write further questions: *what/drink? a lot/other people/ restaurant? waiter/waitress? time/leave? do/next?* In the meantime, check that Ss A and B are preparing their story and emphasise that it must be exactly the same because the police will question them separately. Prompt them with ideas about other things the police might ask about.

C While the police question Student A, Student B should wait outside or on the other side of the room, so he/she can't hear the questions. You could put some background music on to help with this. When Student B answers the questions, tell the police to note any answer that is different from A's, and decide afterwards if they think A and B are the robbers or not. Ask the police from the different groups to report back to the class about their decisions, and see which robbers got away with it!

SOUNDS: /ʌ/ AND /ʊ/

5A Direct Ss to the pictures and point out that the symbols represent the sounds. Play the recording for Ss to listen to the sounds and the words. You could also show Ss that to make /ʊ/ their mouth is rounded with lips pushed forward, then for /ʌ/ their jaw needs to drop.

B You may want to ask Ss to predict which group the words belong to before they listen. You could pause the recording after each group of words, and ask individual Ss to repeat them, rather than Ss repeating in chorus. This will give you more opportunity to correct their pronunciation of the 'target' sounds.

Answers: /ʌ/ month, country, hungry, colour /ʊ/ good, cook, look, full

6A and B Look at the example with the class, then put Ss in pairs to work out the answers. Alternatively, you could put Ss in teams and run this as a competition, writing/reading out one question at a time (Ss close their books).

Answers:
brother, husband, son
Russia
Sunday, Monday
good book
push, pull
July

Homework ideas

- Ss write Carla's confession: why she killed Jim and how she did it.
- Ss write an email from Sara, the receptionist at the hotel, to a friend or family member, telling them about the events of the past two days, i.e. the dead businessman, the police interviews, etc.
- **Workbook** Ex 1–5, p55–56

OVERVIEW

THE RIGHT GIFT

Introduction

Ss practise reading and talking about giving gifts and likes and dislikes, using *like, love, hate + -ing* and vocabulary related to activities.

SUPPLEMENTARY MATERIALS

Resource bank p168

Ex 1A (alternative activity): prepare a handout with alternatives for Ss to tick (see notes).

Warm up

Tell Ss to close their books. Write the following words on the board and put Ss in pairs to talk about what they have in common: *pens, theatre tickets, flowers, dinner, chocolates*. Then direct Ss to the picture of a gift on p96 and tell them (if they haven't already guessed) that this is what the words have in common: they can all be gifts. Use the picture and acting out to illustrate the meaning of verbs that are commonly used with *gift*, i.e. *give, get (receive), wrap, open/unwrap*.

READING

1 You could start by eliciting some more examples of common gifts, e.g. a book, a CD, a bottle of wine, a bottle of perfume. Give Ss one example of when you personally give gifts, then put them in pairs to discuss the questions. After a minute or two, ask a few pairs to share their answers with the class.

Alternative activity

Give Ss the following on a handout or display it on the board:

Tick the alternatives which are true for you:

1 I give gifts to people … on their birthdays.
on special festivals.
in business situations.

2 I buy gifts for … my family.
a lot of my friends.
people at work or school.

When Ss have ticked the alternatives, they can compare and discuss their answers in pairs.

2A Before directing Ss to the text, check the following vocabulary: *death* (the end of someone's life), *unlucky* (means something bad will happen), *immediately* (without waiting). Encourage Ss to put ticks on the text in the margin, next to the things that are the same in their country. Ss can discuss their answers in pairs and with the whole class.

B Make sure Ss cover the text and try to remember the answers together.

C Ss read and check their answers to Ex 2B.

Answers: 2 UK 3 Japan 4 Thailand 5 UK, Mexico 6 Mexico 7 Japan 8 UK

D You may want Ss to do the **Photo bank** exercise (matching names of gifts to photos) before they start this discussion. You could also demonstrate the activity by completing each sentence with your own examples.

> **➡ PHOTOBANK** p146
>
> To learn more about the language of gifts, get Ss to complete Ex 1A and then in pairs discuss Ex 1B.
>
> **Answers:** 1 E 2 O 3 N 4 F 5 B 6 J 7 L 8 C 9 D 10 G 11 K 12 M 13 A 14 H 15 I

GRAMMAR *like, love, hate + -ing*

3A Draw the line on the board and ask Ss to help you complete it with the verbs.

> **Answers:** 2 like 3 don't like 4 hate

B Give Ss a minute or two to look at the rules. You could check their understanding by asking them to choose the correct sentence from each pair below:

I like open gifts. I like opening gifts.

She loves roses. She loves rose.

> **Answers:** 1 plural 2 verb + -ing

C Write the -ing forms *going, driving, sitting, doing* on the board and ask Ss to decide where the stress is on each one as they listen to the recording (on the first syllable). When Ss repeat the phrases, make sure they don't overemphasise the 'g' sound at the end of the -ing forms. The sound should be /ŋ/ rather than two sounds /ng/

> **➡ LANGUAGEBANK** 9.1 p134–135
>
> You could provide a challenge for *stronger students* here by asking them to work out the spelling rules for -ing forms before they look at the **Language bank**. Write the following examples on the board and ask Ss what (if anything) is added or taken away before -ing: *using, giving; buying, opening; getting, wrapping.* Ex 9.1A gives more practice in spelling -ing forms, and Ss could practise the dialogues in Ex 9.1B in pairs, after they've completed them.
>
> **Answers:** A 2 chatting 3 working 4 writing 5 saying 6 having 7 starting 8 stopping 9 cooking 10 emailing
> B
> 1 A: Do you like doing sport?
> B: Well, I like swimming but I don't like running.
> A: Do you like playing tennis?
> B: Yes, I do.
> 2 A: Sam doesn't like speaking on the phone.
> B: Does he like writing emails?
> A: No, he doesn't, but he loves meeting people online.
> B: And does he like playing computer games?
> A: Yes, he does.

PRACTICE

4A Give Ss a few minutes to complete the sentences, working alone or in pairs.

> **Answers:** 2 watching 3 having 4 reading 5 going 6 living 7 getting up 8 wrapping

B Use the first three sentences to demonstrate this, ticking or changing them as appropriate for you. For *stronger students,* if they ask you how to say *It's OK,* introduce *I don't mind + -ing,* e.g. *I don't mind watching sport on TV.*

C Ask Ss to be prepared to tell the class about the two things in common, e.g. *We both like … but we don't like …*

> **Optional extra activity**
> Give Ss some prompts on the board and ask them to rewrite the sentences in Ex 4A again, this time changing different parts of the sentence, i.e. the -ing form or the noun, rather than the main verb. Examples of prompts: *cook, brothers, the news, breakfast, in the country, go to bed, get, the gym.*
> Ss then compare their sentences.

VOCABULARY activities

5A Remind Ss to pay attention to the spelling as they write the -ing forms.

> **Answers:** 2 relaxing 3 playing 4 cooking 5 taking 6 going 7 swimming 8 chatting 9 camping 10 going

> **Optional extra activity**
> In pairs, Ss take turns to mime the activities in Ex 5A for their partner to guess. You could demonstrate by miming one of the activities yourself.

B Check that Ss understand the options here by eliciting an example for each one, e.g. *outside – running; inside – cooking; with someone – going to the theatre; in special clothes – swimming; with a machine – taking photos.* Encourage Ss to find as many examples as they can for each option, then share their ideas with the whole class.

> **Possible answers:** outside: 1, 9, 10 (possibly 2, 4, 5, 7)
> inside: 3, 4, 8, (possibly 2, 5, 7)
> with someone: 6, 8, 9, 10 (possibly 1, 3, 7)
> in special clothes: 6, 7 (possibly 1, 10)
> with a machine: 3, 5, 8

C Invite Ss to ask you about two or three of the activities, so you can provide a model of different answers, e.g. *Yes, I do/ No, I don't/Yes, I love it/No, I hate it.*

Optional extra activity
In pairs, Ss think of at least one more activity for each category in Ex 5B. You could give them some verb prompts on the board to help, e.g. *do, go, eat, wash, listen, clean, write, learn.*

Possible ideas: *doing sport, going to the shops, eating in restaurants, washing the car, listening to music, cleaning the house, writing emails, learning English.*

Then Ss take turns to say one of their activities and their partner guesses how they feel about it, e.g.

A: *Washing the car*

B: *You hate it.*

A: *No, actually, I like it!*

speakout TIP

Give Ss a few minutes to read through the examples of short answers and write them in their phrasebooks. Check their understanding of *It depends* (sometimes I do, sometimes I don't). Then model the short answers for Ss to repeat, focusing on natural intonation. Ss could then practise asking *Do you like … ?* and answering with short answers in open pairs, i.e. across the class, e.g.

A: *Marie, do you like camping?*

M: *It depends. Pietro do you like cooking?*

P: *Yes, sometimes.*

SPEAKING

6A Remind Ss about the 'activity gifts' mentioned in the text in Ex 2A and direct them to the website. Give them a minute or two to find photos of the activities. Check *one-to-one* (a private lesson), *beauty spa* (a place where people have different beauty treatments).

Answers: hot-air balloon trip, driving a Formula-1 car, salsa lessons

B Check *eating out* (eating in cafes and restaurants), then put Ss in pairs to ask and answer.

C Give Ss a few minutes to decide on the best activity and to make a few notes about why they chose it, then to tell their partners, e.g. *I chose salsa lessons for you, because you love dancing and you like doing exercise.*

D You could ask Ss to imagine that they went and did the activity, and now they are going to tell the class about it and why they liked/didn't like it. You could demonstrate this by doing an imaginary example of your own, e.g. *My activity gift was a chocolate-making class. It was a good idea because I love cooking and I love sweets. I enjoyed the activity and I learnt to make some beautiful chocolates. The teacher and the other people in the class were very nice and friendly. The problem was, I ate all the chocolates before I got home!* Give Ss a few minutes to make notes before they tell the class about their 'experience'.

Homework ideas
- Ss write an email to a friend or family member, telling them about an activity gift that they've bought for them. You could give Ss a framework for this, e.g.
Dear (Anna),
Happy (birthday)! I hope you have a (great) day!
I bought you an activity for your (birthday), it's (a hot-air balloon trip).
I chose this because I know you love (flying) and you like (adventure).
To book the (trip), phone (4456 3246). The trips are every day at (3p.m.). Choose the best day for you.
I hope you enjoy it!
Love
- **Workbook** Ex 1–5, p58–59

A WASTE OF MONEY

Introduction

Ss practise listening to people talking about shopping mistakes. They practise talking about shopping and things that are a waste of money, using object pronouns and vocabulary related to money. They also learn how to write captions for things to sell online.

SUPPLEMENTARY MATERIALS

Resource bank p167 and p169

Ex 1A (alternative activity): prepare a handout with statements about shopping (see notes).

Ex 6C: take in photos of objects for Ss to write captions.

Warm up

Tell Ss to close their books and write the title *A waste of money* on the board. Illustrate the meaning of the phrase by telling an anecdote, e.g. *This morning I bought a coffee on my way to school, but I didn't have time to drink it and now it's cold and I don't like it. It was a waste of money.*

Write the following (or similar) statements on the board:

CDs	
Flowers	are a waste of money.
Holidays, etc.	

Put Ss in pairs and tell them to choose two statements and think of reasons why they're true, e.g. *Newspapers are a waste of money because people see the news on TV and read the news on the internet.*

Then invite a few pairs to tell the class their ideas.

VOCABULARY money

1A You could start by telling Ss whether you like shopping and explain why/why not. Then put Ss in pairs to discuss, and invite one or two Ss to report back to the class about their partners' opinions afterwards.

Alternative activity

Prepare a handout with the following sentences and ask Ss to circle the options to make the statements true for them:

1 I love/like/don't like/hate shopping.

2 I go shopping once/twice/three times a week/month/year.

3 I often/don't often go shopping at the weekend/after work or school.

4 I usually go shopping with my friend(s)/with my (mother)/on my own.

5 I like shopping for clothes/shoes/gifts/books/things for the house/(other).

Ss then compare and justify their answers in pairs.

B Tell Ss to focus on the sentences with the verbs in bold, and that they'll have time to read the questions in Part C.

Answers: 2 sell 3 pay 4 cost 5 get

C Put Ss in pairs and tell Student A to close their books and answer Student B as he/she reads out the questions, then swap roles. In this way Ss will need to listen to each other, rather than simply reading the questions in their **Students' Books**. Ask a few pairs to tell the class how many of their answers were the same.

2A Give Ss time to write the past forms, working alone.

Answers: 2 sold 3 paid 4 cost (point out that there are a few irregular verbs like this, that have the same form in the past) 5 gave 6 got

B Make sure that Ss are pronouncing *bought* correctly, i.e. with a silent 'gh'.

C Demonstrate this with one or two Ss first.

➠ PHOTOBANK p147

To practise more about the language of money, get Ss to complete Ex 1A alone and discuss Ex 1B in pairs.

Answers: 1 E 2 A 3 D 4 F 5 C 6 G 7 H 8 B

LISTENING

3A Direct Ss to the pictures and see if they can name any of the objects without looking at the words in the box. Then give them a minute or two to match the words from the box.

Answers: hat A lamp C tent B drums E exercise bike D

B Ss could discuss this in pairs or together as a class. Encourage Ss to justify their opinions, i.e. why they like the object or think it's a waste of money.

C Before you play the recording, check *break – broke* (mime breaking something) and *fix* (reg). Also give an example of a shopping mistake, i.e. something you bought that you didn't use/like. Tell Ss to write the letter of the picture next to speakers 1–5.

Answers: 1 B 2 D 3 A 4 E 5 C

Unit 9 Recording 3

1

A shopping mistake? Um … well my boyfriend wanted to go camping, so I bought him a tent. It was a good tent. I paid seventy pounds for it. Anyway, he put it up in the garden – once, I think. Imagine that, just one time! He never used it again. It was a waste of money. The truth is he really likes hotels!

2

I don't really know … Oh yeah, last year my wife bought me an exercise bike. I thought it was a good idea, too, but you know, I think I used it three times. It was hard work! A real waste of money!

3

Shopping mistakes? Oh, that's easy. Clothes. I often buy clothes and then when I get home I don't like them. For example, last month I went shopping with a friend and I bought a hat. It cost a hundred euros. My friend said it looked beautiful. My boyfriend said it was terrible … so I sold it … on the internet. I got fifty euros for it. It was a real waste of money.

D Start by showing Ss the meaning of *too big/small* and *the wrong size/colour*. You could do this with simple board drawings (e.g. a person with a very small hat and a very big coat) or by borrowing one or two items from Ss, e.g. a jacket that's too small for you, a watch that's too big, a tie/scarf (for *the wrong colour*). Go through the example with the class, then give Ss time to choose a mistake and prepare what they're going to say about it. N.B. If a student doesn't have an example of a shopping mistake, tell them to invent one. Put Ss in groups of 4–5 to talk about their mistakes.

4
A shopping mistake? Oh yes, all the time. For example, I got my sister's little boy some drums. For his birthday. I thought it was a good idea. He loves those drums. He plays them all day. So he's happy … but my sister isn't happy. Now she doesn't talk to me! I phoned her yesterday, but she didn't answer.

5
A shopping mistake. Erm … oh yeah, my mother gave us a lamp. We didn't like it, but I know it cost her a lot of money. Then after a week I broke it. I tried to fix it but it was impossible. Whoops!

GRAMMAR object pronouns

4A Give Ss a minute or two to complete the sentences, working alone. For *stronger classes*, you could tell Ss to cover the box and try to complete as many sentences as they can, from what they know already. You may also want to point out at this stage that pronouns are words that go in place of nouns, e.g. *it* is in the place of *exercise bike* in sentence 1.

Answers: 1 it 2 him 3 her 4 them 5 us

B You could draw the table on the board and write the answers in the second column as you elicit them from the class or ask Ss up to the board to write them.

Answers: object pronoun: you, him, her, it, us, them

C Refer Ss back to the sentences in Ex 5A to help them with the rule. For *weaker classes*, write sentence 4 on the board: *He loves those drums. He plays them every day.* Use the example to show Ss that *He* comes before *loves,* and *them* comes after *plays.*

Answers: Use a subject pronoun *before a* verb.
Use an object pronoun *after a* verb.

D Give Ss time to read the examples and note which sounds are linked or dropped. You could also model the examples without the linking (i.e. pronouncing the 'h' in *him/her*) to show Ss that it sounds unnatural.

> **LANGUAGEBANK** 9.2 p134–135
>
> Give Ss a few minutes to read the summary of object pronouns in the **Language bank**. If you have a mixed level class, you could give Ex 9.2A to the *weaker students* and Ex 9.2B to the *stronger students* and give them a key to check their answers.
>
> **Answers:** A 2 Give it to ~~him~~ *her.* 3 Deena lived with ~~we~~ *us* for three years. 4 Come and dance with ~~I~~ *me.* 5 correct 6 I don't like ~~these~~ *them.* 7 correct 8 I played with ~~he~~ *him* yesterday. 9 Diana's in my class. I like ~~she/~~ *her* a lot. 10 The exit is over there, in front of ~~your/~~*you.* B 2B: I didn't like *it.* 3B: Oh no! I put *them* in my other coat. 4B: Sorry, I sent you a text. Didn't you get *it?* 5B: He phoned *me* this morning from home. He isn't well. 6B: No, I asked *her* but she didn't want to go. 7B: A taxi met *us* at the airport. 8B: Wait a minute, class. Did I give *you* your homework?

PRACTICE

5A Ss can complete the sentences alone or in pairs.

Answers: 2 them 3 it 4 me 5 you 6 us 7 her 8 him

B Go through the example with the class, or you could do a different one about you. Point out that they can only change the second part, i.e. not the question, apart from numbers 7 and 8, where they might want to change the name of the student.

C Ss should read their sentences aloud to their partner, rather than simply showing them the sentences in their notebooks.

WRITING captions

6A To show Ss the meaning of *caption*, you could take in a page from a newspaper or magazine that has a photo with a caption underneath it, and elicit from Ss that the caption tells you about what's in the photo. Then you could ask Ss to cover the text and predict what the caption for the photo says, (e.g. *Honda motorbike for sale. Five years old,* etc.) before reading the four captions and finding the matching one.

Answer: caption 3

B Go through the example on the board, erasing *the new trainers* and replacing it with *them.* Ss rewrite the captions alone, then check their answers in pairs.

Answer: 2 A signed photo of Johnny Depp. I met *him* in Los Angeles last year. *He* gave me two photos and I want to sell one of *them.* 3 For sale: my Honda 500T. I bought *it* in 1998. *It* is a beautiful motorbike but I don't use *it* much now. 4 The 2009 Tour Book of Beyoncé I AM. I saw *her* in Caracas. *She* was fantastic but my new flat is too small for all my books.

C You could take in some photos of objects to help Ss with ideas, e.g. a sofa, a handbag, an iPod, a jacket, a boat, a child's dress. Give Ss a framework for their captions, i.e.

- a description of the object
- when/where/how you got it
- why you want to sell it.

Monitor Ss as they write the captions and provide any vocabulary they need, and/or help them to make corrections.

D Ss either read each other's captions in groups or display them round the class, for other Ss to walk round and read. You could tell Ss to choose one object that they want to buy, and tell the class about it.

SPEAKING

7A Give Ss a few minutes to write their answers, while you circulate and help. Encourage them to give some information to support their answer, as in the example in Ex 7B.

B Ss can use the sentence stem *Tell me* to prompt their partner for all the questions.

> **Optional extra activity**
> Ss choose one of the questions from Ex 7A then walk round the class asking all the other Ss that question, and making a note of their answers. Afterwards they summarise what they found out and tell the class, e.g. *Seven people really want to buy a new computer, and five people want to buy clothes.*

Homework ideas
- Ss write two more captions for photos of objects for sale.
- Workbook Ex 1–5, p60–61

WHAT WOULD YOU LIKE?

Introduction

Ss practise listening to and making requests, using *I'd like* and *Would you like … ?* and names of shopping departments. They also learn to use hesitation phrases.

SUPPLEMENTARY MATERIALS

Resource bank p170

Warm up

Direct Ss to the photo of Macy's and ask them what they know about it. Check that Ss understand the idea of a department store (they could tell the class the names of famous department stores in their country), and put them in pairs to think about the advantages and disadvantages of shopping in department stores, as opposed to smaller, specialty shops, or shopping online.

Culture note

Macy's is a U.S. chain of department stores founded by Rowland Hussey Macy in 1858. Its flagship store is located in Herald Square in New York City, but the company has over 800 stores throughout the US. Macy's star, the most recognizable part of the store's logo, was inspired by a tattoo on Macy's arm which he got when he worked on whaling ships. The store is famous in popular culture, referred to in many films and songs. It was the first store to introduce an in-store Santa in 1862. It has also produced the annual Macy's Thanksgiving Day Parade in New York City since 1924 and sponsored the Macy's Fireworks Spectacular, the largest fireworks display on July 4, since 1976.

VOCABULARY shopping departments

1A Start by eliciting the names of the items from Ss: A – *chair*, B – *TV*, C – *travel bag*, D – *toy car*, E – *ring*, F – *towels*. Put Ss in pairs to talk about the best shops for these things in their town/city (if they're studying away from home they could tell each other about places they've found so far in the town/city where they're staying).

B Ss work on this in pairs, writing the letter of the item next to the department name.

Answers: A Furniture & Lighting B Home Entertainment C Travel & Luggage D Toys E Jewellery & Watches F Bed & Bath

C Point out that Ss will hear the departments starting with the ones on the ground floor and going up.

2 Go through the example, then put Ss in pairs to practise. Pairs who finish quickly could add more examples of their own, e.g. *I want to buy a lamp.*

Optional extra activity

Ss work in pairs and Student B closes his/her book. Student A asks where certain departments are and Student B tries to remember, e.g.
A: *Where's the (Menswear and Shoes) department?*
B: *I think it's on the (ground) floor.*
A: *Yes, that's right!*

FUNCTION making requests

3A Tell Ss they're going to hear a conversation between Lisa and Tom, and give them time to read through the options in questions 1–3.

Answers: 1 c) 2 a) 3 a)

B Focus Ss on the three sentences and point out that they need to complete them with one word in each case. Play the first part of the recording (between Lisa and Tom) again.

Answers: 1 What 2 Would 3 like

C Give Ss a minute or two to discuss their ideas in pairs. As you go through the answers, point out that *I'd like a computer game* means 'now', whereas *I like computer game**s*** means 'in general'. Also, if you ask *Would you like this DVD?* you are offering it to the person, whereas *Do you like this DVD?* is asking for an opinion.

Answers: 1 *I'd like* means *I want*. 2 *I'd like* is polite.

> **LANGUAGEBANK** 9.3 p134–135
>
> Give Ss time to read through the summary, and check that they understand the difference between *What would you like?* (open choice) and *Which one would you like?* (limited choice). You could use Ex 9.3 for conversation practice in pairs. N.B. Point out that *Can I help you?* is a common way for a shop assistant to start a conversation, and *Can I have … ?* is another way to make a request.
>
> **Answers:** 2 'd 3 like 4 have 5 Would 6 I'd 7 Do 8 thanks

Unit 9 Recording 6

A: Hi, Tom. It's Lisa.
B: Oh hi, Lisa. How are you?
A: Fine thanks. Listen, what would you like for your birthday?
B: Oh, I don't know. Let me think … I don't know.
A: I'm in Bridge's Department Store, so it's a good time to tell me …
B: Um … well, maybe something from the World Cup.
A: For example?
B: Er …
A: Well, would you like a football shirt, or … ?
B: Um … no. Oh, I know! I'd like a DVD.
A: Of the World Cup?
B: Yeah.
A: OK.
B: Great, thanks.
A: No problem. Bye.
B: Bye.

A: Excuse me, can you help me? Where's the Sports department?
C: It's over there. Behind the Toys department.
A: Thanks.

D: Can I help you?
A: Yes, I'd like a DVD of the World Cup, but there aren't any DVDs here.
D: No, the sports DVDs are in Home Entertainment. In the DVD section.
A: Where's that?
D: It's opposite Computers and Phones. Over there.
A: Thanks.

A: Yeah, I'd like a DVD of the World Cup, but there are two different DVDs here. Which DVD is best, do you think?

E: Er … let me see … this one has all the important matches.

A: How much is it? Ah, I see. Twenty euros. OK, can I have this?

E: Yes, you pay over there.

A: Oh, right. Thanks.

E: No problem.

4A Ss write the four conversations in their notebooks. They can then practise the conversations, remembering to look up from the page as much as possible, so they're not reading aloud. They could also change one or two of the items in each conversation and practise them again, e.g.

1 *coffee, tea*
2 *bike*
3 *half an hour*
4 *sweaters*

Answers:
1
A: Would you like a coffee?
B: No thanks, but I'd like a tea.
2
A: What would Sue like for her birthday?
B: I think she'd like a bike.
3
A: Would you like a break?
B: Yes, let's stop for half an hour.
4
A: Can I have one of those sweaters?
B: Yes, which colour would you like?

B When Ss have identified whether the speaker is polite or not, elicit/point out that the voice falls then rises a little at the end when the speaker sounds polite. Ss could practise just saying *coffee?* and *please*, concentrating on the fall-rise pattern, before they practise saying the whole sentence.

Answers: 1 P 2 NP 3 NP 4 P

C Instead of saying *polite/not polite*, Student B could respond *Of course* if Student A sounds polite, and either ignore Student A or say *No!* if they don't sound polite. You could demonstrate this by inviting one or two Ss to say the sentences to you and responding accordingly.

LEARN TO use hesitation phrases

5A Elicit/Point out that when you don't have an immediate answer for someone it's better to say something, however small, than to stay silent. Give Ss a minute or two to underline the phrases

Answers: 2 Let me think. 3 Um … 4 well … 5 Er … 6 let me see

speakout TIP

Put Ss in pairs to think of hesitation phrases/sounds in their language(s). If Ss are from different countries, they can demonstrate them for their partner/the class.

B Ss work in pairs to do this. After each question pause the recording long enough for both Ss in the pair to answer.

Unit 9 Recording 9

1 What's your favourite fruit?
2 Where were you last Saturday afternoon?
3 Do you want a new car?
4 What did you study in the last lesson?

C Give Ss time to find their questions, then tell them to take turns asking and answering, using hesitation phrases.

SPEAKING

6A Tell Ss to complete the conversation orally, so that the hesitation sounds more natural.

You could write the complete conversation on the board for Ss to check, then erase it before they start practising.

Answers:
A: What would you like for your birthday?
B: I'd like a new pen.
A: Which colour would you like?
B: I'd like a black one, please.

B Ss take turns to be A and B, using the prompts.

C You could elicit/give some ideas for possible presents and options, e.g.
bag – colour
wallet – colour
shirt – size – small/medium/large
DVD – type of film – comedy/drama/romance
CD – type of music – rock/pop/jazz/classical
book – type of book – cookery/biography/novel
phone – make – Nokia/Samsung/Motorola

D Monitor the practice closely so you can give feedback on Ss' use of phrases for making requests, and for hesitation.

N.B. Ask Ss to bring in a favourite possession (or a photo of it) for the next lesson.

Homework ideas
• Ss write a description of a well-known department store in their town/city, saying where it is, how old it is, how many floors there are, if there's a café or restaurant, what their favourite department is and why, etc.
• **Workbook** Ex 1–3, p62

DAYS THAT SHOOK THE WORLD

Introduction

Ss watch an extract from the BBC documentary television series *Days That Shook The World*, which features various milestones in history. The extract looks at how the arrival of the iPod changed the music world. Ss then learn and practise how to talk and write about a favourite possession.

SUPPLEMENTARY MATERIALS

Ex 2C (optional extra activity): prepare a handout for Ss (see notes).

Ex 3B: be prepared to answer questions about a favourite possession.

Warm up

Tell Ss to close their books, then put them in pairs and give them a minute to write down as many ways of listening to music as they can think of. After a minute, invite Ss to share their ideas and make a list on the board.

Possible answers: *on an iPod/MP3 player, on the radio, on a CD player, at a concert, at a music festival, at a club.*

Ask Ss to discuss which way(s) they prefer to listen to music and why.

DVD PREVIEW

1A Direct Ss to the pictures and check that they can pronounce *jukebox*. They could work in pairs to decide where the items go on the timeline, using phrases such as: *The … was first/next/after that … It was in the 1950s/1970s*, etc.

B Start by focusing on the title of the text and explain that it means *times when very important things happened in the world*. You could elicit one or two examples. Give Ss a few minutes to read and check the information against their timelines, as well as identify the object that is not mentioned. Before moving to the next stage, you could ask Ss how they think the iPod changed people's lives.

Ideas: *You can have a lot more songs than on a CD or cassette player. It's easy to change the songs. You can get very small, light iPods which are very easy to carry. You can listen to other things apart from music on the iPod. You can get music, etc. from the internet on an iPod.*

Answers: 1950 C 1960 E 1970 E 1980 A, F 2000 D
The video cassette is not there.

▶ DVD VIEW

2A You could tell Ss to number the photos of the items as they see them in the DVD extract.

Answers: jukebox (1), Walkman (2), iPod (3), CD (4), video cassette (5)

B Give Ss time to read through the sentences and try to complete them before you play the extract again. Check *touch control, headphones, rubbish* (you could use mime to demonstrate all three of these). They can compare answers in pairs and/or with the whole class.

Answers: 1 favourite 2 different 3 white 4 lessons
5 Tourists 6 send 7 old

C Give Ss a minute or two to discuss this in pairs, then share their ideas with the whole class.

Possible ideas: *listen to music (pop, rock, classical, jazz, reggae, R&B, folk, etc.), listen to plays, stories, lessons, the news, discussions.*

Alternatively, you could ask Ss to discuss whether they agree with the statement that 'the machines of today are the rubbish of tomorrow'.

Optional extra activity

Prepare a handout with the following activity:

1 Complete the sentences, then tick the ones that are true for you.

I listen to music …

____ *the car.*

____ *the bath.*

____ *work.*

____ *the gym.*

____ *the train.*

____ *the bus.*

when I ____ *my homework.*

when I go ____ *a walk or run.*

when I go ____ *the beach.*

2 Compare your answers with a partner.

Answers:
in the car/bath; at work/the gym; on the train/bus; do my homework; go for a walk or run; go to the beach.

DVD 9 Days That Shook The World

N=Narrator M=Man

N: In the 1950s, there was the jukebox. In the 1980s, there was the Sony Walkman. Then in October 2001, Apple introduced the iPod. The iPod changed everything. People walked round with thousands of their favourite songs in a little white box in their pockets.

When the compact disc arrived in the 1980s it was new, but the iPod was really different. It was fun. It looked good with its touch control and white headphones. Other MP3 players became popular, everyone had one.

In the first five years, Apple sold seventy million iPods.

Schools and universities started to use MP3 players. Students listened to their lessons at home. Tourists listened to audio tours in cities.

In the music world, bands used the internet to send their music to people's computers and MP3 players. And then came the Smartphone. The Smartphone was a music player, video player, internet, personal organiser, and phone all in one machine.

The old technology of the eighties and nineties is now rubbish. Maybe the machines of today are the rubbish of tomorrow.

M: It's been a huge success.

speakout a possession

3A Start by brainstorming some examples of possessions with Ss, especially the type that can become 'special' to people for some reason, e.g. *a ring, a necklace, a watch, a book, a jewellery box, a money box, a doll, a teddy bear, a bag, a tennis racquet, a fishing rod, golf clubs, special shoes or clothes (ballet shoes, a ball gown)*. Provide vocabulary as Ss need it and make a list on the board. Give Ss a few minutes to answer the questions alone. You could also suggest what to include in *Other information*, e.g. *size, colour, material (wood, leather, gold, silver), descriptive adjectives (useful, unusual, cute, fun)*.

B You could start by inviting different Ss to ask you the questions about a favourite possession of yours.

C You may need to play the recording twice for Ss to answers all the questions. Give them time to compare answers before listening a second time.

> **Answers:**
> Possession: camera
> Where did you get it? New York
> Where is it now? In his bag.
> What do you do with it? He takes pictures of friends and places.
> Why do you like it? It's easy to use, it takes good pictures.
> Other information: He puts his pictures on his website. His camera is his travel partner.

D Give Ss time to read the **Key phrases**, then play the recording again.

> **Answers:** One of my favourite (things/possessions ✓) is …
> It's (very small/big/red).
> I keep it (in my bag ✓/pocket/at home).
> I bought it (last year ✓/in New York ✓).
> (My brother/wife/best friend) gave it to me …
> for (my birthday/Christmas)
> I like it because it's (easy to use/useful/beautiful ✓).

Unit 9 Recording 10

One of my favourite possessions is my camera. It's very small, and I keep it in my bag. I bought it last year in New York. I like it because it's easy to use and it takes very good photos. I take photos of my friends, and of places and of me. I have a lot of photos of me in different places. I put them on my website. I travel a lot, and I usually travel alone, but my camera is my travel partner.

> **Optional extra activity**
> Put Ss in pairs to think of different examples to put in the brackets in the **Key phrases**, then invite the pairs to share their ideas with the class and compile them on the board.
>
> Possible ideas:
>
> *It's (black/silver/metal).*
>
> *I keep it (in a drawer/in a box/in my car).*
>
> *I bought it (ten years ago/a long time ago/in a market/on holiday).*
>
> *(My mother/boyfriend/daughter) gave it to me …*
>
> *(for Valentine's Day/when I left university/ for good luck in my exams)*
>
> *I like it because it's (fun/cute/lucky/easy to carry).*

4A First, give Ss time alone to prepare what they want to say about the possession: encourage them to make notes rather than writing full sentences and provide help as required. If Ss have brought their possession or a photo of it to class, they can think about how they will use it in their presentation. If they don't have the possession or a photo of it with them, they could draw a simple sketch of it. Then move Ss around so they're working with new partners, and give them time to tell each other about their possessions. Encourage the partners to give feedback about the talk, i.e. what was interesting, surprising and also anything they didn't understand. Ss can then adjust what they say about the possession before they move into groups in the next stage.

B Put Ss in groups of four or five. Tell Ss that while each person is talking about their possession, the listeners should write one question about the possession to ask the person when they've finished. When all the Ss have finished, each person in the group decides which possession is the most interesting/unusual and tells the rest of the class about it. Monitor the speaking activities carefully and make notes of good language use and any problem areas, for praise and correction at the end.

writeback a favourite possession

5A Direct Ss back to the questions in Ex 3A and tell them to tick each question that is answered in the text.

> **Answers:** Where did you get it?
> What do you do with it?
> Why do you like it?
> Other information:
> It doesn't answer: Where is it now?

B Remind Ss to use the example description as a model. You could suggest that they write about a different possession from the one they talked about in Ex 4, then when they've finished, collect in the descriptions and redistribute them. Ss then read out the description they've received, and the rest of the class has to guess whose possession it is.

> **Homework ideas**
> • Ss write about another favourite possession or about someone else's (e.g. a best friend or family member) favourite possession.

LOOKBACK

SUPPLEMENTARY MATERIALS

Ex 2B (optional extra activity): prepare matching exercise for Ss A and B (see notes).

LIKE, LOVE, HATE + -ING

1A Tell Ss to write the questions in their notebooks.

Answers: 2 What do you like reading? 3 What TV programme do you like watching? 4 Who do you like phoning? 5 What do you like eating for dinner? 6 Do you like travelling by plane? 7 What sport do you like doing? 8 What music do you like listening to?

B Tell Ss to ask each other the questions in random order, so they can't predict which question is next and have to listen to each other. Ss could report back to the class on things they have in common, and any of their partner's answers that they thought were surprising.

ACTIVITIES

2A You could run this as a competition in teams. Write or display the words on the board, one at a time. When a team member guesses a word, they put up their hand to answer and say the missing vowels only. They win a point for each correct vowel and continue until they make a mistake (and another team can continue) or finish the phrase.

Alternative idea
Run the activity as a team game, but for each phrase just write the correct number of dashes on the board. Teams guess one missing letter at a time, winning a point for each correct letter and losing a point if the letter isn't in the phrase.

Answers: 1 camping 2 cooking 3 going on long walks 4 chatting online 5 running 6 going to the theatre 7 playing computer games 8 relaxing 9 taking photos 10 swimming

B Tell Ss to think of an object (or place) they need for five of the activities in Ex 1A before they start asking and answering. Help with vocabulary as required. Go through the example or demonstrate the activity by inviting one or two Ss to ask you the questions about an activity.

Optional extra activity
If your Ss need extra support with this activity, tell Student A to answer questions about activities 1–5, and Student B activities 6–10. Then give A and B the following matching exercises on slips of paper, to help them with places and objects for their activities:

A

Match each activity 1–5 to a place and an object:
in the park	in the kitchen	in a campsite
on the beach	in an internet café	trainers
a computer	a sleeping bag	a cookbook	a map

....

B

Match each activity 6–10 to a place and object:
on the sofa	in the city	on the train	in a pool	at a wedding
a camera	an iPod	a ticket	a swimsuit	a good book

MONEY

3A You could run this as a competition in teams. Write or display the words on the board, one at a time. When a team member guesses a word, they put up their hand to answer and spell the verb. They win a point if the spelling is correct, and a point if they can give the correct past form of the verb.

Answers: 2 give 3 sell 4 cost 5 get 6 pay

B Give Ss a minute or two to complete the sentences, working alone.

Answers: 2 costs 3 pays 4 give 5 get 6 sell

C Tell Ss to think of a reason why they agree with the sentence, or to change the sentence so they agree with it, e.g. *Food costs too much. I agree because I paid (x amount) for (bread) yesterday.*

OBJECT PRONOUNS

4A You may want to review subject and object pronouns before Ss start this. Put Ss in pairs to 'test' each other, e.g.
A: *he*
B: *him* (etc.)

Answers: 2 d) 3 c) 4 e) 5 b) 6 a)

B Ss work alone on this. Help with vocabulary if required.

C Go through the example or demonstrate the activity with a student.

SHOPPING DEPARTMENTS

5A You could run this as a race in pairs or as a competition in teams. To win points, Ss need to spell the word correctly.

Answers: 1 Jewellery & Watches 2 Computers & Phones 3 Furniture & Lighting 4 Travel & Luggage 5 Home Entertainment 6 Bed & Bath 7 Menswear & Shoes 8 Beauty 9 Children's Clothes & Shoes 10 Toys

B Give Ss a few minutes to discuss this. If you have any Ss who don't like shopping in department stores, they could tell their partners about good websites they've found for buying things from some of the categories (furniture, lighting, luggage, etc.) online.

MAKING REQUESTS

6A Give Ss a few minutes to correct the mistakes, working alone.

Answers: B: Yes, I would like this pen. A: OK. Is it ~~he~~ a present? B: Er … yes. A: Which wrapping paper would you ~~would~~ like, red or green? B: I'd like the green paper. A: Who ~~Where~~ is the gift for? B: For me ~~I~~. Today is my birthday!

B Encourage Ss to look up from the page as much as possible, and cover the conversation when they feel confident with it.

C Demonstrate how to change parts of the conversation, e.g. *I'd like **these books**.*

D Ask a few pairs to act out their conversations for the class.

OVERVIEW

10.1 A NEW JOB
GRAMMAR | can/can't
VOCABULARY | collocations
HOW TO | talk about ability

COMMON EUROPEAN FRAMEWORK
Ss can find specific, predictable information in simple everyday material such as advertisements; can ask and answer questions about themselves and other people, things they can do.

10.2 TIME FOR A CHANGE
GRAMMAR | be going to
VOCABULARY | life changes
HOW TO | talk about plans

COMMON EUROPEAN FRAMEWORK
Ss can understand and extract the essential information from short recorded passages dealing with predictable everyday matters that are delivered slowly and clearly; can describe plans.

10.3 HELLO AND GOODBYE
FUNCTION | conversations
VOCABULARY | saying goodbye
LEARN TO | respond naturally

COMMON EUROPEAN FRAMEWORK
Ss can make an introduction and use basic greeting and leave-taking expressions; can ask how people are and react to news.

10.4 MIRANDA ⊙ BBC DVD
speakout | something new
writeback | an interview

COMMON EUROPEAN FRAMEWORK
Ss can extract the essential information from TV extracts where the visual supports the commentary; can give a short, rehearsed basic presentation on a familiar subject; can describe past activities and personal experiences.

10.5 LOOKBACK
Communicative revision activities

 BBC VIDEO PODCAST
People talking about the jobs they wanted to do.

A NEW JOB

Introduction
Ss practise reading and talking about job adverts and listening to job interviews. They also practise talking about ability, using *can* and related collocations.

SUPPLEMENTARY MATERIALS
Resource bank p171 and p173

Ex 2A: bring a driving license for vocabulary checking.
Ex 4D (optional extra activity): prepare a handout with extracts from the recording in Ex 3, with gaps for Ss to complete (see notes).

Warm up
Review names of jobs. Put Ss in pairs and give each pair a blank piece of paper. Tell them to think of five jobs, check their spelling in a dictionary, and write them, with the letters jumbled, on the paper. Each pair then passes the paper to the next pair, who try to guess the jobs and order the letters correctly, then pass the paper back for the writers to check. Bring the class together and make a list on the board of all the jobs they thought of. Check that Ss understand all the jobs by asking what the person does, where they work, etc.

VOCABULARY collocations

1A You could start by telling Ss to cover the word webs and look at the verbs in the box. Elicit one or two examples of a noun or phrase that goes with each verb, e.g. *cook pasta, ride a bike, speak English*, etc. Then direct Ss to the example and put them in pairs to complete the other word webs.

Answers: 2 play 3 speak 4 read 5 remember 6 make 7 drive 8 ride Activities in the photos: make coffee, read a map, ride a motorbike, play golf

B Demonstrate the activity with a *strong student* taking the part of Student B. Point out that Student B should try to remember the words without looking at the word webs.

READING

2A Start by checking the following vocabulary: *need* (demonstrate by trying to write on the board without a pen, and asking Ss: *What's the problem?*), *driving licence* (show an example), *memory* (compare with *remember*: if you remember things well, you have a good memory). Give Ss a few minutes to read the adverts and discuss their answers with a partner.

B You could go through sentence 1a) as an example with the class. Ss work alone or in pairs.

Answers: 1a) You need to speak ~~three~~ two languages. b) You *don't* need a car. *You need to drive. / You need a driving licence.* 2a) You *don't* work in the kitchen every day. *You sometimes work in the kitchen.* b) You *don't* need to live in the city. *You need to know the city well.* 3a) correct b) *Some of* the group's songs are ~~from the 90s~~ new.

3A Tell Ss to write the numbers 1–3 in their notebooks and write the name of the job next to each number as they listen. Ss could also underline key words/phrases in the job adverts to help them decide which job the person wants.

Answers: 1 pizza delivery person (No, he doesn't get the job.) 2 singer/guitarist (Yes, he gets the job.) 3 tour guide (We don't know if she gets the job.)

B Give Ss a minute or two to discuss this question with a partner before they listen again to check their ideas.

Answers: 1 He has an accident. 2 He sings and plays guitar. 3 She speaks three languages and she has a driving licence but she doesn't remember the interviewer's name.

Unit 10 Recording 1

Conversation 1

A: So, Greg. Thanks for coming in.
B: No problem.
A: Right, I have some questions for you.
B: OK.
A: Er … first of all, can you ride a motorbike?
B: Yes, um … yes, I can. Of course.
A: That's good. And do you know the city well? Can you find a place, fast?
B: Yes, I can. No problem.
A: And in this job you sometimes work alone …
B: That's not a problem.
A: … but you meet a lot of people.
B: I like people.
A: OK, good. Oh, and we sometimes get very busy and we need help in the kitchen – cleaning or cooking. Is that OK?
B: Yeah, no problem. I worked in a café last year and I made sandwiches … and pizzas.
A: Great! Can you start tomorrow?
B: Sure. Wow, I got the job?
A: Yes, congratulations! Come and look at the motorbike.
B: Oh, it's big.
A: Yeah, here you go. Try it.
B: Oh, er, OK. It's a bit difficult to ride. But I'm sure I can learn.
A: Be careful!
B: Aaah!
A: Oh, no! Greg, are you OK? Next interview, I think.

Conversation 2

A: So, you think this is the job for you.
B: Yeah, yeah I do.
A: OK, can you sing?
B: Yeah, I can. And I can play guitar.
C: OK, great. Let's hear something.
B: All right, here we go.
C: Not bad. OK, that's good. Nice. And what about dancing?
B: Ah … I can dance, but not very well.
A: Mmm. OK, but you can sing well and you're good on guitar.
C: OK, we'd like to try you … for a month.
B: That's great!

Conversation 3

A: So, what languages can you speak?
B: English, Japanese, Russian.
A: Great. And can you drive?
B: Yes.
A: OK. And can you remember facts and information?
B: Yes, I can. I have a very good memory.
A: So, can you remember my name?
B: Er … Did you say your name? Erm … Sorry, I can't remember.
A: Oh, dear … OK, let's try some other questions.

GRAMMAR can/can't

4A First, demonstrate the meaning of *can/can't* by acting out two examples, e.g. draw something badly on the board, then write the sentence *I can/can't draw* and ask Ss which alternative is correct. Then say something fairly complicated in English and write *I can/can't speak English*, for Ss to choose the correct alternative. Then give Ss two minutes to complete the tables.

Answers:

Can	you	sing? make pizzas?
Yes, No,	I	can. can't.

+	I/You/He/She	can	play guitar.
–	We/They	can't	drive.

Watch out!

Ss may think they need to use *to* with the verb, e.g. *I can to sing*. You could put the following sentences on the board and ask the class which are correct:

I can to sing.

I can sing.

Can you dance?

Can you to dance?

B You could write the rule on the board and elicit the correct answer.

Answer: your ability

C When Ss have repeated after the recording, they could practise saying the three words in quick succession to their partner (like a tongue twister) and see if their partner can hear the difference between them.

Teaching tip

If Ss have difficulty producing the weak form of *can*, tell them to try saying /kn/. It will also be easier when they practise saying it in a sentence because the main verb will carry the stress.

D Refer Ss to sounds 1, 2 and 3 in Ex 4C before you play the recording. When Ss have checked their answers, they could practise repeating the sentences. Point out that *can* is only pronounced /kæn/ in the short answer: in questions and affirmative statements, it's pronounced /kən/.

Answers: 2 2 3 1 4 1 5 3 6 3

⟶ LANGUAGEBANK 10.1 p136–137

Direct Ss to the note about using *well, quite well, very well* and *not very well* after *can*. You could give Ss Ex 10.1A for homework and use Ex 10.1B in class. When Ss have completed the conversation, they practise it in pairs, then two or three pairs act it out for the class, as dramatically as possible.

> **Answers:** A 2 can you speak 3 can ride 4 can't remember 5 can take 6 Can you read 7 can never understand 8 can't see
> B B: Let me try. Yes, I *can*. A: *Can* you walk on it? B: I don't know. Oh, no, I *can't*. A: OK, just sit down and relax. B: I *can't* relax! Where's my mobile? A: I *can't* see it. You *can* use my mobile. B: It's no good. A: What's the problem? B: I *can't* get a phone signal here. *Can* you go and get help? A: Yes, no problem. Don't move!

Optional extra activity

Prepare a handout for Ss with the following extracts from the recording about job interviews in Ex 3. Put them in pairs to help each other complete the conversations with the missing verbs (twelve in total), then refer them to the audio script to check, or play the recording again. Ss could also practise the dialogues with their partners.

1
A: Er … first of all, can you ___ a motorbike?
B: Yes, um … yes, I can. Of course.
A: That's good. And do you know the city well? Can you ___ a place, fast?
B: Yes, I can. No problem.

2
A: Great! Can you ___ tomorrow?
B: Sure. Wow, I got the job?
A: Yes, congratulations! Come and look at the motorbike.
B: Oh, it's big.
A: Yeah, here you go. Try it.
B: Oh, er, OK. It's a bit difficult to ride. But I'm sure I can.

3
A: OK, can you ___?
B: Yeah, I can. And I can ___ guitar.
C: OK, great. Let's hear something.
B: All right, here we go.
C: Not bad. OK, that's good. Nice. And what about dancing?
B: Ah … I can, but not very well.

4
A: So, what languages can you ___?
B: English, Japanese, Russian.
A: Great. And can you ___?
B: Yes.
A: OK. And can you ___ facts and information?
B: Yes, I can. I have a very good memory.
A: So, can you ___ my name?
B: Er … Did you say your name? Erm … Sorry, I can't.

PRACTICE

5A Go through the example with the class, then give Ss a few minutes to complete the questions, working alone or in pairs.

> **Answers:** 2 Can he sing? 3 Can Barbara ride a horse? 4 Can you dance? 5 Can you and your friend speak Italian? 6 Can George read Chinese?

B When Ss have completed these and checked their answers, they could practise asking and answering in pairs. *Stronger students* can cover the answers and try to remember them.

> **Answers:** 2 he can 3 she can't 4 I can, I can 5 we can't, we can speak 6 he can, he can't

Optional extra activity

Ss work in groups of three or four. Student A thinks of a job and the others guess what it is by asking up to ten questions with *Can you … ?* and a verb from Ex 1A. Student A guesses which job they're referring to and answers *Yes* or *No*, e.g.
Student B: *Can you play the guitar?*
Student A: *No, I'm not a musician.*
Student C: *Can you ride a motorbike?*
Student A: *No, I'm not a delivery person.*
Student D: *Can you drive a taxi?*
Student A: *Yes, I'm a taxi driver.*

⟶ PHOTOBANK p147

Ss match photos to sentences with *can/can't* and ability verbs.

> **Answers:** 1 I 2 G 3 D 4 H 5 F 6 C 7 E 8 B 9 A 10 J

SPEAKING

6A Direct Ss to the quiz and give them a minute or two to look at the questions. Elicit how to give positive answers as well as the negative one in the example, e.g. *Can you dance? Yes, I can dance quite well/very well.* Put Ss in pairs to go through the questions and note a number for their partner's answer next to each question. Monitor the pairwork carefully and make notes of good language use and problem areas for feedback later.

B Tell Ss to look at the sections where their partner got ten points or more. Then Ss tell each other which job(s) is/are good for them. You could encourage Ss to think of other jobs for their partners that are not mentioned in the key.

C Go through the example with the class, then give Ss a few minutes to talk about the questions in pairs. Bring the class together and invite Ss to report back on whether the quiz was right about them or not.

Homework ideas

- Ss write a job advert, following the examples in Ex 2A. You could give them a framework, e.g.
  Title
  Can you _____ ?
  Do you _____ ?
  Are you _____ ?
  We are _____ .
  We need a _____ .
  Contact us at (email address).
- **Workbook Ex 1–4, p63–64**

TIME FOR A CHANGE

Introduction

Ss practise listening to people talking about their goals. They practise talking about their plans and goals for the future, using *be going to* and vocabulary related to life changes. They also learn how to check their written work.

> **SUPPLEMENTARY MATERIALS**
>
> Resource bank p172
>
> **Ex 5A**: prepare your own 'road' with five goals for the future to show the class.

Warm up

Tell Ss to close their books and write the title *Time for a change* on the board. Ask for one or two examples from the class of things that people change (e.g. about themselves, their lives, things around them, etc.). Then put Ss in pairs to brainstorm more examples. After two or three minutes, invite pairs to share their answers with the class.

Possible examples: *people change their job, the city or country where they live, their house, the furniture and colours in their house, their car, their school, their hair (colour or style), the way they spend their free time, etc.*

VOCABULARY life changes

1A Tell Ss to cover the text in Ex 1A and focus on the photos. Elicit from the class what the person wants to do in the future in each case and establish that these things are *goals*. Then direct Ss to the text and identify the goals in the photos.

> **Answers:** spend more time with the family and friends, lose weight, stop smoking, save money, get fit, get organised, work less and relax more

B You could tell Ss about one of the things on the list that you want to do, then put them in pairs to ask each other.

> **Optional extra activity**
> Ss work in pairs. Student A gives a clue about one of the goals in Ex 1A and Student B guesses which one it is. Then Student B gives a clue, and so on, e.g.
> A: *You don't eat cakes and sweets.*
> B: *Lose weight!*
> A: *Right!*

LISTENING

2A Check that Ss understand what they have to do by asking what Tom's goal is from Ex 1A (learn something new). Point out that some people may have more than one goal.

> **Answers:** 2 Fiona 10 3 Liam 3, 4 4 Rudi 2 5 Alex 9, 3

B Give Ss time to read the sentences before they listen again. They may already be able to decide if some of the sentences are true or false, then check when they listen again.

> **Answers:** 1 F 2 T 3 F 4 F 5 F 6 T 7 T 8 T

C Give Ss a few minutes to discuss the question, then invite a few individuals to report back to the class.

Unit 10 Recording 4

Conversation 1

A: Hi, do you have a minute?

B: Yeah, sure.

A: What's your name?

B: Tom.

A: OK, Tom. Can you look at this list? It's people's top ten goals in life.

B: Oh, OK.

A: So, do you have a goal for this year?

B: A goal? Yes, I want to learn something new. My girlfriend can cook really well, but she doesn't like cooking. So I'm going to learn to cook.

A: That's interesting. Any special type of cooking?

B: Yeah, Japanese food. I lived in Japan and I love Japanese food.

A: I see, well …

Conversation 2

A: So, Fiona, do you have a goal for this year?

C: I'm going to change jobs.

A: That's a big change!

C: Yeah, well, I work in an office, and I don't like it. I'd like to work outside.

A: Great.

C: My friend Sheila is going to help me.

A: Well, good luck with that.

C: Thanks!

Conversation 3

A: Liam, do you have a goal for this year?

D: Yes, I do.

A: So, what are you going to do?

D: Well, I work with computers, sometimes twelve hours a day and I often take work home. It isn't good …

A: Right.

D: … so this year I'm going to spend more time with my friends and I'm not going take work home.

A: Great.

Conversation 4

A: Rudi, what are your goals?

E: Er… I'm going to get fit. I never do sport. I can't play tennis or anything, but I'm going to start exercising. Something easy. Take a walk every day.

A: Sounds good.

Conversation 5

A: What's your goal this year, Alex?

F: I have two goals really.

A: Oh, and what are they?

F: One is to save more money. The other is to see my friends more.

A: That's great. And what are your plans? With your friends?

F: Well … hmm … maybe go shopping together.

A: Go shopping? Then you aren't going to save money!

F: Yeah, but I'm not going to stop shopping!

GRAMMAR *be going to*

3A You could either put the four sentences on the board and go through the two questions with the whole class, or put Ss in pairs to discuss them first. You may also want to check the idea that *be going to* is for plans, by asking a question such as *Is this my idea/ opinion about the future, or my plan (something I decided before)?*

> **Answers:** 1 future 2 + a, b; – c, d

B You could draw the table on the board and write the answers into the gaps as you elicit them from the class. You could also check the form with *we* and *they* and add them to the table.

Answers:

I'm You're She's	going to	change jobs. work less. get fit.

Watch out!

Ss may leave out *be*, e.g. *I going to change jobs.* You could write one or two examples without *be* on the board and ask Ss if they're correct to raise their awareness of the potential omission. Monitor the practice activities carefully for mistakes like this.

C You could write the examples on the board and invite two Ss to come out and change them to the negative form.

Answers: He isn*'t* going to be there.
We are*n't* going to come.

D When Ss have listened to the sentences, ask them if they could hear *to* in *going to change* … etc. Point out that, although it is there, it isn't stressed, so it's a very small sound.

Teaching tip

If Ss have difficulty producing the weak sound, tell them to try just saying /t/. There will naturally be a small 'explosion' of air after the consonant, which will sound like a schwa /ə/.

⟹ **LANGUAGEBANK** 10.2 p136–137

You could use Ex 10.2A for a listening correction activity. Ss close their books and you read out one sentence at a time. Ss put up their hands and either tell you the correct version of the sentence or say it's correct. Ss could do Ex 10.2B in pairs, then practise the conversation together.

Answers: A 2 Charlotte's going *to* be a writer. 3 I ~~are~~ '*m* going to stay home tomorrow. 4 We aren't going to arrive before seven o'clock. ✓ 5 Antonio's going to leave work at five. 6 I'm not going to pay! 7 Kiera and Sam ~~is~~ *are* going to drive to Chicago. 8 My daughter isn't going to sell her flat. ✓
B 2 to 3 not 4 he 5 're 6 buy 7 's 8 going

PRACTICE

4A Ss can complete the sentences alone or in pairs.

Answers: 2 I'm not going to do the homework tonight. 3 Tonight, the teacher is going to watch TV. 4 I'm not going to write any emails tomorrow.   5 Tomorrow afternoon, I'm going to relax. 6 On Friday, my friends and I are going to see a film.

B Show Ss how to change the example sentence, e.g. *After class, I'm going to have a sandwich.* or *After class, I'm not going to have a coffee.* Give Ss a few minutes to work on the sentences alone.

C Go through the example, pointing out that they need to ask *What about you?* to find out their partner's answer. Tell them to make a note of their partner's answers, as they'll need to remember them for the next stage. N.B. Although the question form is not covered in this lesson, if a *stronger class* asks you about it, you could elicit *What are you going to do?*

D Put Ss in groups of four or five to tell each other about their plans.

SPEAKING

5A Start by putting the following verb prompts on the board, to help Ss with ideas: *get, learn, change, spend, stop, work, meet, see, go to, visit.* You could demonstrate this by preparing your own 'road' with future goals and drawing/displaying it on the board and explaining it to the class. Ss could put their 'road' of future goals on a separate piece of paper, to give themselves more space to write, or to draw simple pictures representing the goals (this will also be easier for Ss to carry round with them if necessary in the next stage).

B This could be done in groups, or Ss could stand up and walk round the class, talking to different people. Monitor the activity closely and make notes of good language use and problem areas, for praise and correction later.

WRITING checking your work

6A First check that Ss understand *punctuation*, by writing punctuation marks on the board and eliciting their names (capital letter, apostrophe, question mark). Ss can work alone, then compare their answers in pairs before checking with the whole class.

Answer: Thanks for your email. Here'*s* the information about my plans. I'm going *to* be in Istanbul on *S*unday for three days. Can we ~~to~~ meet? My hotel is the FiveStar in Topsu Street. I'*m* going to visit the Blue Mosque on Monday and I'*d* like to look around the markets. Can we have lunch together one day*?* ~~Are~~ *Is* Tuesday good for you? Email me or ~~texted~~ me.

speakout TIP

To help Ss to think of other things to check in their writing, put the following on the board to show mistakes with spelling, word order and vocabulary, and elicit corrections:
tomorow, munth
We can meet? I'm going not to have lunch.
say two languages, pass time with friends

B You could tell Ss to imagine they're visiting a different city, and think of the places they'd like to see there. For *weaker classes*, tell Ss to follow the email in Ex 6A, changing the place names and days.

C Ss swap emails and check them for mistakes. You could suggest that they use a code, e.g. *P* (punctuation), *V* (verbs), *S* (spelling), *WO* (word order), *VO* (vocabulary) and write the letters in the margin, on the same line as the mistake. Then they give the email back and correct their own mistakes.

D You could give Ss some ideas about what to include here, e.g.
Dear ____ ,
Nice to hear from you. I hope you enjoy your visit to ____. Yes, ____ is good for me. Let's meet at (name of café/restaurant) at (time).
See you then,
____

Homework ideas
• Workbook Ex 1–6, p65–66

HELLO AND GOODBYE

Introduction

Ss practise listening to and using phrases for starting and ending conversations. They also learn to respond naturally.

SUPPLEMENTARY MATERIALS

Resource bank p174

Warm up: be prepared to tell Ss an anecdote (see notes).

Ex 2A: bring a bank card and a business card for vocabulary checking.

Ex 2A (alternative approach): prepare cut up copies of the three complete conversations for each pair of Ss.

Ex 6B (optional extra activity): prepare prompts on slips of paper for each student (see notes).

Warm up

You could start by telling Ss a short, simple anecdote about the last time you spoke to a stranger, e.g. to ask the time, to offer help, etc.

Then write the following questions on the board:

When did you last speak to a stranger? Where were you?
Why did you speak? Did you see the person again?
Would you like to see the person again?

Give Ss time to think about their answers to the questions, then put them in pairs to ask and answer. Monitor the activity and ask any Ss who had a particularly interesting story to tell the rest of the class.

FUNCTION   conversations

1A If Ss are from the same country, they can brainstorm as many ways as possible of saying hello and goodbye and starting a conversation with a stranger. If Ss are from different countries, they can teach each other how to say hello and goodbye in their language, and compare acceptable ways of starting conversations.

B Tell Ss to note down any key words or phrases that help them to decide if the people are friends or strangers, e.g. *How are you? Nice to meet you.*

Answers: 1 F 2 S 3 S

C Give Ss a minute or two to read through the options before playing the recording again. Vocabulary to check: *get off a bus/train* (mime, also compare with *get on*), *bank card* vs *business card* (show examples).

Answers: 1 b) 2 a) 3 c)

2A Ss could work in pairs to complete the conversations. Give them time to check their answers in the audio script, or if you think it would benefit Ss to hear the complete conversations, play the recording again.

Answers: 2 time 3 have 4 have 5 going 6 this 7 think 8 around 9 friend 10 talk

Alternative approach

Prepare copies (one per pair of Ss) of the completed conversations from Ex 2A and cut them up into separate lines. In pairs, Ss first separate the three conversations, then put them in order. They then listen to the recording to check, moving the lines around if necessary as they listen.

B Go through the examples with the class and point out that they need to find four more examples of each.

Answers:
1
Excuse me, do you have the time?
So where are you going?
What do you think of the music?
Are you from around here?
2
I'm sorry, I have a lesson at two.
Oh look, this is my station.
I'm sorry, I can see an old friend over there.
Nice to talk to you.

C You could remind Ss that the stress is usually on the words that carry the meaning of the sentence, and give them an opportunity to predict where the stress will be, before they listen to the recording.

Answers: <u>What</u> do you <u>think</u> of the <u>music</u>?
Are you from <u>around</u> <u>here</u>?
Is <u>that</u> the <u>time</u>?
<u>Nice</u> to <u>talk</u> to you.

⟹ LANGUAGEBANK 10.3 p136–137

Give Ss time to read through the summary of phrases for starting and ending conversations. You could use Ex 10.3 for conversation practice in pairs.

Answers: 2 This is a nice place. 3 What do you think of the music? 4 I can see an old friend over there. 5 Nice to talk to you. 6 Good to talk to you, too. 7 Is that the time? 8 I have a meeting in ten minutes.

Unit 10 Recording 6

Conversation 1

A: Hi, Duncan.
B: Hi, how are you?
A: Good thanks. Hey, this is a great place.
B: Yes, it's really good. I often come here.
A: … well, that was delicious. Let's have coffee.
B: OK … wait, is that the time? I'm sorry, I have a lesson at two. Here's some money for lunch.
A: No, that's all right. Keep in touch!
B: See you in two weeks, after the holidays, yeah?
A: Oh yes, that's right. See you then …

Conversation 2

A: Excuse me, do you have the time?
B: Yes, it's half past four.
A: Thanks. So … erm … where are you going?
B: Me? I'm going to …
… so you're from Madrid. That's interesting.
A: Yes, well, I come from Cordoba. I moved to Madrid when I was ten.
B: I see … Oh, look, this is my station.
A: Look, here's my card.
B: And here's mine.
A: Very nice to meet you.
B: Nice to meet you, too.
A: I hope we meet again.
B: I hope so, too.
A: Goodbye.
B: Bye!

Conversation 3

A: What do you think of the music?
B: It's not bad.
A: Hi, I'm Doug.
B: Oh, hello. I'm Jo.
A: So, are you from around here?
B: No, I'm not actually. I'm from …
A: … yes and I was in China the next year. I speak Chinese, you know.
B: Oh, really?
A: And I speak four other languages. French, German, Spanish …
B: I'm sorry, I can see an old friend over there. Nice to talk to you.
A: Oh … and you.
B: See you later.
A: See you soon.

3A Working in pairs or alone, Ss write the full conversations in their notebooks.

> **Answers:**
> A: This is a good party.
> B: Yes, it is. What do you think of the food?
> A: It's good.
> B: I'm (your name).
> A: Hi, I'm (your name).
> B: Are you from around here?
> A: Yes, I live in (place).
> A: Oh, is that the time?
> B: Yes, I have a class at half past six.
> A: And my train leaves at quarter past.
> B: Nice to talk to you.
> A: Nice to talk to you, too.

B Ss should use the prompts for practice, rather than reading the full conversation from their notebooks. Once Ss are feeling confident with the conversation you could suggest that they cover their side of the prompts, so they can only see their partner's prompts and practise again. Ss could also change some of the words in the prompts, e.g. *food (music), good (great/terrible), class (meeting/appointment), half past six (seven o'clock), train (bus), quarter past (half past).*

LEARN TO respond naturally

4A Elicit some ideas for number 1 from the class as an example, then put Ss in pairs to discuss the rest. Point out that in this case *respond naturally* means without having to think about what to say or saying something that people always say in this kind of situation.

B Ss may need to listen more than once to write the responses accurately.

> **Answers:** 1B: Yes, it's really good. 2B: Nice to meet you, too. 3B: I hope so, too. 4B: Here's mine.

speakout TIP

Ask Ss how these two-line conversations can help their speaking (because Ss can learn them and use them from memory, without having to think about what to say/how to say it).

C Encourage Ss to cover the conversations in Ex 4A and just practise from the prompts.

VOCABULARY saying goodbye

5A Ss can work in pairs and try to help each other complete the phrases before checking in the audio script. Point out that the only phrase that is not fixed is 2 (… *in a few weeks, … in an hour, … in two months,* etc.), and that *see you soon* and *see you later* are used interchangeably, despite the apparent difference in meaning.

> **Answers:** 1 see you soon 2 see you in two weeks 3 keep in touch 4 bye 5 see you later

B Ss can do this in pairs, or walking round the class, talking to different people. The idea is <u>not</u> to repeat A's phrase but to vary the way of saying goodbye.

SPEAKING

6A Give Ss a few minutes to prepare what they are going to say about the music, food, their plans for the weekend, what they did last weekend, etc.

B If possible, set up the room to suggest a party rather than a classroom, e.g. move some furniture, play some music. You could demonstrate walking up to a student and saying *Hi (X), what do you think of … ?* and wait for the student to respond, then gesture for the rest of the class to start talking. If you play music, you could pause it every minute or so, as a 'cue' for Ss to move on to talk to someone else. Monitor and make notes of good language use and any problem areas for praise and correction later.

> **Optional extra activity**
> Set up a situation in which the Ss are at a party where they don't know anybody else (e.g. at a conference, or in the first week at university). Prepare prompts like the following on slips of paper and give one to each student:
> *You don't like parties.*
> *You're bored.*
> *You're very hungry because you didn't eat breakfast or lunch today.*
> *You don't have any friends, so try to make friends with people at the party.*
> *You like talking about your pet goldfish.*
> *You were late for the party because of traffic. Tell everyone you meet about it.*
> *You're very unhappy because you broke up with your boyfriend/girlfriend.*
> *You are very interested in computers.*
> *The music's very loud and you can't hear what people say.*
> *You like talking about the weather.*
>
> Tell Ss they should use their prompt in the way they talk/act at the party, but they shouldn't repeat exactly what it says to other Ss. Collect the prompts.
>
> When the 'party' has finished, display all the prompts on the board and ask Ss to identify the person who had each one.

> **Homework ideas**
> * Ss imagine they are one of the people in conversation 2 or 3 from Ex 1. They write an email to a friend telling them about meeting someone new: where they met, what they talked about, what they thought of the other person, etc.
> * Workbook Ex1–3, p67

MIRANDA

Introduction

Ss watch an extract from the BBC comedy series *Miranda*, which shows the main character trying to change her life. Ss then learn and practise how to talk about a time when they learnt something new and write a magazine interview.

> ### SUPPLEMENTARY MATERIALS
>
> **Warm up:** prepare sets of cards with collocations (see notes).
>
> **Ex 2A (optional extra activity):** prepare a handout with sentences about the DVD extract for Ss to choose the correct alternatives (see notes).
>
> **Ex 3A:** bring in/download pictures of ideas for new things to learn.
>
> **Ex 3B:** be prepared to answer questions about a time when you tried to learn something new.

Warm up

Review collocations from lessons 10.1 and 10.2. Prepare one set of cards per pair with the following collocations:
stop smoking, get fit, change jobs, play an instrument, ride a bike, get organised, make a coffee, drive a bus, lose weight, save money, spend time with friends, learn something new.

Ss put the cards in a pile face down in front of them and take turns to pick a card. The person with the card says the part of the collocation after the verb and their partner has to remember the correct verb and say the full collocation, e.g.
A: *time with friends*
B: *spend time with friends*

DVD PREVIEW

1A Ss could start by covering the prompts and trying to think of one thing for each situation, then tell the class their ideas. When Ss look at the prompts, you may want to check:
feel stupid (you could mime this), *too expensive* (you can't pay for it), *the wrong clothes* (give an example, e.g. jeans for a wedding). Give Ss a few minutes to decide which problems go with each situation.

> **Possible answers:**
> learn something new: all the prompts apart from *It's too expensive*
> change jobs: all the prompts apart from *The teacher doesn't like you*, *It's too expensive*
> go to a new place: *You have the wrong clothes*, *You don't know the people*, *It's too expensive*
> spend time with friends: *You're bored*, *You have the wrong clothes*
> try to get fit: all the prompts apart from *You don't know the people*

B Before Ss read the information, check: *the star* (the most important person), *thirty-something* (between 31 and 39).

> **Answers:**
> 1 Miranda wants to change her life.
> 2 She tries
> • to learn something new
> • to go to a new place
> • to spend time with friends
> • to get fit

▶ DVD VIEW

2A Give Ss time to read through the problems and places before they watch the extract. You could play the extract without sound the first time: Ss can match the problems and places without hearing what Miranda says.

> **Answers:** 1 c, d, e 2 b 3 a, c, d

> **Optional extra activity**
> Prepare a handout with the following sentences about the DVD extract, and ask Ss to choose the correct alternative in each case:
> 1 She ran/didn't run up the stairs.
> 2 She opened/didn't open the door of the gym.
> 3 She ate/didn't eat sushi.
> 4 She gave/didn't give someone soy sauce.
> 5 She danced/didn't dance with Chris.
> 6 She danced/didn't dance with the teacher.
> Answers:
> 1 didn't run, 2 didn't open, 3 ate, 4 gave, 5 didn't dance, 6 danced

B Ss try to remember/predict which phrases Miranda said.

C When Ss have checked their answers, you could also ask them who says the other phrases. (b) – the man at the gym, f) – her friend at the dance class, g) – the dance teacher, h) – her friend at the dance class)

> **Answers:** a) c) d) e)

> **Optional extra activity**
> In pairs, Ss choose one of the following situations and role-play the conversation between the two people:
> • Miranda and her flatmate, telling her about the things she tried and what happened;
> • The man at the gym and his wife/girlfriend, telling her about Miranda's visit to the gym;
> • The woman working at the sushi restaurant telling her friend about Miranda at the restaurant;
> • Another student from the dance class, telling a friend about what happened at the lesson.
> Invite Ss to act out their conversations for the class.

DVD 10 Miranda

M=Miranda R=Receptionist W=Woman
D=Dance instructor P=Miranda's partner

M: I am off to the gym, yes, the gym. Oh yes, look at me go. Ah. Excuse me, I don't think these doors are working.

R: Are you OK?

M: Oh – that way.
Oh, yes … feeling that.
Help! Make it stop please! Someone make it stop! Help! I mean what do they do? I mean does anyone really know what they do?
Whaa!
No, I'm stuck. My … necklace.

W: …'s on the floor.

M: Oh stop … actually sorry, sorry. OK …

W: Don't pull it just un- just undo it at the back.

M: I can't. There's too much down the hole. So sorry, sorry. Sorry. Hello, afternoon. I've unhooked, I've unhooked, sorry about this, sorry, sorry. Sorry about this. Can I … whilst I'm here, OK. Hello again. Right, where were we?

W: Leaving.

M: Quick!

D: 'Fantastico, muy sensual.'

P: Wow! She is amazing.

D: Stop, stop! '¡Bailas como un hipopótamo!' You will not learn when you dance with her. Chris! You are a natural.

P: Really?

D: You mind?

M: Well I do a bit.

D: Silence! 'Musica.'

M: Carry on. Nothing to see here.

speakout something new

3A Start by brainstorming some examples of new things people learn. You could bring in/download pictures to represent some of the following and display them on the board, to help Ss with ideas: a sport (e.g. sailing, skiing), a game (e.g. cards, chess), ride a horse/a bike, a musical instrument, dancing, painting/drawing, making clothes/jewellery/pottery, photography, cooking (e.g. Italian/Indian/Chinese food), another language. Give Ss time to make notes, working alone.

B You could start by inviting different Ss to ask you the questions about a time you tried to learn something new.

C You may need to play the recording twice for Ss to answer all the questions fully. Give them time to compare answers before listening a second time.

> **Answers:** 1 She learned guitar three years ago because she can sing and she likes music. 2 Alone (at first) but she wasn't very good. 3 She had a teacher. He was good. 4 The teacher gave her homework. She learned to play well after four months. She still plays.

D Give Ss time to read the **Key phrases**, then play the recording again.

> **Answers:** I wanted to learn (to play guitar ✓/to cook) because …
> I went to a class.
> I tried to learn it (alone ✓/with a friend).
> I was/wasn't ✓ (very) good at it.
> The teacher was (great ✓/good/not very good).
> After (four/six) months I (played guitar ✓/did it) really well.
> I still (do it/play) every day. ✓

> **Optional extra activity**
> Remind Ss about some of the prompts in Ex 1A by asking them to complete the following sentence stems with some of them:
> *I went to a class but (the teacher didn't like me/I made mistakes).*
> *I tried to learn it alone but (I didn't understand what to do/I wasn't good at it).*
> They could also change the prompts to the negative:
> *The teacher was great because (I didn't feel stupid/I wasn't bored/I made mistakes but it was OK).*

4A First, give Ss time alone to prepare what they want to say: direct them back to their answers to the questions in Ex 3A and tell them to use the **Key phrases** and their own ideas to expand the answers into a story. When they practise telling their story to their partner, encourage the partners to give feedback, e.g. suggest some other information they could include, or explain something more clearly.

B Put Ss in groups of four or five. Tell Ss that while each person is talking about their experience, the listeners should make notes and write one question about what the person tried to learn to ask them when they've finished. Point out that Ss will need this information about each other for Ex 5B. Monitor Ss as they tell their stories and make notes of good language use and any problem areas, for praise and correction at the end.

Unit 10 Recording 9

Three years ago I bought a guitar. I wanted to learn to play guitar because I can sing and I like music. I tried to learn it alone. I had a book and I practised every day. I learned some songs, and I played guitar and sang the songs. I was happy, but then my boyfriend said I wasn't very good at it. He said I needed a teacher. So I found a teacher, and studied guitar with him. The teacher was great but it was very different because he gave me homework every week. After four months I played guitar really well. I still play every day.

writeback an interview

5A Give Ss time to read the interview, then discuss the questions in pairs.

> **Answers:** 1 To use *Twitter*. Because his or her friends use *Twitter*.
> Answers to 2 and 3 will vary among Ss.

B Ss should use the notes they made while they were listening to other Ss in Ex 4B. Point out that they should also extend the interview beyond the last line of the example in Ex 5A, i.e. they should include questions and answers about how the person learnt and how successful they were. You could then invite some individuals to read out their interview with a partner (not the student in the interview) and ask the rest of the class to guess who it was.

> **Homework ideas**
> • Ss write an interview with another student from their group in Ex 4B.

LOOKBACK

COLLOCATIONS

1A You could run this as a race. The first pair to write in the correct verbs and bring them up to show you wins the race.

> **Answers:** 2 I ~~ride~~ tennis every weekend. *play*
> 3 It's easy to ~~ride~~ maps. *read*
> 4 I ~~play~~ two languages. *speak*
> 5 I ~~cook~~ all my clothes. *make*
> 6 I ~~remember~~ my bike to work. *ride*
> 7 I would like to ~~make~~ a bus. *drive*
> 8 It's easy to ~~drive~~ phone numbers. *remember*

B You could either elicit the words/phrases from the class as a whole, or put Ss in pairs and give them a time limit.

> **Possible answers:**
> play football, the guitar, computer games
> read music, words in Arabic
> speak Spanish, Japanese
> make a pizza, a coffee, a sandwich
> ride a horse, a motorbike
> drive a car, a taxi
> remember information, English words, birthdays

C Ss could also use the verbs they thought of in Ex 1B to change the sentences and make then true, e.g. *I often cook pasta. I play football every weekend.*

CAN/CAN'T

2A Tell Ss to write the questions in their notebooks.

> **Answers:** What songs can you sing?
> What sports can you play?
> What food can you cook?
> What important dates can you remember?

B Tell Ss to ask each other the questions in random order, so they can't predict which question is next and have to listen to each other. Ss could report back to the class on things they have in common, and any of their partner's answers that they thought were surprising.

> **Alternative idea**
> Tell Ss to include one answer which is not true. Their partner then has to guess which answer it is, but they only have two chances to guess. Their partner wins a point if they don't guess correctly.

LIFE CHANGES

3A Ss could do this alone or in pairs.

> **Answers:** 2 change jobs 3 save money 4 learn something new 5 spend more time with friends 6 work less and relax more 7 help others 8 stop smoking 9 lose weight 10 get fit

B You could suggest that Ss put the life changes in order from *easy* ➔ *difficult* before they start discussing. For **stronger classes,** tell them to justify their answers, e.g. *It's easy to learn something new if you want to do it.*

BE GOING TO

4A Put Ss in pairs to write the sentences and help each other with the correct verbs.

> **Answers:** He's going to go to the café. He's going to meet Sue and Jenny.
> He's going to go to the gym. He's going to get fit.
> He's going to go to the cash machine. He's going to get 200 euros.
> He's going to go to the newsagent's. He's going to get/buy a newspaper.
> He's going to go to the pharmacy. He's going to buy/get aspirin.

> **Optional extra activity**
> Tell Ss to close their books and write the following prompts on the board:
> | | | |
> |---|---|---|
> | *125 euros* | *bread and coffee* | *do a class* |
> | *shampoo* | *Tim and Mike* | *a magazine* |
> Ss write the man's plans, remembering the places that he's going to go to and matching the prompts to them, e.g. *He's going to go to the pharmacy. He's going to buy shampoo.*

B You could demonstrate this by writing four places for yourself. You may also want to brainstorm some names of places with the class, e.g. *the library, the doctor's, the dentist's, the swimming pool, the cinema, (name) school, the garage,* etc.

C Demonstrate the activity with a student taking the part of B.

SAYING GOODBYE

5 You could run this as a competition in teams. To win points, Ss need to spell the corrected word correctly.

> **Answers:** 1 See you later. 2 Bye. 3 See you ~~one~~ *next* week. 4 Keep ~~on~~ *in* touch. 5 See *you* soon.

CONVERSATIONS

6A Give Ss a few minutes to complete the conversation, working alone.

> **Answers:**
> A: Hi!
> B: Oh, hi. How *are* you?
> A: Good, thanks. This is a *nice* café.
> B: Yes, I sometimes come here for lunch.
> A: Really? What *do* you think of the food?
> B: Er … it's good. Wait, is *that* the time?
> A: No, that clock's wrong. It's two o'clock.
> B: Oh no, my train leaves in five *minutes*!
> A: No problem. There's a train every half hour.
> B: Sorry, I can see an old friend over *there*.
> A: Oh, OK. *Nice* to talk to you.
> B: And to you. See *you* soon …

B Encourage Ss to look up from the page as much as possible, and cover the conversation when they feel confident with it.

C Demonstrate how to change the parts in bold, e.g.
A: *Very well, thanks. This is a nice restaurant.*
B: *Yes, I sometimes come here for dinner.*

D Ss can either change partners or stand up and walk around the class, practising the conversation with different people, and changing it as they go along. Monitor this speaking practice and be prepared to give feedback on Ss' language use.

REVIEW 5: UNITS 9–10

Introduction

The aim of the review units is for Ss to revise and practise the grammar, vocabulary and pronunciation from the previous two units in a different context. The context for this review unit is Ss' progress in English so far and plans for improving their English in the future.

SUPPLEMENTARY MATERIALS

Ex 4A: prepare strips of paper with ideas to help Ss (see notes).

Warm up

Tell Ss to close their books and write the title *What can you do in English?* on the board. Also write the following verb prompts and put Ss in pairs to think about what they can do: *talk about, describe, ask, answer, pronounce, tell, write.*

Invite Ss to share their ideas with the rest of the class.

Possible answers: *talk about (e.g. my job), describe (e.g. a place), ask (e.g. someone's name and address), answer (e.g. about my likes and dislikes), pronounce (e.g. the alphabet in English), tell (e.g. a story), write (e.g. an email to a friend).*

READING AND GRAMMAR

1A Before Ss start the questionnaire, check the following vocabulary: *count* (demonstrate), *order* (demonstrate), *routines* (things you do every day/week), *sound* (demonstrate *sound happy, sound sad*). You could suggest that Ss put a tick (✓) in the box if they're confident that they can do it, a question mark (?) if they're not sure/not very confident, and a cross (x) if they think they can't do it.

B Go through the example, then suggest a few different answers that Ss could give to their partner, depending on how confident they feel:
Yes, definitely.
Yes, but I need more practice.
I'm not really confident about that yet.
Not really.

Give Ss time to ask and answer all the questions: they could ask some of the questions in random order, so their partners can't predict which question is next and have to listen more carefully. Ss could report back to the class about things they can both do, e.g. *We can both order food and drink in a café.* (Note the position of *can* – before *both*).

C First check that Ss understand *improve* (make better). Give them a few minutes to think about the skills and complete the sentences, working alone.

D Once again, Ss can see what they have in common.

2A To give Ss a simple reading task while they read the text, ask them which three things from the box in Ex 1C the student writes about (Answer: *reading, listening, pronunciation*). Ss then work alone to substitute the pronouns and compare answers with a partner.

Answers: 2 me 3 she 4 us 5 they 6 we 7 them 8 us 9 him 10 He

B Give Ss a few minutes to discuss the questions, then invite them to share their ideas with the class.

Possible answers: 2 The most important words in each sentence are stressed by the speaker, so this helps you to follow the overall meaning of the text.
3 You can imitate the person's pronunciation and try to match the speed, rhythm and tone, so you sound more natural.

LISTENING AND GRAMMAR

3A Tell Ss that the people are talking about areas of English they want to work on/improve, then play the recording.

Answers: 2 Speaking 3 Listening 4 Grammar 5 Writing

B You could ask Ss to work in pairs and discuss which alternative they think is best, before they listen again and check the speakers' answers.

Answers: 1 seven 2 write 3 coffee break 4 at the same time 5 write 6 day

C You could discuss this question with the class as a whole, and ask Ss to justify their answers.

Review 5 Recording 1

1 I want to learn a lot of vocabulary, so I'm going to learn seven new words every day. I like reading, so I'm going to look at the BBC news website and write down new words.

2 Speaking is a problem for me. In the coffee break, I'm not going to speak in my language. I'm going to speak in English. All the time!

3 I can't understand English very well, so I'm going to practise listening. I'm going to listen to my CD and read the audio scripts at the same time.

4 My grammar is bad. Very bad! I'm going to look on the internet and do some extra grammar practice.

5 I want to improve my writing, so I'm going to write a diary every night, in English. I'm going to write about my day.

SPEAKING

4A As well as directing Ss to Ex 3A for ideas, you could put the following prompts on strips of paper and pass them round the class for Ss to use if they match their goals and appeal to them as a good idea:

- Read and write to an internet forum about something you are interested in.
- Have a speaking partner in the class and speak English for ten minutes every day.
- Use the *speakout* CD to practise sounds.
- Watch the *speakout* podcasts at home and read the audio script at the same time.
- Write new words in a vocabulary book.
- Read an easy English book.

B Put Ss in groups of four or five to tell each other their plans. Monitor the activity and invite any student who has particularly good ideas to tell the whole class about them at the end.

5 Direct Ss to p117 and give them a minute or two to look at the game and the instructions. Then check the instructions by asking Ss about squares 1 and 2, e.g.
T: *What do I do for number 1?*
Ss: *You talk about your town/city or country for thirty seconds.*
T: *And for number 2?*
Ss: *You say and spell three transport words.*
N.B. Tell Ss that they should use a watch or timer function on a mobile phone to time the speaker for thirty seconds. Put Ss into groups of three or four to play the game.

If you don't have any dice, tell each group to tear a small piece of paper into six pieces and write a number from 1–6 on each one. Then they can put the pieces of paper in an envelope or small bag and each person can pick a number when it's their turn. Ss can use a coin or other small object as their counter.

Monitor the groups carefully and make notes of good language use and any problem areas for praise and correction later.

SOUNDS: /ɑː/ AND /ɜː/

6A Direct Ss to the pictures and point out that the symbols represent the sounds. Play the recording for Ss to listen to the sounds and the words. You could also show Ss that to make /ɑː/ their mouth is open (as if they're at the dentist's), and that for /ɜː/ the sound is like someone's reaction when they hear about something that sounds horrible to eat (e.g. spaghetti with chocolate).

B You may want to ask Ss to predict which group the words belong to before they listen. You could pause the recording after each group of words, and ask individual Ss to repeat them, rather than Ss repeating in chorus. This will give you more opportunity to correct their pronunciation of the 'target' sounds.

Answers: /ɑː/ last, party, guitarist, can't, dance
/ɜː/ first, learn, girlfriend, work, circle

7A and B Look at the example with the class, then put Ss in pairs to work out the answers. Alternatively, you could put Ss in teams and run this as a competition, writing/reading out one clue at a time, e.g.: *a fruit with /ɑː/ that begins with a 'b'* (Ss close their books).

Answers:

	/ɑː/
a country	Argentina
a fruit	banana
a month	March
a form of *be*	are
an adjective	far
a time of day	afternoon
a verb	laugh

	/ɜː/
a nationality	German
a colour	purple
a type of clothes	shirt
a day	Thursday
a form of *be*	were
an adjective	thirsty
a number	thirteen/thirty

Homework ideas
- Ss write an email to a friend, telling them about their plans for improving their English.
- Ss start a diary in English.
- Ss look at some websites in English and report back to another student, or to the class if there is another lesson after this one.
- Workbook Ex 1– 4, p68–69

PAGE	UNIT	PHOTOCOPIABLE	LANGUAGE POINT	TIME
155	6	Sunny Spain	**Grammar: *a/some; Is there a … ?/Are there any … ?*** • practise *a/some* • practise the question form *Is there a … ?/Are there any … ?* • practise short answers • review vocabulary for objects	30
156	6	Spot the difference	**Grammar: *there is/are, a/an, some, a lot of, not any*** • practise *a/an, some/a lot of/not any* • practise *there is/are* • review vocabulary for shops and services	25–30
157	6	Give us a clue	**Vocabulary: places** • practise vocabulary for places in the context of a crossword • practise asking and answering questions to elicit crossword clues	30
158	6	Paris in the spring	**Functional language: completing travel timetable information** • practise asking and answering about travel information • review vocabulary for transport • review telling the time	30
159	7	Did you know?	**Grammar: past simple regular verbs** • practise the past simple of regular verbs • practise saying dates	20
160	7	Where were you?	**Grammar: past simple: *was/were*** • practise the past simple *was/were* in the context of a board game • practise dates • review time phrases	30
161	7	Great fun	**Vocabulary: adjectives and common collocations** • practise adjectives and common collocations with nouns	30
162	7	How was it?	**Functional language: giving opinions** • practise asking and answering about opinions • review verb phrases	25–30
163	8	Alibi	**Grammar: past simple** • review vocabulary for transport • practise past simple of regular and irregular verbs	25–30
164	8	Firsts	**Grammar: past simple questions and answers (irregular verbs)** • practise the past simple question and answer form for irregular verbs in the context of a questionnaire • review verb phrases	20–25
165	8	Missing objects	**Vocabulary: prepositions of place** • practise prepositions of place • review vocabulary for objects	20–25
166	8	Village life	**Functional language: giving directions** • practise asking for and giving directions • review vocabulary for places	20–25
167	9	Opinions	**Grammar: subject/object pronouns** • practise subject and object pronouns • practise expressing likes and dislikes • review vocabulary for objects, activities and food	25–30
168	9	Do you like … ?	**Grammar: *love, like, hate* + *-ing*/noun** • practise asking about and expressing likes and dislikes • review vocabulary for activities and animals and verb phrases	25
169	9	Money, money, money!	**Vocabulary: money** • practise vocabulary for money • practise speaking skills by asking and answering a questionnaire	25
170	9	What would you like?	**Functional language: making offers and requests** • practise making offers and requests • review vocabulary for places, objects and adjectives for feelings	30
171	10	Rules	**Grammar: *can/can't*** • practise *can* and *can't* • review vocabulary for places and verb phrases	30–40
172	10	Good intentions	**Grammar: *be going to*** • practise talking about future plans with *going to* • review verb phrases and question words	25–30
173	10	Collocations	**Vocabulary: verb phrases** • practise verb phrases • practise asking and answering about abilities	25–30
174	10	See you later, alligator!	**Functional language: starting and ending conversations** • reviewing holding conversations in different settings	25–30

You're French. You're a footballer and an actor. Your name is Eric Cantona.	You're Jamaican. You're a singer. Your name is Bob Marley.	You're Spanish. You're an artist. Your name is Picasso.
You're German. You're a scientist. Your name is Einstein.	You're Argentinian You're a footballer. Your name is Maradona.	You're British. You're a spy. Your name is James Bond.
You're Austrian. You're a doctor. Your name is Sigmund Freud.	You're Italian. You're an artist and an inventor. Your name is Leonardo da Vinci.	You're English. You're a writer. Your name is Shakespeare.
You're Italian. You're a musician. Your name is Vivaldi.	You're American. You're an actress. Your name is Marilyn Monroe.	You're American. You're a singer. Your name is Elvis.

Are you ... ?

Einstein
Vivaldi
Maradona
Marilyn Monroe
Shakespeare
Bob Marley
James Bond
Leonardo da Vinci
Sigmund Freud
Elvis
Picasso
Eric Cantona

NATIONALITY	JOB	NAME

CAR	BUS	HAT	CHEESE
CLOCK	SPAGHETTI	FLAG	COFFEE
FLOWERS	PASSPORT	DANCER	SUSHI
GERMANY	GREAT BRITAIN	MEXICO	FRANCE
SWITZERLAND	ITALY	CANADA	BRAZIL
THE NETHERLANDS	CHINA	SPAIN	JAPAN

Worksheet A

1 Complete the words and match them to the pictures.

1 a c _ _ i _	Picture _____
2 a _ e _	Picture _____
3 an _ _ _ _ b _ _ _	Picture _____
4 a p _ _ c _ _	Picture _____
5 a d _ _ r	Picture _____
6 a w _ _ k _ o o _	Picture _____

2 Ask your partner for the missing words.

Picture B _____   Picture F _____

Picture C _____   Picture I _____

Picture D _____   Picture L _____

Worksheet B

1 Complete the words and match them to the pictures.

1 a _ _ a b _ _ _	Picture _____
2 a l _ _ _ t _ _ _	Picture _____
3 the b _ _ _ r _	Picture _____
4 a _ a _	Picture _____
5 a s _ _ _ d _ _ _ _ 's b _ _ _ k	Picture _____
6 an _ t _ c _ b _ _ _ _ d	Picture _____

2 Ask your partner for the missing words.

Picture A _____   Picture H _____

Picture E _____   Picture J _____

Picture G _____   Picture K _____

✂

STUDENT REGISTRATION FORM

Name: _Ana Garcia_

Email address: _agarcia21@mail.es_

Country: _Spain_

Occupation: _Student_

Mobile phone number: _0657 453 210_

STUDENT REGISTRATION FORM

Name: _Thiago Alves_

Email address: _talves@mail.com_

Country: _Brazil_

Occupation: _Doctor_

Mobile phone number: _0786 4351112_

STUDENT REGISTRATION FORM

Name: _Jessica Pirelli_

Email address: _pirelli@email.com_

Country: _Italy_

Occupation: _Teacher_

Mobile phone number: _0781 953612_

STUDENT REGISTRATION FORM

Name: _Akemi Fukuda_

Email address: _afukuda21@mail.jp_

Country: _Japan_

Occupation: _Teacher_

Mobile phone number: _090 456 383 82_

Ask questions to complete the forms.

STUDENT REGISTRATION FORM

Name: _____

Email address: _____

Country: _____

Occupation: _____

Mobile phone number: _____

STUDENT REGISTRATION FORM

Name: _____

Email address: _____

Country: _____

Occupation: _____

Mobile phone number: _____

STUDENT REGISTRATION FORM

Name: _____

Email address: _____

Country: _____

Occupation: _____

Mobile phone number: _____

A _____ B _____ C _____

D _____ E _____ F _____ G _____ H _____ I _____

1 Carolyn is the mother. She's the cook. She's in the kitchen.	5 Petra is his wife. She's the waitress. She's in the hotel restaurant.
2 Her husband is Matthew. He's the manager. He's in the office.	6 Lionel is her brother. He's the barman. He's in the bar.
3 Rosanna is their daughter. She's the porter. She's at the entrance.	7 Paula is her sister. She's the gardener. She's in the garden.
4 Orlando is their son. He's the waiter. He's in the hotel restaurant.	8 Her parents are Scott and Danielle. They're on holiday! They're in the swimming pool.

Worksheet A

1 **Look at the hotel plan. Find out which rooms these people are in.**

Where is the mother?

The mother _____.

The brother _____.

The husband _____.

The daughter _____.

The children _____.

	The son	**Hotel Colorado**		The parents
Room 52	Room 99		Room 84	Room 73

The wife		The father		The sister	
Room 33	Room 100	Room 19	Room 13	Room 28	Room 67

2 **Tell your partner which rooms the family members are in.**

The father is in room nineteen.

Worksheet B

1 **Look at the hotel plan. Tell your partner which rooms the family members are in.**

The mother is in room fifty-two.

The mother		**Hotel Colorado**	The brother	
Room 52	Room 99		Room 84	Room 73

	The husband		The daughter		The children
Room 33	Room 100	Room 19	Room 13	Room 28	Room 67

2 **Find out which rooms these people are in.**

Where is the father?

The father _____.

The sister _____.

The wife _____.

The son _____.

The parents _____.

y

Worksheet A

1　Put the letters in the correct order to make feelings. Where is the stress? Match the word to the picture.

phayp _____　　sihtryt _____

iretd _____　　dbroe _____

2　Ask your partner for the other words: *What's picture … ? How do you spell it?*

Worksheet B

1　Put the letters in the correct order to make feelings. Where's the stress? Match the word to the picture.

ldco _____　　tho _____

ghrnuy _____　　nagyr _____

2　Ask your partner for the other words: *What's picture … ? How do you spell it?*

Grammar: *that is/those are; possessive 's; because*

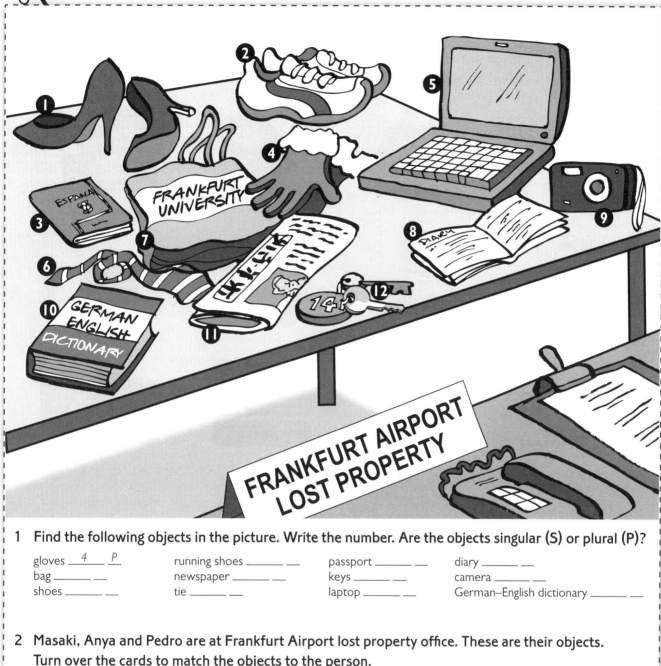

1 Find the following objects in the picture. Write the number. Are the objects singular (S) or plural (P)?

gloves __4__ _P_   running shoes _____ __   passport _____ __   diary _____ __
bag _____ __   newspaper _____ __   keys _____ __   camera _____ __
shoes _____ __   tie _____ __   laptop _____ __   German–English dictionary _____ __

2 Masaki, Anya and Pedro are at Frankfurt Airport lost property office. These are their objects.
   Turn over the cards to match the objects to the person.

Masaki is from Japan.	Masaki is a footballer.	Masaki is on holiday.	Masaki is in The Mirage Hotel.
Anya is German.	Anya is an English student.	Anya lives in Frankfurt. Frankfurt is a very cold city.	Anya is a student at Frankfurt University.
Pedro is from Marbella in Spain.	Pedro is a computer engineer.	Pedro writes a diary.	Pedro is on business.

Worksheet A

Add the vowels to complete the objects. Then ask and answer about the other objects:
What's this? It's a ... What are these? They're ...

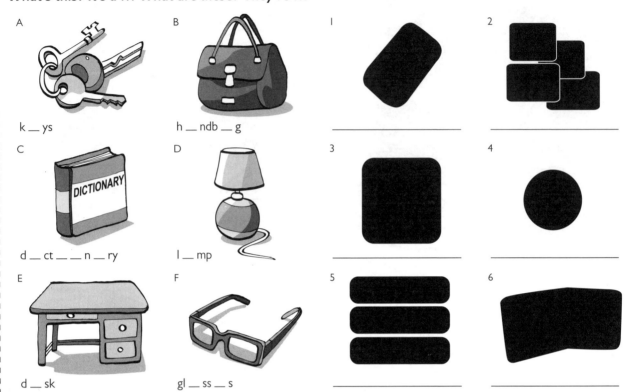

A   k __ ys

B   h __ ndb __ g

1   _____

2   _____

C   d __ ct __ __ n __ ry

D   l __ mp

3   _____

4   _____

E   d __ sk

F   gl __ ss __ s

5   _____

6   _____

Worksheet B

Add the vowels to complete the objects. Then ask and answer about the other objects:
What's this? It's a ... What are these? They're ...

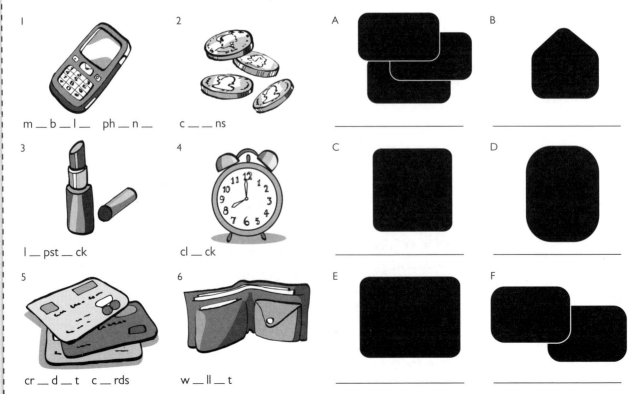

1   m __ b __ l __ ph __ n __

2   c __ __ ns

A   _____

B   _____

3   l __ pst __ ck

4   cl __ ck

C   _____

D   _____

5   cr __ d __ t   c __ rds

6   w __ ll __ t

E   _____

F   _____

1   Work in pairs. Find twelve items of clothing.

t-shirtshoesshirtcoathatshortssuittieglovesbootsskirtglasses

2   Look at the pictures. Work in pairs. Match the clothes to one of the people.

Anna   **Tina**   **Chris**   **Dan**

3   Work in groups. Are your answers the same?

1 **Put the sentences from the dialogue in order.**

   a) W: Here you are. An egg sandwich and a white coffee. _____

   b) C: Yes, an egg sandwich, please. _____

   c) C: Brown bread, please. _____

   d) W: Anything to drink? _____

   e) W: That's ten euros, please. _____

   f) W: Can I help you? ___1___

   g) W: Thank you! _____

   h) C: Yes, a white coffee, please. _____

   i) C: How much is that? _____

   j) C: Here you are. _____

   k) W: White or brown bread? _____

2 **Practise the dialogue with a partner.**

3 **Work in pairs. One of you is the waiter and the other is the customer. Use the menu to order.**

Café Royale

Price list

Black coffee 3.00 €

White coffee 3.60 €

Sparkling water 1.60 €

Still water 1.10 €

Cola 1.75 €

*   *   *   *

Chicken sandwich (brown) 6.70 €

Chicken sandwich (white) 6.40 €

Cheese sandwich (brown) 6.60 €

Cheese sandwich (white) 6.40 €

Egg sandwich (brown) 5.50 €

Egg sandwich (white) 5.20 €

*   *   *   *

Chocolate cake 4.50 €

Carrot cake 4.30 €

Worksheet A

Use the pictures to talk about Victoria. Mark the similarities with Judy with a ✓ and the differences with an ✗. *She lives in a house.*

Worksheet B

Use the pictures to talk about Judy. Mark the similarities with Victoria with a ✓ and the differences with an ✗. *She lives in a flat.*

Worksheet A

1 Complete the questions with the correct preposition: *at/in/on/every*.

	YOU	NAME
What do you do _____ the mornings before work?		
Where do you go _____ Saturday night?		
What do you do _____ the weekend?		
Do you go to the cinema _____ week?		
Do you do your English homework _____ night?		
Do you watch television _____ evening?		
Do you meet your friends _____ Saturdays and Sundays?		

2 Answer the questions for you.

3 Ask the other students. Find another student who has the same answer as you.

Worksheet B

1 Complete the questions with the correct preposition: *at/in/on/every*.

	YOU	NAME
What do you do _____ the evenings after work?		
Where do you go _____ Friday nights?		
Do you play sport _____ the weekend?		
Do you go to English class _____ week?		
Do you use the computer _____ night?		
Do you drink coffee _____ day?		
Do you work _____ Saturdays?		

2 Answer the questions for you.

3 Ask the other students. Find another student who has the same answer as you.

Worksheet A

BARCELONA	BEIJING	CARACAS	DUBLIN
13.45		07.15	

HONG KONG	ISTANBUL	MEXICO CITY	NEW YORK
20.00		06.45	

MOSCOW	MUMBAI	NAIROBI	SÃO PAOLO
15.30		15.00	

Worksheet B

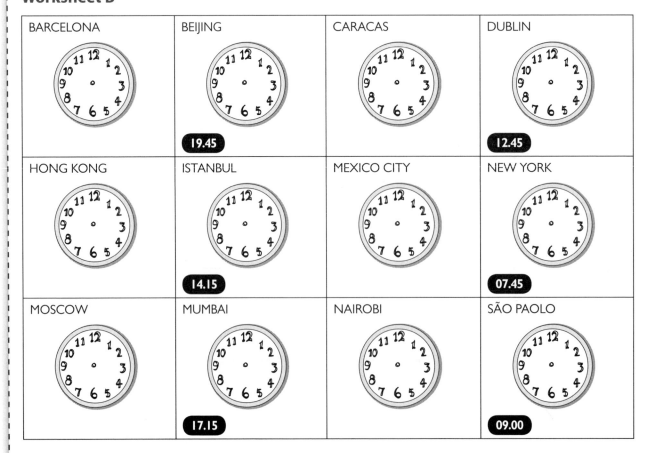

BARCELONA	BEIJING	CARACAS	DUBLIN
	19.45		12.45

HONG KONG	ISTANBUL	MEXICO CITY	NEW YORK
	14.15		07.45

MOSCOW	MUMBAI	NAIROBI	SÃO PAOLO
	17.15		09.00

1 **START**	2 I have breakfast.	3 I listen to the radio.	4 I start work at 09.00.	5 I always _____ .
10 I never _____ .	9 I have dinner in a restaurant.	8 I have lunch at home.	7 I watch television in the evening.	6 I get up late on Sundays.
11 I eat fish on Fridays.	12 I go to bed before midnight.	13 I eat pasta.	14 I speak in English.	15 I sometimes _____ .
20 I walk to work.	19 I often _____ .	18 I sing in the shower.	17 I eat healthy food.	16 I do my homework.
21 I'm late for classes.	22 I don't _____ often.	23 I drink coffee.	24 I go to the cinema.	25 **FINISH**

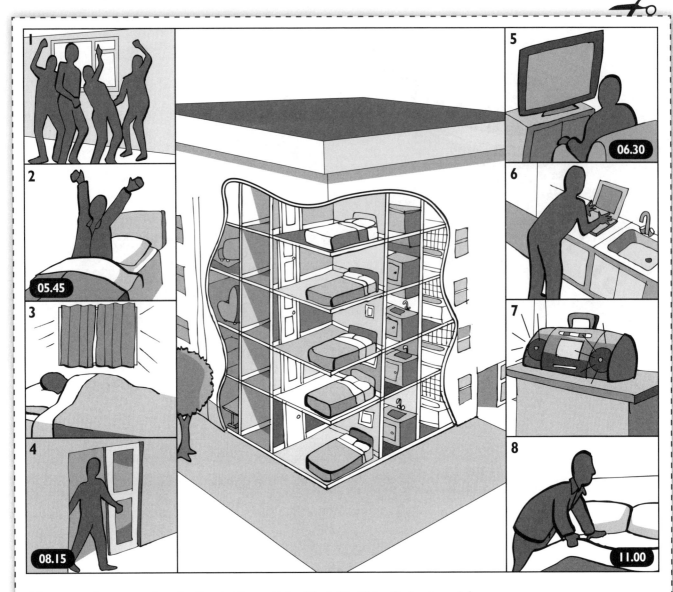

There are four people who live in these flats: Ned, Matilda, Robert and Anya.
Listen to your partner and match the activities and the flat to the person.

A

His name is Ned.
He lives on the second floor.
He plays very loud music at night.
He has parties every Saturday.

B

Her name is Matilda.
She lives on the ground floor.
She gets up at 05.45 in the morning.
She watches the news on television
at 06.30 in the morning.

C

His name is Robert.
He lives on the third floor.
He goes to work at 08.15 in the morning.
He goes to bed at 11.00.

D

Her name is Anya.
She lives on the first floor.
She works at home.
She doesn't get up early.

Worksheet A

Find the answers to the clues you have.
Then ask your partner for the other clues.

Across

2 The French eat a lot of this. (6)
3 _____ (8)
6 Some people put this in tea or coffee. (5)
7 _____ (6)
8 People eat a lot of this in Italy (but it isn't pasta). (5)
9 _____ (4)
10 This is a kind of meat. (5)

Down

1 _____ (7)
3 This is a kind of pasta. (9)
4 _____ (9)
5 It is usually white or brown. (5)
6 _____ (5)

Worksheet B

Find the answers to the clues you have.
Then ask your partner for the other clues.

Across

2 _____ (6)
3 Make this with bread and ham or cheese. (8)
6 _____ (5)
7 Some people eat this for breakfast with milk. (6)
8 _____ (5)
9 This food lives in the sea. (4)
10 _____ (5)

Down

1 White meat. (7)
3 _____ (9)
4 This is a popular fast-food. (9)
5 _____ (5)
6 Healthy vegetables, served cold. (5)

Functional language: asking for information

Worksheet A

| Complete your hotel information sheet. | Ask questions to complete the information about your partner's hotel. |

Name: _____

Restaurant: YES/NO

Breakfast times: _____

Lunch times: _____

Dinner times: _____

Gym: YES/NO

Opening hours: _____

Exchange: _____

Times: _____

Hairdresser: YES/NO

Times: _____

Guided tour: YES/NO

Price: _____

Name: _____

Restaurant: YES/NO

Breakfast times: _____

Lunch times: _____

Dinner times: _____

Gym: YES/NO

Opening hours: _____

Exchange: _____

Times: _____

Hairdresser: YES/NO

Times: _____

Guided tour: YES/NO

Price: _____

Worksheet B

| Complete your hotel information sheet. | Ask questions to complete the information about your partner's hotel. |

Name: _____

Restaurant: YES/NO

Breakfast times: _____

Lunch times: _____

Dinner times: _____

Gym: YES/NO

Opening hours: _____

Exchange: _____

Times: _____

Hairdresser: YES/NO

Times: _____

Guided tour: YES/NO

Price: _____

Name: _____

Restaurant: YES/NO

Breakfast times: _____

Lunch times: _____

Dinner times: _____

Gym: YES/NO

Opening hours: _____

Exchange: _____

Times: _____

Hairdresser: YES/NO

Times: _____

Guided tour: YES/NO

Price: _____

Grammar: *a/some; Is there a ... ?/Are there any ... ?*

1 Petra goes on holiday to Spain. Match pictures 1–12 with the words below.

passport ___   credit cards ___   laptop ___   watch ___

sunhats ___   swimsuit ___   mobile phone ___   jewellery ___

Spanish–English   sunglasses ___   pen ___   magazines ___
dictionary ___   book ___   handbag ___   make-up ___

clothes ___   wallet ___   suncream ___

2 Choose eight items that Petra takes on holiday. Write them in the correct column.

a ...   some ...

_____   _____

_____   _____

_____   _____

_____   _____

3 Ask students about the eight items they chose.

Is there a passport? Yes, there is. / No, there isn't.
Are there any clothes? Yes, there are. / No, there aren't.

Worksheet A

Find ten differences.

Worksheet B

Find ten differences.

Worksheet A

Find the answers to the clues you have. Then ask your partner for the other clues.

Across

1   There are a lot of computers here. (8, 4)

5   _____ (8)

9   _____ (8)

10   _____ (10)

Down

2   _____ (4, 7)

3   _____ (5)

4   There is a whiteboard here. (9)

6   _____ (11)

7   There are a lot of students here. (10)

8   _____ (7)

9   You buy medicine here. (8)

Worksheet B

Find the answers to the clues you have. Then ask your partner for the other clues.

Across

1   _____ _____ (8, 4)

5   _____ (8)

9   _____ (8)

10   There are newspapers and magazines here. (10)

Down

2   _____ _____ (4, 7)

3   There are a lot of beds here. (5)

4   _____ (9)

6   _____ (11)

7   _____ (10)

8   There are planes here. (7)

9   _____ (8)

Worksheet A

1 You want to travel to Paris. Ask your partner to complete the missing travel information.

TRANSPORT	LEAVE FROM	TIME	ARRIVE AT	TIME	PRICE
PLANE	London Heathrow	19.40	Paris-Orly	21.50	€139 single
TRAIN					
COACH	London Victoria	21.30	Paris Gallieni	07.30	€48
TRAIN AND FERRY					

2 Decide which way you want to travel.

Worksheet B

1 You want to travel to Paris. Ask your partner to complete the missing travel information.

TRANSPORT	LEAVE FROM	TIME	ARRIVE AT	TIME	PRICE
PLANE					
TRAIN	London St Pancras	10.25	Paris Gare du Nord	13.45	€99.50
COACH					
TRAIN AND FERRY	London Charing Cross	13.10	Paris Gare du Nord	23.20	€75

2 Decide which way you want to travel.

Worksheet A

1 **Find the past simple of these verbs. Complete the sentences with the correct verb.**

dance	play	wait	start	talk	stop	cry	walk

D	A	N	C	E	D	A	Q	R	D	S
S	O	E	B	P	P	C	R	I	E	T
T	Z	W	X	T	L	B	H	W	W	A
O	D	A	T	A	A	W	V	J	A	R
P	N	I	T	L	Y	B	Z	D	L	T
P	Y	T	F	K	E	E	H	T	K	E
E	G	E	I	E	D	K	U	I	E	D
D	Z	D	C	D	C	R	I	E	D	S

1 Lyn O'Bryne from England ___ ___ ___ ___ ___ seven years to find her lost dog in 2001.

2 Some people ___ ___ ___ ___ ___ ___ ___ using the internet in 1995.

3 The film director Alfred Hitchcock ___ ___ ___ ___ ___ ___ for one second when he received an Oscar in _____ .

4 People ___ ___ ___ ___ ___ ___ ___ smoking in bars and restaurants in Ireland in _____ .

5 People ___ ___ ___ ___ ___ for 55 hours at a party in India in July 2004.

6 Spain and The Netherlands ___ ___ ___ ___ ___ ___ in the 2010 World Cup Final.

7 The actress Halle Berry ___ ___ ___ ___ ___ when she received an Oscar in _____ .

8 Neil Armstrong first ___ ___ ___ ___ ___ ___ on the moon on July 20th _____ .

2 **Put the dates into the sentences above. Read your sentences to B to check. Were you correct?**

1969	2001	1940	2004

Worksheet B

1 **Find the past simple of these verbs. Complete the sentences with the correct verb.**

dance	play	wait	start	talk	stop	cry	walk

D	A	N	C	E	D	A	Q	R	D	S
S	O	E	B	P	P	C	R	I	E	T
T	Z	W	X	T	L	B	H	W	W	A
O	D	A	T	A	A	W	V	J	A	R
P	N	I	T	L	Y	B	Z	D	L	T
P	Y	T	F	K	E	E	H	T	K	E
E	G	E	I	E	D	K	U	I	E	D
D	Z	D	C	D	C	R	I	E	D	S

1 Lyn O'Bryne from England ___ ___ ___ ___ ___ ___ seven years to find her lost dog in _____ .

2 Some people ___ ___ ___ ___ ___ ___ using the internet in _____ .

3 The film director Alfred Hitchcock ___ ___ ___ ___ ___ ___ for one second when he received an Oscar in 1940.

4 People ___ ___ ___ ___ ___ ___ ___ smoking in bars and restaurants in Ireland in 2004.

5 People ___ ___ ___ ___ ___ ___ for 55 hours at a party in India in July _____ .

6 Spain and The Netherlands ___ ___ ___ ___ ___ ___ in the _____ World Cup Final.

7 The actress Halle Berry ___ ___ ___ ___ ___ when she received an Oscar in 2001.

8 Neil Armstrong first ___ ___ ___ ___ ___ ___ on the moon on July 20th 1969.

2 **Put the dates into the sentences above. Read your sentences to A to check. Were you correct?**

2010	2004	2001	1995

Where were you?

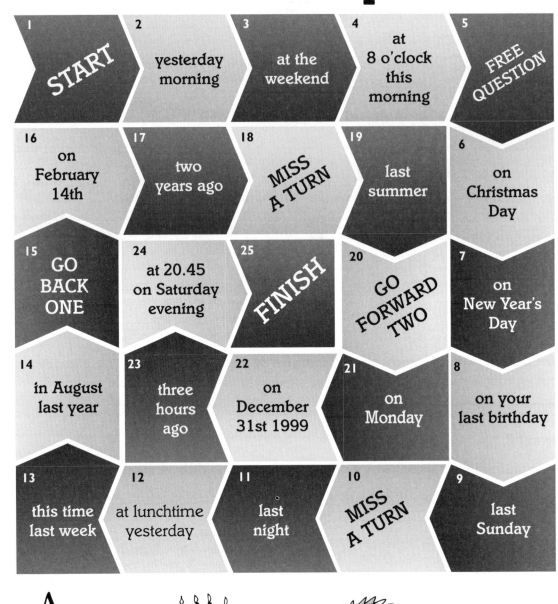

1 START	**2** yesterday morning	**3** at the weekend	**4** at 8 o'clock this morning	**5** FREE QUESTION
16 on February 14th	**17** two years ago	**18** MISS A TURN	**19** last summer	**6** on Christmas Day
15 GO BACK ONE	**24** at 20.45 on Saturday evening	**25** FINISH	**20** GO FORWARD TWO	**7** on New Year's Day
14 in August last year	**23** three hours ago	**22** on December 31st 1999	**21** on Monday	**8** on your last birthday
13 this time last week	**12** at lunchtime yesterday	**11** last night	**10** MISS A TURN	**9** last Sunday

difficult	exam	easy	exam
delicious	food	terrible	food
noisy	bar	quiet	bar
interesting	book	boring	book
lovely	dress	horrible	dress
sad	film	happy	film

Worksheet A

1 *How was your last meal in a restaurant?*

a It was delicious.
b It was all right.
c It was awful.

2 *How was the last programme you watched on television?*

a It was interesting.
b It was OK.
c It was boring.

3 *How was your last English homework?*

a It was easy.
b It was all right.
c It was difficult.

4 *How was your last holiday?*

a It was fantastic.
b It was OK.
c It was terrible.

5 *How was your last birthday present?*

a It was lovely.
b It was all right.
c It was horrible.

6 *How was the last restaurant you went to?*

a It was very quiet.
b It was OK.
c It was very noisy.

Count the number of a, b and c answers.

Mostly as: You are a 'glass half-full' person. You have a positive outlook on life. Or maybe you are just very lucky! But don't be afraid to say when you don't like something!

Mostly bs: You are neither a 'glass half-full' nor a 'glass half-empty' person. You have a neutral outlook on your life but don't be afraid to say what you like and don't like!

Mostly cs: You are a 'glass half-empty' person. You have a slightly negative outlook on life. Or maybe you are just unlucky! But don't be afraid to say when you like something!

Worksheet B

1 *How was your lunch yesterday?*

a It was delicious.
b It was all right.
c It was awful.

2 *How was the last film you watched in the cinema?*

a It was interesting.
b It was OK.
c It was boring.

3 *How was your last English exam?*

a It was easy.
b It was all right.
c It was difficult.

4 *How was last weekend?*

a It was fantastic.
b It was OK.
c It was terrible.

5 *How was your last present?*

a It was lovely.
b It was all right.
c It was horrible.

6 *How was the last party you went to?*

a It was very quiet.
b It was OK.
c It was very noisy.

Count the number of a, b and c answers.

Mostly as: You are a 'glass half-full' person. You have a positive outlook on life. Or maybe you are just very lucky! But don't be afraid to say when you don't like something!

Mostly bs: You are neither a 'glass half-full' nor a 'glass half-empty' person. You have a neutral outlook on your life but don't be afraid to say what you like and don't like!

Mostly cs: You are a 'glass half-empty' person. You have a slightly negative outlook on life. Or maybe you are just unlucky! But don't be afraid to say when you like something!

1 Last Saturday evening between 7p.m. and 11p.m. somebody robbed a bank in Piccadilly Circus in London. The police think Jacques robbed the bank. Below are his tickets and receipts. Complete the list of transport he used.

———————— ————————
———————— ————————
———————— ————————

2 Complete the police report about what Jacques did on Friday and Saturday with the past simple of the verbs in the box.

take (x2) go have travel arrive (x2) stay rent pay drive buy

Jacques __took__ a taxi from his house in Toulouse to the airport at three o'clock on Friday afternoon. He _____ by plane to Paris. In Paris he _____ a train to Calais. Then he _____ from Calais to Dover by ferry. He _____ in Dover at half past eleven at night and he _____ in a small hotel. The next morning he _____ a car and _____ to London. When he _____ in London he _____ lunch in an Italian restaurant. At half past seven he _____ some flowers. He _____ the underground to Piccadilly Circus at a quarter to eight. At half past ten he _____ for dinner for two in a French restaurant by credit card.

3 What do you think? Did Jacques rob the bank?

Worksheet A

Ask your partner about the first time he/she …	When did you first … ?	Where did you first … ?	☺
went on holiday			
had dinner in a restaurant			
went camping			
spoke English			
saw a film in the cinema			

Worksheet B

Ask your partner about the first time he/she …	When did you first … ?	Where did you first … ?	☺
rode a bicycle			
went to school			
made a meal for other people			
went to another country			
met an English-speaking person			

Worksheet A

1   Ask your partner about the objects in the box. Draw them on the picture.

| keys | glasses | jacket | dictionary | bag |

2   Compare pictures with your partner. Are they the same?

Worksheet B

1   Ask your partner about the objects in the box. Draw them on the picture.

| laptop | jeans | bicycle | magazine | running shoes |

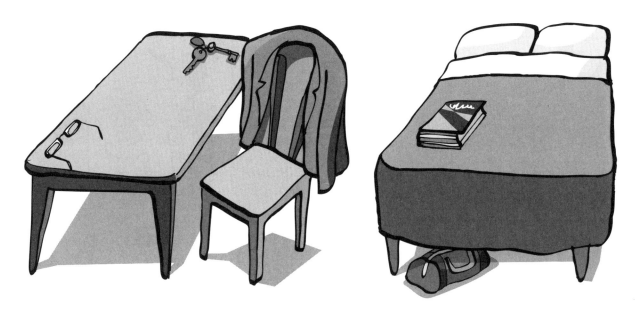

2   Compare pictures with your partner. Are they the same?

Worksheet A

Match the conversations to the people in the picture. Then write the question or answer.

—— _____

There is a swimming pool next to the school.

—— _____

Yes, the payphone is opposite the bakery.

—— Excuse me. Where's the pharmacy?

_____

—— Where is the bus stop?

_____

Worksheet B

Match the conversations to the people in the picture. Then write the question or answer.

—— Where is the swimming pool?

_____

—— Is there a payphone?

_____

—— _____

It's between the restaurant and the bakery.

—— _____

The bus stop is in front of the school.

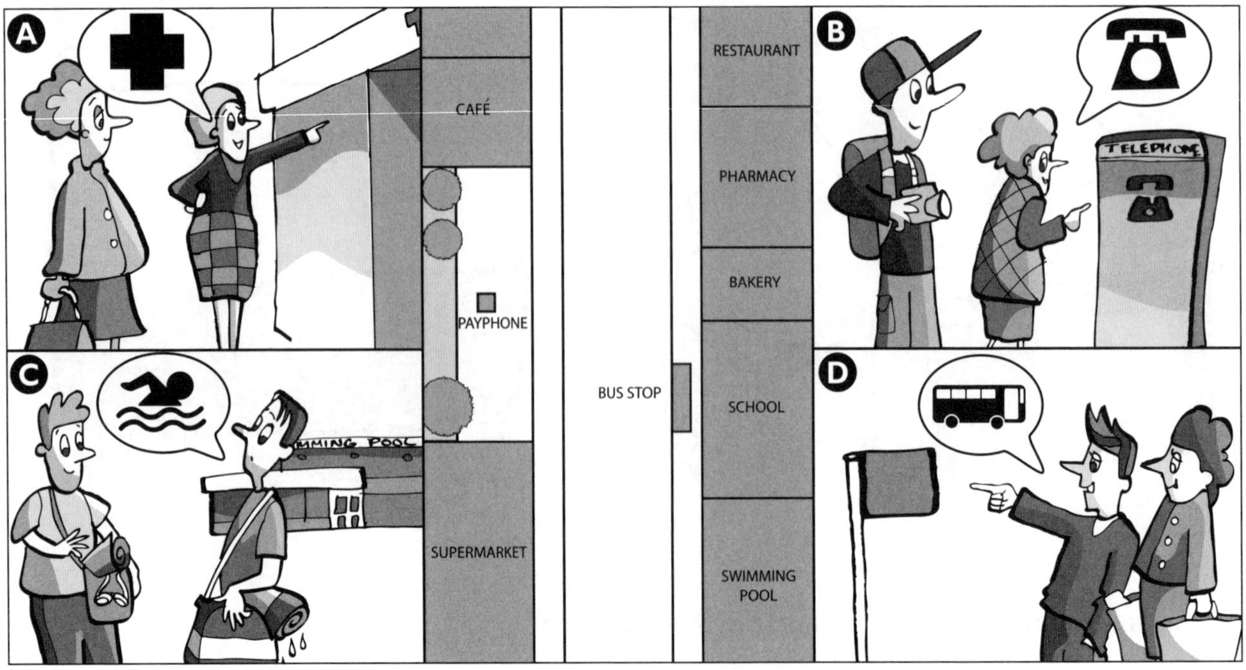

1 Write an example of a person or thing you love or dislike for each category.

1 a film _____
2 a vegetable _____
3 a singer _____
4 a book _____
5 a sport _____
6 an activity _____
7 a city _____
8 an animal _____
9 a sportsperson _____
10 a type of food _____
11 an actor _____
12 a type of music _____

2 Ask your partner: *What do you think of ... ?*

Useful language

I like I love I hate I don't really like I don't like	him/her/it/ them.	I think it's I think she's I think he's I think they're	(really/very) good. fantastic. OK/all right. (really/very) bad. terrible.

1   Complete a sentence with *like/love/don't like/hate* so that it is true for you.
    Pass the worksheet to your left.

	NAME
I _____ running.	_____
I _____ buying presents.	_____
I _____ camping.	_____
I _____ chatting online.	_____
I _____ dogs.	_____
I _____ late night parties.	_____

2   Complete a sentence with a noun or gerund so that it is true for you.
    Pass the worksheet to your left.

	NAME
I love _____ .	_____
I like _____ .	_____
I don't like _____ .	_____
I hate _____ .	_____
I like _____ a lot.	_____
I don't really like _____ .	_____

Money and you

1

It's near the end of the month. You don't have any money left.
You see a pair of shoes you really like.

- **a** You buy them with your credit card.
- **b** You don't buy them. You don't like spending money you don't have.

2

You buy a pair of expensive trousers in July.
In October, you try them on. They're too small.

- **a** You hope to lose some kilos.
- **b** You try to sell them on the internet.

3

You buy two tickets for a concert. Your friend wants to pay you later.
A month later your friend still owes you the money.

- **a** You don't like talking about money. You don't ask your friend for the money.
- **b** You phone and email your friend regularly to remind him/her to pay you.

4

A friend gives you a jumper for your birthday, but you don't like it.

- **a** You put it in your wardrobe, but never wear it.
- **b** You give it to another person for his/her birthday.

5

You buy a beautiful watch in the sales. It cost £300. Normally it costs £600.
You never wear it. You decide to sell it because you need a new computer.
The computer costs £550.

- **a** You sell it for £300. You don't like asking for more than what it cost you.
- **b** You sell it for £600. That's what it costs in the shops now.

6

It's May and you need a new television because your old television doesn't work.

- **a** You buy it now. You hate waiting and you love watching television.
- **b** You wait until the sales in July.

Mostly as

You probably spend too much money every month. You want things instantly and you hate waiting, but sometimes it's a good idea to be patient and only spend what you have.

Mostly bs

You are very careful with money. You probably never spend more than what you have. Remember sometimes it's good to spend some money and enjoy yourself.

Worksheet A

Would you like something to eat?	Which colour would you like?
Can I help you?	What would the teacher like for her birthday?
Excuse me. Where's the children's clothes section?	The sports department is on the second floor.
Coffee, please. Black coffee.	Let me think. Yes! I'd like the sushi, please.
Yes, of course. Which would you prefer? A banana or an apple?	No thanks. I think it's a waste of money.

Worksheet B

No thanks. I'm not hungry.	I'd like the green one, please.
Yes, please. I'd like to buy a camera.	I don't know. Maybe a CD. She loves classical music.
It's on the third floor.	I'd like to buy a football.
Would you like some tea or coffee?	What would you like to eat?
Can I have some fruit, please?	Would you like some wrapping paper for the present?

I'm going to ...	My answer ✓ = YES ✗ = NO	Ask your partner: What about you? If your partner answers YES, ask the follow-up question.
... save money.	————	_____ Why? _____
... get fit.	————	_____ How? _____
... cook tonight.	————	_____ What? _____
... do sport this weekend.	————	_____ What? _____
... clean your house.	————	_____ When? _____
... study English this evening.	————	_____ How long? _____
... get more organised.	————	_____ How? _____
... learn something new.	————	_____ What? _____
... give somebody a present.	————	_____ What? _____
... study English when this course finishes.	————	_____ Where? _____
_____ ?	————	_____ _____ ? _____

1 Cross out the incorrect phrase in column 2.

CAN YOU SAY ... ?		✔ = YES ✗ = NO
play	tennis football chess ~~swimming~~	
ride	a bicycle a horse a car a motorbike	
speak	French three languages in English for 20 minutes your teacher	
cook	ice cream pasta Japanese food vegetables	
make	tea your homework sushi jewellery	
read	music Chinese words maps a phone call	
drive	a bicycle a car a train a bus	

2 Use the correct verb phrases to ask your partner about his/her abilities.
Mark his/her answers: ✔ or ✗ in the table.

Can you play tennis? Yes, I can. = ✔ No, I can't. = ✗

A

AT A PARTY

Start a conversation with someone you have just met. Talk about the food, music and so on.

Useful language:

What do you think of … ?

A

ON A TRAIN

Start a conversation with the person in front of you. Talk about the destination, where they are from and so on.

Useful language:

Excuse me! Where are you going?

A

IN A RESTAURANT

Start a conversation with the person you are having dinner with. He/She is a business colleague. Talk about the food, work and so on.

Useful language:

What do you think of … ?

A

ON THE STREET

You see your neighbour's daughter on the street. Stop and talk to her about school, hobbies and so on.

Useful language:

Hello! How are you?

What do you do at … ?

A

IN THE UNIVERSITY CAFÉ

You are a teacher with a new student from one of your classes. Talk about the university, plans for the future and so on.

Useful language:

Do you like … ?

A

IN A TRAVEL AGENCY

You are in a busy travel agency. Talk to another customer about travelling, holiday plans and so on.

Useful language:

Where are you going on holiday?

B

Answer your partner's questions. When you leave say:

Nice to meet you.

or

Is that the time? Bye!

B

Answer your partner's questions. When you leave say:

Keep in touch.

or

I have a class now. Bye!

B

Answer your partner's questions. When you leave say:

See you soon!

or

Oh look! This is my station.

B

Answer your partner's questions. When you leave say:

I hope we meet again!

or

I have to go now. Bye!

B

Answer your partner's questions. When you leave say:

Nice to talk to you!

or

I can see a friend over there.

B

Answer your partner's questions. When you leave say:

See you later!

or

Oh no! I'm late! Goodbye!

Unit 1

FAMOUS HISTORICAL FIGURES

Materials: One role card per student and one worksheet per student

Distribute the worksheets and the role cards. Tell Ss to complete the first row of the table with their information, but not to show it to anyone else. Explain that they are at a party with each of the famous people on their worksheet. (You could play low background music.) Elicit the following questions and write them on the board using another example, e.g. Brad Pitt. *What's your nationality? What's your job? Are you Brad Pitt?* Explain to Ss that they have to complete the information on the sheet with similar questions.

If you have less than twelve Ss, do one or two role cards as examples with the class. Give extra role cards to *fast finishers*. It is not necessary for Ss to find all the people. If you have a smaller class or less time, Ss could be told to find a limited number, e.g. six.

As an extension, Ss work in pairs and try to remember who each student is, their job and nationality.

WHERE'S IT FROM?

Materials: One worksheet per group of three, cut up and backed onto card. Separate the cards into objects and countries. (Optional: one colour for picture cards and one colour for map cards.)

Put Ss into groups of three. Give a set of cards to each group and tell them to match the object to the country. Check answers as a class.

Explain that Ss are going to play a memory game. Ss turn the cards face down. The map cards go on one side and the object cards go on the other side of a flat surface. Taking turns, they turn one of the map cards and one of the object cards. If the cards match, they say The _____ is from _____ . They keep the pair and they have another go. If the cards don't match, they say The _____ isn't from _____ . They turn the cards face down and it is the next student's turn. Ss play until all the cards have been matched. The winner is the student with the most cards.

As an extension, Ss have five minutes to write down as many combinations as they can remember. They get two points for each correct answer.

> **Suggested answers:**
>
> car – Germany; bus – Great Britain; hat – Mexico; cheese – France; clock – Switzerland; spaghetti – Italy; flag – Canada; coffee – Brazil; flowers – The Netherlands; passport – China; dancer – Spain; sushi – Japan

HOW DO YOU SPELL IT?

Materials: one copy of worksheet A and worksheet B per pair of students

Put Ss into two groups, A and B. Distribute the worksheets and ask them to complete the words, and match them to the pictures. Go round and help with spelling and pronunciation, and check answers carefully as Ss finish.

Put Ss into AB pairs and tell them to ask each other for the names of the silhouette objects in their picture. Model the language they'll need to do this first (e.g. *What's picture E? It's a chair. How do you spell it? C-H-A-I-R*). Go round and check spelling and pronunciation. Check answers as a class.

> **Answers:**
>
> Student A: 1 a chair, Picture E   2 a pen, Picture K 3 a notebook, Picture G   4 a pencil, Picture H 5 a door, Picture A   6 a workbook, Picture J
>
> Student B: 1 a table, Picture D   2 a laptop, Picture F 3 the board, Picture C   4 a bag, Picture I   5 a student's book, Picture L   6 a noticeboard, Picture B

IDENTITY CARD

Materials: one role card and one worksheet per student

Put Ss into groups of four. Distribute one role card and one worksheet to each student. Tell Ss they are the student on the role card and they have just enrolled at a language school. They have to complete the registration forms for the other students. Focus on the blank forms and elicit the questions necessary to complete them. Write the questions on the board: *What's your name? How do you spell it? What's your email address?* (Check Ss know how to say @ (at), and . (dot).) *What's your country? What's your job/occupation? What's your phone number?* Write your details on the board as if they appeared on the registration form. Demonstrate the questions with a student. Ss complete the forms in groups. Check answers as a class.

> **Answers:**
>
> As shown on completed registration forms.

Unit 2

A FAMILY BUSINESS

Materials: one copy of the illustration per group and one role card per student

Put Ss into groups of eight. Give each student a worksheet of the hotel picture and a role card. Tell Ss they have to identify the people in the picture by exchanging information. Tell Ss to do this in numerical order. Do the first one as an example. Read the information about Carolyn and check Ss are able to identify her correctly. Check the spelling of Carolyn and feed in: *How do you spell that?* and write the question on the board. Ss continue in groups until they have labelled all the people in the picture. Get feedback.

As an extension, ask Ss to turn over their role cards and exchange information about the people in the picture in pairs or groups. Do the first one as an example. Prompt Ss by writing these questions on the board: *What's his/her job? Where is he/she?*

> **Answers:**
>
> A Rosanna   B Matthew   C Carolyn   D Petra   E Orlando F Paula   G Danielle   H Scott   I Lionel

HOTEL ROOMS

Materials: one copy of worksheet A and worksheet B per pair of students

Put Ss into AB pairs and distribute the worksheets. Focus Ss on the examples. Tell them to exchange information with their partner to fill in the hotel plan and complete the sentences. Monitor the Ss. Check answers as a class. Vary feedback by asking: *Who is in room … ?* and *Where is … ?*

As an extension, Ss ask each other the following questions. They record their partner's answers. Feedback as a class.

1 *What's your telephone number?*

2 *What's the number of your house/flat?*

3 *How many students are there in your class?*

4 *How many children are there in your family?*

> **Answers:**
>
> Room 52 the mother; Room 99 the son; Room 84 the brother; Room 73 the parents; Room 33 the wife; Room 100 the husband; Room 19 the father; Room 13 the daughter; Room 28 the sister; Room 67 the children

ARE YOU HAPPY?

Materials: one copy of worksheet A and worksheet B per pair of students

Put Ss in groups A and B. Distribute the worksheets and ask them to unjumble the words in pairs AA and BB. Do the first one in A and in B as examples. Write the words on the board. Model the pronunciation and elicit the stress. Ss mark the stress then they repeat for the rest of the words. Monitor and check. Ss then match the words to the pictures.

Put Ss in pairs AB and tell them to ask each other for the names of the remaining adjectives. Model the language they'll need to do this first, e.g. *What's picture 1? happy*, etc. *How do you spell it? H-a-p-p-y.* Check answers as a class and encourage correct pronunciation. Drill the more difficult words.

As an extension, Ss take it in turns to mime a feeling for their partner to guess.

> **Answers:**
>
> Student A: 1 happy   3 bored   4 thirsty   7 tired
>
> Student B: 2 cold   5 hot   6 angry   8 hungry

LET'S GO!

Materials: one set of cards per group of three or four

Put Ss in groups of three or four. Give each group a set of cards. The face cards are in a pile face down. The response cards can either be divided among the Ss or put face up on a flat surface. Ss take it in turns to turn over a face card and leave it on the table face up. The others find correct responses and put them with the face card. There are three responses for each face card, but they must be in the correct order. Some responses are possible in more than one dialogue. Monitor. The first team to complete all six dialogues wins.

Put Ss into pairs. Ss then practise the dialogues. Write an example on the board and drill it, paying particular attention to intonation.

Tip: Ss can look at the card to read it, but should look at the other speaker when they speak.

> **Possible answers:**
>
> 1 I'm hungry. / Me too! / Let's eat a pizza! / Good idea!
>
> 2 I'm cold. / Me too! / Let's go inside. / Yeah! OK!
>
> 3 I'm tired. / Are you? / Yes, let's take a break. / OK.
>
> 4 I'm thirsty. / Let's go to a café. / Good idea! Let's have a soft drink. / Oooh! Yes, please!
>
> 5 I'm bored. / Let's go! / Where? / Let's go to the cinema.
>
> 6 I'm hot. / Me too! / Let's drink some cold water! / Good idea!

Unit 3

LOST PROPERTY

Materials: one copy of the worksheet per student and one set of cards per group of students

Distribute the worksheets. Tell Ss to work in pairs to match the vocabulary to the pictures and decide if the words are singular (S) or plural (P). Put Ss into groups of three or four with a set of cards. They take it in turns to turn over one card at a time and match the person to an object. Do an example on the board and elicit: *that* – singular and *those* – plural. Feed in *because*. Write on the board:

That passport is *Pedro's* because *he's Spanish*.

   OBJECT   WHOSE   REASON

Those keys are *Masaki's* because *he's in The Mirage Hotel*.

   OBJECT   WHOSE   REASON

Check answers as a class.

> **Answers:**
>
> 1 running shoes 2 (P); passport 3 (S); diary 8 (S); bag 7 (S); newspaper 11 (S); keys 12 (P); camera 9 (S); shoes 1 (P); tie 6 (S); laptop 5 (S); German–English dictionary 10 (S)
>
> 2 Students' own answers.

MYSTERY OBJECTS

Materials: one copy of worksheet A and worksheet B per pair of students

Distribute the worksheets. Put Ss into pairs AA and BB to complete their words with the correct vowels. Monitor and check. Then put Ss into AB pairs and tell them to ask and answer about the silhouettes using *What's this? It's a …* and *What are these? They're …* Ss first say the corresponding letter (A–F) or number (1–6) and then ask the correct question. Model an example with a student. Feed in *How do you spell that?* Check answers as a class.

> **Answers:**
>
> Student A: A keys; B handbag; C dictionary; D lamp; E desk; F glasses
>
> Student B: 1 mobile phone; 2 coins; 3 lipstick; 4 clock; 5 credit cards; 6 wallet

CLOTHING STYLES

Materials: One copy of the worksheet per pair of students

Distribute the worksheets. Ss work in pairs to find the twelve items of clothing. Check answers and put the words on the board. Check for correct pronunciation.

Point to the pictures of the clothes and ask: *What's this? What are these?* Write the questions on the board and establish that *this* is singular and *these* is plural. After asking a few times, teacher to student, the Ss could ask each other in open pairs around the class.

Look at the pictures of the people. In pairs, Ss match the people to the clothes. Do an example with the class and write on the board *I think this is* (person's) (clothes). *I think these are* (person's) (clothes). Put Ss into groups to compare answers then check as a class. With *stronger classes*, ask for further explanations, e.g. *I think these are Tina's gloves because she likes sports.*

Answers:

1 t-shirt; shoes; shirt; coat; hat; shorts; suit; tie; gloves; boots; skirt; glasses

2 Students' own answers.

CAFÉ ROYALE

Materials: one copy of the worksheet per student

Distribute the worksheets. Focus on the photo to set the context (ordering in a café). *Elicit waiter (W)* and *customer (C)*. Tell Ss to put the dialogue in order. The first line is done as an example. Get feedback. Chorus drill the conversation.

Set up the classroom as far as possible to look like a self-service café. Ss should stand up facing each other as if at a counter. Ask Ss to practise the conversation, ensuring that they first look at the line, but then look at their partner when they speak. Ss should be encouraged to accompany the dialogue with appropriate gestures and mime. Gradually, as they become more familiar with the script, the customer for example, can cover their part and respond to the waiter and vice versa, until they are independent of the script. Then ask Ss to order just using the menu. Monitor throughout and help with pronunciation. You could invite a few pairs to perform their dialogue for the class.

Answers:

1 f) 2 b) 3 k) 4 c) 5 d) 6 h) 7 a) 8 i) 9 e) 10 j) 11 g)

Unit 4

SIMILARITIES AND DIFFERENCES

Materials: one copy of worksheet A and worksheet B per pair of students

Revise the verb phrases used (see Answers). Use mime and drawing to elicit the verb phrases.

Put Ss into pairs AB. Distribute the worksheets. Explain that Victoria and Judy are best friends, but that they are similar in some ways and different in other ways. Tell Ss to describe the person in their picture to their partner. Do an example with a student: *Victoria wears glasses.* Student: *Judy wears glasses.* With *stronger classes* you could elicit *too.* Ss have to find five similarities and five differences. Check answers as a class and focus on the third person singular *s* on verbs in affirmative and the use of the auxiliary *doesn't.*

Answers:

Similarities: has/wears glasses; drives a car; doesn't smoke; works in an office; has two children.

Differences: Victoria drinks coffee, Judy doesn't drink coffee. Victoria lives in a house, Judy lives in a flat. Victoria plays the piano, Judy plays the guitar. Victoria plays golf, Judy plays basketball. Victoria eats Japanese food, Judy eats Italian food.

THINGS IN COMMON

Materials: two sets of cards per group of students

Review the verb phrases before starting the game (see Answers). Show Ss each card and elicit and drill the verb phrase.

Put Ss into groups of four. Divide the cards equally between each student. Ss take it in turns to say a phrase about each of their cards. The person with the same card says *Me too!* and both Ss discard that card. The winner is the person who discards all their cards first. Demonstrate how the game works by doing a few examples with the Ss. Select a card and say, e.g. *I like cats.* The student with the same card says *Me too!* Put the cards together and repeat with another card. Return the cards to the Ss before starting the game. Monitor closely.

At the end of the game, ask who was first to finish in each group. Get feedback by asking Ss in each group to act out some of the two-line dialogues in pairs.

Answers:

like: cats, fish and chips

play: tennis, golf

drive: a taxi, a bus

have: two brothers, a mobile phone

work: in a hospital, in a hotel

go: shopping on Fridays, to the theatre

live: in the mountains

study: at school

FIND SOMEONE WHO

Materials: one copy of worksheet A and worksheet B per pair of students

Put Ss into pairs AA and BB to complete the questions. Check answers as a class. Even though the questions are different on worksheets A and B, the preposition for each time phrase is in the same order, so just ask for the time phrase and not the whole question.

Ss answer the questions for themselves with short phrases. Do one question from A and one from B as an example. Monitor closely and when the Ss have completed their answers, tell Ss to mingle and ask the other Ss their questions. For each question they must find someone who has the same answer as them. Then they write that person's name. Do one or two examples as a class to illustrate.

Get feedback. Ask a few Ss who had similar answers to them.

Answers:

in; on; at; every; at; every; on

TIMES AROUND THE WORLD

Materials: one copy of worksheet A and worksheet B per pair of students

Put Ss into pairs AB and distribute the worksheets. Make sure Ss can't see each other's worksheet. Tell Ss to complete their worksheet by asking each other questions and drawing the hands to display the time on their blank clocks. Elicit the question and answer for the first two clocks on each worksheet and write them on the board: *What time is it in* (the city)? *It's* (time) *in* (city).

Answers:

Barcelona: 13.45; Beijing 19.45; Caracas 07.15; Dublin 12.45; Hong Kong 20.00; Istanbul 14.15; Mexico City 06.45; New York 07.45; Moscow 15.30; Mumbai 17.15; Nairobi 15.00; São Paolo 09.00

Unit 5

GAME BOARD

Materials: one copy of the board, one coin per group and one counter per student

Put Ss into groups and distribute the board. Ss toss a coin to move: heads moves one space and tails moves two spaces. Ss have to repeat the sentence they land on with an adverb of frequency in the correct place so that it is true for them. In every fifth sentence, Ss have to add the correct verb so that the sentence is true for them. Do one or two examples on the board to demonstrate what Ss have to do. For every correct sentence, the student gets another turn. Monitor closely. The first student to finish is the winner.

Get feedback to some of the sentences. You could ask Ss if anything their partners said surprised them.

NOISY NEIGHBOURS

Materials: one copy of the worksheet per student and one role card per pair of students

Draw a block of flats on the board and pre-teach *live on the ground/first/second/third floor*. Explain to the Ss that they are going to match four neighbours to their flats and the activities they do there.

Put Ss into pairs. Give each student the worksheet and give each pair of Ss one role card. Ss match the person on their role card to the activities and flats on the worksheets. Monitor and check they are matching correctly.

Remove the role cards and put the Ss into groups ABCD. Tell Ss to exchange the information about the person who was on their card with the other three Ss. Ss must match the neighbour to the flat and activities.

Check answers as a class.

Answers:

A: 1, 7, second floor; B: 2, 5, ground floor; C: 4, 8, third floor; D: 3, 6, first floor

CROSSWORD

Materials: one copy of crossword A and crossword B per pair of students

Put Ss into pairs AA and BB and distribute the crosswords. Ss complete their crossword using the clues provided. Monitor and check.

Put Ss into pairs AB. (*Weaker Ss* could be in groups AABB so As and Bs can find answers in pairs.) Elicit the question and write on the board: *What's* (number) *across/down?* Drill the question.

Ss A and B take it in turns to read the clue. Their partner has 30 seconds to guess the answer (*stronger Ss* could try to give extra information to guide their partner before providing the answer).

Check answers as a class.

As an extension, Ss read out the words and their partner has to provide the definition.

Answers:

Across: 2 cheese   3 sandwich   6 sugar   7 cereal   8 pizza   9 fish   10 steak

Down: 1 chicken   3 spaghetti   4 hamburger   5 bread   6 salad

BE MY GUEST

Materials: one copy of worksheet A and worksheet B per pair of students

Put Ss into pairs AA and BB. Ss design a hotel brochure by completing the information for their hotel. Then they prepare the questions to find out information about another hotel. Monitor closely and make sure Ss form the questions correctly. With *weaker classes*, model a few example questions.

Put Ss into pairs AB to complete the form. Demonstrate the activity by doing a few examples with Ss, e.g. *Do you have a restaurant in the hotel? Yes, I do./No, I don't.* Remind Ss to use expressions like *Great! Oh good! Lovely!* Get feedback. Ask Ss which hotel they prefer and why.

Unit 6

SUNNY SPAIN

Materials: one worksheet per student

Distribute the worksheets. Explain to Ss that they are helping Petra select items to take on holiday to Spain. Ss work in groups to label the pictures. Check answers with the class. Then Ss decide which eight items Petra takes on holiday and write the list under *a/some*. Elicit whether each item takes *a* or *some* so Ss can check their lists.

Put Ss into pairs. Ss have to ask questions to find similarities and differences in what Petra takes on holiday. Elicit the questions and short answers and write them on the board. Model and drill: *Is there a (passport)? Yes, there is./No, there isn't. Are there any (sunhats)? Yes, there are./No, there aren't.* Ss find out how many similarities there are between theirs and their partner's suitcases. Elicit some answers from different pairs and give whole class feedback on errors/good language used.

Answers:

passport 6; sunhats 4; Spanish-English dictionary 11; clothes 3; credit cards 7; swimsuit 9; sunglasses 5; book 2; laptop 12; mobile phone 1; pen 8; magazines 10

SPOT THE DIFFERENCE

Materials: one copy of worksheet A and worksheet B per pair of students

Review *There is/are, a/an, some, a lot of, not any* using objects around the classroom. With a weaker class, introduce the topic of airports and review the vocabulary of what you can find in airports (people, shops, airplanes, etc.).

Put Ss into pairs and distribute the A and B worksheets so each pair has one of each. Tell Ss to find the ten differences between their picture and their partner's picture. Ss take turns to describe their picture. They mark their differences on their picture. Check answers and write them on the board.

Tip: You could add a competitive element here by setting a time limit and awarding points for the correct answers. The pair with the most correct answers wins!

As an extension, *stronger Ss* could exchange information using the question form.

Answers:

Picture A

There is a newsagent's. There are some payphones. There is a snack bar. There are a lot of people.

Picture B

There is a pharmacy. There is an internet café. There is a cash machine. There are a lot of airplanes. There is a restaurant. There is a bus.

GIVE US A CLUE

Materials: one copy of crossword A and crossword B per pair of students

Put Ss into pairs AA and BB and distribute the crosswords. Ss complete their answers using the clues provided. Monitor and check.

Put Ss into pairs AB. (*Weaker Ss* could be in groups AABB so As and Bs can find answer in pairs.) Elicit the question and write on the board: *What's (number) across/down?* Drill the question.

Ss A or B take it in turns to read the clue and give their partner up to 30 seconds to guess the word(s). For the clues which are pictures, Ss make their own definition or use mine or drawing. Check answers as a class.

Answers:

Across: 1 internet café   5 hospital   9 payphone
10 newsagent's

Down: 2 cash machine   3 hotel   4 classroom
6 supermarket   7 university   8 airport   9 pharmacy

PARIS IN THE SPRING

Materials: one copy of worksheet A and worksheet B per pair of students

Put Ss into pairs AA and BB and distribute the worksheets. Tell Ss they want to travel to Paris but they need more information about how to get there. If necessary, review *train, ferry, plane*. Write *TRAIN, Where from?* and *Time?* on the board. Elicit the questions: *Where does the train leave from? What time does the train leave?* Ask As to work together to prepare the questions they need and Bs do the same. Focus on the above two questions and elicit the answers from the Ss: *It leaves from London. It leaves at 19.40.* If necessary, review all the questions: *Where does it arrive? What time does it arrive? How much does it cost?*

Put Ss into pairs AB. Ss ask each other the questions to complete the timetable. Elicit answers from different pairs and give whole class feedback on errors/good language used.

Unit 7

DID YOU KNOW?

Materials: one copy of worksheet A and worksheet B per pair of students

Put Ss into pairs AA and BB. Distribute the worksheets. Ss find the past form of the verbs in the wordsearch and complete the sentences with the correct verb in the past simple. Check answers as a class, with Ss only saying the correct verb for each clue NOT the whole sentence. Ss then choose the missing date for their sentences. Ss change into pairs AB. They read their full sentences to each other to check if the date was correct. Check answers as a class.

Answers:

D	A	N	C	E	D	A	Q	R	D	S
S	O	E	B	P	P	C	R	I	E	T
T	Z	W	X	T	L	B	H	W	W	A
O	D	A	T	A	A	W	V	J	A	R
P	N	I	T	L	Y	B	Z	D	L	T
P	Y	T	F	K	E	E	H	T	K	E
E	G	E	I	E	D	K	U	I	E	D
D	Z	D	C	D	C	R	I	E	D	S

1 waited   2 started   3 talked   4 stopped   5 danced
6 played   7 cried   8 walked

WHERE WERE YOU?

Materials: one copy of the board, one coin per group and one counter per student

Put Ss into groups and distribute the board. Ss toss a coin to move: heads moves one space and tails moves two spaces. When a student lands on a square, another student in the group has to ask him/her the question: *Where were you … ?* The student answers: *I was …* It's a good idea to write: *I don't remember.* on the board. Invite Ss to ask you one or two questions first to model the task. On a free question the Ss in the group can ask about any time they want. If a student answers *I can't/don't remember*, they return to the square they were on before. The first student to finish is the winner.

Invite Ss from different groups to tell the class about Ss in their group, e.g. *At 8 o'clock this morning Anna was at home.*

GREAT FUN

Materials: one set of cards per group of students

Put Ss into groups of three or four. Distribute the cards. First Ss sort the cards into adjectives and nouns. Check answers as a class. Then Ss match the nouns and adjectives. Tell Ss that each noun has two adjective collocations that are opposites. Sometimes there is more than one possible combination, but each adjective must have a suitable collocation, so for example, *delicious* can only go with *food*. Check answers as a class. Ensure Ss have the correct adjective collocations (see Answers). (If Ss give a different answer which collocates correctly, e.g. *boring film*, tell them that it is a correct answer but not the answer for this activity). Check pronunciation.

Turn cards face down in a grid. Ss play pelmanism: Each student takes it in turn to turn over two cards and try and find the correct collocation. The student must say the words on the card out loud. If the two words do not collocate, they must be turned face down and left in exactly the same place. When a student gets a match, he/she keeps it and has another go until he/she gets a mismatch. The winner is the student with the most cards at the end. Ask Ss in each group who won.

As an extension, ask Ss to form sentences using the collocations.

Answers:
difficult/easy exam; delicious/terrible food; noisy/quiet bar; interesting/boring book; lovely/horrible dress; sad/happy film

HOW WAS IT?

Materials: one copy of worksheet A and worksheet B per pair of students

Put Ss into pairs AB and distribute the worksheets. Ss interview each other and note their partner's answers. (Questions are very similar but not identical to give stronger motivation for listening. The three optional answers are the same.) Ss then count how many as, bs and cs their partner has. Remind Ss that the quiz is for fun and they shouldn't take the results very seriously.

Invite Ss to tell the class if they were mostly a, b, or c and if they agree with the conclusion.

Unit 8

ALIBI

Materials: one worksheet per student

Distribute the worksheets. Read the blurb about the robbery. Explain *alibi*. Ss work in pairs to find the means of transport. Check answers as a class.

Focus on the verbs. With *weaker classes* ask Ss to put the verbs in the past simple before they complete the story. Encourage Ss to work in pairs or groups to do task. Check answers as a class.

Ask Ss to speculate on whether Jacques robbed the bank or not. There is no definite answer, but probably not – he was probably having a romantic dinner with his girlfriend, hence the flowers and the bill in the restaurant for two people.

As an extension, Ss could reconstruct the story in groups using the tickets, receipts and map.

Answers:

1 taxi, plane, train, ferry, car, underground

2 Jacques *took* a taxi from his house in Toulouse to the airport at three o'clock on Friday afternoon. He *went/travelled* by plane to Paris. In Paris he *took* a train to Calais. Then he *went/travelled* from Calais to Dover by ferry. He *arrived* in Dover at half past eleven at night and he *stayed* in a small hotel. The next morning he *rented* a car and *drove* to London. When he *arrived* in London he *had* lunch in an Italian restaurant. At half past seven he *bought* some flowers. He *took* the underground to Piccadilly Circus at a quarter to eight. At half past ten he *paid* for dinner for two in a French restaurant by credit card.

FIRSTS

Materials: one copy of worksheet A and worksheet B per pair of students

Put Ss into pairs AB and distribute the worksheets. Elicit a few example questions. With *weaker classes*, you could put Ss into groups A and B to prepare the questions. Monitor closely. Elicit some answers from different pairs and give whole class feedback on errors/good language used.

As an extension, group pairs and get Ss to present their partner to the group.

MISSING OBJECTS

Materials: one copy of worksheet A and worksheet B per pair of students

Put Ss into pairs AB and distribute the worksheets. Ss should sit face-to-face. Elicit the questions: *Where is … ?* and *Where are … ?* using objects around the classroom. Ss cover their eyes while you put the objects in a different place. Ss ask about the missing objects and elicit the prepositions of place. In *weaker classes* you could get groups of A and B to review the location of the objects in their picture.

Ss ask their partner about the objects in the box above their picture. Based on their partner's answer, they draw the object in the correct place on their picture. Afterwards they compare pictures. Elicit some answers from different pairs.

As an extension, Ss can turn over their sheets and see how much they remember about the location of the objects.

Possible answers:

A The glasses are on the left of the table. The keys are on the right of the table. The jacket is on the chair. The dictionary is on the bed. The bag is under the bed.

B The laptop is on the table. The jeans are on the floor next to/near the chair. The bicycle is between the table and the bed. The magazine is on the bed. The running shoes are under the bed.

VILLAGE LIFE

Materials: one copy of worksheet A and worksheet B per pair of students, one copy of the picture per pair of students

Put Ss into pairs AA and BB and distribute the worksheets and pictures. Tell them to match their sentences to scenes A–D in the picture. Do an example to demonstrate the activity. Monitor and check. Then direct Ss to the map and ask them to complete the conversations by writing the questions or answers. Do an example. Accept any answers that are grammatically correct. Monitor and check while Ss are completing the conversations.

Change Ss into pairs AB. Ss read the printed original versions to each other so they can check if their questions and responses are the same as the original. Note other versions may also be correct.

Get feedback. Ss act out the conversations, first looking at the text, but saying the sentences while looking at their partner. As they become more confident they can practise without looking at the text.

Answers:

C Where is the swimming pool? There is a swimming pool next to the school.

B Is there a payphone? Yes, the payphone is opposite the bakery.

A Excuse me. Where's the pharmacy? It's between the restaurant and the bakery.

D Where is the bus stop? The bus stop is in front of the school.

Unit 9

OPINIONS

Materials: one worksheet per student

Distribute the worksheets. Review the categories and ensure Ss understand the vocabulary. Elicit a few examples of films they like or dislike. Tell Ss to think of one example for each category. Monitor and check.

Present and drill the question *What do you think of … ?* Practise the pronunciation paying attention to linking and weak forms. Ss ask you two or three questions first. Answer the questions with reference to the Useful language box: *I like it. I think it's really good.*

Put Ss into pairs AB to ask each other their opinions. Feedback with the whole class and ask Ss to tell you some of the opinions their partners expressed.

DO YOU LIKE … ?

Materials: one worksheet per student

Put Ss into groups of six. Distribute the worksheets. Tell Ss to complete a sentence in each section so that two sentences are true for them. Tell them not to write their name at this stage. Don't let anybody see what they have written. When they have written their answer they pass the paper to the left and complete the next sentences and so on until all the sentences have been completed. Monitor for correct spelling of the verb + *-ing* form and ensure the nouns are without the definite article.

Redistribute the completed sheets and tell Ss to ask *yes/no* questions to find who wrote each statement. When they find a person who fits the sentence, they write their name. Remind Ss of the structure: *Do you like … ?* and the short answers: *No, not at all; No, not really; Yes, I do; Yes, sometimes; Yes, a lot.*

MONEY, MONEY, MONEY!

Materials: one worksheet per student

Put Ss into pairs and distribute the worksheets. Pre-teach *you don't have any money left.* Ss read the situations and record each other's answers. When Ss have finished they count how many as or bs their partner got and read the key at the bottom of the page.

Ask a few Ss if they or their partner spend too much or too little and/or if they agree with the key. Remind Ss not to take the quiz too seriously!

WHAT WOULD YOU LIKE?

Materials: one set of cards per pair of students

First demonstrate the language by making an offer, e.g. *Would you like my pen?* and eliciting a response. Write the offer and response on the board. Put Ss into pairs AB and distribute the cards (cards A to Ss A and cards B to Ss B). Tell Ss that five of their cards are offers or requests and five of them are responses. Ss separate the cards into offers/requests and answers before they start the task. Monitor and check (in *weaker classes* put Ss into pairs AA and BB to sort the cards). A must not see B's cards and B must not see A's cards. Ss take it in turns to say an offer or request and their partner has to respond with the correct answer. When they find a fit they put the two cards together face up. When all the cards have been paired off, check answers as a class.

As an extension, Ss can play a game of pelmanism. Ss place the cards face down in a column. In pairs, they take it in turns to turn over one card at a time and try to find a match. If they guess correctly, they have another turn until they have a mismatch. If the two cards don't match, they must be left in exactly the same place face down. This activity can be used before or instead of the above activity or at a later date.

Answers:

Would you like something to eat? No thanks. I'm not hungry.

Which colour would you like? I'd like the green one, please.

Can I help you? Yes, please. I'd like to buy a camera.

What would the teacher like for her birthday? I don't know. Maybe a CD. She loves classical music.

Excuse me. Where's the children's clothes section? It's on the third floor.

I'd like to buy a football. The sports department is on the second floor.

Would you like some tea or coffee? Coffee, please. Black coffee.

What would you like to eat? Let me think. Yes! I'd like the sushi, please.

Can I have some fruit, please? Yes, of course. Which would you prefer? A banana or an apple?

Would you like some wrapping paper for the present? No thanks. I think it's a waste of money.

Unit 10

RULES

Materials: one set of cards per group of students

Put Ss into groups of three and distribute the cards. Ss write the words to identify the places. Do the first one as an example. Check answers as a class.

Review the verbs which could be used for each picture, e.g. *restaurant: eat, have lunch/dinner*. Model a sentence for one of the pictures, e.g. *You can have dinner here. You can't play a game here*. Write on the board *You can … here. You can't … here*. Get Ss to place the cards face down on the table. Ss take it in turns to take a card and make two sentences (make sure the other Ss don't see the card). For example: *You can swim here. You can't run here*. The Ss in the group have to guess the place. The person who guesses correctly wins the card. The person with the most cards is the winner.

Ask different groups who won and give whole class feedback on errors/good language used.

Answers:

a restaurant, a cinema, a disco, a park, a library, a swimming pool, a train, a school, a clothes shop, a hospital, an English class, plane

GOOD INTENTIONS

Materials: one worksheet per student

Write on the board: *We are going to talk about our intentions*. Highlight *be going to* and ask if it refers to present, future or past actions. Distribute the worksheets. Check Ss remember the vocabulary. Ss complete the second column so that it is true for them. Give an example of a positive and negative response to show that they use a tick for yes and a cross for no. Ss write their own last question.

Put Ss into pairs. They take turns to exchange information and make a short note of their partner's answer. If their partner answers yes, they ask the follow-up question. Do an example before they start the activity.

Elicit some answers from different pairs. Model the third person singular for *be going to* and write it on the board. Put Ss into groups of four and ask them to share three or four of their partner's answers with their group.

As an extension, get Ss to find common answers in their group and report them to the class using *My friends and I are going to …*

COLLOCATIONS

Materials: one worksheet per student

Put Ss into pairs and distribute the worksheets. Tell Ss that three of the phrases are correct and one is incorrect. Go through the example. Ss cross out the incorrect collocations. Check answers as a class.

Tell Ss to ask each other about their abilities and to record their partner's answers with a tick for yes and a cross for no. Model the question and short answers on the board using the first question as an example. Get Ss to ask you two or three of the questions. Ss continue in pairs. Monitor and encourage Ss to use: *Yes, I can. No, I can't.*

Elicit some answers from different pairs and give whole class feedback on errors/good language used. Highlight that the third person singular form doesn't use s. Then, Ss work with a new partner and share three or four of the most interesting answers with their new partner.

As an extension, invite Ss to tell the class what their partner and they have in common *We can both swim*. Highlight the position of *both* after can.

SEE YOU LATER, ALLIGATOR!

Materials: one role card per student

You could put the title of the activity *See you later, alligator!* on the board and ask Ss if it is saying *hello* or *goodbye*. Model the phrase to elicit why we say *alligator* (because it rhymes with *later* and it is amusing). If the word *alligator* is unfamiliar, you could show a picture of one.

Ask Ss to stand in two lines facing each other. Give each student a role card. Those with card A start a conversation according to the information on the card with the person opposite them. The Ss with card B have to respond. Model with a student. Clap your hands after about one minute (depending on how the Ss are getting on, it could be longer or shorter). The student with card B has to choose one of the responses as a way of saying *Goodbye*. Sometimes either response will be appropriate and sometimes only one of them. The Ss then exchange cards with their partner. The student at the end of one of the lines comes to the front of that line so that Ss change partners.

The process can be continued until the Ss are back facing their first partner, until all the cards have been used by each student, or at your discretion.

Invite Ss to say which conversation they had was most interesting or amusing.

TESTS INDEX

LISTENING

1 ▶ 65 **Listen and tick the correct answer, a), b) or c).**

1 How much is the brown clock?

£22.20	£22.50	£25.50
a) ___	b) ___	c) ✓

2 What's Paul's nationality?

Chinese	Italian	American
a) ___	b) ___	c) ___

3 What's the student's first name?

Candy	Kandi	Kandy
a) ___	b) ___	c) ___

4 When does Neil do sport?

every day	never	on Saturdays
a) ___	b) ___	c) ___

5 The hat is …

Alice's	Sandra's	Pedro's
a) ___	b) ___	c) ___

6 Henry is …

tired	cold	bored
a) ___	b) ___	c) ___

[| 5]

2 ▶ 66 **Listen and write T (true) or F (false) next to each sentence.**

1 Martha and Dan are at a café.   _T_
2 Their food and drink is €12.60.   ___
3 The café closes at 5.45.   ___
4 Dan is cold.   ___
5 Martha sometimes eats chocolate cake.   ___
6 Martha likes cheese.   ___

[| 5]

PRONUNCIATION

3 ▶ 67 **Listen and underline the word or letter with a different sound.**

1 are   K̲   car   R
2 cake   bread   steak   take
3 our   they're   their   where
4 you   U   do   no
5 what   hot   that   not
6 he's   this   these   keys
7 play   G   J   day
8 what   at   hat   that
9 knows   goes   those   shoes
10 blue   Q   go   too
11 they   C   key   T

[| 5]

VOCABULARY AND GRAMMAR

4 **Underline the different word in each group.**

1	Russia	China	exercise	Argentina
2	printer	singer	engineer	taxi driver
3	bored	eighty	cold	thirsty
4	listen	have	speak	write
5	box	lamp	desk	weekend
6	chips	sweater	jacket	shirt
7	sister	father	waiter	brother
8	red	green	brown	read
9	café	bread	steak	cheese
10	gym	gift shop	lunch	hairdresser's
11	forty	twelve	trousers	thirteen

[| 5]

5 **Add the missing letters.**

1 Saul has one son and two d _a_ _u_ _g_ _h_ _t_ _e_ rs.
2 A: What's his job?
   B: He's an a _ _ _ r.
3 A: Are you OK?
   B: No, I'm not. I'm very t _ _ _ d.
4 I always eat c _ _ _ _ l with milk for breakfast.
5 A: Are they from A _ _ _ _ _ _ _ a?
   B: Yes, they are. He's from Sydney and she's from Melbourne.
6 A: How old is she?
   B: She's n _ _ _ _ y - f _ _ e.
7 He works on W _ _ _ _ _ _ _ ys and Thursdays.
8 A: What's 'SingFest'?
   B: It's a music f _ _ _ _ _ l. The bands are really good this year.
9 I work in the morning and I study in the e _ _ _ _ _ g.
10 My favourite colour is y _ _ _ _ w.
11 The g _ _ _ _ d tour begins at 2 p.m.

[| 5]

6 Underline the correct answer, a) or b).

1 ____ you from Spain?

  a) <u>Are</u>   b) Do

2 She ____ up at six o'clock.

  a) goes   b) gets

3 Do you like ____?

  a) football   b) in a flat

4 You do exercise at ____.

  a) the office   b) the gym

5 You ____ hungry!

  a) 're always   b) always are

6 Who's ____ man over there?

  a) this   b) that

7 They don't have lessons ____ the weekend.

  a) in   b) at

8 What ____ those?

  a) 's   b) are

9 I ____ go to the hairdresser's.

  a) don't often   b) often don't

10 We ____ eat steak, but not very often.

  a) sometimes   b) usually

11 Are they ____ books?

  a) Maria's   b) Marias

                           | 5 |

7 Correct the grammar mistakes.

        does

1 What time ~~do~~ Pete have dinner?

2 Where Kim is?

3 She doesn't likes chips.

4 Look at me! This are my new trousers.

5 Glen's 44 and Farah is 42. They're son's 19.

6 We have two children. Her son's name is Raj.

7 They always are happy.

8 It's name is Hotel Orlando.

9 It's my dads house.

10 Yes, I'm.

11 She not hungry.

                           | 5 |

8 Complete the sentences with the correct positive (+) or negative (-) form of the verbs in brackets.

1 He always ___phones___ me on my birthday. (+) (*phone*)

2 That ___isn't___ true. (-) (*be*)

3 My keys _____ in the box. (-) (*be*)

4 Katy _____ French. (+) (*study*)

5 She _____ healthy food. (-) (*eat*)

6 Nina _____ a motorbike. (+) (*have*)

7 I _____ fish. (-) (*like*)

8 She _____ a DVD every evening. (+) (*watch*)

9 I _____ tired. (-) (*be*)

10 You _____ a teacher! (-) (*be*)

11 He _____ at university. (+) (*be*)

12 Christa _____ sport. (-) (*do*)

                           | 10 |

9 Write questions. Use the prompts.

1 what / your / name

  What's your name?

2 what time / she / get up

  _____

3 where / they / from

  _____

4 you / doctor

  _____

5 you / live / with your parents

  _____

6 this / Minna's / chair

  _____

                           | 5 |

10 Underline the correct alternatives to complete the email.

Dear Anita,

Help! I have a problem with [1]*my/his* girlfriend. And it's the same problem every week.

We [2]*often/always* watch a DVD at my house on Saturday evenings – every week. And every week [3]*on/at* eight o'clock, my [4]*girlfriend's/girlfriend* phone rings and she answers it. She talks to [5]*her/his* friend for ages!

And does she say sorry? No, she doesn't! She [6]*never/sometimes* says sorry! It drives me crazy!

What do I do? What do you think?

Max

                           | 5 |

READING

11 Read the article and match headings 1–5 to paragraphs A–E.

Famous families

By Alex Walker
21st April

A

Brothers Joel and Ethan Cohen are film-makers from the USA. Joel's wife, Frances McDormand, is an actor. She is also from the USA. Joel and Frances have an adopted son, Pedro. He comes from Paraguay.

B

Patrick Tse is a Chinese actor from Hong Kong. Patrick's son, Nicholas Tse, is an actor, a singer and a songwriter. Nicholas is married to actor and singer Cecilia Cheung. They have two sons, Lucas and Quintus. Nicholas has dual nationality – he is Canadian and Chinese. He and his family live in Hong Kong.

C

Swedish actor Stellan Skarsgård is an actor. Three of his children, Gustaf, Bill and Alexander, are actors, too. The brothers often appear together in Swedish films.

D

Musician Ravi Shankar comes from India. He has two daughters, Norah Jones and Anoushka. They are singers, and Ravi often gives concerts with Anoushka.

E

The Coppolas are a famous American family in the film industry. Francis Ford Coppola is a film director and his wife Eleanor is an artist. Their daughter Sofia and son Roman are film directors. Sofia is also a singer and actor.

1 A family of actors and singers _____
2 Musical father and daughters _____
3 Film-making brothers _____
4 Father and sons – all actors ___C___
5 A film-making family _____

| | 4 |

12 Read the article again. Write true (T) or false (F) next to each sentence.

1 Joel Cohen and his wife are American. _T_
2 Joel Cohen's child is from Paraguay. ____
3 Nicholas Tse's father is a singer. ____
4 You never see any of the Skarsgård brothers in the same film. ____
5 Anoushka often sings at concerts with her father. ____
6 Sofia Coppola's mother is an artist. ____

| | 5 |

13 Read the signs and answer the questions with one, two or three words.

MUSIC FESTIVAL
CITY PARK
THIS SATURDAY ★ 11 A.M.–11.30 P.M.

Gloria's gifts

Sorry!
We are CLOSED
on Mondays

FREE
English LESSONS
TUESDAYS
and
THURSDAYS
2 P.M.–4 P.M.

Today's specials
Chicken & vegetable pasta 4.95
Steak & chips 8.99
Fish & chips 7.50
Fruit cake 2.75

Guitar teacher
I'm Martín and I'm from Argentina.
I teach Spanish guitar to all ages.
Tel: 8724 99260
Email: pablobb@hayoo.com

1 What's Martín's nationality?
  He's from Argentina.
2 When does the music festival start?
  _____
3 How much are the English lessons?
  _____
4 How much do the fish and chips cost?
  _____
5 When is the gift shop closed?
  _____
6 What does Martín teach?
  _____
7 What's his phone number?
  _____

| | 6 |

COMMUNICATION

14 Underline the correct response, a) or b).

1 What's the problem?

   a) I'm hot.   b) Wonderful.

2 I'm hungry.

   a) Good idea.   b) Me too.

3 I'd like a cheese sandwich, please.

   a) Still or sparkling?

   b) Brown bread or white?

4 Let's have a break now.

   a) OK.   b) Me too.

5 Anything else?

   a) No thank you.   b) That's six euros.

6 How much does it cost?

   a) Half past six.   b) Six thirty.

| | 5 |

15 Complete the conversations with the phrases from the box.

| help you   as in   Excuse me   Sorry?   time is it |
| How much   time's   Thanks   please   wonderful |
| When |

Waiter: Can I ¹ _help you_ ?

Man: Yes, I'd like a coffee, ² _____ .

Woman: ³ _____ does the swimming pool open?

Receptionist: At half past eight.

Woman: What ⁴ _____ now?

Receptionist: It's eight o'clock.

Woman: ⁵ _____ does it cost?

Receptionist: It's free.

Woman: Free? That's ⁶ _____ .

Receptionist: What's your first name?

Man: Gerry.

Receptionist: Is that J-e-r-r-y?

Man: No, it's G ⁷ _____ 'good'. G-e-r-r-y.

Man: ⁸ _____ .

Woman: Yes?

Man: What ⁹ _____ the lesson?

Woman: Quarter past nine.

Man: ¹⁰ _____ When?

Woman: Quarter past nine.

Man: Quarter past nine. ¹¹ _____ .

| | 10 |

WRITING

16 Add the missing linkers to the blog entry.

| and   but   that   because   first   then |

BLOGGER

It's Friday evening ¹ ___and___ I'm tired! I'm tired ² _____ I work from Monday to Friday. I like my job ³ _____ it's very difficult.
So, what do I do at the start of the weekend? ⁴ _____ , I go to the shops and I buy my favourite food and drink – meat, vegetables, cola, cake. After ⁵ _____ , I make and eat a big dinner. I play music and watch TV, ⁶ _____ I phone my friends and talk about what to do on Saturday and Sunday … I don't go to bed late.

▶ Posted one hour ago
   via my mobile

| | 5 |

17 Write a blog entry about your weekend. What do you do? What do you eat? Write 50–80 words.

BLOGGER

_____

_____

_____

_____

_____

_____

_____

_____

_____

_____

_____

_____

_____

_____

▶ Posted one hour ago
   via my mobile

| | 10 |

| **Total:** | 100 |

LISTENING

1 ▶ **65 Listen and tick the correct answer, a), b) or c).**

1 How much is the brown clock?

£22.20	£22.50	£25.50

a) ____ b) ____ c) ✓

2 What's Lily's nationality?

Chinese	Italian	American

a) ____ b) ____ c) ____

3 What's the student's family name?

Wallace	Wallis	Wallice

a) ____ b) ____ c) ____

4 Where does Neil work?

in a shop	in a taxi	in an office

a) ____ b) ____ c) ____

5 Alice is at …

the gym	the cinema	the hotel

a) ____ b) ____ c) ____

6 The keys are …

Henry's	Diana's	the hairdressers's

a) ____ b) ____ c) ____

☐☐ **5**

2 ▶ **66 Listen and write T (true) or F (false) next to each sentence.**

1 Martha and Dan are at a café. _T_
2 Their food and drink is €12.80. ____
3 The café closes at 5.30. ____
4 Dan and Martha are cold. ____
5 Martha never eats chocolate cake. ____
6 Martha doesn't like cheese. ____

☐☐ **5**

PRONUNCIATION

3 ▶ **67 Listen and underline the word or letter with a different sound.**

1 are _K_ car R
2 cake bread steak take
3 our they're their where
4 you U do no
5 what hot that not
6 he's this these keys
7 play G J day
8 what at hat that
9 knows goes those shoes
10 blue Q go too
11 they C key T

☐☐ **5**

VOCABULARY AND GRAMMAR

4 **Underline the different word in each group.**

1	Russia	China	exercise	Argentina
2	thirty	keys	eleven	sixteen
3	brother	mother	son	doctor
4	dinner	gym	gift shop	hairdresser's
5	chicken	restaurant	fish	meat
6	work	blue	black	white
7	steak	hat	T-shirt	jacket
8	tired	hot	seventy	hungry
9	picture	actor	clock	desk
10	singer	waiter	computer	businessman
11	listen	speak	red	read

☐☐ **5**

5 **Add the missing letters.**

1 Saul has one son and two d _a_ _u_ _g_ _h_ _t_ _e_ r s.
2 A: Are they from A __ __ __ __ __ __ __ a?
   B: Yes, they are. He's from Sydney and she's from Melbourne.
3 He works on Tuesdays and W __ __ __ __ __ __ __ ys.
4 A: What's her job?
   B: She's an e __ __ __ __ __ __ __ r.
5 My favourite colour is w __ __ __ e.
6 A: What's 'SingFest'?
   B: It's a music f __ __ __ __ __ __ l. The bands are really good this year.
7 He always eats fish and v __ __ __ __ __ __ __ __ __ s for dinner.
8 I work in the morning and I study in the a __ __ __ __ __ __ __ n.
9 The g __ __ __ __ d tour begins at 4 p.m.
10 A: Are you OK?
    B: No, I'm not. I'm b __ __ __ d.
11 A: How old is he?
    B: He's s __ __ __ y - n __ __ e.

☐☐ **5**

6 Underline the correct answer, a) or b).

1 ____ you from Spain?

  a) <u>Are</u>   b) Do

2 I ____ bored.

  a) never am   b) 'm never

3 Are they ____ pens?

  a) Ginos   b) Gino's

4 I ____ eat fish, but not very often.

  a) sometimes   b) usually

5 What ____ those?

  a) are   b) 's

6 They don't work ____ day.

  a) on   b) every

7 He ____ up at eight o'clock.

  a) gets   b) goes

8 Do you like ____?

  a) coffee   b) in a house

9 Let's ____ Exercise 3A now.

  a) work   b) do

10 Who are ____ men over there?

  a) these   b) those

11 We ____ go to the swimming pool.

  a) don't often   b) often don't

`5`

7 Correct the grammar mistakes.

             does

1 What time ~~do~~ Pete have dinner?

2 It's name is Café 29.

3 Yes, I'm.

4 She not tired.

5 It's my mums car.

6 Look at me! This are my new shoes.

7 Eli's 12 and Caz is 14. They're dad's 49.

8 We have two children. Her son's name is Pip.

9 He doesn't likes fish.

10 Where my keys are?

11 He always is bored.

`5`

8 Complete the sentences with the correct positive (+) or negative (-) form of the verbs in brackets.

1 He always __*phones*__ me on my birthday. (+) (*phone*)

2 That __*isn't*__ true. (-) (*be*)

3 Jacob _____ his homework in the evening. (-) (*do*)

4 You _____ a doctor! (-) (*be*)

5 George _____ Spanish. (+) (*study*)

6 She _____ meat. (-) (*eat*)

7 He _____ in the classroom. (+) (*be*)

8 I _____ cheese. (-) (*like*)

9 She _____ TV every evening. (+) (*watch*)

10 Ken _____ a motorbike. (+) (*have*)

11 My shoes _____ black. (-) (*be*)

12 I _____ cold. (-) (*be*)

`10`

9 Write questions. Use the prompts.

1 what / your / name

   What's your name?

2 where / they / from

  _____

3 you / singer

  _____

4 what time / he / go to bed

  _____

5 this / Karim's / book

  _____

6 you / work / in an office

  _____

`5`

10 Underline the correct alternatives to complete the email.

Dear Anita,

Help! I have a problem with ¹*my/his* boyfriend. And it's the same problem every week.

We ²*always/usually* go to the city together on Monday mornings – every week. We go in my ³*boyfriend/boyfriend's* car. And every week my boyfriend drives ⁴*his/her* car very fast. I ⁵*often/don't* like it but every week he does the same thing.

We get to the city and I'm not happy. He knows I'm not happy but does he say sorry? No, ⁶*sometimes/never*! It drives me crazy!

What do I do? What do you think?

Beatrice

`5`

11 Read the article and match headings 1–5 to paragraphs A–E.

Famous families

By Alex Walker
21st April

A

Brothers Joel and Ethan Cohen are film-makers from the USA. Joel's wife, Frances McDormand, is an actor. She is also from the USA. Joel and Frances have an adopted son, Pedro. He comes from Paraguay.

B

Patrick Tse is a Chinese actor from Hong Kong. Patrick's son, Nicholas Tse, is an actor, a singer and a songwriter. Nicholas is married to actor and singer Cecilia Cheung. They have two sons, Lucas and Quintus. Nicholas has dual nationality – he is Canadian and Chinese. He and his family live in Hong Kong.

C

Swedish actor Stellan Skarsgård is an actor. Three of his children, Gustaf, Bill and Alexander, are actors, too. The brothers often appear together in Swedish films.

D

Musician Ravi Shankar comes from India. He has two daughters, Norah Jones and Anoushka. They are singers, and Ravi often gives concerts with Anoushka.

E

The Coppolas are a famous American family in the film industry. Francis Ford Coppola is a film director and his wife Eleanor is an artist. Their daughter Sofia and son Roman are film directors. Sofia is also a singer and actor.

1 A film-making family _____
2 Father and sons – all actors ___C___
3 Musical father and daughters _____
4 Film-making brothers _____
5 A family of actors and singers _____

> 4

12 Read the article again. Write true (T) or false (F) next to the sentences.

1 Joel Cohen and his wife are American. _T_
2 Nicholas Tse lives in Canada. ____
3 Nicholas's father and wife are actors. ____
4 You sometimes see the Skarsgård brothers in the same film. ____
5 Anoushka often sings at concerts with her father. ____
6 Sofia Coppola's brother is an actor. ____

> 5

13 Read the signs and answer the questions with one, two or three words.

MUSIC FESTIVAL
CITY PARK
THIS SATURDAY ★ 11 A.M.–11.30 P.M.

FREE *English* LESSONS
TUESDAYS and THURSDAYS
2 P.M.–4 P.M.

Gloria's gifts
Sorry!
We are CLOSED
on Mondays

Today's specials
Chicken & vegetable pasta 4.95
Steak & chips 8.99
Fish & chips 7.50
Fruit cake 2.75

Guitar teacher
I'm Martín and I'm from Argentina.
I teach Spanish guitar to all ages.
Tel: 8724 99260
Email: pablobb@hayoo.com

1 What's Martín's nationality?
He's from Argentina.

2 How much are the English lessons?
_____

3 When is the gift shop closed?
_____

4 How much does the steak and chips cost?
_____

5 When does the music festival finish?
_____

6 What does Martín teach?
_____

7 What's his email address?
_____

> 6

COMMUNICATION

14 Underline the correct response, a) or b).

1 What's the problem?
   a) <u>I'm hot.</u>   b) Wonderful.

2 I'd like some mineral water, please.
   a) Still or sparkling?
   b) Brown bread or white?

3 How much does it cost?
   a) Quarter past four.   b) Four fifteen.

4 Anything else?
   a) No thank you.   b) That's five euros.

5 I'm thirsty.
   a) Good idea.   b) Me too.

6 Let's have a break now.
   a) OK.   b) Me too.

                                   5

15 Complete the conversations with the phrases from the box.

~~help you~~   as in   Excuse me   Sorry?   time is it How much   time's   Thanks   please   wonderful When

Waiter: Can I ¹ _help you_ ?
Man: Yes, I'd like a cola, ² _____ .

Receptionist: What's your family name?
Man: Jerry.
Receptionist: Is that G-e-r-r-y?
Man: No, it's J ³ _____ 'job'. J-e-r-r-y.

Man: ⁴ _____ .
Woman: Yes?
Man: What ⁵ _____ the concert?
Woman: Quarter past two.
Man: ⁶ _____ When?
Woman: Quarter past two.
Man: Quarter past two. ⁷ _____ .

Woman: ⁸ _____ does the gym open?
Receptionist: At half past nine.
Woman: What ⁹ _____ now?
Receptionist: It's nine o'clock.
Woman: ¹⁰ _____ does it cost?
Receptionist: It's free.
Woman: Free? That's ¹¹ _____ .

                                 10

WRITING

16 Add the missing linkers to the blog entry.

~~and~~   but   first   then   that   because

BLOGGER

It's Sunday evening ¹___*and*___ I'm not happy! I'm not happy ² _____ it's the end of the weekend. I like my job ³ _____ I don't like Monday mornings!
So, it's the end of the weekend … but what do I do at the start of the weekend? ⁴ _____, I phone my friends and talk about what to do on Saturday and Sunday. ⁵ _____ I make and eat a big dinner. It's usually fish and chips or chicken and chips. After ⁶ _____, I play loud music and watch TV. I don't go to bed late.

▶ Posted one hour ago
  via my mobile

                                 5

17 Write a blog entry about your weekend. What do you do? What do you eat? Write 50–80 words.

BLOGGER

_____
_____
_____
_____
_____
_____
_____
_____
_____
_____
_____
_____
_____
_____

▶ Posted one hour ago
  via my mobile

                                 10

Total: **100**

LISTENING

1 ▶ 55 **Listen and tick the correct answer, a), b), or c).**

1 Why was the woman in China?

work	holiday	family
a) ___	b) ✓	c) ___

2 Adam's wife wants him to travel by …

taxi	bus	underground
a) ___	b) ___	c) ___

3 What did Selma do on her holiday?

camp	meet people	walk
a) ___	b) ___	c) ___

4 Fiona's going to get … soon.

fit	a new job	a monthly pass
a) ___	b) ___	c) ___

5 What did Alice do with the gift from Ricardo?

change it	break it	lose it
a) ___	b) ___	c) ___

6 What can't the man do?

play the drums	play the guitar	sing
a) ___	b) ___	c) ___

[ ] 5

2 ▶ 56 **Listen and write T (true) or F (false) next to each sentence.**

1 It's the 1st August.   _T_
2 Lisa's birthday is on the 21st August.   ____
3 Lisa didn't dance at her party last year.   ____
4 She's going to cook a meal for a lot of friends for
  her birthday this year.   ____
5 Angela gave Lisa clothes last year.   ____
6 Lisa would like a day at a beauty spa.   ____

[ ] 5

PRONUNCIATION

3 ▶ 57 **Listen and write the regular past simple verbs in the correct sound group.**

~~stopped~~ ~~waited~~ ~~played~~ liked moved started cried worked finished wanted lived talked listened

/t/	/ɪd/
stopped	waited

/d/	
played	

[ ] 5

VOCABULARY AND GRAMMAR

4 **Underline the different word in each group.**

1	speak	read	<u>ride</u>	write
2	local	delicious	all right	great
3	swim	run	relax	cost
4	hotel	luggage	pharmacy	newsagent's
5	March	June	November	beauty
6	second	sixth	laugh	first
7	furniture	single	passenger	ticket office
8	opposite	remember	behind	near
9	cry	dance	gift	wait
10	drive	train	bus	bike
11	buy	arrive	sell	get

[ ] 5

5 **Add the missing letters.**

1 How much do those bags c _o_ _s_ t?
2 My goal for this year? I want to lose w _ _ _ _ _ t.
3 A: Do you have plans for next year?
  B: No, not really. I need to get o _ _ _ _ _ _ _ _ d.
4 You can write 't _ _ _ d' like this – '3rd'.
5 My birthday's in A _ _ _ _ l.
6 He usually goes to work by u _ _ _ _ _ _ _ _ _ _ d.
7 I don't like ch _ _ _ _ _ _ g o _ _ _ _ _ e. I like
  talking to people on the phone or face-to-face.
8 A: Is that book i _ _ _ _ _ _ _ _ _ ng?
  B: Yes, it's very good.
9 A: Is the window on the left of the door?
  B: No, it's on the r _ _ _ _ t.
10 A: I'd like to call her, but my mobile's at home.
  B: It's OK, there's a p _ _ _ _ _ _ _ e over there.
11 How many p _ _ _ _ _ _ _ ers were in the car?

[ ] 5

6 Underline the correct alternative, a) or b).

I Where ____ you yesterday?

   a) <u>were</u>   b) was

2 Let's meet ____ the station.

   a) on   b) at

3 What did you ____ him?

   a) gave   b) give

4 She writes about her travels ____ the internet.

   a) at   b) on

5 I love ____ old buildings on holiday!

   a) seeing   b) going

6 Let's ____ some coffee.

   a) cook   b) make

7 'B' is ____ 'A' and 'C' in the alphabet.

   a) behind   b) between

8 Let's talk about it ____ the car.

   a) in   b) at

9 See you ____ !

   a) two weeks   b) later

10 Where do you ____ your clothes?

   a) pay   b) get

11 She wants to help ____ .

   a) money   b) others

| | 5 |

7 Complete the blog with the correct past simple form of the verbs in brackets.

From waiter to teacher

Three years ago I [1] _was_ (be) a waiter in a restaurant. I [2] _____ (not be) very happy so I [3] _____ (decide) to change jobs.

I [4] _____ (look) at job adverts every day for three months, but I [5] _____ (not see) any interesting ones. Then one day I [6] _____ (see) an advert for teaching assistants in India.

I wrote a letter with my details, and two days later someone phoned me. They [7] _____ (ask) me to go for an interview, and they [8] _____ (give) me a job.

It was a voluntary job so they [9] _____ (not pay) me – I just [10] _____ (have) food and a place to live.

Then, I [11] _____ (do) some training and I became a 'real' teacher. That's my job now and I love it!

| | 10 |

8 Correct the grammar mistakes.

I What ~~were~~ _did_ you do yesterday?

2 He has a lot brothers and sisters.

3 Jill can running 10km.

4 You're going have a good time.

5 No, there aren't some good shops near here.

6 I hate wrap gifts.

7 We lived next of the school.

8 Do you like my bike? My dad gave it to him for my birthday.

9 The meal didn't be expensive.

| | 4 |

9 Choose the correct words to complete the story.

| ~~don't~~ wasn't on arrived didn't a any |

Planes, trains and me

I really love going to different countries but I [1] _don't_ like travelling by plane. In fact, I hate it!

Last year I went [2] _____ holiday with my friend, Luca. Luca wanted to fly, but I [3] _____ want to go by plane so I travelled by train. Big mistake!

The journey took nine hours. I didn't have [4] _____ food with me and there wasn't [5] _____ café on the train.

When I [6] _____ at the hotel, I was very tired and hungry. It [7] _____ a good start to the holiday!

| | 6 |

10 Complete the questions for the answers. Use two, three or four words.

I A: Where _____ _were you_ _____ last week?

   B: I was on holiday.

2 A: Where _____?

   B: I went to Dublin.

3 A: _____ hot?

   B: No, it wasn't hot. It was cold!

4 A: _____ in Dublin?

   B: Yes, there's an airport in Dublin.

5 A: _____ people friendly?

   B: Oh yes, the people were really friendly.

6 A: _____?

   B: I ate the local food.

| | 5 |

READING

11 Read the article and match a)–f) with gaps 1–6.

New Year – New You?

It's the 31st of December. Tomorrow is the start of a new year. For many people this is a good time to choose some personal goals. ¹_b_ Maybe you'd like to get organised or perhaps you want to save some money. ²____.

'I can't think of any New Year's resolutions. ³____. I don't want to change anything.'

Audrey, 65

'I always have lots of plans at the start of a new year. This year I'm going to get healthy. So, I'm going to go to the gym three times a week. I'd like to lose weight. I'm going to go swimming every Sunday because I love doing that. ⁴____, and I'm not going to drive to work. I'm going to walk or go by bike.'

Bea, 29

'I work in a bank, but I hate thinking about money all the time. I'm going to look for a completely different sort of job this year. ⁵____.'

Nathan, 26

'I'm not going to make any New Year's resolutions this year. Last year I made about five New Year's resolutions. I didn't keep any of them! It was the same the year before that … and the year before that.'

Stefan, 32

'I'm going to learn to swim. ⁶____ and I don't like being in the water. But now I have my own children, I think it's important for me to learn.'

Maddie, 28

a) I didn't have lessons when I was a child
b) ~~Are there any lifestyle changes you want to make?~~
c) I'd like to help others in some way
d) This year I'm going to stop eating chocolate
e) I'm very happy being me
f) We asked five people about their New Year's resolutions

[ ] **5**

12 Read the article again. Write T (true) or F (false) next to each sentence.

1 Bea's goal is to walk or cycle to work next year. _T_
2 Maddie can't swim. ____
3 Audrey isn't happy with her life. ____
4 Nathan loves his job. ____
5 Bea likes swimming. ____
6 Stefan can't keep New Year's resolutions. ____

[ ] **5**

13 Read the text then complete the blog entry with words from the box.

THE SHANGHAI **NO. 1** DEPARTMENT STORE
830 Nanjing Road, Shanghai

There are about 300 shops on Shanghai's Nanjing Road. Most of them are modern buildings, full of expensive items, like fashion and electronic goods from around the world.

The Shanghai No.1 Department Store (or 'First' Department Store) offers shoppers a very different experience. It is an old building, and most of the items for sale are Chinese, not international.

The store opened in 1934. It was called The Sun, and was one of just four big department stores in Shanghai at the time.

Departments: Clothes, Gifts, Food, Toys, Books, Jewellery, Homewear, Sports, Menswear, Women's Clothes, Beauty.

~~modern~~	old	First	Menswear	international
The Sun				

We had a great day today – we went shopping on Nanjing Road. There are a lot of ¹_modern_ buildings and shopping centres there. They sell ²_____ things – clothes, computers, phones, things like that. We also found this fantastic ³_____ department store.
It was called ⁴_____ when it first opened in 1934. Now it's called The Shanghai ⁵_____ Department Store.
There were lots of interesting things for sale. I bought a traditional Chinese jacket in the ⁶_____ department.

[ ] **5**

COMMUNICATION

14 Match sentences 1–6 with responses a)–f).

1 Which colour would you like? _c_
2 What would you like? ____
3 How was the fish? ____
4 Hey, this music's really great. ____
5 How was the film? ____
6 Nice to talk to you. ____

a) Can I have a tea, please?
b) Good to talk to you, too.
c) ~~Let me see … the black one, please.~~
d) Yes, it's fantastic.
e) It was boring.
f) Delicious!

[ ] **5**

15 Complete the conversation with the words and phrases from the box.

| can I have | what | do | excuse me | would | sorry |
| where | you know | let me check | behind | when |

Sales assistant:	Can I help you?
Customer:	¹ _Can I have_ a ticket to Zurich, please.
Sales assistant:	² _____ you like a single or a return?
Customer:	Return, please.
Sales assistant:	And when ³_____ you want to come back?
Customer:	Tomorrow.
Sales assistant:	That's sixty-seven fifty, please.
Customer:	OK. ⁴_____ does the next train leave?
Sales assistant:	At ten forty.
Customer:	⁵_____ does it leave from?
Sales assistant:	Gate thirty.
Customer:	⁶_____? Gate thirteen?
Sales assistant:	No, thirty.
Customer:	Thank you. Oh ... ⁷_____!
Sales assistant:	Yes?
Customer:	Where is gate thirty?
Sales assistant:	It's over there, ⁸_____ the snack bar.
Customer:	'Snack bar'? ⁹_____'s a 'snack bar'?
Sales assistant:	It's ... ¹⁰_____, a place where you can get snacks ... like a café.
Customer:	Ah, yes. I understand. ¹¹_____. The snack bar is in front of gate thirty.
Sales assistant:	Yes, that's right.

| 10 |

16 Underline the correct alternatives to complete the email.

---

¹*Hi/Dear* Mr Kovacs,

I'm going to be back in the office on ²*Monday/monday*, not tomorrow, ³*so/because* there aren't any planes tonight.

I met Elise Bernhardt yesterday and I gave ⁴*her/Elise Bernhardt* the pictures. There weren't any problems with them, ⁵*because/so* we had some time to talk about other things.

⁶*Take care/Regards*,

Carla

| 5 |

17 You are on holiday in a city. Write an email to a friend. Write about two or three of the things from the box. Write 50–80 words.

| the food   a problem   what you did yesterday |
| a plan for tomorrow   the transport |

| 10 |

| Total: | 100 |

LISTENING

1 ▶ 55 **Listen and tick the correct answer, a), b) or c).**

1 Where did the woman meet her husband?

at work	at a bus station	on a train
a) ____	b) ____	c) ✓

2 There aren't any … this evening.

taxis	buses	underground trains
a) ____	b) ____	c) ____

3 Selma stayed at … for her holiday.

a campsite	home	a hotel
a) ____	b) ____	c) ____

4 Fiona isn't going to get …

a monthly pass	a new job	organised
a) ____	b) ____	c) ____

5 What did Ricardo do with the gift for Alice?

change it	wrap it	lose it
a) ____	b) ____	c) ____

6 What can the man do?

sing	play the drums	read music
a) ____	b) ____	c) ____

[5]

2 ▶ 56 **Listen and write T (true) or F (false) next to each sentence.**

1 It's the 1st August. _T_

2 Lisa's birthday is on the 20th August. ____

3 Last year she had a party. ____

4 Lisa likes dancing. ____

5 Lisa would like to have a party again this year. ____

6 Angela is going to talk to her sister about Lisa's gift. ____

[5]

PRONUNCIATION

3 ▶ 57 **Listen and write the regular past simple verbs in the correct sound group.**

~~stopped~~ ~~waited~~ ~~played~~ liked moved started cried worked finished wanted lived talked listened

/t/	/ɪd/
stopped	waited

/d/
played

[5]

VOCABULARY AND GRAMMAR

4 Underline the different word in each group.

1 speak	read	<u>ride</u>	write
2 April	January	December	jewellery
3 boring	fantastic	second	all right
4 cost	pay	cry	sell
5 third	ninth	fit	fourth
6 gift	passenger	return	gate
7 snack bar	bike	payphone	pharmacy
8 talk	wait	near	dance
9 toy	swim	run	play tennis
10 taxi	ride	plane	underground
11 behind	between	near	boring

[5]

5 Add the missing letters.

1 How much do people p _a_ _y_ for English lessons here?

2 My birthday's in M _ _ _ _ h.

3 You can write 'f _ _ _ t' like this – '1st'.

4 A: Do you like being a waiter?
   B: No, I don't. I want to c _ _ _ _ e my job.

5 He doesn't s _ _ _ k Spanish.

6 A: These pictures of your family are very good.
   B: Thanks. I like t _ _ _ _ _ g ph _ _ _ s.

7 Sorry, I don't r _ _ _ _ _ _ _ r your family name.

8 She rides a m _ _ _ _ _ _ _ _ e to work.

9 Let's get some money from that c _ _ h
   m _ _ _ _ _ e.

10 A: Is it a good hotel?
   B: No, it's t _ _ _ _ _ _ e!

11 Let's get a coffee at that i _ _ _ _ _ _ _ t c _ _ é.

[5]

6 Underline the correct alternative, a) or b).

1 Where ____ you yesterday?
   a) <u>were</u>   b) was
2 See you ____!
   a) three days   b) later
3 He's a taxi driver ____ Moscow.
   a) in   b) at
4 I love ____ new people on holiday.
   a) meeting   b) speaking
5 My goal for this year? I want to ____ weight.
   a) lose   b) save
6 He plays the piano but he can't ____ music.
   a) read   b) speak
7 Those phones ____ a lot of money.
   a) buy   b) cost
8 Where did you ____ it?
   a) got   b) get
9 I was ____ university in 1994.
   a) at   b) in
10 Come and sit ____ me!
   a) near   b) between
11 There's a lot of football ____ TV.
   a) at   b) on

[ ] 5

7 Complete the blog with the correct past simple form of the verbs in brackets.

From waiter to teacher

Three years ago, I ¹ _was_ (be) a waiter in a restaurant. I ² _____ (want) to change jobs because I ³ _____ (not be) very happy, but I ⁴ _____ (not know) what job to do. Then one day, I ⁵ _____ (meet) someone on the train. She was a teaching assistant in India. She ⁶ _____ (talk) about her job and it sounded very interesting.
I sent an email with my details, and three days later someone ⁷ _____ (phone) me. I went for an interview, and they ⁸ _____ (give) me a job. It ⁹ _____ (be) a voluntary job at first so I ¹⁰ _____ (not get) any money – just food and a place to live.
Then, I did some training and ¹¹ _____ (become) a 'real' teacher. That's my job now and I love it!

[ ] 10

8 Correct the grammar mistakes.

1 What ~~were~~ _did_ you do yesterday?
2 The tickets didn't be expensive.
3 The door is on the right to the window.
4 There is three bookshops near here.
5 I hate get up at six o'clock.
6 She's going cook dinner.
7 Pete can swimming 10km.
8 She has a lot brothers and sisters.
9 Do you like my shoes? I bought it yesterday.

[ ] 4

9 Choose the correct words to complete the story.

| ~~don't~~ on was decided any it a |

Planes, trains and me
I really love going to different countries but I ¹ _don't_ like travelling by plane. In fact, I hate ² _____!
Last summer I went ³ _____ holiday with my friend, Luca. Luca wanted to fly, but I ⁴ _____ to take the train. Big mistake! The journey took nine hours. There wasn't ⁵ _____ café on the train and I didn't have ⁶ _____ food with me. When I arrived at the hotel I ⁷ _____ very tired and hungry. It wasn't a good start to the holiday!

[ ] 6

10 Complete the questions for the answers. Use two, three or four words.

1 A: Where _____were you_____ last week?
   B: I was on holiday.
2 A: Where _____?
   B: I went to Amsterdam.
3 A: _____ people friendly?
   B: Oh yes, the people were really friendly.
4 A: _____?
   B: No, there isn't an underground in Amsterdam.
5 A: _____ cold?
   B: No, it wasn't cold. It was hot!
6 A: _____ a good time?
   B: Yes, thanks. I had a very good time.

[ ] 5

READING

11 Read the article and match a)–f) with gaps 1–6.

New Year – New You?

It's the 31st of December. Tomorrow is the start of a new year. For many people this is a good time to choose some personal goals. ¹ _b_ Maybe you'd like to get organised or perhaps you want to save some money. ²____.

'I can't think of any New Year's resolutions. ³____. I don't want to change anything.'

Audrey, 65

'I always have lots of plans at the start of a new year. This year I'm going to get healthy. So, I'm going to go to the gym three times a week. I'd like to lose weight. I'm going to go swimming every Sunday because I love doing that. ⁴____, and I'm not going to drive to work. I'm going to walk or go by bike.'

Bea, 29

'I work in a bank, but I hate thinking about money all the time. I'm going to look for a completely different sort of job this year. ⁵____.'

Nathan, 26

'I'm not going to make any New Year's resolutions this year. Last year I made about five New Year's resolutions. I didn't keep any of them! It was the same the year before that … and the year before that.'

Stefan, 32

'I'm going to learn to swim. ⁶____ and I don't like being in the water. But now I have my own children, I think it's important for me to learn.'

Maddie, 28

a) This year I'm going to stop eating chocolate
b) ~~Are there any lifestyle changes you want to make?~~
c) I didn't have lessons when I was a child
d) I'd like to help others in some way
e) We asked five people about their New Year's resolutions
f) I'm very happy being me

[   ] 5

12 Read the article and write T (true) or F (false) next to each sentence.

1 Bea's goal is to walk or cycle to work next year. _T_
2 Bea likes swimming. ___
3 Nathan loves his job. ___
4 Stefan can't keep New Year's resolutions. ___
5 Maddie can't swim. ___
6 Audrey isn't happy with her life. ___

[   ] 5

13 Read the text then complete the blog entry with words from the box.

THE SHANGHAI NO. 1 DEPARTMENT STORE
830 Nanjing Road, Shanghai

There are about 300 shops on Shanghai's Nanjing Road. Most of them are modern buildings, full of expensive items like fashion and electronic goods from around the world.

The Shanghai No.1 Department Store (or 'First' Department Store) offers shoppers a very different experience. It is an old building, and most of the items for sale are Chinese, not international.

The store opened in 1934. It was called The Sun, and was one of just four big department stores in Shanghai at the time.

Departments: *Clothes, Gifts, Food, Toys, Books, Jewellery, Homewear, Sports, Menswear, Women's Clothes, Beauty.*

~~modern~~   old   First   Menswear   international   The Sun

We went shopping on Nanjing Road today. We visited a lot of ¹ _modern_ buildings and shops. We also found this fantastic ²_____ department store. It's called The Shanghai ³_____ Department Store.
The shop was called ⁴_____ when it first opened in 1934. It has lots of interesting things for sale. I bought a traditional Chinese jacket in the ⁵_____ department.
The modern shops on Nanjing Road are great – they sell ⁶_____ things – clothes, computers, phones, things like that. But I really loved this famous old department store.

[   ] 5

COMMUNICATION

14 Match sentences 1–6 with responses a)–f).

1 Which colour would you like? _e_
2 What would you like? ___
3 How was the fish? ___
4 Hey, this music's really great. ___
5 How was the film? ___
6 Good to talk to you. ___

a) Yes, it's fantastic.
b) Nice to talk to you, too.
c) Delicious!
d) Can I have a tea, please?
e) ~~Let me see … the black one, please.~~
f) It was boring.

[   ] 5

15 Complete the conversation with the words and phrases from the box.

~~can I have~~	that's right	when	want	like
for example	excuse me	where	you know	sorry
opposite				

Sales assistant: Can I help you?

Customer: [1] _Can I have_ a ticket to Zurich, please.

Sales assistant: Would you [2]_____ a single or a return?

Customer: Return, please.

Sales assistant: And when do you [3]_____ to come back?

Customer: Tomorrow.

Sales assistant: That's sixty-seven fifty, please.

Customer: OK. _____ does the next train leave?

Sales assistant: At ten forty.

Customer: And where does it leave from?

Sales assistant: Gate fifteen.

Customer: [5]_____? Gate fourteen?

Sales assistant: No, fifteen.

Customer: Thank you. Oh … [6]_____!

Sales assistant: Yes?

Customer: [7]_____ is gate fifteen?

Sales assistant: It's over there, [8]_____ the snack bar.

Customer: 'Snack bar'? What's a 'snack bar'?

Sales assistant: It's … [9]_____, a place like a café where you can get snacks, [10]_____ drinks, cakes, chips …

Customer: Ah, yes. I understand. Let me check. The snack bar is in front of gate fifteen.

Sales assistant: Yes, [11]_____.

> **10**

16 Underline the correct alternatives to complete the email.

[1]*Hi/Dear* Mr Kovacs,

I met Claude Dupont yesterday and I gave [2]*Claude Dupont/him* the papers. There weren't any problems with them [3]*because/so* we had some time to talk about other things.

I'm going to be back in the office on [4]*friday/Friday*, not tomorrow, [5]*because /so* there aren't any trains tonight.

[6]*Regards/See you soon*,

Carla

> **5**

17 You are on holiday in a city. Write an email to a friend. Write about two or three of the things in the box. Write 50–80 words.

the food	a problem	what you did yesterday
a plan for tomorrow	the transport	

> **10**

> **Total: 100**

ANSWER KEY

Mid-course Test A

LISTENING

1

Audioscript

1

A: Excuse me.

B: Yes, can I help you?

A: How much is the clock?

B: This one? It's twenty-two pounds twenty.

A: No, not that one. The brown one.

B: This one? It's … twenty-five pounds fifty.

A: OK.

2

A: Hello, I'm Lily.

B: Hi, Lily. I'm Paul. Nice to meet you.

A: Nice to meet you, too. Where are you from?

B: I'm from the USA.

A: Oh, where in the USA?

B: Texas. Where are you from, Lily?

A: I'm from China.

B: Oh, right. I have some friends in China.

3

A: Hello, I'm here for the German lesson.

B: OK. What's your surname, please?

A: It's Wallis.

B: Is that W-a-l-l-i-s?

A: Yes, that's right.

B: And your first name, please.

A: It's Kandy.

B: Is that C-a-n-d-y?

A: No, K as in 'king'. K-a-n-d-y.

B: Kandy Wallis. OK, you can go through to Room 4.

A: Room 4? Thanks.

4

A: Do you like football, Neil?

B: Football? Yes, I do. I always watch the big matches on TV – you know, on Saturdays.

A: But I mean, do you *play* football?

B: Oh, no. I don't do any sport!

A: Really? But exercise is important. How do you get to work? Do you walk to the office?

B: No, I don't. I drive or I go by taxi. And I drive to the shops.

A: Oh, Neil! You're terrible!

5

A: What's that?

B: Sorry? What?

A: What's that thing on the floor?

B: I think it's a hat.

A: Oh, yes. It's Sandra's hat.

B: No, it isn't. Sandra's hat is blue.

A: You're right. Let's have a look. Oh yes, it's Pedro's.

B: Where *is* Pedro? Is he at the gym?

A: No, he's at the cinema with Alice.

B: Oh, right.

6

A: Are you OK, Henry?

B: No, I'm really tired.

A: Let's have a break for ten minutes.

B: Good idea.

A: Are these your keys?

B: No, they're Diana's.

A: Oh, OK. Where is she?

B: At the hairdresser's.

2 c   3 c   4 b   5 c   6 a

2

Audioscript

Waiter: So, that's two coffees, two cheese sandwiches and one chocolate cake. Anything else?

A: No, thanks. That's all.

Waiter: OK. That's 12 euros 60, please.

A and B: OK.

B: Oh, excuse me.

Waiter: Yes?

B: What time do you close?

Waiter: At half past five.

B: Thanks.

A: Are you OK, Martha?

B: No, I'm not. I'm really cold.

A: Are you? I'm OK. Well, let's go inside.

B: Good idea.

A: Are you OK now?

B: I'm still a bit cold, but it's OK.

Waiter: OK … Two coffees, two cheese sandwiches and one chocolate cake.

A and B: Thank you.

B: That cake is very big!

A: Yes. Do you want some?

B: No thanks. I never eat cake.

A: Oh.

B: And I don't like chocolate.

A: Really?

B: It's true!

A: What do you like?

B: Just things like bread, cheese and fruit, really.

A: Oh, right. Well, let's start work. Is that your pen?

B: Yes.

2 T   3 F   4 F   5 F   6 T

PRONUNCIATION

3

2 bread   3 our   4 no   5 that   6 this
7 G   8 what   9 shoes   10 go   11 they

VOCABULARY AND GRAMMAR

4

2 printer   3 eighty   4 have   5 weekend
6 chips   7 waiter   8 read   9 café
10 lunch   11 trousers

5

2 actor   3 tired   4 cereal   5 Australia
6 ninety-five   7 Wednesdays   8 festival
9 evening   10 yellow   11 guided

6

2 b   3 a   4 b   5 a   6 b   7 b   8 b   9 a
10 a   11 a

7

2 Where's/is Kim?
3 She doesn't like chips.
4 These are my new trousers.
5 Their son's 19.
6 Our son's name is Raj.
7 They're/are always happy.
8 Its name is Hotel Orlando.
9 It's my dad's house.
10 Yes, I am.
11 She's not/isn't hungry.

8

3 aren't/are not   4 studies
5 doesn't/does not eat   6 has
7 don't/do not like   8 watches
9 'm/am not   10 aren't/'re not
11 's/is   12 doesn't/does not do

9

2 What time does she get up?
3 Where are they from?
4 Are you a doctor?
5 Do you live with your parents?
6 Is this Minna's chair?

10

2 always   3 at   4 girlfriend's   5 her
6 never

READING

11

1 B   2 D   3 A   4 C   5 E

12

2 T   3 F   4 F   5 T   6 T

13

2 (It starts at) 11 a.m.
3 They're free. / nothing / 0
4 7.50
5 Mondays / On Mondays. / Every Monday.
6 (He teaches) guitar / Spanish guitar(.)
7 (It's) 8724 99260 (.)

COMMUNICATION

14

2 b   3 b   4 a   5 a   6 b

15

2 please   3 When   4 time is it
5 How much   6 wonderful   7 as in
8 Excuse me   9 time's   10 Sorry?
11 Thanks

WRITING

16

2 because   3 but   4 First   5 that   6 then

17 (sample answer)

I like the weekend but I never go out on Friday evenings. I usually eat pizza and watch TV.

On Saturdays I get up at eight o'clock. First, I have a small breakfast – cereal and juice. Then I do sport with my friends. We always have lunch together in a café after that. I sometimes go to the shops in the afternoon.

On Sundays I have a big breakfast – eggs, sausages and toast. I drink coffee and read the newspaper.

Mid-course Test B

LISTENING

1

Audioscript
See Test A.
2 a   3 b   4 c   5 b   6 b

2

Audioscript
See Test A.
2 F   3 T   4 F   5 T   6 F

PRONUNCIATION

3

2 bread   3 our   4 no   5 that   6 this
7 G   8 what   9 shoes   10 go   11 they

VOCABULARY AND GRAMMAR

4

2 keys   3 doctor   4 dinner   5 restaurant
6 work   7 steak   8 seventy   9 actor
10 computer   11 red

5

2 Australia   3 Wednesdays   4 engineer
5 white   6 festival   7 vegetables
8 afternoon   9 guided   10 bored
11 sixty-nine

6

2 b   3 b   4 a   5 a   6 b   7 a   8 a   9 b
10 b   11 a

7

2 Its name is Café 29.
3 Yes, I am.
4 She's not/isn't tired.
5 It's my mum's car.
6 These are my new shoes.
7 Their dad's 49.
8 Our son's name is Pip.
9 He doesn't like fish.
10 Where are my keys?
11 He's/is always bored.

8

3 doesn't/does not do   4 aren't/'re not
5 studies   6 doesn't/does not eat   7 is/'s
8 don't/do not like   9 watches   10 has
11 aren't/are not   12 am/'m not

9

2 Where are they from?
3 Are you a singer?
4 What time does he go to bed?
5 Is this Karim's book?
6 Do you work in an office?

10

2 always   3 boyfriend's   4 his   5 don't
6 never

READING

11

1 E   2 C   3 D   4 A   5 B

12

2 F   3 T   4 T   5 T   6 F

13

2 They're free. / nothing / 0
3 Mondays / On Mondays. / Every Monday.
4 8.99
5 (It finishes at) 11.30 p.m.
6 (He teaches) guitar/Spanish guitar(.)
7 (It's) pablobb@hayoo.com (.)

COMMUNICATION

14

2 a   3 b   4 a   5 b   6 a

15

2 please   3 as in   4 Excuse me   5 time's
6 Sorry?   7 Thanks   8 When
9 time is it   10 How much
11 wonderful

WRITING

16

2 because   3 but   4 First   5 Then   6 that

17

See sample answer in Test A.

End of Course Test A

LISTENING

1

Audioscript

1

A: How did you meet your husband?

B: We met on a train. There was a problem at one of the stations and we started chatting … and we didn't stop!

A: Were you in this country?

B: No, we were in China. I was on holiday and he was there because of work.

2

A: Hi, it's me.

B: Adam, where are you? Are you on the underground?

A: No, there aren't any trains tonight. The underground is all completely closed. It's crazy. I'm at the bus station.

B: Why don't you take a taxi?

A: Well … they're so expensive. It's OK, I can wait for a bus.

B: Go on, get a taxi! You don't do it very often.

A: OK, you're right. See you soon.

3

A: Hi, Selma. How was your holiday?

B: Great, thanks.

A: Did you go camping?

B: No, we didn't in the end because the weather was so bad – really cold. We stayed at home but we had some good days out.

A: That's nice. What sort of things did you do?

B: We went for some long walks in the country. We didn't see anyone else – it was just us and the children. Then we cooked some nice meals in the evening.

A: Right …

B: It was a really relaxing week. Really, it was!

4

A: Hi, Fiona. Do you take the bus to work every day?

B: Yes, I do. It's so expensive!

A: Do you have a monthly pass?

B: A 'monthly pass' … no. What's that?

A: You know – you buy a ticket for a whole month – for 30 or 31 days … It's a cheap way to use the buses every day.

B: Oh, I didn't know about that.

A: So, are you going to buy one today?

B: No, I'm not. You see, I'm going to change jobs soon.

A: Oh, really? What are you going to do?

B: I don't know yet, but I'm going to get organised and find a job that's not in the city centre.

A: Good idea!

5

A: Is that a new watch, Alice?

B: Yes. Do you like it?

A: Very nice! Where did it come from?

B: It's a long story …

A: Go on!

B: Well, it was Ricardo … He gave me a watch for my birthday …

A: Ah!

B: … but I didn't like it.

A: Oh.

B: I know. It was sad, really. He arrived at my house with this gift – all nicely wrapped …

A: Did the shop do it?

B: No, he did it himself. So I took off all this beautiful paper and opened the box and then I saw the watch inside … and I just really didn't like it. Ricardo looked at me and he knew.

A: Oh, poor Ricardo!

B: It was OK. In the end we laughed about it. And at the weekend we went shopping together, and I changed it for this one.

A: It really is very nice.

B: Thank you.

6

A: What do you think of the music?

B: It's great!

A: I'd like to be on stage with them, really.

B: Yeah? What do you play? Or do you sing?

A: I can't sing. But I play the guitar.

B: Oh, right.

A: And the drums, too.

B: That's great. I love listening to music but I don't really play anything. I can't read music at all.

A: Oh no, I can't do that either. I just listen to things, remember them and play them.

B: Wow!

2 a   3 c   4 b   5 a   6 c

2

Audioscript

A: It's the first of August today, Lisa. A new month.

B: August – a fantastic month!

A: Ah, yes, it's your birthday in August, isn't it? Is it the 20th?

B: No, the 21st.

A: Oh, yes. I remember your party last year. It was so good, Lisa. I danced all night.

B: Me too! And I don't even like dancing!

A: Are you going to have a party again this year?

B: No. It's too much hard work getting everything ready. But I am going to do something.

A: Like what?

B: I'm just going to cook dinner for two or three friends – including you, of course.

A: Ah, nice … What would you like for your birthday, by the way? Last year I gave you those blue trousers. Would you like clothes again this year? Or maybe some books?

B: I don't know … I've got so many things. Let me think …

A: What about an activity gift?

B: What do you mean?

A: An activity gift means I don't give you an object, I give you an experience.

B: I still don't understand.

A: You know, like a day at a beauty spa or driving a Formula 1 car or going in a hot air balloon …

B: Mmm! A day at a beauty spa sounds good …

A: OK. I can ask my sister. I think she knows a good place.

B: Thanks, Angela, that's a really kind idea! I can't wait!

2 T   3 F   4 F   5 T   6 T

PRONUNCIATION

3

/t/ liked, worked, finished, talked

/d/ moved, cried, lived, listened

/ɪd/ started, wanted

VOCABULARY AND GRAMMAR

4

2 local   3 cost   4 luggage   5 beauty
6 laugh   7 furniture   8 remember   9 gift
10 drive   11 arrive

5

2 weight   3 organised   4 third   5 April
6 underground   7 chatting online
8 interesting   9 right   10 payphone
11 passengers

6

2 b   3 b   4 b   5 a   6 b   7 b   8 a   9 b
10 b   11 b

7

2 wasn't   3 decided   4 looked
5 didn't see   6 saw   7 asked   8 gave
9 didn't pay   10 had   11 did

8

2 He has a lot **of** brothers and sisters.

3 Jill can **run** 10km.

4 You're going **to** have a good time.

5 No, there aren't **any** good shops near here.

6 I hate **wrapping** gifts.

7 We lived next **to** the school.

8 Do you like my bike? My dad gave it to **me** for my birthday.

9 The meal **wasn't** expensive.

9

2 on   3 didn't   4 any   5 a   6 arrived
7 wasn't

10

2 did you go   3 Was it
4 Is there an airport   5 Were the
6 What did you eat

READING

11

2 f   3 e   4 d   5 c   6 a

12

2 T   3 F   4 F   5 T   6 T

13

2 international   3 old   4 The Sun   5 First
6 Menswear

COMMUNICATION

14

2 a   3 f   4 d   5 e   6 b

15

2 Would   3 do   4 When   5 Where
6 Sorry   7 excuse me   8 behind   9 What
10 you know   11 Let me check

WRITING

16

2 Monday   3 because   4 her   5 so
6 Regards

17 (sample answer)

Hi Mimi,

We're in Budapest and it's fantastic. Today we walked in the city for three hours. It was very cold so we went to a lot of cafés for hot drinks and cakes!

We saw some beautiful old buildings in the city and I took a lot of photos.

Last night we went to a restaurant and ate some local food. It was great.

Tomorrow we're going to visit a famous swimming pool here.

Love,

Sal

End of Course Test B

LISTENING

1

Audioscript

See Test A.

2 c   3 b   4 a   5 b   6 b

2

Audioscript

See Test A.

2 F   3 T   4 F   5 F   6 T

PRONUNCIATION

3

/t/ liked, worked, finished, talked
/d/ moved, cried, lived, listened
/ɪd/ started, wanted

VOCABULARY AND GRAMMAR

4

2 jewellery   3 second   4 cry   5 fit   6 gift
7 bike   8 near   9 toy   10 ride   11 boring

5

2 March   3 first   4 change   5 speak
6 taking photos   7 remember
8 motorbike   9 cash machine   10 terrible
11 internet café

6

2 b   3 a   4 a   5 a   6 a   7 b   8 b   9 a
10 a   11 b

7

2 wanted   3 wasn't   4 didn't know
5 met   6 talked   7 phoned   8 gave
9 was   10 didn't get   11 became

8

2 The tickets **weren't** expensive.
3 The door is on the right **of** the window.
4 There **are** three bookshops near here.
5 I hate **getting** up at six o'clock.
6 She's going **to** cook dinner.
7 Pete can **swim** 10km.
8 She has a lot **of** brothers and sisters.
9 Do you like my shoes? I bought **them** yesterday.

9

2 it   3 on   4 decided   5 a   6 any   7 was

10

2 did you go   3 Were the
4 Is there an underground
5 Was it   6 Did you have

READING

11

2 e   3 f   4 a   5 d   6 c

12

2 T   3 F   4 T   5 T   6 F

13

2 old   3 First   4 The Sun   5 Menswear
6 international

COMMUNICATION

14

2 d   3 c   4 a   5 f   6 b

15

2 like   3 want   4 When   5 Sorry
6 excuse me   7 Where   8 opposite
9 you know   10 for example
11 that's right

WRITING

16

2 him   3 so   4 Friday   5 because
6 Regards

17

See sample answer in Test A.

Pearson Education Limited
Edinburgh Gate
Harlow
Essex CM20 2JE
England
and Associated Companies throughout the world.

www.pearsonelt.com
© Pearson Education Limited 2012

First published 2012

ISBN: 978-1-4082-1690-3

Set in Gill Sans Book 9.75/11.5

Printed in Slovakia by Neografia

Acknowledgements
The publisher would like to thank the following for their kind
permission to reproduce their photographs:

(Key: b-bottom; c-centre; l-left; r-right; t-top)

Alamy Images: Glowimages RM 146; **Fotolia.com:**
CandyBox Images 168 (woman jogging), Megan Lorenz
167tr, TheSupe87 167cr, WavebreakMediaMicro 168 (family
camping); **Getty Images:** Echo 168 (man walking a dog), John
Eder 167br; **iStockphoto:** Steve Debenport 168 (woman
opening a present); **Shutterstock.com:** samotrebizan 167l

All other images © Pearson Education

Every effort has been made to trace the copyright holders and
we apologise in advance for any unintentional omissions. We
would be pleased to insert the appropriate acknowledgement
in any subsequent edition of this publication.

Illustrated by Eric@kja-artists